Armed Ambiguity

Armed Ambiguity

Women Warriors in German Literature and Culture in the Age of Goethe

✦

Julie Koser

NORTHWESTERN UNIVERSITY PRESS
EVANSTON, ILLINOIS

Northwestern University Press
www.nupress.northwestern.edu

Printed in the United States of America

10 9 8 7 6 5 4 3 2 1

Library of Congress Cataloging-in-Publication Data

Names: Koser, Julie, author.
Title: Armed ambiguity : women warriors in German literature and culture in the age of Goethe / Julie Koser.
Description: Evanston, Illinois : Northwestern University Press, 2016. | Includes bibliographical references and index.
Identifiers: LCCN 2015041098| ISBN 9780810132344 (cloth : alk. paper) | ISBN 9780810132320 (pbk. : alk. paper) | ISBN 9780810132337 (e-book)
Subjects: LCSH: Women in literature—History—18th century. | Women in literature—History—19th century. | German literature—History and criticism—18th century. | German literature—History and criticism—19th century. | Violence in literature. | Femininity in literature. | Women—Germany—Social conditions—18th century. | Women—Germany—Social conditions—19th century.
Classification: LCC PT151.W7 K675 2016 | DDC 830.9/352042—dc23
LC record available at http://lccn.loc.gov/2015041098

∞ The paper used in this publication meets the minimum requirements of the American National Standard for Information Sciences—Permanence of Paper for Printed Library Materials, ANSI Z39.48–1992.

CONTENTS

ACKNOWLEDGMENTS

The completion of this book would have not been possible without the institutional support of the University of Maryland, College Park, and the University of California, Berkeley. I am especially grateful to the University of Maryland Graduate School for the 2011 summer Research and Scholarship Award; to the School of Languages, Literatures, and Cultures for the 2011 semester research grant as well as multiple awards to fund my research presentations; and to the University of California, Berkeley, for the Dean's Normative Time Fellowship, all of which enabled me to conduct research in Germany and the United States and complete various portions of this book. Additionally, I am indebted to the interlibrary loan staff at McKeldin Library for their tireless efforts to track down and obtain materials consulted and analyzed in this book. Along these same lines, a thank you goes to the Germanic Collections Librarians James Spohrer at Doe Library and Kelsey Corlett-Rivera at McKeldin Library as well as Alexander Fiebig at the Staatsbibliothek Berlin for their assistance. I would also like to thank the Arts and Humanities Research Council in conjunction with the Steering Committee of the research project "Representations of Women and Death in German Literature, Art and Media after 1500" for the opportunity and financial support to participate in the 2007 colloquium on "Women Fighting: Warriors and Terrorists" at Trinity College, Oxford.

Additional thanks go to my colleagues in the Department of Germanic Studies and in the School of Languages, Literatures, and Cultures for their support. A special thank you goes to colleagues both in and outside the field who generously agreed to read, provide valuable feedback on, and pose insightful questions about various parts of the book: Karin Baumgartner, Mary Helen Dupree, Viktoria Harms, Michele Mason, Mehl Penrose, Patricia Anne Simpson, Heather Sullivan, and W. Daniel Wilson. I am especially grateful to Dan Wilson, who continues to inspire and encourage me. I appreciate the feedback on translations offered by Elke Frederiksen, David Gramling, and Donald Backman. Thank you to Michele Mason for being a sounding board and critical reader. My appreciation also goes to the anonymous reviewers for their thoughtful and productive suggestions. Thank you to Henry Carrigan, Gianna Mosser, and the staff at Northwestern University Press for your support of my project. To Paul Short, a special thank you for your invaluable advice and the generous donation of your time.

A version of chapter 1 appeared as "Spectre and/or Ideal: Representations of Revolutionary Women in the German Press, 1789–1794," *German Life and Letters* 63, no. 2 (April 2010): 105–21, and has been published with the permission of Blackwell Publishing Ltd. Portions of chapter 5 appeared as "Rebellious Bodies: The Human Form as Site of Social and Political Conflict in Heinrich von Kleist's *Die Hermannsschlacht* and *Penthesilea*," in *Rebellion and Revolution: Defiance in German Language, History and Art*, ed. Melissa Etzler and Priscilla Layne (Newcastle upon Tyne: Cambridge Scholars Publishing, 2010), 62–88, and has been published with the permission of Cambridge Scholars Publishing. I am grateful for their permission to include revised versions of these articles here.

They say it takes a village to raise a child, but it is also true that it takes a village to write a book. I am deeply indebted to my family, near and far, for their unlimited capacity for patience and encouragement as well as their generosity of spirit and time. Most importantly, to Ben and Madeleine, I could not have done this without your unwavering support, patience, and love.

ABBREVIATIONS AND CONVENTIONS

BNP Benedikte Naubert. *Philippe von Geldern. Oder Geschichte Selims, des Sohns Amurat.* 2 vols. Leipzig: Weygandsche Buchhandlung, 1792.

BNT Benedikte Naubert. *Geschichte der Gräfin Thekla von Thurn oder Scenen aus dem dreyssigjährigen Kriege.* 2 vols. Leipzig: Weygandsche Buchhandlung, 1788.

CC Carl von Clausewitz. *Vom Kriege: Hinterlassenes Werk.* Munich: Ullstein, 1980.

CCE Carl von Clausewitz. *On War.* Edited by Beatrice Heuser. Translated by Michael Howard and Peter Paret. Princeton, N.J.: Princeton University Press, 1989.

CMF Caroline de la Motte Fouqué. *Das Heldenmädchen aus der Vendée.* 2 vols. Leipzig: Gerhard Fleischer der Jüngere, 1816.

CW Engel Christine Westphalen. *Charlotte Corday. Tragödie in 5 Akten mit Chören. Mit einem Kupfer.* Hamburg: B. G. Hoffmann, 1804.

HK Heinrich von Kleist. *Penthesilea.* In *Sämtliche Werke und Briefe.* Edited by Hans Rudolf Barth, Ilse-Marie Barth, and Hinrich C. Seeba. Vol. 2, *Dramen 1808–1811: Penthesilea; Das Käthchen von Heilbronn; Die Hermannsschlacht; Prinz Friedrich von Homburg.* Frankfurt am Main: Deutscher Klassiker, 1987.

HKB Heinrich von Kleist. *Briefe von und an Heinrich von Kleist 1793–1811.* Vol. 4 of *Sämtliche Werke und Briefe.* Edited by Klaus Müller-Salget and Stefan Ormanns. Frankfurt am Main: Deutscher Klassiker, 1997.

HKE Heinrich von Kleist. *Penthesilea.* Translated by Joel Agee. New York: Perennial, 1998.

HPM *Historisch-politisches Magazin, nebst litterarischen Nachrichten.* Edited by Albrecht Wittenberg. Hamburg, 1787–95.

HSZ *Berlinische Nachrichten von Staats- und gelehrten Sachen.* Berlin: Haude & Spener, 1790–93.

HZ Heinrich Zschokke. *Charlotte Corday oder die Rebellion von Calvados. Ein republikanisches Trauerspiel in vier Akten. (Aus den Zeiten der französischen Revolution.) In Jamben.* Stettin: Johann Sigismund Kaffke, 1794.

JG Johann Wolfgang von Goethe. *Herrmann und Dorothea.* In *Sämtliche Werke: Briefe, Tagebücher, und Gespräche.* Edited by Waltraud Wiethölter and Christoph Brecht. Vol. 8, *Die Leiden des jungen*

Werthers, Die Wahlverwandschaften, Kleine Prosa, Epen. Frankfurt am Main: Deutscher Klassiker, 1994.

JGE Johann Wolfgang von Goethe. *Verse Plays and Epic*. Edited by Cyrus Hamlin and Frank Ryder. Translated by David Luke. New York: Suhrkamp, 1987.

KGD Karoline von Günderrode. "Darthula nach Ossian." In *Sämtliche Werke und ausgewählte Studien*. Edited by Walter Morgenthaler. Vol. 1, *Texte*. Basel: Stroemfeld/Roter Stern, 1990.

KGH Karoline von Günderrode. *Hildgund*. In *Sämtliche Werke und ausgewählte Studien*. Edited by Walter Morgenthaler. Vol. 1, *Texte*. Basel: Stroemfeld/Roter Stern, 1990.

KGM Karoline von Günderrode. *Mora*. In *Sämtliche Werke und ausgewählte Studien*. Edited by Walter Morgenthaler. Vol. 1, *Texte*. Basel: Stroemfeld/Roter Stern, 1990.

SJ Friedrich Schiller. *Die Jungfrau von Orleans*. In *Werke: Nationalausgabe*. Edited by Benno von Wieseand and Lieselotte Blumenthal. Vol. 9, *Maria Stuart. Die Jungfrau von Orleans*. Weimar: Böhlau, 1948.

SJE Friedrich Schiller. *The Maid of Orleans*. In *Schiller: Five Plays*. Translated by Robert David MacDonald, 617–733. London: Oberon Books, 1998.

SL Friedrich Schiller. "Das Lied von der Glocke." In *Werke: Nationalausgabe*. Edited by Norbert Oellers. Vol. 2, bk. 1, *Gedichte: In der Reihenfolge ihres Erscheinens 1799–1805*. Weimar: Böhlau, 1983.

SLE Friedrich Schiller. *Das Lied von der Glocke*.Translated by Thömas James Arnold. London: D. Nutt, 1842.

TH Therese Huber. *Die Familie Seldorf*. Edited by Magdalene Heuser. 2 vols. Hildesheim: Georg Olms, 1989.

VZ *Königlich Privilegirte Berlinische Zeitung von Staats und gelehrten Sachen*. Berlin: Voss, 1789–93.

Where possible, I have used published translations of original source material. Instances in which I altered translations have been noted accordingly. In cases where translations are unavailable, I have provided my own translations. Unless otherwise indicated, all translations are my own.

Spelling variations and typographical errors in the original have been maintained. In certain instances, the notation [*sic*] has been inserted for the sake of clarification to indicate the error in the original.

Armed Ambiguity

Introduction

Mythologizing the Woman Warrior

The nineteenth-century dramatist Heinrich von Kleist's depiction of the Amazon warrior queen Penthesilea setting upon her enemy and would-be lover Achilles in the last bloody encounter on the battlefield of the Trojan War is arguably one of the most brutal and simultaneously poignant scenes in German literature. Fueled by desire and wounded by perceived betrayal, Penthesilea mercilessly tears the object of her affection to pieces with her teeth alongside her dogs of war. This battle-hardened warrior woman is subsequently pushed to the edge of insanity at the realization of her violent transgression. Her grief and remorse wield themselves as symbolic daggers to mortally pierce her already wounded heart. Gathered around the armed maiden's corpse, her fellow Amazons lament the death of their queen by memorializing her grace, compassion, and tenderness, attributes seemingly at odds with the qualities she had displayed only moments before and which had horrified even the most experienced of these warring women.

This dramatic rendering of the woman warrior does not stand alone as an isolated instance. In the wake of the French Revolution, many such polysemous depictions of women and violence embodied the climate of apprehension, uncertainty, and instability that held western Europe, and German-speaking territories in particular, captive at the beginning of the nineteenth century. A full contingent of women warriors of page and stage triggered persistent anxieties as well as powerful fantasies about women's use of violence—and forms of "perceived" female transgression more generally—that destabilized the status quo of entrenched structures of power. Evoking simultaneous feelings of aversion and attraction, women warriors, as the embodiment of female transgression writ large, appear at once as ghastly prospect and feminine ideal, deceitful criminal and valorous patriot, deviant villain and sacrificing heroine, bloodthirsty hyena and defender of the domestic good, paragon of love and repository of unregulated passions, aberration of nature and emancipatory fantasy. Far from being the exception, the trope of the woman warrior became a central vehicle by which men and women writers sought to renegotiate the role of women in the social and political life of the emerging German nation.[1]

Armed Ambiguity is an interrogation of how reactionary visions of "ideal femininity" existed alongside subversive fantasies of new femininities in the ideological battle being waged over the reorganization of German society around 1800. As a harbinger of the modern political era, the French Revolution altered irrevocably the social and political structure of Europe and sparked several distinctive discursive shifts in depictions of women's violence. This study is a critical engagement with ambiguous manifestations of women and violence, the rhetorical strategies employed by eighteenth- and nineteenth-century writers in their negotiations with the specter of women at war, and the broader claims being staked to the female body as the site of competing social and political discourses in an age of radical instability and rapid transformation. At issue in literary confrontations with the warlike woman is not only her incursion into the field of battle as armed combatant. The figure of the female warrior is but one extreme example of late eighteenth- and early nineteenth-century women's "unruly" behavior that stands in for both overt and more subtle forms of female transgression during this period. From the political activism of female revolutionaries, such as Olympe de Gouges, demanding their rights of citizenship and equality in neighboring France, to bourgeois and aristocratic women writers taking up the pen and asserting their voices in the literary and intellectual life of German society, defiant, disorderly women posed a threat to the social order.

The many literary depictions of warlike women serve as signposts mapping disruptions across the cultural landscape at the close of the eighteenth century. These reference points cannot be read as a linear progression from point A to B; instead, they represent the complex and often contradictory responses of the German public to the unsettling of societal, political, and personal hierarchies, systems of power, and ways of being. Women's participation in political matters and on the battlefield challenged the most fundamental tenet of eighteenth- and nineteenth-century notions of manhood: namely, the assumption that only men were capable of protecting and defending their homeland and their families.[2] By its very nature, an analysis of the concepts of femininity and warfare simultaneously necessitates a reexamination of masculinity in times of military conflict. The fragmented definitions and contested renegotiations of the identities of the male warrior and patriot resulting from his encounters with the armed woman will therefore also be examined.

Beginning with German press reports detailing participation by women in the escalating violence in neighboring France, women as warriors repeatedly underwent marked transformations in the German imagination. From the storming of the Bastille (1789) to the war in the Vendée (1793–96) and culminating with women's patriotic defense of country and family in the German Wars of Liberation (1813–15), the figure of the warring woman vacillated continuously between passive and active forms of violence that appeared to coincide with ideological shifts in the German political context. Prior to this revolutionary turmoil, eighteenth-century German authors had traditionally depicted violence perpetrated by women as indirect or passive acts, for example, the jilted mistresses Marwood and Orsina of G. E. Lessing's bourgeois dramas *Miss Sara Sampson* and *Emilia Galotti* or the notorious virago Adelheid in Goethe's *Götz von Berlichingen*. They either take revenge with poison or seduce others to carry out their vengeful plots. Violent women, with the exception perhaps of Euripides's Bacchae or the iconic figures Judith and Salome, were rarely portrayed wielding their own weapons to inflict the fatal blow until the final decades of the eighteenth century, which saw a drastic increase in the number of fictional warlike women who took up the sword.

Deploying methods informed by New Historicism, discourse analysis, and feminist and cultural studies, *Armed Ambiguity* examines tropes of the woman warrior constructed by print culture—including press reports, novels, dramatic works, and lyrical texts—during this decades-long conflict in European history. By focusing primarily on works conceptualized, composed, or published by German writers, both male and female, between the outbreak of the Revolution in France and the defeat of Napoleon and subsequent expulsion of French forces from German territories, which engaged either explicitly or implicitly with the fractured historical context, this analysis sheds new light on how women's bodies became a semiotic battleground for competing social, cultural, and political agendas in one of the most critical periods of modern history. The works treated in this book evince a critical awareness of the power invested in representation as they strategically exploit the artificiality of the very gender roles they attempt to obscure or expose. This study does not exhaustively catalog and offer analyses of every literary instantiation of the woman warrior appearing around 1800; such a project exceeds the scope of this particular book and would, indeed, necessitate a multivolume work in order to document all such manifestations.[3] Instead, I identify the dominant strategies by which German society participated in a process of mythification in its attempts to make sense of and negotiate its own ambivalence toward the seemingly unsettling union of women and armed violence, more specifically of women and warfare.

My deliberate deployment of the term "myth" in this book is twofold. By referring to literary narratives and fictional depictions of the woman warrior as myths, I foreground the politics of representation that is intimately and precariously linked to and driven by underlying ideological agendas, complex processes of identity formation, sanctioned or foreclosed modes of agency, and structures of power. To borrow the words of Roland Barthes, myth, as a semiological system used to convey a message, "is not defined by the object of its message, but by the *way in which* it utters this message."[4] Therefore, this book is centrally concerned with the distinct rhetorical strategies by which the men and women writers of the period not only engaged with but also mythologized the fraught notion of women as agents of death, namely through demonization, deification, domestication, subversive inscription, and resignification. These literary maneuvers construct new myths of the warlike woman as specter and cautionary tale, patriotic saint and heroic martyr, maternal defender of domestic, patriarchal values and the status quo, emancipatory fantasy of new forms of female existence, and a repository for deadly uncontainable desires and fears of the "eternal feminine" respectively. At the same time, the concept of mythification functions in this book as an effective tool to highlight specific processes by which conservative social theorists manufactured a view of society as organized around rigid, fixed, naturalized gender roles that served a reactionary social agenda, which will be problematized in greater detail in the following section.

There are, to be certain, textual anomalies of the warring woman that do not fit seamlessly within the models presented here, just as there are occurrences of the woman warrior that fit within multiple categories at once. Indeed, I assert the latter is the case for many of the armed women in this study. However, these strategies of literary representation offer productive departure points from which to decipher the woman warrior's ambiguous status that allowed for the multiplicity of meaning both imposed on and evoked by the constellation of warlike women and the use of deadly force at the turn of the eighteenth to the nineteenth century. The women warriors in this book are barometers of the social and political climate in German-speaking territories and reveal how literary texts and cultural artifacts foregrounding women's armed insurrection problematized the discursive construction and illusionary dichotomization of "public" and "private" spheres predicated on myths of "masculine" and "feminine" ideals.

Debating Gender: Mythopoesis and the Woman Warrior around 1800

In times of crisis, whether relating to issues of political legitimacy, national identity, military upheaval, or economic stability, women's bodies become reluctant objects of regulatory forces that attempt to regain control of civil society. Unruly, disorderly, or disruptive women become symptoms of systemic instability that is in need of containment. The assertion and regulation of social practices function as a means of restoring order, which is achieved through the implementation of both official and unofficial policies. The enactment of legal doctrines such as the 1794 *Allgemeines Landrecht für die Preußischen Staaten* (*General Provincial Law for the Prussian States*) or the 1804 Code Napoléon sought to establish a unified set of legal and social conventions with the purpose of codifying what individuals in power deemed "appropriate" behavior.[5] However, what proves far more compelling than these officially regulated forms of control are the unofficial modes of asserting power. Where laws and regulations failed to maintain the status quo, ideology and myth were mobilized to contain and suppress the "unruly" female body. The gender debates in which social theorists were engaged at the end of the eighteenth century established themselves as effective means to reestablish stability and ensure the docility of potentially rebellious, subversive bodies. Questions of anatomy, physiology, and psychology played a crucial role in establishing both men's and women's active participation in or exclusion from the military conflicts around 1800.

Enduring perceptions about Woman's inherent "maternal nature," that is, as giver of life, which stood in direct contradiction to the practice of warfare that required the dealing of death, informed social practices and political policies.[6] Indeed, in most Western cultures, war and politics, including issues of citizenship and military service, have been viewed with relatively few exceptions as masculine pursuits.[7] However, such overdetermined, essentialist notions, which suggest a cohesive, natural concept of man and woman, conveniently neglect historical evidence revealing the diversity of women and the roles they have played in times of warfare. Women have not only been passive victims of military strife but have also constituted an integral, albeit illegal, part of the support structure of the military up until the eighteenth and nineteenth centuries.[8] As sutlers, "comfort women," combat nurses, cross-dressing women soldiers, grieving widows, and innocent victims of violence in war-torn regions, women have engaged in or been directly impacted by warfare in one form or another.

By the end of the eighteenth century, the basis for participation in what was considered the newly emerging public sphere, including sites of armed struggle and military service, was being reconstructed upon a fallacious foundation of scientific, psychological, and social discourses promoting a myth of "Nature" in order to define what it meant to be a man or woman.[9] Invoking "natural determination" as the constant thread running throughout Enlightenment gender debates, various "enlightened" writers—moralists, philosophers, social theorists, and members of the scientific community—worked in concert to solidify a hierarchical, bifurcated social structure founded on the strict dichotomization of *Geschlechtscharaktere* (sex-based characters) resulting in such oppositional dyads as masculine/feminine, active/passive, natural/deviant, political/domestic.[10] A discourse of difference, but also complementarity, came to dominate gender theories at the height of the debates. In her extensive analysis of gender discourses during this period, sociologist Claudia Honegger identifies French anatomist Pierre Roussel's highly influential study *Système physique et moral de la femme* (1775), translated in 1786 into German as *Physiologie des weiblichen Geschlechts* (*The Physiology of the Female Sex*), as marking the beginning of this "Sonder-Anthropologie" in European thinking about gender, which postulated the incommensurability of the sexes.[11] The transition to this divergent model of gender is illustrated by Roussel's theory of difference based on observed anatomical features in which "Nature" conferred upon man the strength needed to meet the demands of public life, while woman was bestowed with a yielding and passive "nature" that destined her for a life of domesticity.[12]

The French anatomist attributes these "observed" anatomical deviations and correlative characteristics to "Nature," ignoring any influence exerted by underlying social power structures; gender therefore appears static, fixed, and eternal. Turning a blind eye to external, social factors for these observed variations, his study denies categorically the possibility that woman might participate in "typically male" activities, such as politics or warfare.

Conservative social theorists built their case for the continued bifurcation of public and private life on the "scientific facts" uncovered by anatomists such as Roussel. Exemplifying the more reactionary, essentialist tenor of the bourgeois gender discourse, government official and university instructor Ernst Brandes's 1787 essay *Ueber die Weiber* (*On Women*) dismissed Cartesian duality by positing a direct correlation between woman's physical and mental capabilities. Like Roussel, Brandes invoked "Nature" to explain woman's social subordination, thereby obfuscating the social structures at work in the gendering of the public, political sphere as masculine. "Nature," not patriarchal society, Brandes led his readers to believe, conferred upon woman a weak body and an inferior mind, making her doubly disqualified for political life.[13] Perhaps even more effective in solidifying women's social subjugation were Wilhelm von Humboldt's claims of complementary sex traits which proffered an illusion of gender equality. In his 1795 essays *Über den Geschlechtsunterschied und dessen Einfluß auf die organische Natur* (*On Gender Difference and Its Influence on Organic Nature*) and *Über die männliche und weibliche Form* (*On the Male and Female Form*) Humboldt grounded his theory of the sexes on the belief that they are different yet equal by necessity. Building upon a basis of complementary but hierarchical oppositions, Humboldt emphasized harmony and balance between existing *Kräfte* (forces) present within each individual. Following Humboldt's logic, if man is endowed with greater intellectual and rational capabilities, then due to the laws of "Nature," woman could not possess these same qualities without transgressing the order of things. Instead, she must balance his cold objectivity with a greater tendency towards emotion and fantasy. If man is strong-willed and assertive, woman must yield and endure.[14] Although Humboldt cautioned against assuming the possibility of masculinity or femininity in a "pure" form—which Gail K. Hart sees as evidence that Humboldt and others fundamentally understood that "gender attributes are cultural additives rather than congenital features"—Humboldt's assignment of complementary characteristics foreclosed the possibility for a reversal or an equalization of power relations by the female sex; if ambiguity exists, it is in the androgynous ideal only attainable by the male sex.[15]

If such works prepared the foundation for the oppositional relationship between woman and man, then philosopher and social theorist J. G. Fichte's exposition on *Naturrechtslehre* (doctrine of natural right), as it pertained to the sexes, cemented in the social consciousness the bifurcated, hierarchical social division between them for decades and even centuries to come. Fichte's contribution to the unfolding discourse on bourgeois virtues and gender roles proved perhaps the most insidious and influential of all. Expounding on the institution of marriage as it related to the State in the first appendix to his 1796–97 treatise *Grundlage des Naturrechts* (*Foundation of Natural Right*), Fichte articulates his theory of the sexes, their assigned roles, and separate spheres in society. Love, Fichte asserts time and again, is the basis and driving force to which all other drives are subsumed and which constitutes and defines women's very existence.[16] Their inherent, inalienable drive to love becomes the justification for their exclusion from public life and the explanation for women's natural subordination to men in all matters.[17]

While scholars have commented on Fichte's essentialist gender theories at great length, what proves particularly critical for a study of the woman warrior are the means by which writers grappled with gendered concepts of love and sacrifice in their literary visions of women, violence, and political conflict. The concepts of love and self-sacrifice are synonymous in Fichte's construction of women: "Liebe aber ist es, wenn man um des andern willen, nicht zufolge eines Begriffs, sondern zufolge des Naturtriebes, sich aufopfert" (Fichte, *Grundlage* 4.100; "But love is self-sacrifice for the sake of another, not on the basis of a concept, but as a result of a natural drive" [Baur, *Foundations of Natural Right* 269]).[18] For Fichte, the beneficiary of this self-sacrifice is, without question, the male subject. It is therefore man's duty to ensure that woman be able to fulfill her biological destiny: "Je größer das Opfer, desto vollkommener die Befriedigung ihres Herzens" (Fichte, 4.103; "The greater the sacrifice, the more complete is the satisfaction of her heart" [Baur, 272]). Fichte's narrative of woman's natural, durable disposition to love and to sacrifice herself infiltrated literary representations of the woman warrior. Writers explored the tension inherent in the gendered bourgeois discourse of love and sacrifice in their literary negotiations with transgressive warlike women, whose use of force and incursion into the public, and often political, sphere of military engagement signaled a violation of social and political order. In this way, the fictional bodies of women warriors became objects upon which conservative and progressive social forces exerted their control.

At the same time that dominant narratives, such as Fichte's, lauded biology as destiny, a few individuals appeared to resist the power of such myths. In his 1792 plea for the improvement of women's social status, German writer and social critic Theodor von Hippel openly challenged claims that women were predetermined for social subordination. Highlighting the contradiction between woman's social obligations and advantages as well as her status under the law as an immature subject, Hippel lifted the naturalizing veil to expose men's ambivalence as the true culprit in woman's legal and social subordination:

> Wenn mich nicht alles trügt, so hat die *Furcht* der Männer, durch die Weiber *unterjocht zu werden*, die ersteren zu jener Überhäufung

> mit Wohltaten gebracht. [. . .] *Furcht*! Fiel dies Wort auf? Es sollte auffallen.—Seht, ich will mein Herz ausschütten und zur Ehre des männlichen Geschlechtes bekennen, daß keine bösere Absicht als *die Furcht, das andere Geschlecht würde uns beherrschen*, den Grund zu unserer Herrschaft über dasselbe gelegt hat.[19]
>
> If I am not sadly deceived, it was the *fear* on men's part of *being subjugated* by women, which brought the former to overwhelm the women with benefits and privileges. [. . .] *Fear!* Does the word strike home? It is meant to do just that. Behold, I shall lay open my heart and[,] to the honor of the masculine sex [, confess] that no more evil intention lay behind our dominion over the opposite sex than the fear that they would become our masters.[20]

Holding his male counterparts responsible for the social inequities between the sexes, Hippel is perhaps the only male author to identify and speak out so explicitly against the structures of patriarchal power mobilizing "Nature" as an instrument of structural domination. That social theorists and members of the scholarly community sought to construct a hierarchical discourse of difference, while others simultaneously exposed the mutability and artificiality of gender as a tool of subordination, created the possibility for the ambiguous woman warrior to capture the fascination of proponents of these competing social agendas and to become the site of their contestation.

As these examples demonstrate, the body, but more specifically the female body, became the locus of conflict in attempts to identify, index, and categorize the differences between the sexes and to assert power over the individual.[21] Perceived anatomical differences, labeled as "natural," led to assumptions about the distinct mental and emotional constitutions of the two sexes: man was distinguished by his developed musculature, physical strength, and larger brain resulting in his assigned status as rational, decisive, and courageous active subject. Woman, in contrast, was characterized by delicate nerves, a fragile skeleton, smaller skull[22] and—most importantly for anatomists and social theorists—her reproductive organs, which conferred upon her the role of emotional, morally superior yet physically vulnerable, passive object. The ostensible evidence for both physical and psychological distinctions between the sexes laid the groundwork for justifying social, political, and legal contrasts. In one typical example of circular logic, social ideology and scientific theory came to validate one another: women were best suited for a life of domesticity because of their weaker musculature and they were equipped with weaker musculature because they were destined for the domestic sphere. By creating and reiterating fictions of "biological destiny" and "natural determination," theorists not only justified women's exclusion from martial activity, and the political arena, as natural, but they also obscured the grounds upon which they built their arguments.

Textual and visual iterations of nurturing, obedient, maternal women, particularly when juxtaposed with depictions of disorderly, bellicose women as deviant and abnormal, affirmed the hierarchical, bifurcated "natural" order of the gendered world. The success of these gender myths, for example the notion of a bourgeois "ideal femininity," turned on their ability to appear as uncontested, eternal truths. As Barthes has argued, the process by which myth appears as a naturalized truth is both continuous and ever changing: myths appear unchanged, static; yet, mythical speech is constantly being restructured to conform to and be readily adopted by the specific historical moment which produces it.[23] The proliferation of such manufactured realities naturalized and obfuscated the power structures and specific sociohistorical discourses that produced them. In this way, texts around 1800 that reproduced images of an "ideal femininity" as passive, fragile, and emotional asserted what was "natural" and simultaneously coded as *un*natural anything deviating from this norm, thereby targeting women's bodies as the objects upon which unseen forms of social regulation and symbolic power were being exerted.

At the same time that such "truths" about gender were being disseminated to regulate gender roles in line with reactionary social agendas, the very constructedness of these discourses allowed for another more subversive possibility, namely the strategic appropriation of gender myths as forms of contestation. Women's discursive bodies were reclaimed in this sense as sites of renegotiation and reinscribed with alternate visions of femininity, which not only sought to expose the fallacy of the myths but to exploit them in the construction of new, more empowering modes of being. Reading late eighteenth-century gender discourses with Judith Butler's theories of performativity and discursive acts, I argue that while myths of gender binaries sought to "naturalize" a set of practices and norms through the act of naming, they simultaneously offered women writers an opportunity to reclaim their bodies, both material and discursive, by articulating their own notions of what it meant to be a woman.[24]

An exploration of the subversive impulses manifested in works by many women writers of this period offers insight into women's strategic awareness of and negotiations with dominant social narratives. Such textual traces of resistance, contestation, appropriation, and reimagining expose the myth of the gendered public-private divide even as it was being proclaimed and enforced by contemporaries. Furthermore, if gender discourses of the eighteenth century are treated as forms of injurious speech, then attempts by women writers to resignify the term "femininity," and all that it implied, signaled ruptures in the social structures of domination that "perform[ed] a reversal of effects."[25] Certain women writers strategically appropriate and recontextualize myths of love and sacrifice as specifically feminine attributes as a means of "opening up the possibility of 'agency,' where agency is not the restoration of a sovereign autonomy in speech, a replication of conventional notions of mastery."[26] This redoubling of the gendered rhetoric enabled them to problematize the notion of separate spheres which denied women their rightful place in public life and their valuable contribution to the political and social welfare of their homeland. Close readings of women warriors in the works of Therese Huber, Karoline von Günderrode, and Caroline de la Motte Fouqué elucidate the authors' strategic "misappropriation" of love, both in the form of patriotism and familial love, as the motivation behind their heroines' armed participation and sacrificial offering on the battlefield. By reinscribing love to signify an empowering, subversive feminine attribute, these authors constructed emancipatory fantasies, which envisioned and legitimized new forms of femininity transcending the binaries promulgated by conservative social discourses.

In focusing on the figure of the woman warrior as a site of symbolic contestation, I do not deny materialist claims that "bodies matter." Indeed, the materiality of women's bodies was of central importance in the scientific community's assertions of her inherent passivity and also served as "evidence" for claims made by social theorists, such as Brandes, regarding women's inherent domesticity. It is exactly this intersection of the material and the discursive to which *Armed Ambiguity* is attuned and which is so critical to our understanding of how eighteenth-century gender debates established dominant narratives to which literary manifestations of bellicose women responded. Despite the criticism lodged against Butler in recent decades for neglecting the materiality of the physical body, her theories of performativity and discursive practices when paired with an attentiveness to the concerns of real, material bodies offers valuable insights into the ways in which women's bodies were co-opted in the service of and directly impacted by competing ideologies. Indeed, as proponents of material feminism have advocated, productive and nuanced insights into the complex relationship between the social and natural worlds may be culled more successfully from approaches that attend to both material and discursive forces.[27]

Revolutionary Ruptures: German Responses to the Violence of the French Revolution

The gender narratives focusing on women's bodies, with which the authors discussed in this book engage, capture the unease and apprehension generated by the political chaos and ruptures in the fabric of German society during this period. The destabilizing effects of this revolutionary period were one of the driving forces necessitating the reestablishment of clearly defined gender roles as a form of social control.[28] Literary representations of warring women are negotiations with this transformative moment in modern European history, a period in which print culture engendered new fantasies of warlike women in the hotly contested battle for German public opinion.

Due to its rapid expansion in the eighteenth century, the press assumed a more powerful role in German public opinion-making about the French Revolution, but its reports of women's participation in revolutionary violence also established the tone with which subsequent literary treatments of armed women would engage.

Even before Parisian crowds stormed the Bastille on July 14, 1789, German newspapers and journals were awash with reports of the violent changes underway in France. The magnitude of the events unfolding to the west of German borders was not lost on nobles, intellectuals, or members of the literary community, and reporting on the Revolution became an ideological battleground for German public sentiment.[29] Most initial responses to the politically charged events, as documented in travelogues, diaries, and newspaper and journal reports can be divided into three categories: enthusiastic reactions to dramatic changes hastened by the Revolution and hopeful calls for similar reforms to be undertaken in German-speaking territories; supportive reception of the revolutionary transformations but protective defense of the status quo within German borders; and lastly outright rejections of the articulation and implementation of republican principles in either France or Germany.[30] Enthralled by the possibility that principles espoused by early Enlightenment thinkers might be put into practice, idealistic Germans rushed to Paris to participate in the euphoria characterizing the early stages of the Revolution, while others wearily waited for the political plague to infect German society.[31]

The period between 1792 and 1793 marked a critical turning point in German public opinion about the Revolution. Even proponents of the newly founded French Republic were hard-pressed to maintain their support in the aftermath of a series of violent events culminating in the public spectacle of Louis XVI's beheading in early 1793, which paved the way for the bloodiest phase of the Revolution. Compounding daily reports of carnage in the streets of Paris, displays of public executions, and a general culture of fear propagated by fanatical Jacobins was France's declaration of war against the Austrian-Prussian coalition in April 1792. The Revolution and its violence took on a sense of immediacy for Germans, who could no longer turn a blind eye to the threat of bloodshed "over there." The brutality being perpetrated within French borders now had direct implications for the daily lives of German families. Sons, fathers, brothers, and husbands became soldiers mobilized to battlefields in France, while German borders were penetrated by foreign aggressors and communities were subjugated to the control of French occupying forces.[32] The often brutal and cynical behavior of the French occupiers quickly disabused German underclasses of any notions they might have had about "liberation" by their French "brothers."[33]

Most German intellectuals, who had initially welcomed the Revolution, distanced themselves from the violence. Rather than agitate for social change through revolt or protest by the masses, as their French neighbors had done,

Germans retreated to the comforting idea of a more gradual, controlled structural transformation offered by the notion of enlightened absolutism. Central to this retreat was the assumption that neither the average French nor German citizen was ready for the responsibilities that accompanied greater freedom and rights.[34] Even staunch German Jacobins, such as Georg Forster, were forced to acknowledge that their hopes of a French Republic on German soil were dashed by the bloodshed that had become the order of the day in the months and years following the French king's execution.[35] This disillusionment with the Revolution found an outlet in German representations of the French Girondist sympathizer Charlotte Corday, who assassinated the prominent journalist and Jacobin Jean-Paul Marat in his bathtub in July 1793. Journalists and literary authors, from both moderate and more radical camps, attempted to efface the violent, criminal nature of Corday's political act in their fictional treatments of the young female assassin in order to recuperate her for their political and social agendas.

It was not lost on the political elite that such radicalism could easily erupt in Germany. This anxiety went beyond concern about the upheaval of the existing political order and extended to specifically encompass fears that German women might follow the example set by their French counterparts and publicly demand their rights. As market women took to the streets to demand fair grain prices in order to feed their families, others armed with farm implements and some with weapons marched to Versailles in October 1789 to demand the royal family's return to Paris. Indeed, historian Klaus Epstein has implied a direct link between the French women's October march to the king's palace and the most serious example of revolutionary subversion on German soil, the Saxon peasant revolt of 1790.[36] Meanwhile female revolutionaries like Théroigne de Méricourt and the founding members of the women's political club Société des Citoyennes Républicaines Révolutionnaires (Society of Revolutionary Republican Women), Claire Lacombe and Pauline Léon, appeared before the Legislative Assembly in 1792 to petition women's right to bear arms.[37] Even Hippel, the adamant defender of women's right to direct political representation, in his response to reports of women publicly agitating for their freedoms, conveys the ambivalence aroused by the prospect of disorderly women.[38] He admonishes male members of the French Legislative Assembly for not immediately bestowing the same rights on women in order to avoid public scenes of disobedience. Hippel is so dismayed by the prospect of women resorting to unruly behavior that he reverts to the same rhetoric of woman's "Nature," which he criticized previously, in order to stave off this apprehension: "Doch ist es die Frage, ob die Pariser Damen schon die Selbstüberwindung gehabt haben, so weit zur Natur zurückzukehren, daß sie die gute Sache menschlich und bürgerlich beherzigen können.—Wahrlich, zu deutschen Weibern ist größeres Vertrauen zu fassen" (Hippel, *Über die bürgerliche Verbesserung* 123–24; "Nevertheless, the question remains whether the fashionable ladies of Paris can [discipline] themselves and return far enough back to nature to be able to ponder the matter in humane and [civilized] fashion. Surely we can have more faith in the women of Germany" [Sellner, *On Improving the Status of Women* 121; translation modified]). The socially progressive Hippel's retreat to "Nature" reveals how deeply entrenched such gender myths had become by the end of the eighteenth century and how quickly they could be reactivated to confront the looming threat of disorderly, violent women.

In this moment of political chaos, the collapse of the ancien régime not only precipitated a deterioration of established class structures but also facilitated the inversion of social conventions, in particular narratives constructed around gender and separate spheres. The carnivalesque atmosphere generated by the political and military disorder at the turn of the century created a space in which women could subvert the political hierarchy and social order, if only temporarily. The concept of the carnival serves as an entry point into elucidating how military conflicts characterizing the end of the eighteenth century enabled women's violent participation in the public sphere of warfare to assume the form of symbolic disobedience. Furthermore, it helps to illustrate how depictions of women at war responded to these perceived transgressive maneuvers by supporting or subverting entrenched institutions of power. To be sure, critics have downplayed the transgressive potential of Mikhail Bakhtin's notion of the carnival, arguing it can never truly allow for permanent change or inversion of power structures because it is sanctioned by ruling institutions. However, I contend that the French Revolution and resulting violent campaigns must be considered as truly transgressive acts because they were intended to permanently overthrow aristocratic structures of power via sanctioned and unsanctioned acts of violence, as is evidenced by the storming of the Tuileries, the September massacres, and perhaps most clearly by *la Terreur* (the period known as the Terror) carried out by the ruling Jacobin party. The topsy-turvy, inverted nature of the early Revolution was not sanctioned by the authorities or those "on top." As Natalie Zemon Davis argues in her work on forms of female transgression in the early modern period, the subversive potential of role inversion is made possible by the phenomenon of the carnival and the concept of "play."[39] Thus, women who acted out were indeed undermining the social order and institutions of authority in ways that were perceived as truly threatening and not just feigned performances.

Women's active participation in the public sphere of warfare threatened to disrupt the established absolutist power structure and expose its tenuous control over societal conventions. German news reports cast female revolutionaries as "deviant" or "anti-ideals" while simultaneously juxtaposing these female specters with visions of "ideal femininity" in the form of passive, maternal female patriots. In her work on female transgression in eighteenth-century Britain, Katharine Kittredge has argued the need to examine not only the depiction of the "feminine ideal" but also to consider how the construction of the "anti-ideal" serves as a "mechanism that shapes perception and enforces conformity."[40] Expanding on Kittredge, I argue that interrogating instantiations of the woman warrior, which ultimately complicate the archetypes of "feminine ideal" and "anti-ideal," reveals the discursive strategies employed by authors in the perpetuation or contestation of dominant gender myths used to regulate and exert social domination. My critical treatment of these reports excavates the deep-seated ambivalence about women and violence, but also disorderly women more broadly, and their destabilizing effect on the status quo. More importantly, this book illuminates how the phenomenon of ambiguity can be seized upon in order to subvert or resignify dominant narratives.[41]

Women Warriors as Gender-Benders: Literary Cross-Dressing and the Battlefield

A critical examination of ambiguous women warriors and the ways in which women's material and discursive bodies served as sites of symbolic struggle necessitates a brief meditation on the role of transvestism and its relationship to gendered identity. The appearance of literary and historical cross-dressing women warriors around 1800 is one example of the transgressive possibility proffered by periods of political turmoil. At the end of the eighteenth century there was a direct correlation between women's armed participation in the martial conflicts and the phenomenon of cross-dressing.[42] In France, this connection can perhaps best be explained by the legal restrictions leveled by the National Convention in 1793 outlawing women's participation in the Revolutionary Army. Circumnavigating this ban, women intent on fighting to defend the emerging Republic resorted to cross-dressing in order to take up arms alongside fellow male soldiers. Similar examples have been documented among German forces during the Napoleonic Wars, with the names Eleonore Prochaska and Anna Lühring becoming synonymous with heroic virtue and patriotic sacrifice.[43] While the German press likened French republican amazons to bloodthirsty animals, tales of German women's heroism some two decades later ceased to evoke the same anxiety and fear. Cross-dressing German women warriors, literary scholar Elisabeth Krimmer argues, were rehabilitated for patriotic causes because they no longer posed a danger to the patriarchal structure.[44] Instead of linking demands to bear arms with demands for political equality, women who took up arms were depicted as fighting an external enemy threatening German values and autonomy.

Krimmer locates such models of female patriotism at the conclusion of the Wars of Liberation; however, as I shall argue, the literary reframing of cross-dressing women warriors as patriotic defenders of the domestic good began slightly earlier and is exemplified by the women warriors of Benedikte Naubert's 1788 historical novel *Geschichte der Gräfin Thekla von Thurn* (*Story of the Countess Thekla of Thurn*) and 1792 historical novel *Philippe von Geldern. Oder Geschichte Selims, des Sohns Amurat* (*Philippe of Guelders; or the Story of Selim, the Son of Murad*). Naubert's reluctant literary cross-dressers illustrate the precarious and complex nature of cross-dressing and remind us that transvestism has the potential to destabilize and challenge binaries, but that it can be co-opted just as readily to foreclose subversive readings and to secure the status quo.[45] Krimmer's warning to proceed with caution when interrogating instances of literary cross-dressing is well-heeded. It is not my intention to argue that literary cross-dressing is always a transgressive act, nor do I suggest it necessarily implies a subversive intention; for example, my readings of Naubert's reluctant cross-dressing warrior women Thekla and Philippe challenge such an essentialist position. However, I do accept that textual manifestations of cross-dressing women warriors masquerading as male soldiers complicate and present the opportunity to reveal as unstable the reliance on appearance as a means to accurately identify and categorize individuals and the roles they occupy based on gender, as my analyses of the gender-bending warriors in the works of Naubert, Schiller, and others demonstrate.

Sartorial transgressions prove particularly useful vehicles for those women writers who seek to mount a critique of the bifurcated structures of social hegemony. As this book argues, women writers Therese Huber, Karoline von Günderrode, and Caroline de la Motte Fouqué highlight the artificiality of discursively constructed notions of "femininity" and "masculinity" and call into question the basis for coding the public sphere as exclusively masculine based on these assumptions by playing with the gender ambiguity of their cross-dressing heroines. Similarly, Krimmer argues that the very act of cross-dressing instantiates the ambivalence toward gendered identity being articulated in gender debates during this same period. Literary "cross-dressers often carry metaphorical meaning. They embody categorical instabilities and poetological crises. It is only to be expected that the eighteenth century—a society plagued by epistemological uncertainties—would be mesmerized by the ambiguous 'nature' of the cross-dresser."[46]

While cross-dressing proves a useful narrative strategy by which certain women writers exploited the ambiguity of warring women to imagine new forms of female agency, what function do these cross-dressers perform in works by male authors? Do they similarly signal "category crises" elsewhere,[47] and what ideological agendas do they advance? How is ambivalence articulated in literary visions that do not rely on cross-dressing? *Armed Ambiguity* answers these questions in its critical investigation of Friedrich Schiller's armed maiden Johanna in the 1801 historical drama *Die Jungfrau von Orleans* (*The Maid of Orleans*) and Johann Wolfgang Goethe's domestic amazon in the 1797 epic poem *Herrmann und Dorothea*. In my reading, Johanna and Dorothea exemplify ambiguity by engaging in violence coded as masculine while simultaneously retaining their "feminine" appearances. Such depictions of the androgynous warrior and the authors' unsuccessful literary attempts to contain the transgressive potential of the disorderly woman further complicate the eighteenth-century notion of gender as a stable signifier. Along these lines, I focus on Heinrich von Kleist's amphibolic Amazon queen Penthesilea, a specter of the androgynous ideal,[48] to suggest that her degeneration leading to a primal act of violence and ultimate self-destruction signals the dangers posed by individual acts of transgression and the immutability of systemic forms of power.

Deciphering Enigmatic Women Warriors

Reading ambiguous representations of warring women through these critical lenses, *Armed Ambiguity* excavates literary texts' negotiations with historical gender discourses, discourses that sought to naturalize a rigid set of social practices and cultural norms, and how these fictional works problematized the arbitrariness of such conventions and their underlying structures of domination. In doing so, I build upon the seminal work of German feminist scholars, whose initial interrogations of literary depictions of "the feminine" by eighteenth- and nineteenth-century men and women writers anticipated what Butler would later refer to as the discursive construction of gender. Of central importance to this study is the work of Inge Stephan, whose research, along with Sigrid Weigel, was instrumental in assessing how writers reproduced or challenged the aestheticization of femininity in their texts and the implications of these depictions for women's self-images.[49] More specifically, Stephan's focus on warlike women in texts by German male authors offered the first feminist analysis of the means by which gender ambivalence intersected with political upheaval around 1800.[50] Beginning with the 1989 bicentennial of the French Revolution, Stephan's groundbreaking work was expanded on by scholars working to elucidate further the varied significance of warring women in literature of this period.[51]

Scholarship on women and violence has been moved forward most recently in the interdisciplinary three-volume series on women and death, which surveys women's relationship to violence, both as perpetrator and victim, over a period of some 500 years. In an impressive collection of essays on German literature, art, and cultural practices in *Women and Death 2: Warlike Women in the German Literary and Cultural Imagination since 1500*, Sarah Colvin and Helen Watanabe-O'Kelly have assembled perhaps the most comprehensive study of the woman warrior's trajectory in the German cultural context from the German reception of the Amazons to the political self-fashioning of the left-wing terrorist Ulrike Meinhof. In a similar vein, Watanabe-O'Kelly's important monograph *Beauty or Beast? The Woman Warrior in the German Imagination from the Renaissance to the Present* (2010) places heavier emphasis on literary manifestations of warlike women and what they reveal about specific cultural and historical contexts. However, the extensive scope of such studies results in the woman warrior only receiving cursory attention in any one historical period.

While these projects prove invaluable in facilitating a better understanding of the nexus between gender and warfare in various cultural and political contexts throughout German history, they also raise important questions about individual historical conditions in which images of warring women are manifested. I build on these pioneering works by offering a detailed treatment of the discursive spaces occupied by armed women during one of the most decisive periods in modern European cultural and political thought. Furthermore, by bringing together depictions of women warriors constructed by both male and female writers, *Armed Ambiguity* engenders new, critical assessments of both classical and neglected works. The very structure of this study seeks to erase the traditional hierarchical gendered divisions between canonical and peripheral, privileged and marginalized, by creating a space for these authors to engage in dialogue with one another via their women warriors. By focusing attention on the semiotic battles waged over the female body, I aim to reinvigorate scholarly investigations into the human body as a site of both contestation and renegotiation of power and agency at the beginning of modern German history.

Chapter One

✦

The Power of the Press

Eighteenth-Century German Print Culture Constructs the Woman Warrior

Beginning with the first reports of the July 1789 storming of the Bastille in Paris, the French Revolution became a source of fascination and contestation for watchful politicians, critical scholars, and the anxious general public. The Revolution altered irrevocably every facet of European culture. One such alteration was the destabilization of borders: the geopolitical border between French and German territories was under attack as was the gendered boundary between public and private spheres of activity. This instability that threatened to undermine social order in France also endangered the gender norms within German-speaking territories. German newspapers and journals played a decisive role in shaping public opinion about the Revolution by targeting revolutionary women's presence and participation in matters of politics and war. In an attempt to defend and reinforce reactionary political ideologies and social norms against revolutionary fervor threatening to engulf German regions, the German press mobilized diametrically opposed representations of female participants in the public sphere: "violent" warlike women and "well-mannered" patriotic ladies. The press depicted armed women's presence in the political realm as "unnatural" and "dangerous" while at the same time it privileged images of the patriotic mother and wife whose support of the political cause was depicted as "natural" and "nonthreatening." These competing images of revolutionary women, as either specter or ideal, served as expressions of the hopes and fears Germans felt toward the events unfolding in neighboring France and border regions of Germany. Yet more importantly, this binary structure undergirding the German press's characterization of women's relationship to political change and armed conflict would become the dominant narrative with which subsequent literary negotiations with fictional and historical women warriors would engage for decades.

The earliest traces of the German public's preoccupation with the French Revolution are to be found in eyewitness and travel reports circulated by regional newspapers and journals, political treatises, and literary works. Of the aspects of the Revolution that engrossed the press and literary community, the woman warrior emerges as a prominent and recurring image. Literary manifestations of the armed, defiant woman set against backdrops of political upheaval in works by male and female authors thematized, in one fashion or another, the simultaneously traumatic and potentially liberating effects of the French Revolution. Firsthand accounts published by the popular press proved just as influential as the fictional depictions of the armed woman by the literary community. The images of armed, revolutionary women in the print media played an increasingly powerful role in reinforcing gender roles—and the gendering of the public, political sphere as masculine—because of its ability to reach a broader audience. Its portrayal of women in the political violence and social turmoil of the French Revolution, the French Revolutionary Wars, and the Napoleonic invasion of German territories impacted the reading public's attitude toward women's presence and participation in the public sphere, most specifically involving matters of political equality, including the right to bear arms.

Newspaper and journal representations of women bearing arms convey the hopes and fears, two diametrically opposed yet intertwined emotions, of Germans toward the unrest developing across and within their own borders. The German press's depiction of female participants in the Revolution can be categorized predominantly into two contrasting myths of femininity: the "ideal" feminine embodied by the dutiful, patriotic "Bürgerin" and the "anti-ideal" depicted as the outspoken, ominous "Weib" of the working class.[1] Images of a gentle, feminine "Bürgerin" depict women performing normative gender roles and socially "acceptable" forms of passive, female patriotism that confirmed the social and political order and simultaneously perpetuated the illusion of equality.[2] In contrast, the figure of the working class woman warned readers of the potential threat posed by women who sought to move beyond their social rank and assert their access to the newly proclaimed civil liberties. These artificial archetypes express and play upon the fears of readers, more specifically male readers,[3] that German women's increased participation in the public life of German society might weaken or even upset the gendered sociopolitical hierarchy. Depictions of violent market women competing alongside images of passive, obedient housewives and mothers functioned simultaneously as invisible forms of domination and sites of contestation. They became at once objects and agents of myth's power.[4] Narratives demonizing warlike women confirmed the fabricated truth of an "ideal femininity"—just as readily as did prevailing myths of docile housewives—and secured disobedient women's status as deviant or, at the very least, peripheral. Thus, the press strategically vilified the armed woman and privileged the patriotic mother and wife in an effort to contain the potential threat posed by violent female revolutionaries to the social order.

As revolutionary women's actions threatened to erode the carefully constructed myths of a bourgeois "ideal femininity," German newspapers and journals controlled and mediated the news of such events, opting frequently to reinforce traditional gender myths. Helga Brandes argues that the press rejected the female revolutionaries by portraying them negatively. This allowed the reading public to counter its fear while bolstering the established gender hierarchy of late eighteenth-century German society.[5] Brandes has accurately observed that the construction of both negative and positive images of women is a means by which the press attempts to manipulate the reader and to promote a specific political agenda—in this case, an antirevolutionary program instilling fear in order to reinforce existing power structures. However, while she claims that the periodical plays the central role as the "Meinungsträger" (opinion maker) in the formation of ideology,[6] I assert the importance of the regional newspaper alongside political and literary journals in shaping the reading public's opinion about women's participation in the public sphere and the reassertion of conservative social and political values through carefully manufactured myths of warlike women.

The German Press as "Meinungsträger" and Mythmaker

Two of the most widely circulated Prussian newspapers, the *Berlinische Nachrichten von Staats- und Gelehrten Sachen*, also known as the *Haude und Spenersche Zeitung* (*HSZ*), and the *Königlich privilegirte Zeitung von Staats und gelehrten Sachen*, also known as the *Vossische Zeitung* (*VZ*), provide fertile ground for an investigation into the press's reception of revolutionary women and its strategic deployment of myths about women and violence in order to reaffirm a reactionary social order. As the largest German state, Prussia played not only the dominant role in the Coalition Wars against France but also had widespread influence in matters of politics and culture.[7] Furthermore, reports from a number of more widely circulated journals including Albrecht Wittenberg's *Historisch-politisches Magazin, nebst litterarischen Nachrichten* (*HPM*), published in Hamburg (1787–95), and Johann Wilhelm von Archenholz's *Minerva*: *Ein Journal historischen und politischen Inhalts*, published first in Hamburg and then in Leipzig (1792–1858), serve as useful resources for a consideration of the print media's fixation with the figure of the armed woman.

Newspapers, like periodicals, informed the reading public in nuanced ways. Scholarship has focused primarily on the function of political and literary journals during this period of social upheaval. This trend could be due to the common misperception of newspapers as neutral historical sources rather than as literary texts in need of interpretation. As I argue, the press's ability to present information as "objective" or "truthful" exemplifies its utility as an effective vehicle for mythmaking by constructing and deploying manufactured realities that remained uncontested. In actuality, newspapers, like journals and traditional literary genres, produced subjective interpretations of events that were guided by underlying ideological agendas. A study conducted by Ursula E. Koch et al. similarly reveals that Prussian newspapers, the *HSZ* in particular, narrativized their news of the Revolution by combining factual reporting with subjective opinions of informants and incorporating interpretations and interspersed arguments.[8] While newspapers' main function was to inform the public about current events, they were also subject, at least theoretically, to varying degrees of censorship depending on the region and the political leanings of the reigning nobility. For example, both the *HSZ* and *VZ* complied with Prussian censorship laws imposed by Friedrich Wilhelm II. These restrictions directly impacted what and how news was presented to their readers. The news reaching the public was no longer dependent solely on the editor's political and social agenda but was now the product of yet another subjective filter, the local nobility. Political journals, on the other hand, became outlets for exercising political opinion and criticism.

An unprecedentedly greater number of people had access to news reports than in previous centuries, resulting in a more timely exchange of information and in the press's increasing power to shape public opinion.[9] Similarly, the press also had the power to influence how individuals developed a sense of self in relation to others, particularly in relation to the foreign Other.[10] When viewed from this perspective, reports of armed women in the German media not only contributed to a perception of the neighboring French, but also caused the German reader to reflect on his or her own position toward such reports. If the Revolution were to spread to Germany, would men succumb to the will of armed women? Would German women follow the examples set by their French counterparts and take up weapons to defend their families and country? These are implicit questions with which the German reader was confronted on a daily basis.

As the influence of the press grew, so too did criticism of its abuse of influence from intellectuals and social theorists. Christoph Martin Wieland's 1790 editorial in *Der Neue Teutsche Merkur* highlights how some journalists reporting on events in France succumbed to sensationalism or at the very least exaggeration in order to increase their profits.[11] He argues that it is the author's responsibility to the reader to acknowledge his or her bias instead of disguising personal opinion as fact. Wieland calls for the "return" to objective and truthful reporting.[12] His efforts to expose and remove social and political agendas from reports of revolutionary events could do very little to stop the publication of outright propaganda, but his voice was one of many signaling an uneasiness with the power of the press at this unprecedented historical juncture.

The prevalence of reports demonizing and idealizing women's participation in the events of the Revolution was a function of the publishers' desire to increase profits while also satisfying the agenda of social moralists seeking to reinforce conservative values and social order. The press's circulation of reports about dangerous armed women in particular was an attempt to contain the subversive potential such images might generate among female readers.[13] In his work on "disorderly" women in the broadsheets of early modern England, Stuart Kane argues that the negative depiction of "wife-as-shrew" was "such a heavily coded and extensively represented image that her subversive capability was largely containable."[14] Furthermore, Kane contends that broadsheets, which were consumed primarily by readers of the lower classes, focused on the "disorderly" conduct of lower-class women in the hope that readers would "internalize these broader cultural anxieties about them, and [would] potentially reproduce these anxieties in their own daily lives," resulting in a kind of "consensual self-regulation by the lower classes, men and women alike."[15] Like the murder ballads of early modern England, eighteenth-century reports of the armed "Weib" as specter circulating in pamphlets, fliers, newspapers, and journals across German territories cultivated a discourse of fear and anxiety that attempted to regulate the roles of women of all classes in public life. With many of the subscriptions held by reading societies, coffee houses, inns, and taverns, newspapers transcended class boundaries and bridged the gap between educated middle- and upper-class audiences and readers belonging to the uneducated lower classes.[16]

Revolutionary Specters: Amazons, Hyenas, and Furies

A prominent feature of the press's coverage of the Revolution were references to "women" as a broadly defined group that generalized the presence of any woman in the public sphere of the Revolution and marked her as the "anti-ideal."[17] Informants for newspapers and political journals rarely single out individual women in their accounts. Groups of female participants are described in general terms such as a "Haufen" (mob), a "Schar" (band), a "Schwarm" (swarm), or as members of the "Pöbel" (mob). The appearance of terms such as "Weib" or "Weiber," "Frauenzimmer," and "Frauensperson" are, more often than not, accompanied by such qualifiers as "selbst" and "sogar" (even) and "besonders" (especially). For example, a report in the *VZ* from Paris dated July 17, 1789, describing the storming of the Bastille and the visible change in the people's attitudes notes that "Selbst die Frauenzimmer sahen die Köpfe, die umher getragen wurden, mit sichtbaren Zeichen von Vergnügen" ("Even the ladies saw the heads that were being carried around with visible signs of amusement").[18] Almost the same construction is used to describe this procession in the *HPM*: "sogar das weibliche Geschlecht lächelte, und bezeugte seinen Beyfall bey diesem schrecklichen Anblicke" ("even the female sex smiled and showed its approval at this terrible sight").[19] The only difference between the "objective" newspaper report and the "subjective" journal account is the term used to identify the female spectators. Avoiding references to class altogether, the anonymous author of the *HPM* article expresses disbelief at the actions of the entire female sex. Rather than displaying visible signs of revulsion at the bloody scene—a reaction which would have upheld commonly asserted myths about the female "Nature" as being best suited for the duties of life in the domestic sphere—the women in question insert themselves into the political violence unfolding in the streets of Paris. Thus, their roles as witnesses to and their endorsement of violence marks a departure from and provides a sharp contrast to the archetypal pacifist, maternal figure of the familial household, who gives life instead of taking it.

These depictions are not limited to Parisian women and indicate the growing fear in Germany that this was not just a French problem. Dispatches from border provinces such as Brabant and cities like Liège and Strasbourg inform Prussian readers of the spread of violence to women from these regions. In reports from Strasbourg dated February 2, 1791, both the *HSZ* and *VZ* depict unrest in the area where women protested against the National Constituent Assembly's edict restricting the special rights of the clergy. The *HSZ* notes the appearance of more than one hundred "Amazoninnen" (amazons) armed with "Bratspießen" (roasting spits) and mounted on horses,[20] while the *VZ* describes the women's threats to burn the commissariat alive for stealing from the church.[21] Depicting these women as amazons alludes to the popularity of the mythic warriors among female revolutionaries who appropriated the image of the warrior woman as an empowering model of female agency and fashioned themselves as modern-day Amazon warriors.[22] More importantly, however, the reports emphasize the threat posed by women's participation in the politics and military conflicts of the Revolution. These accounts of women in Strasbourg arming themselves with weapons similar to those of the Hüningen women, near Basel, reported by the *VZ* almost a year earlier, indicate that the Revolution and its violence could no longer be contained within France nor limited to French women.

The press's attention to the actions of the women from the border regions represents only one stage in the public's lengthy fascination with and criticism of women's participation in the Revolution. Initial coverage of women's ominous agitation minimized the female revolutionaries' threat to social order by depicting their demands as contained to traditionally "domestic" matters of home and familial stability. The events of October 5–6, 1789, in which market women marched from Paris to Versailles to force the king and his family to return to the capital, was the first instance in which women's presence in the public sphere became widely publicized in German newspapers and journals. An account from Paris dated October 9, 1789, reports that some 10,000 women from the lower classes appeared "in ganzen Schaaren auf den Straßen" ("in entire bands in the streets") and "schwärmten durch die Stadt, und nöthigten alle Weiber, die ihnen begegneten, oder die sich in ihren Buden und Läden befanden, gemeinschaftliche Sache mit ihnen zu machen" ("swarmed through the city and forced the women, whom they encountered or who were in their booths and shops, to do collective things with them").[23] The reporter, who previously referred to these women of the lower classes as "berauschte Weiber" (intoxicated women), depicts the powerful nature of the market women and their urgent, aggressive actions. The report moreover describes their forceful entry into the town hall where they demanded bread and commandeered weapons. This report is one of the earliest descriptions of women protesting en masse, although not yet formally organized, for basic necessities such as food and social order. While the verbs "nöthigen," "sich drängen," and "verlangen" convey the underlying threat and use of force presented by this group of women, the objects of their demands minimize the danger they pose: ensuring food and safety for their families were duties that continued to fall within women's responsibilities as caretakers, nurturers, and providers. Their threat is further diminished by the fact that the women's demands for and even confiscation of weapons does not result in women committing acts of violence: "Die Weiber liefen mit den Gewehren davon, gaben sie ihren Männern, u. wollten, daß diese mit nach Versailles gehen sollten" ("The women ran away with the firearms, gave them to their husbands, and wanted them to go with them to Versailles").[24] Despite the Revolution's destabilizing effect on the political hierarchy, myths of a stable gender order, in which men were the standard bearers of military force and political change, remained intact, at least for the time being.

Other reports demonstrate that when women shifted their demands away from basic necessities to the right to bear arms and political participation, the press no longer depicted their threat as benign. A report about the same scene appears in the *HPM* and assigns women the leading role in events preceding the October march.[25] Whereas the *VZ* report states that the women handed over the weapons to men, this *HPM* reporter clearly places the deadly weapons in the hands of the more than 2,000 women: "Die meisten hatten Piken, andere Säbel, Flinten, und damit die Rüstung vollkommen seyn möchte: so ließen sie 2 oder 3 kleine Canonen, deren sie sich in der Stadt bemächtiget hatten, vor sich herführen" ("The majority had spears, others sabers, rifles, and in order to complete the armament they allowed 2 or 3 small cannons, which they had taken possession of in the city, to be brought before them").[26] The discrepancies between the two reports are significant: the *HPM* lists the "Haufen" of women at just over 2,000 while the *VZ* assigns a greater number to the "Schaaren"; furthermore, there is an inconsistency as to whether or not and to what extent women took up arms. While the women in both the *HPM* and *VZ* reports are portrayed as asserting their agency by means of force ("nöthigen" and "nahmen mit Gewalt"), the *HPM* states that the women not only took possession of but also wielded the weapons, including the use of cannons. The reporter's acknowledgment that the women's threats of violence are no laughing matter—"Dieß war eigentlich nur eine Farce, und man lachte darüber; es ward aber Ernst daraus" ("This was merely a farce and it was laughed about, but it became serious")[27]—conveys the seriousness of the situation and confirms growing fears about women's role in the public sphere of the Revolution: their participation had already escalated from the role of spectator to that of instigator and perpetrator.

Increasingly, the articles utilized more provocative and disturbing language to portray the "base nature" of the insurrectionary, Parisian "Weiber mit Gewehren" (women with weapons). This was especially true in accounts documenting their cruelty and fury toward the royal family. For instance, the women are reported to have shouted, "sie wollten mit dem Kopfe der Königin Kegel schieben, und aus ihren Eingeweiden weisse Kokarden machen" ("they wanted to bowl with the head of the queen and to make white cockades out of her intestines").[28] Like the *HPM* report, this account points to the perceived intensification of the women's violence. The reporter suggests that these armed women have the means to follow through on their threats of bodily violence against the royal family. The women's demands are still motivated by the right to fair food prices but are now accompanied by calls for violent retribution.

The chaos and social upheaval generated by the Revolution created a kind of carnivalesque atmosphere in which the image of the transgressive female revolutionary became fertile ground for male activism while simultaneously reinforcing the inherent danger of such an uncontrollable, dangerous woman. In the above report male cross-dressers, men disguised in women's clothing, are suggested to be among the thousands of women. While women cross-dressing as men in order to move unrestricted within the public sphere and to circumvent the sanctions against women's participation in combat has been well documented,[29] the presence of cross-dressing men is less prevalent and raises the question: what advantages did disguising themselves as women have for male participants of the Revolution? Citing examples of male cross-dressing from the fifteenth to the nineteenth centuries, Natalie Zemon Davis suggests that men's political transvestism invoked the carnivalesque mode of inversion as a means by which to publicly express dissent while evading potentially negative ramifications for such open defiance. By co-opting the image of the disorderly woman, "the males drew upon the sexual power and energy of the unruly woman and on her license (which they had long assumed at carnival and games) to promote fertility, to defend the community's interests and standards, and to tell the truth about unjust rule."[30] Yet, the German press's reports of male political transvestism sought to undermine the women's agency as independent, engaged citizens by suggesting that they alone could have neither made such threatening demands nor acted in such a violent manner, thereby reinforcing for readers the prevailing gender discourse of a physically weak and emotionally feeble female sex.

When the German press published accounts depicting the violence perpetrated by groups of women involved in the revolutionary mob's attack on the Tuileries three years after the storming of the Bastille, it highlighted the depravity of women and implied that their actions and demeanor were distinct from those of the men who also participated. The king's attempt to flee France, the threat of invasion by Prussian and Austrian forces, and the people's demands that the king be dethroned culminated in the storming of the royal family's residence on August 10, 1792. These reports confirmed for readers that women's participation in the Revolution was not confined to the violent events of 1789, and that they still presented a risk to public order. Reports from August 13, 1792, in which news of the attack on the Tuileries was published, depict the people, and most notably the women, as uncontrolled and crazed: "Das Volk, vorzüglich die Weiber, klatschte und jauchzte bei jedem Todtschlage, daß die Fenster hätten zittern mögen" ("At every death the people, especially the women, clapped and cheered so that the windows could have shaken").[31] The women's perverse pleasure is conveyed further by a report dated four days later documenting the same evening's events: "In den Gesichtern der Weiber bemerkte man nicht das geringste Zeichen von Furcht, u. selten einen Ausdruck von Empfindung" ("Not even the slightest sign of fear and rarely an expression of feeling showed in the faces of the women").[32] While the dispatch acknowledges the unusual response of the entire crowd, the female spectators, alongside children and the elderly, are categorized separately from male "Bürger" (citizens) and are singled out for their dispassionate behavior, which is described in detail, further emphasizing the press's increasingly prevalent portrayal of women in the public sphere as cold and merciless.

Routinely images of women as wild animals, and especially hyenas, savagely and ecstatically engaged in cannibalistic violence against men, were deployed to dehumanize the women in graphic and embellished reports. In these descriptions, women turned predator are relegated to the realm of primal, animalistic drives and desires. An anonymous report dated August 27, 1792, and appearing in the *Welt- und Staatsboth* from Cologne exemplifies this kind of news from France that reached the German public. The revolutionaries are likened to "Hyänen" (hyenas) who kill not out of necessity but out of bloodlust: "Zu solchen Untieren wollen Frankreichs Menschen verwildern. Noch raucht das Blut eines geschlachteten Opfers, und man sieht sich gierig nach einem neuen um" ("France's people want to degenerate into such monsters. The blood of slaughtered victims still steams, and one looks around greedily for a new victim").[33] "Hyäne" became a standard term used in the German press to refer to the bloody and savage behavior of revolutionaries, and women in particular.[34] By casting these women as beasts of prey, reporters exploit and support myths of the "weaker sex" as incapable of controlling its perceived irrational, overly emotional nature. If anything, such reports sought to justify the need for coalition troops to invade France in order to stop the spread of such "degenerate" behavior.

Travel reports, markedly differing in tone, worked in concert with newspaper reportage to confirm the disorder of women. German publicist Konrad

Engelbert Oelsner's series of travel reports from France, which appeared in Archenholz's *Minerva*, provided readers with more than just ostensibly factual accounts of events; his highly subjective commentaries and stylized descriptions bordered on the literary and are particularly notable for framing female revolutionaries as avengers, which situate them as both aggressors against and protectors of men. In his fifth letter, dated Paris, August 14, 1792, Oelsner describes his visceral reaction to the scenes of August 10 and the following days. His account, he states, conveys the "Unordnung [s]einer Seele" (disorder of his soul) that has been "wundgerieben oder vielmehr zerfleischt von einer Reihe schrecklicher Auftritte" ("rubbed raw or rather mauled by a series of horrific scenes").[35] The emotionally laden language Oelsner employs to articulate the atrocities enacted against the men forces him to project himself into the scenes of violence. As he describes the "blutdürstige Brut des Pöbels" ("bloodthirsty spawn of the mob"), he pays particular attention to the women who have been transformed into "schäumende Furien" (foaming furies). Led by the famed female revolutionary Théroigne de Méricourt, the women demand the Swiss Guards be killed as punishment for the deaths of their male relatives: "Wir begehren Rache, gebt Ihr sie uns nicht, so nehmen wir sie selbst an ihnen und Euch!" (Oelsner, "Historische Briefe" 520–21; "We desire revenge, if you don't give it to us, we will take revenge against you and them!").[36] Several layers of mythification are at work simultaneously in Oelsner's account. First, the author's use of the verb "rasen" and the adjective "schäumend" in conjunction with the noun "Furien" to depict the women and their actions resonates with and reinforces the medical community's construction of the female sex as overly emotional and uncontrollable. Second, Oelsner invokes the violent, bloodthirsty female figures of Greek and Roman mythology pervading the German press's reports of women's involvement in the Revolution. Like that of the Maenads and Amazons, the revolutionary women's violence is aimed at male victims. In a further parallel to Greek mythology, the women's act of open defiance of the Swiss Guards' authority, by demanding retribution for their kinsmen, conjures up images of Sophocles's figures Antigone and Electra. In a blurring of familial roles, it is the sisters, wives, and mothers who seek vengeance for the violence inflicted on their families, more specifically on the male members. In threatening to finish what their kinsmen could not, the French "Furies" challenge not only the Swiss Guards' status as guardians of the king but also their "masculinity." The extent of the women's violence appears to be contained within a specific context and confined to a particular audience; however, Oelsner's description extends the possibility of the threat beyond this event and these participants to include anyone who attempts to hinder the revolutionary "Furies" and simultaneously legitimizes fear of the destructive, transgressive nature of women.

Oelsner further galvanizes his audience with his graphic descriptions by suggesting that he is holding back and editing out the truly "unspeakable" atrocities that he witnessed. Oelsner writes that his "blutendes Herz" (bleeding heart) will not allow him to depict the "scheußliche Szene" (abominable scene) that unfolds before him. However, what follows is exactly the scene he claims he cannot describe: "Das Jauchzen der Weiber bedeckt die Wehklagen der Todesangst; sie schlürfen, die Weiber schlürfen mit brutaler Wollust das Grönen der Sterbenden ein, und des Höllenpfuhls Trunkenheit höhnt aus ihrem Munde die letzten Zuckungen der Agonie" (Oelsner, "Historische Briefe" 522; "The rejoicing of the women muffles the groans of terror. They slurp, with brutal lust the women slurp up the moans of the dying, and through their mouths, a devilish drunkenness mocks the last quivers of agony" [Zantop, "Crossing the Border" 222]). Like the *VZ* report from Paris, Oelsner uses "das Jauchzen" to convey the pleasure that the women take in the men's suffering, only this time the women are not merely spectators but also the perpetrators of the men's violent deaths.

Oelsner's account is characterized by heavy erotic undertones of cannibalistic behavior that communicate to the reader a disturbing image of revolutionary women as cruel, bloodthirsty creatures preying on defenseless male bodies.[37] His description of the following day's events extends the eroticized imagery of the women: "In der auf den schrecklichen Tag folgenden Nacht, sollen sie sich auf den Leichnamen, preiß gegeben, die Glieder der Getödteten gebraten, und den Vorschlag sie zu fressen gemacht haben. Noch am Morgen des eilften habe ich Weiber in den Leichnamen wühlen, und die leblosen Theile verstümmeln sehn" ("Historische Briefe" 522–23; "During the night following that horrible day, they reportedly denuded themselves on the dead bodies, roasted the limbs of the killed men, and offered them as food. Even the morning after, I have seen women clawing among the dead, mutilating their limbs" [Zantop 222]). A form of unfettered sexuality is ascribed to the women's actions that simultaneously fascinates and frightens Oelsner. His assurances to the readers that he is furnishing them with "zuverläßige Nachrichten" (dependable news) only compounds the perceived provocation.

A year later, descriptions of women's savagery during the storming of the Tuileries, similar to Oelsner's in wording and imagery, appeared in *Minerva*. A collection of eyewitness accounts portrays the women throwing themselves on male corpses and tearing them apart with their teeth.[38] In the preface to the anecdotes the reader is informed of the legitimacy of the reports, which have been taken from the archives of the Parisian municipality and committee protocols. Although accurate reporting was not always common practice, this "verification of authenticity" may have strengthened Oelsner's claims that his accounts were not merely products of his imagination or an irrational fear of female domination.[39] Oelsner's concerted efforts to link revolutionary women to fears of women's primal drives and destructive nature activated deep-seated anxieties that further solidified the warlike, revolutionary woman as the deviant, unnatural Other while simultaneously strengthening the symbolic power of more "positive" myths of passive, maternal patriots.

Armed Participation: Women's Demands for Equality

As the violence of the Revolution intensified and the threat of war from the outside loomed, women's demands extended beyond calls for fair food prices and included the rights already accorded their male counterparts, more specifically the right to bear arms in order to defend themselves, their families, and their country. Although graphic depictions of revolutionary women's depravity convey a sense of gravity, some reports trivialized their demands for the right to bear arms. The *HSZ* published a report from Paris, dated March 10, 1792, describing the request by a group of women to be allowed the right to carry and to practice using weapons as "lächerlich" (laughable).[40] Commenting at greater length on this request in *Minerva*, Archenholz explains that the French fervor to defend the constitution is not limited to men. As evidence he cites requests made by women in various French prefectures to the Legislative Assembly for permission to defend their cities. Archenholz prefaces the women's speech by calling the reasons for their demands "sonderbar" (unusual). The women, he informs his readers, argue that the Assembly entrusted the constitution to them just as much as it had been entrusted to men: "Nur vertheidigen wollen wir uns. Die bürgerliche Gesellschaft von der wir ein Theil sind, kann uns kein Recht entziehen, das die Natur uns gegeben hat" ("We want only to defend ourselves. The civil society of which we are a part, cannot deny us any right, which Nature has given us").[41] Utilizing the language of Enlightenment discourse, these women assert that their "perceived" weaknesses are not a hindrance to their right to political and military participation; instead, they consider these rights to be inalienable. The women appropriate the term "Nature" so often employed by male authors and the scientific community to justify women's exclusion from the public sphere to make their "reasoned" argument. It is precisely "Nature" that gives them the right to bear arms. The current social order is responsible for their exclusion and not the supposed characteristics of their sex. At the same time, the women accede to certain social norms: they soften the impact of their demands by assuring the Assembly that their political activism will not interfere with their familial responsibilities. This strategic concession on the part of the women was necessary in order to stave off criticism commonly lodged against women in the public sphere that they were bad mothers and wives for neglecting their domestic duties.

Despite the relatively innocuous appearance of women requesting their rights before the Assembly, a sense of fear was growing that weapons placed in the wrong hands could threaten peace and order. Women's demands were neutralized by grouping them with children and deploying "scientific" evidence of their inferiority. The following report in the *VZ* describing scenes from Paris on February 15, 1792, published prior to the storming of the Tuileries and the September massacres, makes apparent that restrictions on the distribution of arms were becoming increasingly necessary: "Knaben, Mädchen und alte Weiber liefen seit einigen Tagen mit dergleichen Waffen [Piken] umher, die in den Händen der niedrigsten Volksklasse augenscheinlich sehr gefährlich werden können" ("Boys, girls, and old women ran around for the last several days with the same weapons that obviously could become very dangerous in the hands of the lowest class of people").[42] Once again, the press categorizes children and women as one group and brands their use of weapons as potentially dangerous. These "passive" citizens are deemed not only too physically weak to defend the republic but also incapable of the maturity necessary for autonomous, legal self-representation. Results of experiments and investigations put forth by members of the scientific community in the late eighteenth and early nineteenth centuries were appropriated by conservative social theorists to lend credibility to claims that women, like children, were incapable of controlling their basic drives and desires.[43] Such theories bolstered the plausibility of news reports depicting women's debauchery and cannibalism, which further justified claims that women were unprepared for the rights and responsibilities of citizenship.

Denials of women's requests to fight, accompanied by criticism of their demands, reasserted women's social subordination based on claims of their inherent passivity that also served to reconfirm their status as objects of male desire. A report from July 30 of the same year appeared in the *VZ* documenting the request by Claire Lacombe, a former actress and president of the Société des Citoyennes Républicaines Révolutionnaires, to be allowed to volunteer "ihre Person, und ihren Arm" ("her self, and her arm") in defense of the republic. Her request was denied by the president, who remarked: "sie schiene mehr dazu gemacht zu seyn, die Tyrannen zu besänftigen, als sie zu bekämpfen" ("she appeared to be better suited to soothe the tyrants than to fight them").[44] As the president's statement makes clear, "Nature" has bestowed on the female sex qualities meant to encourage passivity and calmness, not to incite violence. Furthermore, the innuendo that Lacombe's appearance is best suited to "soothe" her enemy perpetuates the stereotype of actresses as possessing loose morals—a stereotype aimed to discredit women who sought to assert themselves in the public sphere through the theater—while simultaneously sexualizing and eroticizing the woman warrior.[45]

No longer seeking the National Convention's permission for the right to bear arms, these women take action in defense of the Republic. Almost a year after Lacombe's request, the *VZ* report from May 23, 1793, noted the appearance of some 900 women dressed in men's clothing and practicing with weapons: "Sie exercieren alle Tage, und üben sich im Schießen, worin sie schon viele [*sic*] Fertigkeit haben" ("They exercise all day and practice shooting, at which they already are very skilled").[46] Not only were these women practicing marching and rifle shooting, traditionally male occupations, but they were also performing these activities in men's clothing. Their proficiency in these exercises revealed the artificiality of myths constructed around the "delicate" and "inferior" female body and simultaneously threatened to erode the carefully constructed gender discourse centered on diametrically opposed yet complementary gender characteristics used to justify women's exclusion from the very activities in which these women were excelling. While women's cross-dressing functioned not only as a conduit for political and social protest, it also served a very practical purpose, in that it afforded women the unrestricted movement necessary for fighting that women's clothing hampered. As reports demonstrate, cross-dressing women were prevalent among revolutionary forces especially after the 1793 sanctions prohibiting them from fighting. An account in the *VZ* from January 8, 1793, in Frankfurt stated that at least sixteen women masquerading as men were discovered among the captured French soldiers. This discovery was followed by the news that more than a thousand of these women were rumored to be fighting in the French military.[47]

As the number of disguised women among the French troops continued to grow, so did news of the dangers awaiting coalition forces within German territories. In an account in the *VZ* dated June 27, 1793, German troops noted an encounter with French soldiers at the head of the Rhine in their attempt to regain Mainz. Among these troops were reported to be "vornehme Frauenzimmer aus Mainz, worunter man vorzügliche Schönheiten bemerkt haben will" ("exemplary women from Mainz, among whom there are rumored to be exquisite beauties"). However, these women are not simply there to tend to the wounds of the soldiers: "Sie feuern aus gezogenen Büchsen auf unsere deutschen Brüder; es sind aber schon mehrere dieser Amazonen erlegt worden" ("They fire from drawn muskets at our German brothers; however, several of these amazons have already been shot").[48] The women's spheres of activity appear to be shifting: they are no longer protesting in the streets of Paris; they are taking an active role in martial actions against their enemy. In fact, they are German women shooting at fellow Germans—making this account doubly traumatic.

Regardless of their external appearances, women and their willingness to fight became an asset for the sans-culottes who, under pressure from the approaching coalition forces, are reported to have demanded that women take up weapons.[49] As German readers discovered, the phenomenon of women bearing weapons was no longer limited to French female revolutionaries. Mainz Jacobins took advantage of German women's willingness to fight and mobilized them to help defend the French-occupied city.[50] These accounts convey a menacing image of French *and* German women bearing weapons; however, when these reports are compared to or accompanied by news of "acceptable" forms of female patriotism, the danger posed by these "Furies" appears more ominous.

Silk, Sashes, and Patriotic Ladies

Rather than transforming the image of the mythical Amazon into a maternal figure of patriotism as the French had done,[51] the Germans positioned these dangerous warrior women in direct opposition to the demure patriotic lady. With cross-dressing female soldiers attacking the gendered sociopolitical hierarchy, the German press's model of idealized femininity reinforced a normative model that presented women with the illusion of equal participation while protecting the system of power in the male-dominated public sphere. The carefully constructed myths of female German patriotism circulated by the German press sought to ensure that armed women became specters of "degenerate" femininity associated with lower-class French society, which were to be shunned by any German woman who considered herself to be a "respectable" lady.

Class difference plays a central role in reporters' comparisons and criticisms of women's participation in the revolutionary cause. In the *VZ* report dated March 29, 1790, news from Paris describes the praise bestowed on women who resisted the base behavior exhibited by the market women. "Unter schmeichelhaften Lobsprüchen der Gemeinde-Repräsentanten" ("amidst flattering eulogies by the municipal representatives"), a lady identified as "die Hofdame, Frau von Beaupreau" ("court lady, Madame de Beaupreau") and five additional "angesehene Bürgerfrauen" (respected female citizens) are presented with the citizen's medal of honor for staving off greater unrest "unter dem wilden Haufen" (amidst the wild mobs) of market women by buying and distributing bread.[52] The women being honored not only belong to the aristocracy, but they use their wealth to prevent further damage caused by the market women. In addition, the language used to refer to these members of the female sex places the two groups and their subsequent behavior in opposition to one another: the aristocratic women are called "Damen" and "Bürgerfrauen" whereas the women from the lower classes are identified by their livelihood ("Fischweiber") or in derogatory terms ("wilder Haufen").

Class is further emphasized by extolling certain women's financial contribution to the cause. The women's economic influence becomes a visual marker and nonviolent expression of their patriotism. In an account from May 28, 1790, in the *HSZ*, the paper reports the exemplary patriotic conduct of Parisian ladies who attempted to bolster the economy. "Vom patriotischen Geiste beseelt" ("moved by a patriotic spirit") the fifty "Bürgerinnen" attempt to rescue the textile industry by swearing an oath to wear only silk "bis die Fabrik ihre ehemalige Aktivität wieder erhalten habe" ("until the factory has regained its previous productivity").[53] The contribution of these "Bürgerinnen" to the Revolution does not involve physical action; instead, their participation centers on the "passive" use of their bodies as visible patriotic symbols. Draped in expensive fabric in the colors of the Revolution, their bodies appear harmless, representing little threat to the gendered sociopolitical order. A month later, the National Constituent Assembly organized a festival to celebrate the anniversary of the storming of the Bastille. The *VZ* reported that the festival would be "beautified" by the presence of more than 8,000 "Damen" dressed in white taffeta and decorated with sashes in the national colors.[54] Their public appearance on the Champ de Mars, the military parade grounds, marching dutifully behind the National Guard, demonstrates not only what was considered to be their place in the new republic but also signals their symbolic capital to be exploited in support of dominant narratives of republican patriotism. Their passive role is to embody republican ideals and inspire male citizens to action, not to defend the republic themselves. Like the figures of Marianne and Germania, these female bodies become semiotic receptacles for patriotic fantasies and ideological agendas mobilized to unite the people around a common cause and to inspire male citizens to action. At the same time, images of the passive female patriots denied women the right to exercise the principles they were meant to represent.[55]

While newspapers mobilized class in order to elevate or denigrate women's political participation, sometimes there were strategic moves to "unify" women despite their class differences. In both newspapers, the only three references made to women during the September massacres focus not on warrior women or female cannibals; rather, reports inform readers about women's unified, nonviolent contributions to the military effort. The *HSZ* reports that women of all ages had gathered to prepare supplies for the army, while the *VZ* emphasizes the unification of social classes in women's effort to support the military.[56] A third *VZ* report from September 9, 1792, notes that "Bürgerinnen" were invited to construct tents for the army and that many women, regardless of class, participated.[57] By demonstrating that such patriotic efforts transcended class, women of all social levels, but more specifically those from the lower classes who were most susceptible to the lure of revolutionary fervor, were presented with a nonviolent means of contributing to the cause.

Such models of female patriotism found new life in Germany during the Napoleonic Wars and French occupation of German territories. Patriotic clubs channeled women's desire to participate in the public life of the emerging nation and against the foreign oppressor through more traditionally "feminine" activities such as fund-raising while simultaneously promoting a culture of self-sacrifice among wives, daughters, and sisters.[58] Even the actions of those German women who transgressed social mores by taking up arms to fight against the French could be recast in terms of patriotic sacrifice.

Press reports of women's varying forms of participation in the Revolution actively participated in the mythification of the warlike woman as transgressive Other. Stories of violent revolutionary women outnumbered descriptions of silk-clad patriotic ladies; nevertheless, these competing narratives presented the German reader with two decidedly different forms of women's participation in the public sphere. The "anti-ideal" of the armed woman still posed a threat to the social and political division between the sexes and their "appropriate" roles. In contrast, the "ideal" of the well-mannered female patriot was presented as a "safer" model of femininity upon which German women, regardless of class, could fashion their patriotism within the paradigm of princely absolutism and patriarchal order. This dichotomy came to inform and be transformed by fictional responses to the phenomenon of the woman warrior. As the political stakes for German autonomy were raised, these oversimplified, polarized images grew more ambiguous. Enigmatic manifestations of armed women articulated the fraught relationship between German society and the reality of women's violent engagement in the military and political conflicts of the time. Thus, the (anti-)ideals constructed by German press reports established dominant narratives that were transformed by the literary community in its protracted confrontation with the unsettling figure of the woman warrior.

Chapter Two

✦

Armed Ambiguity Personified

The French Assassin Charlotte Corday and German Ambivalence

Verschmolzen sieht man hier die Ideale / Verführerischer Weiblichkeit und Mannheit. In / Dem schönsten Gliederbau die *Brutusseele*!

—Heinrich Zschokke

Nur im Widerspruch / Erscheint mein Ich mit meinem innern *Selbst*.

—Engel Christine Westphalen

The social panic unleashed by revolutionary women's violence generated a profusion of haunting images of aggressive, bloodthirsty Furies in the German press at the close of the eighteenth century. After the young French aristocrat Charlotte Corday brutally assassinated the revolutionary figure Jean-Paul Marat in 1793, a notable discursive shift away from the deviant specter of the warlike woman toward the rehabilitation of the politically active murderess as patriotic martyr for her fatherland occurs. German press coverage and literary dramatizations of Corday employed an array of rhetorical strategies to rehabilitate an otherwise shocking, abhorrent crime—and certainly an act that under other circumstances would have been condemned outright—and recoded it in affirmative terms as patriotic self-sacrifice. In this way, Germans could appropriate the French assassin and her violent murder of a leading figure of the Revolution as a form of patriotism in the service of their own political and social agendas. Yet, what could have motivated a young woman from the countryside to make the journey alone to Paris in order to murder one of the leading, and by many accounts beloved, figures of the Revolution?

Corday's brazen act of terrorism was in fact deeply embedded in the power struggles and political intrigue being waged between the two leading parties of the Revolution. Less than two months prior to Marat's death, the antagonistic conflict between the more radical Jacobins, or Montagnards, and their more moderate counterparts, the Girondists, in the National Convention, had come to a head. Expelled from the Convention within less than a week (May 31–June 2), the Girondist deputies fled to Calvados in the northern region of Normandy. There they plotted to overthrow Maximilien Robespierre (1758–1794) and his loyal supporters, including Marat, who were perceived as pandering to the masses and serving the demands of the violent, ultra-radical sans-culottes. The royalist uprising in the Vendée (1793–96), which had begun in March of that same year, was growing more violent and the likelihood of civil war loomed large. It was against this political backdrop of events that Corday carried out the murder of the man she held solely responsible for the failures of the Revolution, the bloody turn it had taken with the September massacres (1792), and the escalating violence that characterized the early stages of *la Terreur* (1793–94)—which only intensified after Marat's death. On July 13, 1793, Marie-Anne Charlotte de Corday d'Armant (1768–1793), a 25-year-old aristocrat from the commune of Caen in Normandy, entered the Paris apartment of Jean-Paul Marat (1743–1793), a prominent Jacobin and prolific publisher of the influential newspaper *L'Ami de Peuple*. Under the pretense of divulging important information about Girondist conspirators and an impending revolt, Corday was granted access to the physically fragile 55-year-old and stabbed him to death in his bathtub. Four days later, having been tried and found guilty, Corday was beheaded on July 17 at the Place de la Révolution.

With few exceptions, no female assassin has been publicized more in modern German history than this eighteenth-century Gironde sympathizer.[1] The politically motivated act of aggression committed by Corday sent shock waves across Europe and elicited an ambivalent response from the German public, one that was shaped by but also informed ambiguous representations of Corday in press reports and literary texts for decades to follow. Corday's attack on Marat unleashed a flood of publications: newspaper reports, eyewitness accounts, editorials, lyrical treatments, a handful of dramatic works, and countless paintings and etchings. While conservatives rejected Corday's actions outright, moderate and radical supporters of the Revolution alike coopted the female assassin in the service of their political programs and treated her use of deadly force with a compassionate tone.[2] The German public's fascination with Corday is all the more significant because she was neither German nor was her deed carried out on German soil; in fact, not even the victim was German—nor was he French for that matter, a fact Corday later noted[3]—but a Swiss-born French revolutionary. The singularity of the press and dramatists' attempts to reconcile the violent, political nature of Corday's act with their notion of the "weaker sex," when other instances of female violence, such as those committed by French female revolutionaries, were coded as deviant and unnatural transgressions, demands closer scrutiny.

Corday's motives for carrying out the brazen political murder shared an affinity with German public opinion toward the Revolution in 1793 and offers one explanation for the unexpectedly affirmative yet fraught representations of Corday. Whether rightly or wrongly, the politically moderate Corday placed the blame entirely at Marat's feet for the perversion of revolutionary principles by the Montagnards that were manifested in political injustices and mass executions of French citizens. What little German support there had been for the Revolution in the early years dissolved almost entirely. German reactionaries, who had rejected the Revolution from its beginning, viewed Marat's murder by a woman as just one in a long series of examples confirming the political immaturity of the French masses and the depravity to which they had degenerated.[4] While they categorically rejected the glorification of Corday's act on the basis that no individual or state possessed the right to usurp or revolt against its sovereign,[5] they could not entirely condemn the defiant behavior of the young aristocratic woman, who had dispatched one of the Revolution's most influential figureheads.

Meanwhile, radical and moderate German supporters of the Revolution shared Corday's sense of betrayal and disillusionment with the corruption and brutality plaguing the French Republic. Her act of deadly aggression against a perceived enemy of the Republic was deemed a necessary corrective in order to return the Revolution to its proper course.[6] The naturalist and Mainzer Jacobin deputy to the National Convention Georg Forster's correspondence with estranged wife and writer Therese Huber over the course of 1793 evinces this gradual disenchantment with the harsh realities of revolutionary politics experienced by many German friends of the Revolution.[7] Prior to Corday's attack on Marat, the Mainzer deputy's palpable disappointment finds expression in a letter from Paris dated April 16, 1793:

> Ich die Geschichte dieser greuelvollen Zeit schreiben? Ich kann es nicht. Oh, seitdem ich weiß, daß keine Tugend in der Revolution ist, ekelt mich's an. Ich konnte, fern von aller idealischen Träumerei, mit unvollkommnen Menschen zum Ziele gehen, unterweges fallen und wieder aufstehen und wieder gehen. Aber mit Teufeln, und herzlosen Teufeln, wie sie hier alle sind, ist es mir eine Sünde an der Menschheit, an der heiligen Mutter Erde und an dem Lichte der Sonne. [. . .] Immer nur Eigennutz und Leidenschaft zu finden, wo man Größe erwartet und verlangt, immer nur Worte für Gefühl, immer nur Prahlerei und Schimmer für wahres Sein und Wirken—wer kann das aushalten![8]

> Me? Write the history of this abhorrent period? I cannot. Oh, ever since I have become aware that there is no virtue in the Revolution, it appalls me. Far away from all of the idealistic reverie, accompanied by imperfect humans I could have pursued a goal, fallen along the way, stood back up again, and continued. But with devils, and unfeeling devils, like they all are here, it appears to me a sin against

> humanity, against sacred Mother Earth, and against the light of day. [. . .]. To only ever find self-interest and passion, where one expects and demands greatness, only ever words in place of emotion, only ever boasting and glimmer in place of true existence and action—who can endure it!

With this emotional context in mind Forster wrote to Huber three months later concerning Corday's assassination of Marat with renewed hope for the preservation of revolutionary ideals: "Sie liebte die Republik und die Freiheit mit Enthusiasmus und fühlte tief ihre innere Zerrüttung" ("She loved the Republic and freedom with enthusiasm. She felt deeply its inner destruction").[9] Her patriotic sacrifice for the French nation provided the example of greatness for which Forster had yearned. It was this greatness, he asserted, that allowed Corday's political act of violence to be memorialized even by Marat's supporters.[10] Despite Forster's high praise for Corday's daring deed, the German public was keenly aware that her victim had been a powerful man and citizen.

Eighteenth-century public opinion on issues of criminality and punishment were inherently linked to the gender of the perpetrator. To borrow the words of Susanne Kord, "in writing about crime and women, what matters most is the body's gender."[11] If the political assassination of a prominent public figure was coded by readers as a characteristically masculine act, then the gender of the assassin and her victim were of central importance to the Corday reception, including subsequent debates surrounding the moral and legal implications. Furthermore, Kord argues that women's unapologetic use of deadly force, such as in the case of Corday, is never merely a single violation; rather, the female offender is perceived as committing a double transgression: "not only against humanity—as a man would be—but also against gender norms."[12] Corday's offense was thus twofold: she not only defied the law by committing an act of violence resulting in the death of a fellow (male) citizen, but the alleged ideological motivation behind the assault contravened the gendered political order.

The gendering of both physical and metaphorical bodies played a central role in the public's efforts to make sense of Corday's violent act. As Michel Foucault asserts, "it is always the body that is at issue—the body and its forces, their utility and their docility, their distribution and their submission."[13] Depictions of Marat's murder reveal the male body functioning on a number of semantic levels. The most obvious is the infirm, fragile body of the victim. In his weakened, defenseless state, Marat proved an easy target posing little risk to his attacker.[14] Simultaneously, his diseased body operated both as an external sign of his inner moral depravity as well as a metaphor for the political cancer consuming the Republic's body from within and in need of surgical removal. Corday's political murder of a fellow male citizen therefore might be read also as a direct attack on the patriarchal body politic, its laws, social conventions, and gendered order. The threat of this perceived assault was further compounded by her claims that she did what her countrymen were unwilling or incapable of doing. By asserting her position as a political agent willing to take life in order to defend it, Corday provoked a reconsideration of masculinity and patriotism. The wars unleashed by the French Revolution unleashed a crisis in masculinities as German soldiers were engaged in a protracted battle with French forces over the defense of German borders and the expulsion of the foreign invader from the German territories' own political body.[15]

Turning to Corday, we also find the exertion of symbolic forces at work in the seizure, examination, quarantining, and eradication of the unruly female body, as well as the very public autopsy of the perpetrator's reputation in the press. Beyond the public spectacles of her body on trial and more prominently the execution of the disorderly body,[16] Corday's character (soul) became a site of contestation in the literary rehabilitation of the young murderess. The literary community dissected not only her crime but her entire life leading up to that point, and in some instances even beyond her death. They indexed, cataloged, and mapped these points in the minutest detail.[17] In this way, press coverage and dramatic narratives of Corday sought to contain, sterilize, and immunize her aggressive body by exerting control over the memory of the perpetrator. At the same time, however, Corday's rebellious body resisted such attempts to contain fully its subversive potential and offered writers a space in which to probe and contest the same dominant myths of an "ideal femininity" that sought to pacify the defiant, politically active woman.

Ideologically driven purification processes transformed Corday's criminal act into one of patriotic sacrifice. Her metamorphosis from common criminal to heroic martyr for the fatherland occurred literally, as Elisabeth Bronfen might say, "over her dead body."[18] Activating the gendered rhetoric of sacrifice, coded as feminine in bourgeois discourse around 1800, the authors and works considered in this chapter staked their claim to Corday's literary body and soul. It is upon these physical and symbolic surfaces that the drama of the Revolution unfolds and upon which the public's apprehensions about women's incursions into the public sphere of revolutionary politics are projected and explored. The female assassin—a strain of the woman warrior and a kind of irregular combatant—threatened to expose and attack the weaknesses of the patriarchal structures of power and oppression. By elevating Corday to heroic, saint-like heights and investing her image with bourgeois virtues, authors attempted to neutralize the dangers posed by the warlike woman.[19] In their efforts to reframe her as an affirmative model of female heroism, to be mimicked by male citizens, in the service of the *father*land and its restoration,[20] writers complicated the prevailing myth of the woman warrior as specter and renegotiated the fraught constellation between women, violence, and the welfare of the nation.

Corday Reception in the German Press

If German press coverage overwhelmingly demonized revolutionary women for their flagrant disregard of social conventions and incursion into the public sphere of revolutionary politics, then its portrayal of the attack on a prominent Jacobin figure by a young female aristocrat proved far more complicated. Even as some German opponents of the Revolution praised the assassination, not all could condone a woman's use of violence and most certainly not her use of deadly force against a male victim for political aims. Those Germans who viewed the Revolution more positively, on the other hand, appeared to overcome their apprehension about the female aggressor with more ease. These competing visions of Corday were charged with ideological tension between those seeking to maintain the status quo of an entrenched feudal power structure bound to a conservative patriarchal hierarchy and those invested in radically transforming a dysfunctional absolutist system on the verge of collapse.

Two articles appearing in German journals several months after Corday's execution exemplify the ambivalence characterizing the competing discourses about Corday in Germany. Although the essays mobilize opposing images of the female assassin, both texts imply a direct correlation between Corday's violent, political act and her gender. Furthermore, by targeting women readers as the intended recipients of their respective messages, the texts signal that the "fairer sex" is most susceptible to the virulent effects of Corday's impassioned act. Perhaps the most strident condemnation of Corday's political violence appeared in an anonymous article titled "Warnung für einer abscheulichen Mode" [*sic*] ("Warning about an Abhorrent Trend"), published in the November 1793 edition of Weimar publicist Friedrich Johann Justin Bertuch's *Journal des Luxus und der Moden*. Adopting the rhetoric used in press reports to generalize all armed revolutionary women as abject creatures, the author exploits readers' fears of an uncontrolled, destructive female sexuality by casting Corday as a savage, calculating, cold-blooded predator in order to stave off potential imitators. This specter of the sexualized, deadly assassin is countered in a response piece by the author identified only as "K---k" appearing in the 1794 issue of publisher and statesman Friedrich Gentz's *Deutsche Monatsschrift*. Departing from press reports of female patriots in which all forms of violence are eschewed, K---k reframes Corday as a model of feminine virtue and heroic self-sacrifice worthy of emulation by German women in search of an outlet by which to express their love of fatherland. The images of Corday constructed in these texts betray the strategies employed by authors to co-opt Corday for their respective agendas.

The "warning" offered by the *Journal des Luxus und der Moden* article calls attention to press coverage glorifying Corday's use of force for political goals and asserts the dangers such affirmative reports pose to the moral and political order of German society. For the anonymous author, the depiction of Corday as a saint or heroine incited violent, transgressive behavior among German women: "nichts gleicht der Bestürzung, die mich befiel, als ich selbst aus dem Munde teutscher Schönen ihre [Corday] Apotheose vernahm; in ihren Augen jenes wilde Feuer blitzen sah, das sie in einer ähnlichen Lage gewiß einer französischen Bacchantin ähnlich gemacht haben würde" ("nothing compares to the dismay that befell me when I heard firsthand her [Corday's] apotheosis from the mouth of a German beauty; I saw that wild fire spark in her eyes, which in a similar situation certainly would have transformed her into something akin to a French Maenad").[21] Exploiting fears already fed by press reports of cannibalistic female revolutionaries, the author invokes mythical nightmares of the destruction and mutilation of male bodies wrought by uncontrollable, irrational femininity. When unregulated, the Maenad's passions result in the loss rather than the bestowing of life. By foregrounding the destructive nature of Corday and her imitators, the author firmly positions the disorderly, violent woman in the role of unnatural Other in order to counter the portrayal of Corday's crime as a feat of female heroism.

Attempting to curb the spread of Corday's popularity among German women, the author juxtaposes Corday's criminal behavior—she is cast as a "Verbrecherin" (criminal)—with normative, historical models of German bourgeois values.[22] Drawing on emerging nationalist sentiments, the text contrasts the natural inclination and predisposition of German and French women. The German female patriot, unlike her French counterpart, remains "unbefleckt von der Wuth einer gallischen Furie" ("unsullied by the ire of a Gallic Fury") and expresses her love for her fatherland in an appropriate manner reminiscent of virtuous women from bygone ages: "Eine griechische Penelope, und die teutsche Rittersfrau der vorigen Jahrhunderte, die an den politischen Begebenheiten der Welt weiter keinen Antheil nahm, als daß sie ihrem aus dem Kampfe zurückkehrenden Gatten den Schweiß von der Stirn trocknete, und mit zärtlicher Sorgfalt seine Wunden verband, diese seyen Ihre Muster!" (*Journal des Luxus*, "Warnung" 556; "A Greek Penelope, a Germanic knight's wife from a previous century, who only took an interest in the political events of the world in so far as she wiped the sweat from the brow of her returning husband and bound his wounds with care. These are your examples!"). Harkening back to antiquity and an era of medieval chivalry, when men ostensibly were warriors and protectors and women were devoted wives, hearth keepers, and caregivers, the author upholds late eighteenth-century normative gender roles. Woman's greatest contribution to her fatherland, the author suggests, rests in her preservation and confined practice of "ideal" feminine virtues within the familial home. The author further promotes this model of female passivity by appealing to woman's perceived need to appear desirable to men: only women who forsake all forms of violence, including those committed by a "Bacchantin" (Maenad), are desirable to men (555).[23] The article reaffirms an "ideal femininity" that is non-threatening while signaling to German women that only "proper" female patriots, who renounce all claims to the political sphere, make respectable wives. In doing so, the author confirms woman's status as subordinated object of male desire and domination.

In his article "Ueber Charlotte Corday, die Mörderin Marats" ("On Charlotte Corday, Marat's Murderess"), the author K---k restores Corday's subject position and agency as a paragon of female patriotism by redoubling the arguments deployed by his "Warnung" counterpart to criminalize Corday.[24] Addressing his defense of Corday to his female readers, K---k recodes Corday's transgression in gendered terms of self-sacrifice, thereby activating the same rhetoric of feminine virtue mobilized by his opponent.[25] However, in this instance the author strategically appropriates this rhetoric in order to reclaim Corday's act of aggression as an affirmative model of female activism:[26]

> Ich für mein Theil befürchte hieraus für Deutschland so wenig Uebels, daß ich ihm vielmehr Glück deswegen wünsche, und, wenn ich den Beruf dazu hätte, die deutschen Schönen auffordern würde, sich recht oft mit Charlotte Corday zu beschäftigen, und durch das Andenken an die reine Absichten und die edle Selbstverleugnung derselben zu ähnlichen großen Aufopferungen für rühmliche Zwecke sich mit Muth und mit Eifer zu beseelen. Ja wenn sie auch nie so glücklich sind, hierzu Gelegenheit zu haben, so wird doch das hohe Gefühl, das bey jenem Andenken ihren Busen schwellt, die segensvolle Wirkung haben, daß kein böser Vorsatz, kein unedler Trieb neben ihm aufsteigen kann. Es gleicht einer erscheinenden Gottheit, die alles, was unheilig ist, rings um sich her verscheucht, und von ihrem geweihten Wohnsitz in ewiger Entfernung hält.[27]

> For my part, I fear so little evil for Germany as a result of Corday's apotheosis, rather, I wish it far more happiness because of it. If it were my calling to do so, I would prompt German beauties to devote themselves to Charlotte Corday quite often. I would encourage them to be inspired with courage and enthusiasm by the memory of the pure intentions and the noble renunciation of Corday, to carry out similar great acts of self-sacrifice for laudable purposes. If they are never so fortunate to have the opportunity for such self-sacrifice, then the great feeling that swells in their bosom at each remembrance, will have the beneficial effect that no evil intention, no ignoble drive can arise alongside it. The great sentiment is akin to an appearing deity, which banishes everything that is unholy surrounding it and keeps it in eternal distance from its hallowed residence.

Refiguring her bloody act of defiance as divine self-sacrifice, the author establishes an almost antagonistic relationship between the physical and spiritual worlds. Corday, likened to an angel, appears not merely as a heroic human but as an almost supernatural being occupying a "hallowed" higher plane.

The author draws short, however, of promoting women's rights to legal representation, including the right to bear arms. Instead, he contains the threat inherent in such forms of female agency by retreating to an essentialist position which codes sacrifice, the act of offering oneself up for something greater than oneself, as an act compatible with feminine virtue. Corday renounces her claim to her earthly body and allows it to become an instrument, a weapon, to be wielded for the good of the Republic. Yet, in the same instance, this renunciation allows for the body of the perpetrator to be co-opted and infused with new meaning by forces beyond the willing victim's control. As Bronfen argues, the female corpse, particularly when on display as a sacrificial offering, submits itself as an empty vessel to be imbued with meaning for vying political and cultural interests: "Over her dead body, cultural norms are reconfigured or secured, whether because the sacrifice of the virtuous, innocent woman serves a social critique and transformation or because a sacrifice of a dangerous woman reestablishes an order that was momentarily suspended due to her presence." Thus, Corday's transgression, viewed either as horrific crime or noble self-sacrifice, becomes "the site at which cultural norms can be debated."[28] Corday's willing death, however, gestures toward the affirmation of a patriarchal power dependent on woman's subordination, self-denial, and exclusion from the public realm.

Both fervent authors compare Corday with the sixteenth-century woman warrior Joan of Arc to lend credibility to their opposing views about Corday's suitability as a patriotic paragon. Despite the armed maiden's incursion into the battlefield and violation of sumptuary laws of her time by donning men's clothing, the deification of Joan of Arc goes uncontested by both authors. The "Warnung" author's argument revolves around questions of whether such deeds are carried out publicly or privately, in other words, by means of deceit and dissimulation, and whether the acts of aggression are sanctioned. On both accounts, Joan of Arc prevails as the truly virtuous model because she publicly presents herself to her enemy on the battlefield and "bittet um Erlaubniß, in Mannskleidern mit den Waffen in der Hand gegen die Feinde ausziehen zu dürfen" ("asks permission to be allowed to set out in men's clothing with weapons in hand against the enemy").[29] The bellicose woman warrior therefore not only willingly submits herself to the will of the sovereign but to the highest of all patriarchal authorities by functioning as "die Gesandtin der Gottheit" (the messenger of divinity).[30] In this way, she is an agent of the secular and spiritual patriarchs committing violence in their service.

K---k appropriates the same justifications deployed by the anonymous author to deify Joan of Arc but mobilizes them to solidify Corday's status as martyr. If Joan of Arc's feats of military bravery in defense of king and country, which she accomplished with the assistance of thousands of troops at her side, are inspiring, then Corday's single-handed assassination of Marat is nobler still: "Sie allein griff tausend andre an—denn das that sie im eigentlichsten Sinne, indem sie den Marat umbrachte—und konnte sich mit keiner Hoffnung, sich zu retten, schmeicheln" ("She alone attacked thousands of others—for that is what she did in the most literal sense, by murdering Marat—and she could not flatter herself with the hope of being rescued").[31] K---k finds justification for Corday's ascension to saint-like heights because she knowingly carried out a violent, criminal act—the penalty for which was a certain and dishonorable death—and selflessly offered her life for what she perceived to be the greater good of her fatherland.

Although the majority of the German Corday reception vacillates somewhere between vitriolic condemnation and impassioned apologia,[32] there were individuals who approached the subject matter in a seemingly more measured manner. Such writers familiarized readers with the nuanced complexities of the case while offering the public a "judiciously" argued rationale for Corday's deserved standing as martyr for her fatherland. Wieland's temperate commentary accompanying the hyperbolic partisan essay "Scharlotte Korday" ("Charlotte Corday"), penned by an anonymous author referred to only as "—tz," approaches the question of Corday's deviancy or heroism along these lines.[33] In fact, Wieland's assessment of Corday is framed carefully in direct response to Corday's devotee —tz, who invokes the "Geist der verewigten Korday" ("spirit of the immortal Corday") to descend from her heavenly heights in order to instill in Germany's sovereigns the same patriotic fervor and desire to rescue their French neighbors from the tyranny of corruption.[34]

In true Enlightenment fashion, Wieland's moderate essay weighs both sides of the debate surrounding the assassination of Marat while simultaneously articulating the ambivalence characterizing the German reception of Corday. Taking stock of the impact of Corday's violent deed on the German public, Wieland queries: "Woher kommt es denn also, daß, ausser den geschwornen Freunden und Brüdern Marats, schwerlich jemand die Geschichte der Scharlotte Korday gehört oder gelesen hat, ohne *eine unfreywillige Regung* in sich zu fühlen, die ihn *zu gleicher Zeit zum Mitleiden, und zur Bewunderung* für dieses ausserordentliche Mädchen nöthigte?" ("What then accounts for the fact that, with the exception of Marat's sworn friends and brothers, hardly anyone who has heard or read the story of Charlotte Corday has done so without feeling *an involuntary emotion*, which compels him to feel *at once compassion and awe* for this remarkable girl?").[35] Wieland's answer to his own question hones in on the notion of the involuntary reaction by identifying the source of his own contradictory yet concomitant feelings of admiration alongside compassion and delight accompanied by repulsion as directly linked to the nature of the act and the identity of its agent (Wieland, "Ein Paar Anmerkungen" 81 and 83).

Like the "Warnung" author and K---k, Wieland's explicit reference to the perpetrator's sex foregrounds the importance of sex and gender in the reception of Corday's deed. Initially deflecting attention away from the sex-gender issue surrounding the perpetrator and victim, Wieland locates his unease with the assassination itself, a morally objectionable act, which he claims to be the source of his initial aversion to Corday ("Ein Paar Anmerkungen" 83). Yet, his observation that Corday is a person "an welcher ohnehin nichts als ihr Geschlecht weiblich schien" (85; "for whom nothing but her sex appeared to be feminine") does exactly that which he claims not to do: it locates his apprehension about Corday's violent act in the incongruity between Corday's sex—and attributed gender traits—and her ability to commit a violent, political crime conventionally coded as a masculine act.[36] His observation articulates the perceived contradiction between social expectations about women's behavior, both moral and legal, and the positive reception of Corday. Corday's brutal use of force and violent demeanor expose the fissures in bourgeois myths of female passivity, docility, and obedience. This discrepancy between Corday and prevailing notions about the "fairer sex" proves so disconcerting for Wieland that it forces him to search for more probable, and less noble, motives such as "Ehrgeiz" (85; ambition) and "Nachruhm" (86; fame after death), rather than patriotic fervor and love of country, in order to explain her highly political self-sacrifice. Wieland's momentary retreat to ignoble motives points to a widespread practice by his contemporaries to depose any example of female agency that might unmask the artificiality of the gender hierarchy.[37] Ultimately, however, he dismisses the base motives of fame and glory, citing the original letters Corday penned prior to her execution.[38] It is the simplicity of Corday's writing style, mirrored in her staid demeanor conveying "Kaltblütigkeit" (composure) and "Ruhe" (serenenity) which finally earns his respect and admiration (94).[39] Yet the persistent apprehension Wieland experiences toward the assassin is only overcome through the elevation of Corday to saint-like status by casting her as an asexual earthly vessel for a divine force.[40] Through Corday's apotheosis, Wieland can more comfortably express his praise of "diese französische Jael oder Judith" (79; "this French Yael or Judith").[41]

Wieland's invocation of the biblical heroines Yael and Judith participates in the effort among Corday's German sympathizers to manufacture new myths deifying the warlike woman. The saint-like status accorded Corday by her supporters is not merely a result of their contempt for Marat but can be attributed directly to the legacy Corday fashioned for herself just prior to her execution. As if speaking from beyond the grave, Corday's literary estate helped to shape her reception in France and Germany for centuries after her publicly staged death. Among the historical documents chronicling Corday's act, trial, and execution are letters written by the murderess prior to the assassination as well as during her brief incarceration. In these letters Corday places the political nature of her actions front and center by strategically referencing the Roman statesman and iconic assassin Marcus Junius Brutus. Published posthumously in French newspapers and journals, with translations appearing shortly thereafter in the German press,[42] Corday's correspondence and trial proceedings allowed her to position herself and her act of violence in the larger historical tradition of tyrannicide. By invoking Brutus and "einig[e] Alten" (a few ancients) in her letter to Girondist Charles Jean Marie Barbaroux (1767–1794),[43] Corday appropriated a form of *masculine* heroism and civil disobedience in order to lend authority to her transgression of both legal and gender conventions.

Corday further asserts her claim to the heroic subject position by calling into question the masculinity and patriotism of her fellow countrymen. In the same letter to Barbaroux, Corday wages war on the masculinity of her compatriots by arguing that "Es gibt wenig wahre Patrioten, welche für ihr Vaterland zu sterben wissen. Sie sind fast alle Egoisten" ("There are only a few true patriots, who know how to die for their fatherland. They are almost all egoists").[44] This criticism appears in a more striking form in the version of the trial protocol reprinted in Archenholz's *Minerva* under the title "Briefe und Verhör der Charlotte Corday" ("Letters and Interrogation of Charlotte Corday"). In her response to the question of whether she loves the republican form of government, Corday uses the cowardice and inaction of her countrymen and political representatives to magnify her patriotism and justify her deadly deed:

> Ob ich sie liebe? Ich liebe sie und kenne sie besser, als jemand; aber den Franzosen fehlt es an Geist und Energie, Republicaner zu seyn. Ich sehe nichts als Egoisten, die ihr Vermögen auf den Ruinen ihrer Mitbürger zu erheben suchen. Ich sehe in der Versammlung des Convents unwissende und feige Memmen, die da dulden, daß einige wenige Bösewichter die Menschheit mit Füssen treten, und den Bürgerkrieg anzünden. Ich bin müde länger unter einem so sehr herabgewürdigten Volk zu leben.[45]

> Do I love it? I love it and know it better than anyone, but the French lack spirit and energy to be republicans. I see nothing but egoists, who seek to increase their fortunes on the ruins of their fellow citizens. In the National Convention I see ignorant and timid cowards, who tolerate, that a few miscreants trample humankind with their feet and incite civil war. I am tired of living any longer among a people so degraded.

Due to the lack of real patriots, and real men, Corday makes an argument for the necessity of her transgression.[46] By questioning the bravery and patriotism of her countrymen, Corday exposes the interstice between masculinity and patriotism at a moment of social and political instability.

Despite Corday's attempt to fashion her legacy as a female Brutus, German writers also invoked exemplars of female heroism in their reframing of

Corday as patriotic martyr, thereby mitigating her assault on masculinity and society as a whole. Comparisons of Corday to Yael and Judith soon accompanied Corday's self-identification with Brutus as a means to contextualize and rehabilitate her potentially transgressive actions and reframe them within an established, accepted tradition of patriotic female self-sacrifice. Corday firmly located her act within the tradition of male heroism, yet renderings by Wieland, Gleim, Zschokke, Westphalen, and others likened Corday to these biblical heroines. These newly formed narratives about Corday were dialogic in nature, evincing an intertextual awareness, in that they drew upon, had recourse to, and reformulated existing models of self-sacrificing female heroism, which were tailored to the specific historical moment and gender conventions of German society around 1800.[47] Tracing the evolution of the Judith figure at critical moments in German history, Helen Watanabe-O'Kelly notes a striking difference between the biblical assassin and Corday. Watanabe-O'Kelly suggests that Corday's social and political rehabilitation proved far easier for contemporaries than that of her biblical predecessor, because the young aristocrat's act of terrorism contained no evidence of sexual impropriety[48]—although this did not prevent authors such as Zschokke from lending their Corday figures an air of seduction. At the same time, authors avoided comparisons to Judith entirely, as is the case in Westphalen's drama, circumventing the question of female sexuality entirely and foregrounding more seamlessly the virtue of the assassin and heroism of her violent act.

Dramatizations of Corday's Assassination

Despite the press's attempts to succinctly classify and contain Corday into neat archetypes—either as deviant criminal or virtuous saint—the dramatic renderings of Corday reveal a far more complicated and fraught portrait of the warlike woman. The Corday figure undergoes a compelling conversion in fictional reframings by the German, later Swiss, writer and civil servant Johann Heinrich Daniel Zschokke in his 1794 *Lesedrama* (closet drama) *Charlotte Corday oder die Rebellion von Calvados* (*Charlotte Corday or the Rebellion of Calvados*) and the writer and Hamburg salonnière Engel Christine Westphalen in the 1804 dramatic work *Charlotte Corday. Tragödie in fünf Akten mit Chören* (*Charlotte Corday: Tragedy in Five Acts, with Choruses*).[49] The authors' attempts to expunge the criminal element from Corday's deed by recasting it as an act of heroic self-sacrifice carried out by a representative of the "weaker sex" in the service of the nation exposes the instability of gender roles and complicates the warlike woman's relationship to issues of patriotism, violence, and political participation.

As the following dramas reveal, even affirmative treatments of Corday convey the tenuous relationship between sexuality and virtue implied by the legacies of Judith and the warlike woman. Westphalen privileges the virginal, chaste model of Corday in her drama by allowing her heroine to fully renounce sexual desire and channel those earthly passions into a purely patriotic love for the fatherland, thereby facilitating a smooth and rather seamless elevation to patriotic saint. Zschokke, in contrast, engages with the erotic tension characterizing the comparison between Judith and Corday. He places Corday's sexuality front and center by displaying her strategic attempts to exploit her feminine allure and man's desire in order to achieve her political goal. However, even Zschokke ultimately erases any remnants of Corday's perceived immorality and allows her to die a martyr alongside the likes of Yael, Cassius, and Cato.

While explicit references to Corday's divinity work out in the open to assert her candidacy as martyr,[50] it is the more subtle, nuanced strategies Zschokke and Westphalen employ to facilitate Corday's literary reformation and the implications such strategies have for the warlike woman's status as political agent that demand closer scrutiny. In the process of rehabilitating Corday from base murderess to patriotic martyr, both authors raise pressing questions about female agency. Westphalen, in particular, blurs the line between woman as political subject and the issue of instrumentalization in her portrayal of Corday. The author provides no easy answers for her readers and Corday as agent of political change remains ambiguous, despite the comparison of her protagonist to the heroic figures Arria, Cato, and Brutus. What emerges over the course of both dramas is a delicate balancing act between an insistence on woman as an authorized political participant and defusing the transgressive potential associated with such a figure. By emphasizing Corday as the hand of a divine power, as unique, and singular, the authors run the risk of undermining the possibility of female agency as generating from within the individual.

The dramas penned by Zschokke and Westphalen share striking similarities with contemporary newspaper and journal reports of the French assassin and exhibit the writers' awareness of and engagement with these dominant public narratives. Despite their documentary-like quality, the plays by Zschokke and Westphalen simultaneously deviate in strategic ways from the press reports and one another in the version of the "facts" they portray and the means by which these specific components are incorporated into their fictional works. Nevertheless, each writer carves out a unique path for his or her heroic protagonist enabling them to mitigate, at least temporarily, their unease about a woman who takes life in order to express their support for an otherwise horrific crime. The implications of Corday's literary rehabilitation from violent offender to patriotic heroine for issues of female agency and masculine identities are manifested most clearly in three crucial moments represented, or implied, in the dramas: first, the decision-making process leading to Corday's act of violence; second, the transgressive moment of physical violence perpetrated on the body of her victim; and lastly, the aftermath of the deadly political deed encompassing Corday's trial and impending execution.

Setting the Stage

Beyond their shared fascination with Corday's attack on Marat, Zschokke and Westphalen publicly distance themselves from their politically charged dramas. Both Zschokke's *Charlotte Corday oder die Rebellion von Calvados* and Westphalen's *Charlotte Corday. Tragödie in fünf Akten mit Chören* were published either anonymously (Zschokke) or under a pseudonym (Westphalen). For Zschokke, the immediacy of his work to the actual event no doubt necessitated caution and a strategic distancing from the overwhelmingly affirmative dramatization of a French female revolutionary, albeit moderate revolutionary, in a predominantly anti-revolutionary Germany. In Westphalen's case, the matter of anonymity was less an issue of censorship and politics in the relatively progressive nineteenth-century Hansestadt Hamburg and more a result of being a woman writer actively pursuing a genre, the classical drama, considered a privileged masculine domain. An anonymous review of Westphalen's *Corday* published 1805 in *Neue Allgemeine Deutsche Bibliothek* illustrates the expectations and criticisms lodged against women attempting to establish themselves in a genre dominated by the likes of Schiller and Goethe. Citing "public reports" attesting to the author's gender, the review catalogs the pointedly *female* writer's failings in mastering the dramatic form. The redeeming quality allowing the reviewer to recommend the *Corday* play to his readers is the fact that it was composed by a poetess "deren Talent zur Poesie überhaupt keinem Zweifel unterworfen seyn kann; wenn es auch gerade nicht das zur dramatischen seyn dürfte" ("whose talent for poetry absolutely cannot be denied, even if the talent might not be exactly for the dramatic").[51] What proves most remarkable is that the provocative subject matter of the play, penned by a woman, received not a single mention from the critic. Although Zschokke is similarly taken to task for his lack of dramatic talent, and even chastised more severely for his lack of poetic ability, the content and its suitability for the dramatic form suggest the more likely reason for the reviewer's disapproval. After questioning whether such an event is even appropriate for dramatization, the *Neue Allgemeine Deutsche Bibliothek* critic of Zschokke's play remarked a year after its publication: "So viel poetische Freyheiten er sich auch bey Behandlung des Stoffs genommen hat; so ist es ihm doch nicht gelungen, ihn für das Theater interessant zu machen" ("As much poetic license as he has taken in the treatment of the material, he did not succeed in making it interesting for the theater").[52] The display of deadly female aggression directed against a defenseless man "on stage" and "on the page" proved particularly challenging for critics and readers so close in time and distance to the actual events.

In an attempt to mitigate the reader's initial aversion to the subject matter and heroine, the writers carefully framed their portraits of the violent offender by activating the audience's capacity to empathize with Corday. In Westphalen's text, formal structural elements such as prologue, chorus, and epilogue guide the reader's engagement with the provocative events. The prologue's "Genius der Wahrheit" (Genius of Truth) appeals to the audience's compassion to create the possibility for identification between reader and protagonist, thereby initiating the rehabilitation of Corday in German public opinion. Establishing the opposition between "Heldentugend" (heroic virtue) and "Lasters Sckreckensblick" ([*sic*]; specter of vice) in the first three lines of the prologue, the voice of "truth" invokes the rhetoric of bourgeois virtue to plead Corday's case: "Erstickt sie nicht, die sanftern Mitleidstriebe! / Denn selbst Verbrecher fodern [*sic*] noch Erbarmen, / [. . .] Menschlich wollen / Dem Menschen wir des Mitleids Thräne zollen" ("Do not suffocate the gentle instincts of compassion! / For even criminals demand mercy, / [. . .] Humanely we want to extend tears of compassion to our fellow man").[53] Cementing Corday's status as martyred heroine, the Genius of Truth, accompanied by the Genius of Virtue, reappears in the drama's epilogue once more reminding the reader of the ultimate sacrifice of "eine reine Perle" (an untouched pearl) in the battle against "das Laster" (CW, 233).

While Westphalen utilizes the classical structure to frame her appeal, Zschokke aims directly at his readers to make his case in support of Corday. The foreword opening Zschokke's drama overtly establishes the play's tenor and exposes the author's ideological sympathies: "Die heldenmüthige Selbstaufopferung der schönen, philosophischen Schwärmerin, Charlotte Corday, für das Wohl ihres Vaterlandes bleibt eine der rührendsten Anekdoten in der ziemlich unphilosophisch betriebenen Revolution der Neufranken" ("The heroic self-sacrifice of the beautiful, philosophical enthusiast, Charlotte Corday, for the welfare of her fatherland, remains one of the most stirring anecdotes in the rather irrationally conducted Revolution of the New Franconians").[54] Zschokke foregrounds the brave and selfless nature of Corday's feat while also countering criticisms directed at her impressive education (for the time) as well as her engagement in intellectual pursuits defined as the exclusive domain of men. Indeed, one newspaper report published in the *VZ* branded Corday "eine alte Jungfer" (an old maid) who was "mehr fleischig als kernhaft, unreinlich, wie es fast alle weibliche Philosophen und Schöngeister sind" ("more fleshy than robust, uncleanly, as are almost all female philosophers and aesthetes").[55] The anonymous author noted the negative effects of women's engagement with philosophical works, necessarily beyond their limited capabilities, on their physical appearance and moral constitutions. Zschokke's comment, on the other hand, implies that Corday's familiarity with historical examples of patriotic martyrs is exactly that which ennobles her act from murder to tyrannicide. Furthermore, the foreword creates a space in which Zschokke can assert his authority over the subject matter and lend his dramatic styling of Corday credibility by stressing his familiarity with the details of the event that had been publicized "[i]n allen kultivirten Gegenden Europa's [*sic*]" ("in every refined region of Europe").[56] Yet, at the same time, he claims a limited knowledge of certain details in order to justify the creative license he takes in particular scenes while trying to remain within the realm of possibility. This unmitigated engagement with the audience allows the dramatist to step outside his fictional work momentarily, to assert his knowledge of the "facts," but also to anticipate and forestall possible criticism. Westphalen and Zschokke's dramatizations of the political murderess instantiate in unique ways the complex and often contradictory response of the German public toward questions of gender and violence.

The Personal Is Political

Contributing to the literary recuperation of the French assassin and question of female agency is Corday's decision-making process and character development leading up to her attack on Marat. In Zschokke and Westphalen's dramatic works, the Revolution's devastating impact on the Republic's welfare *and* the destabilizing effects of revolutionary violence on Corday's personal world inspire her to political action. Both dramatists foreground the reciprocal and inextricable relationship between the personal and political by emphasizing the loss Corday's family experiences at the hands of Marat and the Jacobins. By linking the political domain of the Revolution with the domestic realm of the family and exploiting the bourgeois gender discourse that tethered women to the welfare and stability of the family, the authors formulate an argument for their heroine's violent incursion into the political life of the Republic.

Westphalen establishes the inextricable bond between personal and political in *Charlotte Corday* on multiple levels. The atrocities Corday witnesses firsthand in Paris, and which continue to haunt her, involve those committed against innocent victims resulting in the destruction of entire families. Lingering in her memory are the lamentations of "der Mütter, Väter, Söhne, / Der bleichen Braut im welken Myrthenkranze, / Durch Marat's Blutdurst jedes Glücks beraubt" ("mothers, fathers, sons, / Of the pale bride in withered myrtle wreath, / Robbed of all happiness by Marat's thirst for blood").[57] Corday attributes the destruction of every hope for personal happiness and prosperity to Marat's political machinations and the Jacobin's policy of bloodshed. Her personal encounter with the horrors of revolutionary violence informs her decision to commit murder and allows her to fashion herself as a protector and avenger of republican families.[58]

While scholars have noted the personal-political correlation in Westphalen's drama, most have neglected the direct impact of revolutionary violence on Corday's aristocratic family as a driving force behind her brutal act of patriotism. The reader of Westphalen's play, however, not only learns that the Corday family patriarch has been stripped of his "Rang, Vermögen, Güter" (position, fortune, and properties) and that his heir, Antoine, "ist ohne Stand"

(CW, 74; is without station), but they also discover that Corday's sister, who lives in Paris, has lost her husband in the Revolution's bloody conflict (CW, 53). Thus, Corday's decision to murder Marat materializes neither as a whim nor as a result of irrational fanaticism. Instead, Westphalen presents Corday's decision as deliberate, informed, and based on concrete personal events both witnessed and experienced by her protagonist.[59]

The patriarchal structures of power, ravaged by revolution, have been rendered weak and ineffectual. Forced to endure emotional, financial, and personal hardships under Jacobin rule, the family's stability has been severely compromised.[60] The attenuated authority of the patriarchal order is instantiated by the father's miscalculated decision to send his daughter to Paris (CW, 19), his passive, fatalist attitude toward the Revolution (CW, 28), and the son's hollow claims of patriotism and bravery that remain unrealized: "Und, glaubt mir, hätt' ich Waffen nur gehabt, / Ich hätte die Verräther schnell durchbohrt, / Nicht eingedenk der eigenen Gefahr" (CW, 43; "And believe me, had I a weapon, / I would have quickly run the traitors through, / Without regard for my own safety"). The men's patriotic rhetoric does not bear out in their actions, or more pointedly in their inaction, and signals the fissures in both the patriarchal familial and political orders. This crisis creates the conditions that allow the Jacobins' corrupt regime to continue unhindered and at the same time necessitate unconventional agents of change, such as female assassins.[61]

The contradiction between the family's culture of resignation, the legends of heroic patriotism that capture Corday's imagination, and the concrete examples of female activism she witnesses in the streets of Paris motivate her decision to develop and carry out her plot against Marat. Countering her mother's claims "Wir ändern nichts" (CW, 20; We alter nothing), Corday articulates a sense of agency that offers the individual the possibility to shape and guide her own destiny. Rather than shed tears for the tragic state of the world, Corday seeks solace in action:

> Nur Eines ist, was sich die Seele nennet—
> Ein Dunkel!——Ob es je die Wolke bricht?
> Sich von der Heimat, die es birget, trennet?
> *Mit Nachdruck.*
> Eins, was den tiefsten Busen mir erglüht,
> Und mit allmächt'ger Kraft mich an sich zieht! (CW, 22–23)

> There is only one thing that calls itself the soul—
> A darkness!——Will it ever break the cloud?
> Separate itself from the homeland, which harbors it?
> *With emphasis.*
> One thing that sets my innermost bosom aglow,
> And draws me toward it with almighty power!

The thought of heroic action bound to a devotion to the homeland emerges here in vague and tentative language. Yet within a span of a few short lines, the clouds obscuring the noble idea part and Corday begins to nurture quietly within her the glowing embers of her brazen deed:

> Ich nenn' es nicht, was mir im Busen glühet.
> Es reife dort allein und still zur That.
> . . . .
> Das Herz muß fest, und groß, und stille handeln,
> So muß Entschluß sich nur in That verwandeln! (CW, 23–24)

> I will not name it, that which ignites in my bosom.
> It matures there alone and quietly to action.
> . . . .
> The heart must act decisively, greatly, and silently,
> In this way determination must transform itself into action!

Westphalen portrays Corday's decision as one made in solitude that asserts a sense of agency signaling to the reader that Corday is not merely a puppet but an autonomous individual.

The heroic sentiments Corday articulates tentatively in this fifth scene become more decisive three scenes later as she is inflamed by ancient standard bearers of patriotic martyrdom (CW, 35–36). The names Cato, Arria, and Antigone embody for Corday a sanctioned form of defiance in service of the Republic that resonates with her sense of duty and loyalty. These serve as models upon which she can fashion her own heroic sacrifice. Dagmar von Hoff argues that Westphalen's play undercuts the potentially empowering model of female agency implied by Corday's political act by presenting it as only an act of mimicry rather than generated from within.[62] However, such a reading fails to account for the seeds of decisiveness that have already taken root in Corday prior to her reacquaintance with the heroic legends. Rather, Westphalen invokes the mythic examples of tyrannicide in order to reframe her female protagonist's transgression within the greater female and male traditions of heroic self-sacrifice and patriotic acts of violence.[63]

Yet, even inspiring models of heroism proffered by the annals of history remain abstract and elusive. It is the immediacy of the female revolutionaries' violent actions Corday encounters that allows her to imagine herself in the role of active political subject altering the fate of her country. Recounting and reenacting for her father the women's brutality, the stage directions suggest Corday's involuntary response to such images of female defiance: "*Sie nimmt schnell ein Messer vom Tische, und macht die Bewegung eines Dolchstoßes*" (CW, 81; "*She grabs quickly a knife from the table and makes the gesture of a dagger thrust*"). The proximity of women and violence both excite and unsettle her: "—Mir schauerts noch bis in das tiefste Mark!—" (CW, 81; "It still sends a chill to my very core!"). Despite her ambivalent response, she begins to question the social precepts asserting female passivity and male heroism (CW, 84). What first manifested itself as a longing to see Marat dead transforms into a concrete declaration of action: "Ja, Ruhe bring' ich meinem Vaterlande!" (CW, 85; "Yes, I will bring peace to my fatherland!"). Corday co-opts the violence perpetrated by the very revolutionaries she detests and redirects it against the man responsible for the women's disorderly behavior in her bid to restore order. Westphalen constructs in gradual layers the motives driving Corday to commit her unspeakable act of violence, thereby giving her protagonist richer texture. By humanizing the perpetrator of a violent crime, Westphalen lays the foundation that will ultimately allow both the author and the reader to reconcile their sense of apprehension toward scenes of violent women with the heroic nature of the deed.

Like Westphalen, Zschokke strategically links Corday's personal welfare with the well-being of the Republic to mitigate his protagonist's illicit recourse to violence for political ends. Zschokke creates a fictional love interest in the character Robert, Charlotte's cousin and childhood friend, in order to bridge the divide between the domestic and political. Although Zschokke sets the stage for Corday's transformation from naive republican to patriotic assassin early in the drama—in the first act, Corday's father quickly disabuses her of idealistic notions of liberation from oppression and unity among the people[64]—it is the figure of Robert who facilitates Corday's metamorphosis into heroic martyr. Having fallen victim to the senseless bloodshed of the Revolution, Robert becomes the personal face of the thousands of innocent victims whose deaths are guaranteed should civil war break out. Mourning Robert, whom she refers to as brother, Corday voices her desire to avenge his death: "Ach, würde jede Thrän' ein Tropfen Gifts / In Marats Kelch!" (HZ, 40; "Oh, if only each tear were a drop of poison / In Marat's cup!"). In the next breath, Corday makes the leap from revenge to patriotism: in every citizen she sees a potential brother:

> Genug!—ist es
> Nicht thöricht, alle seine Thränen
> Für einen *Bruder* weinen, wenn
> Ein *andres* größern Anspruch auf dies Herz
> Und diese Thränen machen darf?—Das *Vaterland*
> Gränzt näher an das Herz, als alles
> Was Blutverwandschaft heißt!—[. . .]
> . . . .
> Das Vaterland liegt an der Kette
> Des Jakobinerkönigs; eine Republik
> Beuge sich vor Marats blutger Majestät.
> Ein Opfer dieser Majestät ward auch
> Mein armer Vetter; die Pariser
> Erwürgten ihn für ihren Abgott!—(HZ, 40)[65]

Enough!—Is it
Not foolish, to shed all of one's
Tears for one *brother*, when
Another may assert a greater claim over this heart
And these tears?—The *fatherland*
Borders the heart more closely than anything
That is called blood-relationship!—[. . .]
. . . .
The fatherland lays in the chains
Of the Jacobin king; a Republic
Bows before the bloody majesty of Marat.
My poor cousin also became a
Victim of this majesty; the Parisians
Strangled him to death for their false idol!–

Robert's murder functions strategically in Zschokke's drama as a metonym for the death of the Republic at the hands of the Jacobins, thereby allowing Corday's love of and revenge for the individual to be transposed onto that of the greater whole. Personal love and loyalty are reframed as and subsumed under a more powerful and all-encompassing love of fatherland.

Zschokke's Corday drama similarly explores the Revolution's inversion of the gender order manifested in the men's inaction and the woman's action. Searching in vain for a true modern-day patriot, Corday laments the dire fate of her country: "Allein mein *Vaterland*, mein armes / Verrathnes Vaterland, und ach, die Tausende, / Die nun—*nun* wieder bluten müssen!—O, / Lebt denn kein *Brutus* mehr?" (HZ, 23; "Alas my *fatherland*, my poor / Betrayed fatherland. And oh, the thousands, / Who now—*now* must bleed again!—Oh, / Is there no *Brutus* alive today?"). While the vacuum created by the absence of effective male heroes in Westphalen's drama presents the opportunity for Corday to insert herself into this role, Zschokke's female patriot first attempts to locate this contemporary Brutus among the male characters closest to her. Yet, the men she encounters—her aged father, her infatuated suitor Corbigni, the well-intentioned general Wimpfen—neither conform to nor fulfill her expectations. Indeed, the lack of suitable male citizens simultaneously justifies and amplifies the heroism of Corday's brazen act of murder:

O Vaterland, wenn *Männer* sclavisch zittern,
Und ihre Feigheit hinter Ehre, Tugend,
Religion verschanzen, um nicht mit des Lebens
Gefahr dich zu erlösen, Vaterland,
So zittern deine *Töchter* nicht! Ich zittre nicht!
Ich zittre nicht! Es ist ein großes, schönes Werk
Vor mir. Ich will das Leben vieler Tausend
Von deinen Kindern retten;—will! (HZ, 58)

Oh fatherland, when *men* tremble slavishly,
And they barricade their cowardice behind honor, virtue,
Religion, so as not to risk life
To rescue you, fatherland,
Your *daughters* do not tremble so! I do not tremble!
I do not tremble! A grand, wonderful deed lies
Before me. I will rescue the life of many thousands
Of your children; I will!

The patriotism and agency Zschokke articulates for Corday is laden with allusions to the family and her gendered identity as woman: it is the daughters, and not the sons, of the fatherland, who will rise up to protect the lives of its children. Women, his drama suggests, are the able-bodied soldiers needed to defend the fatherland and protect the political family.[66] The weakened patriarchal structure can no longer rely on its sons to restore its order. Corday's assertive claim to action is borne out further still by history: "Wahrhaftig, wer da sagt, die Männer sind / Das stärkere Geschlecht, der ist ein Lügner. / Nennt die Geschichte uns nicht Weiber, / Die riesenhaft der Männerallmacht trozten?" (HZ, 57–58; "Truthfully, whoever says that men are / The stronger sex, he is a liar. / Does not history name for us women, / Who defy colossally the almightiness of men?"). Zschokke privileges the legacy of Yael, rather than Judith, as the model of female heroism upon which to fashion Corday's transgression. Ultimately her act of martyrdom is purified of the taint of eroticism associated with Judith and can be read more easily within the greater tradition of female violence as a sanctioned form of patriotic self-sacrifice in service of the fatherland.

If the Revolution's impact on personal lives is justification for political action, as Westphalen and Zschokke's dramas suggest, then the texts' conversion of personal into patriotic devotion to the fatherland further mitigates Corday's violation of the public-private divide. Just as the historical Corday defended her virtue and virginity during her trial—it was suggested that Corday had not acted of her own accord but rather on behalf of or under the guidance of a male lover—the German dramas wage a campaign to recuperate Corday as a model of feminine virtue and secure her status as martyr. Critical to this process is the reframing of Corday's sublimation of personal desire and amorous sentiments into a "purer" form.

The motif of unrequited love takes center stage as an affirmation of Corday's virtue and candidacy for patriotic martyrdom in the dramatic works. Westphalen and Zschokke strategically construct fictional love interests for Corday and potentially intimate moments challenging the heroine's resolve, in order to show Corday's renunciation of earthly desires, thereby elevating her sense of duty and loyalty to her political cause. In Westphalen's play, the dramatist envisions a personal connection between Corday and the German Jacobin Adam Lux (spelled Luchs in the play).[67] As the reader learns, it is

Corday's childhood friend Eugenie, and not Corday herself, who became the object of Luchs's affection, thereby foreclosing the potential for Corday's personal happiness and the fulfillment of her gendered destiny as wife and mother.[68] Liberated from the constraints of such overdetermined gender roles confining her to the domestic sphere, Corday channels her desires toward a greater cause worthy of her offering: "Getroffen von der Liebe Götterstral, / Fühlt sich dies Herz auf ewig nun entzündet! / Glüht itzt in Liebe für ein Vaterland— / Ein Vaterland, des größten Opfers werth!" (CW, 40; "Struck by heavenly radiance of love, / This heart feels forever inflamed! / Ablaze now in love for a fatherland— / A fatherland worthy of the greatest sacrifice!"). Westphalen cloaks patriotic love in religious imagery so that Corday's violation of secular laws as well as religious tenets takes on a supernatural dimension in service of a higher, divine power. Returning once more to the nexus between the personal and political in the concluding moment of this scene, in which Corday has concretely articulated what was initially only a vague, unidentifiable desire, Westphalen mobilizes "love" in order to reiterate the interdependency between domestic and public concerns: "Ich folge dir [Allmächt'ger Liebe], und weih' dem Vaterlande / Die zarten Fäden meiner heimschen Bande!" (CW, 42; "I will follow you [almighty love], and devote to the fatherland / The tender strands of my domestic ties"). The use of the term "heimisch" bridges the domestic space of hearth and home with the native, domestic interests of the Republic. Corday thereby fashions herself and her act of violence as the work of a higher power in the service of an eternal father and the fatherland.

The denial of earthly desire that attenuates Corday's deviant behavior is conspicuously absent in the play's depiction of its male characters. In an interesting move, Westphalen destabilizes yet again the reader's expectations about who should play the role of defender and helpless victim. In a gesture seemingly transcending the gendered discourse of love at the beginning of the nineteenth century, Westphalen asserts (unfulfilled) love and patriotic devotion as the driving forces behind Luchs's willing sacrifice for the Republic. Recounting the tragic loss of his love, Eugenie, Luchs expresses to his friend Lagarde the newfound dedication to his adopted homeland: "Ein Etwas, das seit lang' in mir gebrütet— / An Frankreichs Boden, festgewurzelt, hält— / (*Mit steigender Heftigkeit*) Das jeden Sinn mit Feuerflut umfaßt, / Die mich versengt, wenn ich ihm nicht genüge" (CW, 76; "A certain something, which has incubated within me for some time— / Holds me rooted to France's soil— / (*With growing intensity*) It envelops every sense with a flood of fire, / That sears me, if I do not satisfy it"). Reminiscent of Corday's "unnamed desire," Luchs's patriotic fervor and impetus to act, identified here only as a vague "certain something," emerges as a compelling force of nature beyond his control and threatening to consume him, if not given an outlet for expression. Although Westphalen mobilizes patriotic love to justify Corday's violent act, her projection of the gendered traits of love and sacrifice onto Luchs leaves the male figure appearing fanatical and ineffective.[69] Like Corday, he conceives of a plan to assassinate Marat that requires him to masquerade as a woman—a detail which his friend Lagarde deems demeaning (CW, 134). Yet, more striking is Luchs's indecision and inability to carry out the attack without the counsel and assistance of the level-headed Lagarde, whereas Corday recognizes the need to remain secretive about her plan (CW, 23). The cold objectivity of the rational lawyer Lagarde, the embodiment of enlightened principles, wins out. He dissuades Luchs from pursuing the violent course of action. Luchs's failure to single-handedly conceive and execute his plan, as well as Lagarde's privileging of rational thought over concrete action, confirms the men's status as the embodiment of inaction while simultaneously highlighting Corday's decisiveness.[70] Such passivity, Westphalen's text implies, allowed Marat and the Jacobins to lay waste to the Republic in the first place.

The sublimation of Corday's natural drives and desires to a loftier patriotic purpose that transpires in Westphalen's drama is manifested in a more extreme form in Zschokke's dramatization. Zschokke amplifies Corday's saint-like status by positioning the deadly assassin between two potential love interests: her martyred cousin Robert and her tenacious, self-serving suitor Corbigni. Her ultimate rejection of both men in favor of a heroic death for the Republic—and thereby a renunciation of her future role as wife and mother—works to secure her status as virtuous martyr. Like Westphalen, Zschokke constructs weak male counterparts to justify Corday's violent incursion into the public sphere of revolutionary politics while simultaneously magnifying her heroism and sense of patriotic duty.

Yet, Zschokke's pairing of Corday with her suitor Corbigni is far more complicated. Whereas Westphalen's dramatic apotheosis of Corday eschews any hint of sexuality or desire,[71] Zschokke presents his protagonist as flesh and blood, an object of male desire, and a woman who is conscious of the power she wields over men, an early predecessor, perhaps, of the nineteenth-century femme fatale.[72] Zschokke treads a fine line in his rendering of unrequited love: Corday is both desiring subject in her love for Robert and the object of Corbigni's desire. Corday's longing for Robert as well as Corbigni's passionate pursuit of Corday, however, remain unfulfilled and work in concert to elevate Corday to heroic heights.

Corday's willingness to renounce personal freedom to restore the liberty of her fellow citizens renders her suitor Corbigni, whose desire to possess Corday subordinates every thought and action to achieving this one aim, treasonous and cowardly. As Corday acknowledges when rejecting Corbigni's marriage proposal, her innate devotion to the Republic not only sets her apart from men but from all other women. Her strident patriotism—presented in Zschokke's text as directly opposed to the traits of a suitable wife: "Ich kann, ich werde Sie / Als *Weib* nicht selig machen" (HZ, 46; "I cannot, I will not / Make you happy as your *wife*")—is framed as inherent, rather than unnatural. Underscoring this point is the fact that Corday must remind Corbigni of his duty to the fatherland and his deviation from his role as citizen, patriot, and man in his single-minded pursuit of personal pleasure:

> Corbigni, sind
> Sie wirklich *Mann*, so lassen Sie von diesen
> Fatalen Grillen los. [. . .]
> . . . .
> Republikaner, Deine Braut, Dein Gott, ist
> Die *Republik*! (HZ, 47–48)

> Corbigni,
> If you are truly a *man*, then stop with these
> Disastrous whims. [. . .]
> . . . .
> Republican, your bride, your God, is
> The *Republic*!

For Corday, masculinity and patriotism are inextricably bound to one another: he who does not place fatherland above all else, it follows, must not be a true man like Brutus. The embodiment of ambiguity, Corday's display of manly patriotic devotion alongside her virtuous feminine exterior only inflames Corbigni's desire further:

> Bei Gott, Sie sind das wunderbarste
> Geschöpf, was je mein Auge sah.
> Verschmolzen sieht man hier die Ideale
> Verführerischer Weiblichkeit und Mannheit. In
> Dem schönsten Gliederbau die *Brutusseele*! (HZ, 48)

> My God, you are the most wonderful
> Creature my eye has ever seen.
> Fused together one sees here the ideals of
> Beguiling femininity and masculinity. In
> The *spirit of Brutus* in the most beautiful form!

Corday has become the androgynous ideal: the perfect union and balance of opposing forces. Corbigni's overwhelming attraction to this chimera simultaneously confirms her desirability as a woman—she is not a *Mannweib* (virago) or monster—and her claim to the role as patriotic martyr. However, this same unrestrained admiration underscores his inadequacy as a modern-day Brutus worthy of her affections and respect. It is her awe-inspiring model of masculine patriotic devotion that is meant to incite men to action, but which ultimately results in her claim to the role of political agent and Brutus-like heroic subject position.

While Corday's fervent commitment to the fatherland enables her to sublimate her pursuit of personal happiness, Corbigni's subordination to his drives leaves him apolitical and apathetic. Believing he is about to receive Corday's acceptance of his marriage proposal, Corbigni gladly forsakes his country and his fellow citizens:

> [. . .] Ha, mag das Vaterland
> Doch immerhin zusammenstürzen, mögen
> Die deutschen Adler immerhin die Beute
> Erobern, bliebt nur eine Hütte noch
> Für mich und für Charlotten, o so spotte
> Ich stolz der Erdengötter Herrlichkeit,
> Des Lorbeers der Unsterblichkeit! (HZ, 50)
>
> [. . .] Ha! The fatherland may
> Continue to collapse, the German
> Eagles may continue to capture
> Their prey, as long as one cottage remains
> For me and for Charlotte, oh, so I shall
> Mock with pride the glory of the earthly gods,
> The laurels of immortality!

Zschokke's juxtaposition of Corday and Corbigni destabilizes the gendered spaces of the public and domestic spheres. Corbigni envisions an idyllic, utopian retreat far away from the politics of the Revolution and tucked away safely within the confines of the simple domestic space. Yet the price he must pay to attain this paradise on earth, namely the murder of Marat, is far more than he is willing to offer. Despite Corbigni's clear unsuitability for the task she has in mind, Corday exploits the sway she holds over him in an effort to convince him to carry out the attack.

Seizing on the female body as a semiotic repository for primal drives and desires, Zschokke turns his Corday into the locus for attempts to restore political prosperity. With rather overt erotic implications, Corday attempts to seduce Corbigni into killing Marat: "Ein *Paradies* sollst Du an meiner Hand / Empfangen [. . .]" (HZ, 50; "You shall welcome *paradise* at my hand [. . .]"). Corday willingly barters her sexualized body in an effort to restore the body politic to its former health.[73] In order to demonstrate her sincerity and determination, Corday is prepared to subjugate herself physically and emotionally to the patriotic husband brave enough to liberate her country from oppression: "*Anbeten* will ich ihn, will seine Braut, / Will seine *Sklavin* werden, denn er ist / Befreier meines Vaterlandes!" (HZ, 55; "I want to worship him, want to be his bride, / Want to become his slave, for he is / Liberator of my fatherland!"). Zschokke deploys the metaphor of marriage and physical union of man and wife, transforming the murder weapon, which Corday presents Corbigni as a token of her affection, into a symbolic engagement ring (HZ, 55). The conflation of murder weapon and wedding ring signifies that the future bride and groom's domestic bliss is both contingent upon and imperative for the political prosperity of the Republic.

Zschokke's protagonist fuses personal love with patriotism in order to validate Corday's decision to take Marat's life. Corday internalizes Corbigni's unwillingness to murder Marat in exchange for her hand in marriage as a simultaneous betrayal of the fatherland: "Corbigni / Liebt mich nicht, denn er liebt das Vaterland / Ja nicht" (HZ, 58; "Corbigni / Does not love me, for he does not love the fatherland"). Zschokke turns the gendered association between public and private on its head and projects Corbigni into a feminized role whereby his desire and love for Corday takes precedence over his patriotic duty to the fatherland. Corday views Corbigni as nothing but a "*Knabe*" (*boy*) and seizes upon his inaction to justify her action (HZ, 57).[74]

Westphalen and Zschokke's dramatic treatments of Corday's decision to sacrifice herself for the political welfare of the Republic turn on the conflation of the personal and political. The authors establish this link between private well-being and public safety by emphasizing the devastating impacts of revolutionary violence on Corday's family. Furthermore, the dramatists strategically deploy metaphors of the Republic as a familial unit and civil war as a threat to the sanctity of that family and the lives of its sons, brothers, and fathers. In framing the threat to the Republic as a threat to the family, Westphalen and Zschokke attenuate Corday's violation of social conventions and the political order.

Confronting the Enemy

Westphalen and Zschokke's approaches to displaying or concealing female violence against a male body reveal deeper implications for the literary reframing of Corday as patriot and saint. As von Hoff and others have noted, it was the rule rather than the exception that violent acts committed by female protagonists were not staged.[75] Instead, authors employed various dramatic techniques—such as Kleist's use of teichoscopy in the cannibalistic attack on Achilles in his drama *Penthesilea*—in order to describe the scene occurring offstage for audiences. Rather than leaving the encounter between Corday and Marat to the reader's vivid imagination, Zschokke deviates from dramatic convention by portraying the deadly attack. In staging the encounter, he places the protagonist's heroic act and her honorable surrender front and center for the reader. To avoid violating the aesthetic principles of the classical drama, Westphalen utilizes the chorus of this genre and presents the murder indirectly. Of greater importance for the dramatist than the violent act is the internal conflict it elicits within her protagonist. Highlighting the destabilizing effect the murder has on Corday, Westphalen stresses for her reader Corday's humanity to counter representations of Corday as an emotionless murderess.

In Zschokke's drama, Corday's position as active political subject is necessitated by the Republic's lack of "a few good men." While Robert's conspicuous absence signals that Corday's love cannot be realized, it also creates a void in the public realm for Corday to occupy as an active agent of change. Robert's resurrection at the end of the play only momentarily threatens to erode Corday's resolve as her sublimated sentiments of love resurface. Just seconds before she enters Marat's apartment, she sees a figure, resembling Robert, standing on the street. Alive and well, Robert tries to persuade Corday to return with him to the countryside and back into the loving arms of her family, and thus to return to the private sphere, implying her containment within the domestic space. Corday wavers only briefly as memories of her love for Robert threaten to undermine her determination: "O, mein Schuzgeist [*sic*], stärke mich / Mit Riesenkraft, ich bin ja nur ein schwaches Weib!" (HZ, 107; "Oh, my guardian angel, fortify me / With colossal strength, I am only a weak woman!").[76] Steeling herself for the heroic sacrifice, Corday parts from Robert with only cryptic reference to her impending fate and returns *him* to the domestic sphere. Dismayed by Corday's sudden and inexplicable transformation, Robert breaks down in tears, frantically clinging to Corday's neck (HZ, 115). His display of emotion incurs Corday's admonishment: "Auf, Robert, sei / Ein Mann. Du weinest? pfui doch, *Weiber* müssen / Nur weinen. Lebe wohl!" (HZ, 116; "Get up Robert, be / A man. You cry? Ugh! *Women* alone must / Cry. Farewell!"). Rather than weakening Corday's decision to commit murder, this final encounter with the emotionally distraught Robert confirms for her the need for a strong, decisive patriot to rescue the Republic. In the same instance, this chance meeting underscores for the reader that Corday is not a deviant monster or devoid of human emotion. The sentiments of love tempting Corday to give up her heroic mission remind the reader of the sacrifice she is about to make and the possibility for personal happiness she forsakes in the name of her fatherland and on behalf of her fellow citizens.

Zschokke's tactic for rehabilitating his assassin puts the full force of Corday's violence on display. As Zschokke notes in the foreword to his play, "So unbedeutend immerhin die Folgen jener heroischen That waren: so groß und edel bleibt doch die Handlung selbst" (HZ, 1; "As meaningless as the consequences of that heroic act nevertheless were: the act itself remains great and noble"). Staging the deadly attack in the play's final scene, Zschokke does not temper the menacing appearance of his assassin. Corday, who as the stage directions inform the reader, appears "*aufflammend, mit schreklicher Stimme*" (HZ, 129; "*blazing, with a dreadful voice*"), is a true Fury hovering over her intended victim and condemning him to death. Seconds later, she "*stößt ihm das Messer in den Leib*" ("*thrusts the knife into his body*"). As Marat collapses, Corday proclaims "*im stolzen Triumph lächelnd*" (HZ, 129; *smiling in proud triumph*) the liberation of the Republic from tyranny. The bloody scene, and indeed Zschokke's entire play, concludes with Corday's willing surrender and the victorious pronouncement securing her legacy as patriotic martyr: "[. . .] Kein Tod / Ist unter allen Toden schöner, als / Der Tod fürs freie Vaterland!" (HZ, 130; "[. . .] No death / Is more beautiful among all deaths, than / The death for a free fatherland!").[77] Zschokke is not concerned with an examination of Corday's internal conflict and humanity that dominates Westphalen's drama. Instead, he asserts his heroine's decisive and unwavering certainty as just and patriotic, leaving no room to question her noble intentions.[78]

While Zschokke does not explicitly stage the psychological drama unfolding within Corday after the murder, he does construct scenes condoning the assassin's transgression. The author mobilizes his drama's male characters, more precisely prominent male political and military figures, to confirm Corday's claims that Marat is indeed the sole arbiter of the Republic's destruction. In the third act leading to the play's violent conclusion, Zschokke invents a gathering between the expelled Gironde deputies and sympathizers who plot their revolt against the Montagnards. Led by General Wimpfen (Georges Félix de Wimpffen, 1744–1814), the men convey the chaotic, destabilizing effects of the Revolution that have led to depravity and crimes against the people. In the same instance that the violence perpetrated by Marat and his co-conspirators is condemned, the expelled deputy Guadet (Marguerite-Élie Guadet, 1758–1794) is resigned to the fact that thousands more must die in order to bring about the necessary change that will restore order and peace: "Freund, keine Revolution ist ohne Blut / Vollbracht" (HZ, 85; "Friend, no revolution is accomplished / Without bloodshed"). The men's valiant plans to defeat Marat and rescue the Republic are presented in terms of selfless patriotism and noble deeds:

> [. . .] Wir, die alle hier
> Vor Ihnen stehn, sind rein von *Eigennuz*,
> Von *Selbstsucht*, *Herrschbegier* und *Meuterei*;
> Wir streiten für die *gute Sache*, unser Tod
> Wird einst durch *sie geheiligt*. (HZ, 96)

> [. . .] We, who all
> Stand before you here, are undefiled by *self-interest*,
> By *egoism*, *desire to govern*, and *mutiny*;
> We fight for the *good cause*, our death
> Will one day be *sanctified by the cause*.

In this regard, their motivation for waging a civil war parallels Corday's own desire to liberate the Republic. The men's willingness to shed the blood of thousands of innocent citizens, to pit brother against brother in order to achieve their political goal, highlights the truly noble sacrifice Corday willingly offers: her one life in exchange for thousands.

Like Zschokke's drama, the scenes framing the assassination of Marat in Westphalen's play serve to redeem the violent act as one of necessity and thereby humanize the murderess. In the scenes preceding the murder, Westphalen depicts the intended victim and his Jacobin co-conspirators scheming to execute their Girondist opponents and manipulate public opinion to cover up their crime (CW, 107–18). Positioning Marat alongside Robespierre, Danton, and Saint-Just, Westphalen allows Marat to emerge as the most diabolical and despotic of all the political tyrants in order to warrant Corday's targeting of the sickly publicist.[79] While Danton and Saint-Just express serious reservations about the plot to eradicate their political opposition in the Convention, Robespierre and Marat assert a scorched earth policy dependent on Marat's absolute control of public opinion.[80] Robespierre and Marat figure as the greatest threats to public safety, yet even Robespierre appears harmless when Marat removes his mask in the final scene of act 2 to expose himself as the true monster and ringleader of violence and destruction Corday has claimed him to be.[81] Alone on stage, Marat boasts of his plan to assume complete and total power by dividing and conquering his co-conspirators: "Lacht nur! Gut! Gut! bald seh' ich Euch entzweit. / Auf Euren Trümmern bau' ich meine Herrschaft" (CW, 118; "Go ahead and laugh! Good! Good! soon I will see you divided. / Upon your ruins I will build my reign"). His complete control of the press, which figured prominently in the previous scene, emerges even more clearly as the locus of his power and domination: "Das Volk regier' ich einzig—und das ist / Ein theures Pfand für meine Sicherheit" (CW, 119; "I alone rule the people—and that is / Valuable guarantee for my safety"). Westphalen presents Marat as the greater danger due to his ability to manipulate and mobilize thousands through his role as publicist. His thirst for power and domination knows no bounds, making him the tyrant and despot worthy of Corday's deadly knife: "Und, weh' Dir, Volk!—streng—strenger noch wie Er [Papst Sixtus V.], / Und in ganz anderm Geist möcht' ich regieren!" (CW, 120; "And, woe betide you, nation!—draconian—even more draconian than he [Pope Sixtus V.], / And in a completely different spirit do I desire to govern!").[82] The bloody reign waged by Robespierre will be nothing compared to that which Marat will undertake, if his plan succeeds. Placing Marat alongside the other Jacobin criminals, Westphalen confirms the bleak future facing the Republic under Marat's sway.

Westphalen's strategic framing of Marat not only prepares the reader for Corday's deadly attack but also lays further groundwork for the rehabilitation of a woman's violent political act. The chorus concluding the second act underscores one final time how little Marat values human life and his threat to the citizens of France, whom he mistreats as "nied'res Gewurme" (CW, 121; lowly worms) to be crushed beneath his tyrannical rule. The voices of the chorus condemn Marat to death and call upon avenging Furies to mete out a just punishment for this criminal:

Schrecken ergreift den Verbrecher!—Scheußliches Grausen—
Denn, von der Furie Geissel umschwungen,
Weiß er, rastlos gequälet, ach! nirgend zu hausen—
Bald von zerfleischenden Armen umschlungen;—
Jetzo ergriffen!—verzweifelnd!—im Wahne
Sinkt ihm der Hoffnung hoch flatternde Fahne! (CW, 123)

Terror grips the criminal!—Abominable dread—
For, succumbing to the scourge of the Furies,
He knows, restlessly tormented, alas! no home—
Soon enveloped by mauling arms;—
Now captured!—despairing!—delusional
The high waving flag of hope sinks before him!

These "Göttinnen der Rache" (CW, 122; goddesses of revenge) execute the ordained punishment of the despot, whose death restores order and avenges the crimes committed against humankind. The earthly murderess Corday is replaced by supernatural representatives of justice and retribution, allowing her crime to be both transposed and simultaneously exalted to mythical proportions. Westphalen's strategic representation of Marat, in which she places in his mouth all the fears and concerns expressed by Corday and the play's other characters, and accompanied by the instructive chorus and menacing Furies, confirms for the reader that Corday's actions are necessary to prevent far greater crimes from being committed against the people of the Republic.

Taking still greater care to erase the criminal stain tarnishing her heroine's act, Westphalen underscores that Corday, unlike the Furies, is flesh and blood. The opening scene of the third act, immediately following Marat's death at the hands of the vengeful goddesses, offers the reader unique insight into the psychological effect of the violent act on its perpetrator. A panoply of conflicting emotions unfold within Corday as she reflects on the murder she has just committed. Just as the sight of violent female revolutionaries evoked an ambivalent reaction within Corday, her own act of violence similarly engenders what at first appears to be a momentary crisis of conscience. Her attempt to reconcile her "passive" nature with her use of deadly force collapses into cognitive dissonance. Critical to the staging of Corday's inner turmoil are the play's stage directions, which inform the reader in greater detail about Corday's state of mind.[83] Even as Corday's gestures convey her repulsion at the violence she has just committed, she nevertheless maintains her actions as just and righteous: "Doch itzt auch schuldlos!" (CW, 129; Even now still innocent!). What emerges, however, is not Corday's dismay at the idea of having taken a life—Marat remains a tyrant and monster even in Corday's fragile state of mind—rather, the ambivalence Corday experiences results from the contradiction between her concept of her gendered self and the heroic, violent deed she has just accomplished:

Nur im Widerspruch
Erscheint mein Ich mit meinem innern *Selbst.*
Dieselbe Hand, die von der Kindheit an
Mitleidig oft ein zartes Leben schützte,
Nicht einmal einen Wurm zu tödten wagte—
Diesselbe Hand regiert den Mörder-Stahl!—
. . . .
Den Mord-Stahl? (CW, 129)

Only in contradiction
Does my self appear with my inner *self.*
This same hand, which from childhood onward
Often compassionately defended a delicate life,
Not once dared to kill a worm—
This same hand commanded the murderer's steel!—
. . . .
The murder weapon?

Corday's identity, inherently linked to her feminine role as caregiver, nurturer, and giver of life, is destabilized by her transformation into a dealer of death, or as Karin Baumgartner argues, it is the alienation of her "true (gendered) self from the political persona who committed the deed."[84] The agency implied by "Dieselbe Hand" that wields the murder weapon appears initially far too unsettling for Corday, and in the very next instance she invokes a higher power to distance herself from the violence she has committed: "O, ew'ge Güte! ja, es war *Dein* Werk, / Du lenktest ihn, Du stärktest meine Hand!" (CW, 129; "Oh, eternal benevolence! yes, it was *your* work, / You guided the weapon, you strengthened my hand!"). Corday is only capable of making sense of the contradiction between her passive, feminine self and her violent, heroic alter ego by locating the driving force for her act in an external, supernatural source.[85] Displacing Corday's agency onto a divine power, Westphalen dissociates her heroine from similar acts of violence perpetrated by the bloodthirsty female revolutionaries. Westphalen's framing of her warlike woman as a vessel or instrument for a force residing outside the individual resonates with Schiller's armed maiden Johanna, who functions as the mortal hand of a divine power. Westphalen, like Schiller, reclaims her protagonist's transgression as a divinely ordained act sanctioned in the service of patriotic love.

Westphalen and Zschokke's strategic framing and veiling of Corday's deadly confrontation with Marat facilitates the rehabilitation of the murderess in the concluding portions of the plays and in German public opinion. The authors mobilize male figures associated with the patriarchal order to lend credibility to Corday's offense while at the same time emphasizing that her sacrifice is nobler and more altruistic than all others. In both texts, regardless of their decision to conceal or display Corday's violent transgression, the authors add another dimension to Corday's status as martyr, rather than criminal, by invoking the authority of their play's "informed" male political participants.

Corday's Legacy on Trial

Westphalen and Zschokke further complicate the dominant narratives surrounding Corday by embedding official public as well as personal documents pertaining to the case in their dramas. Telling excerpts from the personal correspondence between Corday and the Girondist Barbaroux as well as Corday and her father were also merged seamlessly into the dramatic works by both authors. Westphalen reproduces Corday's letter to her father almost verbatim, while Zschokke infuses Corday's assertions into the character's dialogue, thereby giving life to the words on the page. Interweaving these official records and intimate texts into their narratives, Westphalen and Zschokke allow their protagonists to speak from beyond the grave.

In Westphalen's play, the final phase of Corday's apotheosis unfolds in scenes staging her trial and the immediate aftermath of her execution. Although these episodes suggest the far-reaching impact of her patriotic sacrifice, the ambiguity characterizing these scenes ultimately implies a return to the status quo, as the intervening decade between Corday's assassination of Marat and Westphalen's composition of the play had demonstrated. Act 4, scene 1 is devoted entirely to Corday's trial and defense, while the remaining scenes of the act are dominated by Luchs and Lagarde's frantic reactions to her impending execution. The act closes with Corday's rejection of Luchs's offer to liberate her. The fifth and final act of Westphalen's play revolves entirely around the despondent male characters and their lamentation as well as glorification of Corday. Concluding the play with the arrest of Luchs and Antoine and Lagarde's morose resignation, Westphalen underscores Corday's agency as active political subject while men remain all talk and no action.

Westphalen's staging of the trial simultaneously constructs a space in which to explore the public's unease with the issue of female agency and violence. In her reproduction of the legal proceedings, Westphalen incorporated in detail and with great accuracy portions of the trial protocol as it had appeared in German journals.[86] Scholars have argued that Westphalen's decision to re-create Corday's testimony before judge and jury not only reclaimed the subject position for her protagonist but it also restored the accused's ability to shape her legacy as patriotic martyr well after her death.[87] Indeed, putting Corday on trial in her drama, Westphalen created the possibility for her protagonist to mount her own defense as a true patriot, rather than a common criminal, and offered one potential resolution to the contested notion of women as political agents.

If the scenes leading up to Corday's trial and execution leave the reader ambivalent about whether Corday acts as an independent agent or merely as an instrument of a higher power, then Westphalen's defense of Corday during the legal proceedings asserts a place for women as agents of political change.[88] Westphalen gives voice to her heroine's own uneasiness with the notion of women's use of violence as she recounts the scenes from Paris (CW, 80–81) and in the immediate aftermath of her own violence (CW, 129). However, what emerges in greater clarity over the course of the play and crystallizes in the trial scene is that the individual, empowered by an overwhelming love of country, is not a passive victim of fate but possesses the power to shape and transform her own destiny. Appearing defiant before the tribunal, Corday defends her decision to murder a fellow citizen. Responding to the judge's questions about what drove her to commit such a brutal crime, Corday invokes the power of patriotic love for the fatherland and her fellow countrymen as her sole justification:

> O frage—wie ein Stral sich erdwärts senkt!
> Nur ein Gesetz erkennt die höchste Liebe,
> Die Liebe für ein theures Vaterland!
> Sie senkt sich nur in eine heiße Brust,
> Da wird der Götterstral zur lichten Flamme!
> So ward auch mir der schöne große Wille!
> Den nun, wie ich gewollt, die That vollendet! (CW, 167–68)
>
> Oh ask—how a ray sinks earthward!
> The highest love recognizes only one law,
> The love of a cherished fatherland!
> It sinks into an ardent bosom,
> Where the divine ray transforms into a bright flame!
> And for me it was that great, grand will!
> Which, as was my pleasure, the act perfected!

Elevating her patriotism to an almost religious state, Corday privileges the authority of the fatherland over the earthly tribunals. She thereby positions herself beyond the purview of Jacobin law and subject only to the Republic. In serving a greater power, namely her republican patriotism, cloaked here with divine symbolism, Corday constructs an image of herself as willing subject of this supreme will. While such imagery initially appears to destabilize her position as political subject, Corday is quick to assert that she alone has carried out the murder of Marat and single-handedly rescued the Republic: "Ich dachte—handelte—ich fragte nicht! / Mein ist die That [. . .]" (CW, 172; "I thought—acted—I didn't ask permission! / Mine alone is the act [. . .]").[89] If we remember her response to her family's resignation (CW, 22–23), we see that she has always asserted a view of the individual's power to shape, guide, and direct the forces of fate. Both her decision to act and the act itself are the result of Corday's will alone, nurtured and empowered by her sense of duty and allegiance.

By reinforcing Corday's own claims of working for a greater good, a nobler cause in service of the Republic, the play's male characters ultimately secure Corday's status as patriotic heroine in the days following her trial and execution. Westphalen seizes on Corday's self-proclaimed desire for her single act of selfless bravery to inspire thousands of patriots to rise up against Jacobin oppression and highlights the female assassin's unsettling and powerful impact on Lagarde. While Luchs's decision to stage a rescue attempt comes as no surprise to the reader—after all, the real Adam Lux published a strident defense of Corday that led to his execution—it is the sudden transformation of the young lawyer Lagarde which suggests the power of Corday's legacy to inspire even the most fervent skeptic. Lagarde, the embodiment of unwavering objectivity and cold rationality, who dissuaded Luchs from committing the same act of murder carried out by Corday, appears completely undone by his inability to stay Corday's execution: "Die That ist strafbar; doch die große Absicht / Verdient den Lorber [*sic*], nicht das Blutgerüst" (CW, 177; "The act alone is criminal; yet the noble intention / Deserves the laurel wreath, not the scaffold"). While the law deals only in black and white, Lagarde sees the liberatory and transgressive potential in the grey area that allows Corday to figure as a heroine.[90] The law may punish the body of the criminal, "Doch tödtet es den Geist des Wirkens nicht" (CW, 177; "Yet it cannot destroy the spirit of the action"). The patriotic ideal of selfless sacrifice that motivates Corday inflames Lagarde's senses.

In striking contrast to the measured tone and scientific-like approach to the question of civil disobedience he exhibited in his discussion with Luchs, Lagarde now appears ruled by his emotions and inclined to hyperbole. The stage directions opening act 5, scene 1, in which Lagarde contemplates in solitude Corday's martyrdom, convey both his physical and emotional "Unruhe" (CW, 205; restlessness), vacillating between calmness and frantic activity. Lagarde is at odds with himself not only over Corday's impending execution but what her fate implies about his own existence as a man:

> Was ich auch treibe, diesen innern Kampf
> Von qualenvoller Unruh, die mich peinigt,
> Von Unmuth—Angst, die zu der festen Brust
> Sich Wege bahnet, weil die Unschuld leidet,
> Zu sänftigen, mich männlich zu beherrschen;
> Wo ich nicht helfen konnte, zu vergessen—
> Das Unausweichliche gelassen dulden—
> Es ist umsonst!—O, theures Bild Charlottens!
> Du Ideal bewundernswürd'ger Größe! (CW, 205–06)

Despite attempts to subdue, this inner battle
Of agonizing unease, which torments me,
Of discontent—apprehension, which carves
Paths to the steadfast chest, because innocence suffers,
Despite attempts to restrain myself like a man;
To forget, where I could not assist—
To calmly endure the inevitable—
It is in vain!—Oh, beloved image of Charlotte!
You ideal of admirable greatness!

Corday's greatness both inspires and calls into question the manliness of those men moved to extreme admiration by her example. Erika Süllwold argues that Corday inspires action;[91] yet, this action remains only illusory, as the men fail to enact real change as a result of Corday's heroic death. Lagarde's ambivalence does not result in a concrete plan of action on how to carry on Corday's patriotic work; instead, he articulates a sense of resignation, passivity, and suffering that invokes tropes of a bourgeois "ideal femininity." It is Corday who remains the active political agent of change, while Lagarde, Luchs, and Antoine never move beyond hollow claims of patriotic duty and devotion.[92]

If Westphalen's staging of Corday on trial restored her heroine's voice and status as political agent, Zschokke accomplishes this similar goal by foregoing a trial scene altogether and opting instead to embed statements made by Corday in her personal letters into the scenes just prior to Marat's assassination. By prefacing the violent encounter with scenes foregrounding her heroism, Zschokke reanimates his protagonist and allows her to reframe her transgression as a necessity. Thus, he prepares the reader for Corday's elevation to martyr even before the heroic deed is carried out. Furthermore, by concluding his drama with the protagonist's triumphant claims of a heroic offering for the fatherland—"*Kein Tod / Ist unter allen Toden schöner, als / Der Tod fürs freie Vaterland!*" (HZ, 130; "*No death / Among all deaths is more beautiful than / Death for a free fatherland!*")—rather than putting Corday's character under the juridical microscope, Zschokke distances his patriotic martyr from the criminal element of her action and avoids debating its efficacy. Recalling Zschokke's foreword to his readers, it is the act itself and not the efficacy of the act that matters (HZ, 1).

Zschokke's reliance on Corday's own voice lends his dramatized portrait of the young female assassin a kind of "authenticity,"[93] at least as far as the images constructed by the German press are concerned. Zschokke adopts the most iconic statements and grand claims linking Corday to her forefathers of antiquity that place her murderous act in the lengthy tradition of sanctioned, heroic acts of tyrannicide: "Nicht das *Schafott*, das *Laster* nur entehrt! / Du findest in Elysium mich wieder, in der / Gesellschaft meines Cassius und Cato" (HZ, 107; "It is not the *scaffold* but only *vice* which is dishonorable! /

You will find me once more in Elysium, in the / Company of my Cassius and Cato").[94] Yet more striking and compelling is Zschokke's reproduction of assertions which spotlight the critique of masculinity articulated by the historical Corday. In her final encounter with the resurrected Robert—a scene which already takes aim at the manhood of the modern French patriot by presenting the emotionally overwrought Robert pleading with Corday and builds on her disappointment with Corbigni's preference for domestic bliss over the Republic's well-being—the warlike woman mounts her final claim to violence as a necessary means to secure the stability of the Republic on the passive and cowardly bodies of her fellow countrymen:

> [. . .] So ist es schändlich,
> Daß ganz Paris nicht einen einzgen Mann trägt,
> Der den *Tyrannen* zittern machte! Die
> Franzosen fürchten sich vor *Koburgs* Heeren nicht,
> Und nicht vor *Braunschweigs* Weltbezwingern,—
> Und beben doch vor einer *einzgen Memme*,
> Die ihre Feigheit hinter Grausamkeit verschanzt.
> Pfui, ewge Schande! Sklaven sind und bleiben
> Die Franken; solchen schwachen Seelen ward
> Die Freiheit nicht geboren— (HZ, 110)[95]

> [. . .] It is therefore shameful,
> That all of Paris does not possess one single man,
> Who made the *tyrants* tremble! The
> French do not fear *Coburg's* armies,
> And not *Brunswick's* conquerors of the world—
> And yet they quake before one *single coward*,
> Who barricades their cowardice behind cruelty.
> Fie, eternal disgrace! The French are and remain
> Slaves; freedom was not born to
> Such weak spirits—

It is not only the cruelty and barbarism of Marat's crimes that demand action be taken; more importantly, it is the Frenchmen's willing enslavement by a coward, weakling, shell of a man, that demands Corday fill the gap left by her fellow male citizens. If once fearless male warriors, who protected republican families and defended the fatherland's borders against menacing threats by foreign enemies, now bow and scrape before a "Memme" like Marat, then drastic corrective measures must be pursued to restore the revolutionary course and along with it the natural order. Such debilitating fear, political passivity, and resigned acceptance of despotic domination diminishes the bravery and ferocity of the former French citizen warrior. By killing Marat, Corday not only liberates the fatherland from an oppressor, rescuing the lives of thousands of potential victims, but she also restores the possibility for men to be men again, although figures such as Corbigni or Westphalen's Luchs and Lagarde leave even this outcome ambiguous.

Although Zschokke could not anticipate how the lengthy debate surrounding Corday would unfold, it seems that opting out of the portrayal of a trial and its aftermath created a more powerful and empowering heroine. It is the act, which speaks for itself, that is at the heart of his dramatization of this modern-day Brutus, Cassius, Cato, and Yael. Rather than obscuring the heroic nature of the murder and the selfless, patriotic motives informing it in a trial scene, in which action is replaced by words, Zschokke's play celebrated the noble act and its martyred patriot. Despite Zschokke and Westphalen's attempts to portray the combination of female agency and violence amidst the chaos of a revolution in crisis in an affirmative manner, their renderings of Corday evince ambivalence about politically motivated warlike women wielding deadly weapons against unarmed male victims.

In an attempt to stake their ideological claims to the murderous act and its perpetrator, journalists and dramatists waged a war over Corday's dead body. Competing antagonistic and affirmative depictions of Corday and her deed engaged with and were informed by questions of female agency debated by contemporary social theorists, politicians, intellectuals, and members of the literary community. While texts vilifying Corday as a bloodthirsty monster drew on and reproduced myths deployed in anti-revolutionary press reports to demonize revolutionary women as specters, the fictional works mobilizing narrative strategies to elevate Corday to mythic, supernatural heights proposed an affinity between the assassin, legendary patriots, and biblical heroines. These competing efforts to bring the defiant, violent female perpetrator into semiotic submission exemplify the polysemy characterizing the woman warrior who resisted symbolic containment. Attempts to mitigate the taint of transgression ascribed to acts of political violence committed by women resulted in enigmatic depictions of Corday that left the issue of the female assassin's agency tenuous at best. After all, murder, regardless of its motives, was nevertheless a violation of the law and moral code. The author's strategic use of love—in the form of patriotism and love of fatherland—to mitigate the transgressive and criminal element of the warlike woman rendered bourgeois myths of an "ideal femininity" problematic while at the same time necessitating a reconsideration of gendered separate spheres and the requirements for active political engagement in and defense of the emerging German nation.

Chapter Three

✦

Armed Virtue

The Woman Warrior as Defender of the "Domestic" Good

The dramatic transformation of the young French assassin Charlotte Corday from fanatical, calculating murderess to glorified patriot and heroic martyr in the decades before and after 1800 represented a significant shift in depictions of women's political violence in Germany that paved the way for the construction of a new female icon. By exploiting the woman warrior's ambiguous status, German authors blurred the early binary of specter-ideal depicted in press reports about female revolutionaries and invented a hybrid woman warrior: the violent woman as a defender of the "domestic" and moral good. Such depictions of paragons of female patriotism reveal the contradictions inherent in rhetorical strategies that constructed women warriors who fought to defend the same reactionary social structures which denied their agency and perpetuated their subordinate status. At the same time, these literary maneuvers to contain the subversive potential of the warlike woman complicate the very myths of an ideal "femininity" and "masculinity" they exploit in their negotiations with a culture in crisis at the end of the eighteenth century.

The literary deployments of warlike women in the works of Benedikte Naubert (1756–1819), Johann Wolfgang Goethe (1749–1832), and Friedrich Schiller (1759–1805) invite closer attention because of the tension they reveal about the rapidly changing realities of German-speaking territories ultimately resulting in the collapse of the Holy Roman Empire in 1806 and accompanied by the gradual emergence of a seemingly more unified, cohesive German territory. Although we cannot speak of *a* German nationalism around 1800, scholars have noted traces of what I would characterize as an "emergent" national sentiment, which developed more intensely in response to the threat posed by French invasion and occupation. The seeds of this gradually maturing conservative national identity were nurtured in the works of German Romantics.[1] The series of lectures that the philosopher and social theorist Johann Gottlieb Fichte held in Berlin in 1807–8 and published under the title *Reden an die deutsche Nation* (*Addresses to the German Nation*), during the French occupation, articulates the awakening interest in the cultivation of a collective national identity based on cultural affinities between disparate German territories and defined in opposition to their shared French occupying enemy. Thus, the term "domestic," as I strategically employ it in my discussion of sanctioned female violence in this chapter, operates on two important levels. First and foremost, I use it to interrogate the ways in which representations of warlike women apply pressure to myths of society's gendered bifurcation into separate spheres: public-private; political-familial; masculine-feminine; battlefield-household. The term "domestic" also acknowledges these emergent, not yet entirely conscious or intentionally formulated, sentiments of German identity that are borne out of a perceived shared threat to political autonomy and personal security.

Authors redirected their armed heroine's aggression outward against an external enemy in order to deploy the woman warrior for traditionalist agendas and to mollify the potential provocation she posed to the patriarchal order. This model of female patriotism stretched well into the early nineteenth century and became more prevalent as military conflict escalated. Already in 1792, after the Prussian defeat at the Battle of Valmy, fear of French invasion deeper into Germany became a reality with the occupation of Mainz and the establishment of the Mainz Republic (1792–93). Epstein has argued that such incursions by French troops, which were met with little resistance by Germans in the region, fed anxieties of German conservatives about the spread of revolutionary violence and principles.[2] Such "conservative hysteria" was further nurtured by Prussia's decisive defeat at the Battle of Jena (1806) resulting in Napoleon's forces seizing control west of the Rhine River and occupying key cities such as Berlin. Napoleon's growing threat to German autonomy proved a critical factor in subsequent portrayals of women's violence as a form of female patriotism.[3] The substitution in perceived danger of the French invader in place of the woman warrior necessitated the construction of new narratives to normalize behavior that previously had been deemed deviant. Now texts sanctioned women's limited participation in the public sphere by depicting patriotic wives, mothers, and daughters as heroic martyrs fighting to defend the fatherland and its conservative values against "infectious" democratic principles, or the *Revolutionsseuche* (revolutionary plague). Literary works, such as those discussed here, explicitly linked women's martial activity to conservative gender myths, exploiting the overdetermined rhetoric of women's maternal nature, in an attempt to subdue the subversive potential of these domestic warriors and forestall women's emancipatory demands. Yet, these very efforts at semiotic delimitation simultaneously problematize, either intentionally or unintentionally, the constructedness of gendered binaries.

Authors activated deeply embedded dispositions about violent women as specters by privileging domestic heroines who either return happily to hearth and cradle once the battle has been won or willingly sacrifice their lives for king and country. Such dispositions dictated the preservation of the internal status quo of a patriarchal gender hierarchy and strict division of spheres. Reframing the disorderly woman as female patriot did not suggest that women would renounce their roles within the domestic sphere in favor of political aspirations. Instead, they would lend their bodies to defend the country in its time of need and return to their homes once the enemy had been defeated. Thus, the danger posed by the invading French enemy proved slightly greater than the fear of the violent armed woman. The latter could be defused through images of women warriors, who fought to defend fatherland and family against a foreign enemy and returned unharmed to their roles as dutiful wives or were elevated to heroic heights in death on the battlefield.

Images of domestic amazons and patriotic martyrs constructed in the works by Naubert, Goethe, and Schiller embody the complexity and ambivalence characterizing German responses to the juxtaposition of women and violence at the turn of the century. Naubert's cross-dressing heroines in the historical novels *Geschichte der Gräfin Thekla von Thurn oder Scenen aus dem dreyssigjährigen Kriege* (1788) and *Philippe von Geldern. Oder Geschichte Selims, des Sohns Amurat* (1792) are only provisional participants in political events, whose presence on the battlefield is portrayed as a necessary yet innocuous transgression. When presented with the opportunity, they readily swap pants and sword for dress and needle. Like Thekla and Philippe, Goethe's domestic amazon Dorothea in the epic poem *Herrmann und Dorothea* (1797) does not actively seek out conflict or her role as woman warrior.[4] Where her cross-dressing counterparts enter the military conflict, Dorothea commits her heroic act of violence openly as a woman within and in defense of the domestic sphere. At the same time, the poem's comparison of the warlike woman's actual heroic actions with the future groom Herrmann's bravado and hollow jingoistic proclamations casts doubt on Dorothea's quiet return to the role of obedient housewife. Naubert and Goethe's works construct reluctant heroines, whose violent actions are presented as defensive maneuvers, rather than acts of aggression, and whose retreat to domestic roles of wife and mother confirm in nuanced ways the uncertain status of the woman warrior. Friedrich Schiller's ambiguous warrior maiden Johanna endures a far more complicated fate in her journey to patriotic salvation in the historical drama *Die Jungfrau von Orleans* (1801). Reading Schiller's tragic heroine against the savage female revolutionaries of his 1799 poem "Das Lied von der Glocke" ("The Song of the Bell"), Johanna appears as an eager woman warrior, whose deadly use of force, albeit sanctioned by both secular and spiritual patriarchal authorities, signals an irrevocable violation of social conventions. Schiller's play envisions the virginal woman warrior as patriotic martyr by framing her selfless acts of aggression as restorative rather than destructive.

These emerging fictions of the domesticated warlike woman presented a double bind for women readers; they were confronted with illusions of female empowerment and increased autonomy while in reality such myths sought to secure women's social subordination. The same dilemma proved particularly precarious for women writers, who either knowingly or unknowingly reproduced traditional myths of an "ideal femininity" constructed and popularized by their male counterparts.[5] The domestic warriors and sacrificial virgin constructed in the works discussed in this chapter enacted a form of *symbolic violence*: both the literary heroines and the female readers function as objects and agents of reactionary myths about gender roles and the division of public and private spheres. As Pierre Bourdieu argues, myth's symbolic power, or symbolic violence, is exerted insidiously over and confirmed by the very individuals subjected to its will.[6] The authors analyzed in this chapter not only participated in the conservative mythmaking process in their attempts to neutralize their warrior women, but their attempts at containment also allow their domestic amazons to be read as strategic negotiations with essentialist gender roles.

These hybrid women warriors, when read in conjunction, complicate notions of female agency and the forms in which women might participate in public life. Despite attempts by Naubert, Goethe, and Schiller to reframe women's violence as patriotic duty, the unsettling ambiguity surrounding these warriors resists containment by conventional resolutions. As the following analyses suggest, fraught images of these warlike women only confirm their equivocal status resulting in their appearance as at once frightening and alluring defenders of the fatherland.

Framing Portraits of the Woman Warrior

Although Naubert, Goethe, and Schiller's texts all exploit the ambiguous image of the woman warrior in an effort to confirm a normative myth of gender dependent on the preservation of separate spheres, they represent distinctive literary frames housing the portraits of their domestic heroines. For Naubert, the historical novel serves as the preferred medium by which to explore the complexity of the warlike woman. Naubert transcended prevailing literary borders by weaving historical subject matter, an emerging academic field around 1800 considered the exclusive domain of male scholars and authors, with the novel, wrongly believed to be a "feminized" genre.[7] The significance of this strategic maneuver is constituted not only by the fact that a woman was writing a historical work but also that she was writing women into history from which they had been previously excluded.[8] Indeed, Naubert's hybrid novel—what Kurt Schreinert has called the "Zweischichtenroman" (two-level novel)[9]—exhibits an early confrontation with the boundaries of political and personal on a number of levels. Moreover,

Naubert's innovative literary strategy to cloak compelling female characters in richly embroidered historical narratives, as exemplified by her novels *Thekla von Thurn* and *Philippe von Geldern*, proved successful.[10] Indeed, Naubert's novels, which she published anonymously, were for the most part well received by critics and often attributed to contemporary male writers. While the anonymous critic of a positive review of *Philippe von Geldern* in the 1793 edition of *Neue Allgemeine Deutsche Bibliothek* focused on the benefits for women readers, commenting that *even* "denkende Frauenzimmer" (thinking ladies) are able to discern between historical fact and fiction and that such novels encourage women to increase their knowledge of the historical subject matter, Naubert's popularity in the eighteenth and nineteenth centuries, as well as her current standing as a prolific German writer, suggests a wide audience including both a male and female readership.[11]

Written just prior to the outbreak of the French Revolution, *Thekla von Thurn*'s narrative anticipates in many ways the impending unrest soon to envelop Europe for the next two and a half decades and the growing presence of women in the public arena of war. The prologue frames the text as a domestic novel foregrounding the lives of a single family mapped onto the events of the Thirty Years' War (1618–48).[12] The events narrated in part 1 of the two-volume novel begin just prior to the Defenestration of Prague (May 1618) and depict the destruction of the protagonist's domestic sanctuary, forcing her to become a participant in the Siege of Magdeburg by General Tilly (November 1630–May 1631). Part 2 maps Thekla's masquerade as her brother Jaromir, missing and presumed dead on the field of battle, and amidst political intrigue between Catholics and Protestants. After an unsuccessful stint as a soldier, the novel concludes with Thekla's safe return to the domestic realm as the wife to her former Catholic enemy and captive Prince Eggenberg, thereby bringing the novel's protagonist full circle.

Naubert's novel especially speaks to the permeability of the boundary between the public sphere of warfare and the private realm of the family. The novel's first part focuses foremost on the fate of the Thurn daughters Thekla and Therese under the supervision of their Catholic-leaning mother Sybille, while their father Jaromir, a converted Protestant, and brothers Bogoslav and Jaromir wage war. The military conflict dominating part 2 functions as catalyst, and to a certain extent justification, for the young Protestant noblewomen's entrance into the public sphere. Even before Thekla assumes the soldier identity of her brother and officially enters the battle, she and her sister are repeatedly impacted by the war's violence. The multiple harrowing abductions of Thekla and her sister, first by the Catholic general Pappenheim and then by a Protestant ally, highlight the realities of warfare in which women were not merely bystanders but directly involved in the violence and political intrigues of war. Indeed, shortly after the publication of Naubert's novel, women were to be found on both sides of the front line in the Revolutionary and Napoleonic Wars.

Despite Naubert's historical novels problematizing the nexus between political violence and personal narratives, her political views, more specifically her stance on the French Revolution, remain opaque. It is striking that the author of numerous works prominently featuring cross-dressing women forced into military conflict remained largely silent on the events precipitating women's increased presence in the galleries of the National Convention, in the streets of Paris, and on the battlefields. There are no surviving documents providing us with concrete evidence of Naubert's attitude about the most transformative political event occurring during her lifetime. Letters published in Nikolaus Dorsch's edited collection of Naubert's correspondence only speak to her apprehension about and disdain for Napoleon's forces, which she and her husband were forced to quarter during the French occupation of Naumburg from 1813 to 1815.[13] Yet, it is exactly in her literary visions of tentative heroines amidst historical conflicts that we find evidence for her response to such inversions of the social order. Images of the woman warrior portrayed in *Thekla von Thurn* and *Philippe von Geldern* evince an unease with women's presence in politically charged military conflicts and the implications for the security and stability of the familial structure. Similarly, scholars like Waltraud Maierhofer, in her analysis of *Thekla von Thurn*, have argued that Naubert's novel did not agitate for women's participation in politics or warfare;[14] instead, it contributed to socially conservative gender narratives by constructing warlike women as "das Ideal der empfindsamen tugendhaften Frau" ("the ideal of the sentimental virtuous woman").[15] Extending Maierhofer's reading to Naubert's novel *Philippe von Geldern*—written after the storming of the Bastille in July 1789, the French market women's march to Versailles in August 1789, and amidst women's demands for civil liberties—I demonstrate how Naubert's novel resisted these transgressive models of femininity and opted instead to represent more traditional visions leaving the patriarchal order intact.

In *Philippe von Geldern* Naubert once again employs the technique of combining a domestic narrative with well-researched historical events by placing her reluctant cross-dressing warrior woman amidst the turmoil surrounding the Ottoman-Hungarian wars, Austrian-Hungarian War, and Burgundian War of the fifteenth century.[16] To date, little has been written about Naubert's novel. It is for this reason that I have chosen to summarize in more detail the events depicted in the work. Part 1 opens shortly after the Battle of Varna (1444), with the abdication of the Ottoman sultan Amurat (Murad II, 1404–1451) and the violent rise to power of his eldest son Mahomed [*sic*] the Conqueror (Mehmed II, 1432–1481). The execution of Hungarian statesman Ladislav Korvinus (Ladislaus Hunyadi, 1431–1457) by King Ladislav of Bohemia (Ladislaus the Posthumous, 1440–1457) concludes the first part of the novel. Shifting its focus to the conflict between Emperor Friedrich III (1415–1493) and his brother Archduke Albrecht VI (1418–1463), part 2 places its protagonists amidst the power struggle for the Hungarian and Bohemian thrones. The novel's seventh and final book concludes in 1481 with the deaths of Charles the Bold, Duke of Burgundy (1433–1477) and Sultan Mahomed. Against this historical backdrop, Naubert recounts the fictional love story between Selim,[17] the younger son of Sultan Amurat, and Philippe von Geldern (Philippa of Guelders, 1467–1547). Beginning in book 4 of the novel, Philippe, disguised as the young page Kalixtus Kolonna (the Christian name given to Kalepin by Pope Callixtus III),[18] takes on greater significance when she fails to warn Emperor Friedrich of the impending attack by his brother, during which the emperor's entourage, including Philippe, becomes trapped in the siege of the Hofburg in Vienna (1462). The story of Philippe's transformation into Kolonna dominates book 6, and in true Enlightenment fashion the novel's final book depicts the union of the newly crowned sultan Selim with his queen Philippe, thus linking East and West, Muslim and Christian.

While Naubert demonstrated an affinity for historically distant backdrops against which to contextualize her women warriors' heroism, for Goethe the epic poem provided the literary canvas upon which he portrayed the chaos and instability engendered by the French Revolution and Revolutionary Wars.[19] *Herrmann und Dorothea* unearths the implications of this political violence on the daily lives of individuals in the German-speaking territories bordering France. Goethe's political conservatism left him ambivalent toward the idea of revolution: he neither supported the idea of rebellion by the masses nor did he condone arbitrary despotism.[20] For Goethe, writing created a space in which he could explore poetically the causes and effects of "dieses schrecklichste aller Ereignisse" ("this most frightening of all events").[21] Responding to unsettling images of women's violent participation in the streets of Paris and on the battlefields, Goethe constructs his "domestic amazon" Dorothea, who at once defends and unsettles social conventions without agitating explicitly for social and political change.

Set in a village in the "idyllic" southern German countryside just east of the Rhine River during the First Coalition campaigns (1792–97),[22] the epic poem recounts the union of Dorothea, a young refugee fleeing the destruction caused by invading French troops west of the Rhine, with Herrmann, the timid, sensitive son of a middle-class innkeeper who harbors social aspirations. Unsettled by Dorothea's imposing figure and story of her heroic exploits against French marauders, as well as the engagement ring on her finger, Herrmann is unable to propose and instead lures Dorothea to the family's home under the pretense of hiring her as a maid. Herrmann's cowardice threatens to ruin the domestic idyll for which he has yearned, when Dorothea confesses her affection for Herrmann. The epic poem concludes with an ironic role reversal: the resolute Dorothea returns to the confines of the bourgeois domestic sanctuary to fulfill her duty as wife and caregiver while the tentative Herrmann asserts his claim as future family patriarch and defender of national values.

Contributing to Dorothea's ambiguity is the author's use of irony in a genre not readily associated with this rhetorical device. Goethe's epic poem inverts the gender of the traditional hero(ine) revealing that established notions of masculinity and femininity are unreliable, and indeed no longer viable, in a Germany unsettled by revolutionary changes. Further examples of irony pervading the text, such as the heroic quality of the hexameter form and the generally non-heroic actions of the poem's middle-class figures, have led scholars to read *Herrmann und Dorothea* as a response to the chaos and disorder spawned by the French Revolution.[23] As the most heroic figure, with perhaps the exception of her deceased, revolutionary-minded first fiancé, Dorothea is best suited for the poem's form.[24] Drawing on these claims, I read the contradictory images of Dorothea as woman and warrior, violent and virtuous, obedient and self-reliant, as creating the possibility for her defensive maneuvers and moral convictions to be co-opted in the service of conservative values and as an example of "appropriate" female patriotism. However, this model simultaneously unsettles the traditional model of male heroism and patriotism that no longer proves viable. As Hohendahl has aptly noted, the violent political and rapid social transformations sweeping across German territories unleashed a "Krise der Männlichkeit" (masculinity crisis). This crisis, in which the *Hausvater* (paterfamilias) as patriarchal authority was displaced in favor of a more centralized governing power, resulted in the "Orientierungsverlust des Sohnes" (disorientation of the son) and necessitated a reconsideration of masculine identity in the new state.[25] The reassessment of masculinity and patriotism that unfolds in Goethe's poem is taken up by Schiller in his dramatization of the Hundred Years' War (1337–1453) and the martyred female patriot.

For Schiller, the historical drama proved a vehicle through which he could stage and explore poetically the human condition as it related to questions of power and moral character. Literary critic Lesley Sharpe has proposed that Schiller's historical dramas and characters emphasize the "complexity and ambiguity of the historical world" and elicit within the reader/audience a "sense of ambivalence through dramatic presentation."[26] Exploiting the enigmatic quality of the historical drama, Schiller stages a woman warrior from whom the stain of transgression has been removed and recasts her in the role of patriotic martyr rather than bellicose warrior. Although well-versed in the historical events providing the backdrop for his armed maiden, Schiller rejected strict adherence to historical fact in the shaping of his protagonists. In his 1793 essay *Über das Pathetische* (*On the Pathetic*), Schiller asserted the view that historical accuracy played only a supporting role to the poetic and aesthetic functions of dramatic works: "Unser Wohlgefallen an idealischen Karakteren verliert nichts durch die Erinnerung, daß sie poetische Fictionen sind, denn es ist die *poetische*, nicht die historische Wahrheit, auf welche alle ästhetische Wirkung sich gründet" ("Because all aesthetic effect is based on the *poetic*, not the historic truth, none of our satisfaction with ideal characters is lost by recalling that they are poetic fictions").[27] Schiller's preference for the poetic over the real may account for the discrepancies scholars have noted between the historical figure Joan of Arc and his dramatic figure Johanna.[28] These same divergences allow for her literary conversion to patriotic saint in contrast to her execution as a common criminal at the stake. In this way, Schiller's choice of historical subject matter to frame and emphasize the development of his conflicted woman warrior shares an affinity, in many ways, with Naubert's use of the historical novel as the backdrop against which to project personal narratives. Indeed, it has been suggested that Schiller was so taken with Naubert's compelling heroine Thekla that he fashioned his own version in the dramatic trilogy *Wallenstein* (1800).[29]

While scholars have been left to speculate about Naubert's political leanings, Schiller's transformation from cautious optimist to skeptical opponent of the Revolution has been documented thoroughly.[30] As the French Republic degenerated into bloodshed, Schiller retreated to the realm of art and aesthetics in search of enlightened reform. The devolution into violence by the French signaled for Schiller the immaturity of the individual still incapable of accepting the responsibilities accompanying personal freedom. It is through this lens that scholars such as Jeffrey L. High have focused their readings of Schiller's later historical dramas in order to identify emergent nationalist sentiments resulting from the foreign occupation of German territories by Napoleon's forces. High suggests that Schiller's fixation with acts of insurrection—particularly in light of the French occupation of Stuttgart (1796) and the invasion of southern territories (1798)—informed his choice of the Hundred Years' War, which figures in his dramatic work as a "liberation movement" and allows his female protagonist to function as a kind of "freedom fighter" against a foreign oppressor.[31]

Schiller's conflicted engagement with the issue of gender is manifested more concretely in his depictions of warring women, which can be read as efforts to reconcile female aggression with bourgeois narratives of feminine virtue. Reading Schiller's dramatic heroine Johanna from *Die Jungfrau von Orleans* with the revolutionary women of his most popular poem "Das Lied von der Glocke" reveals strikingly complex and contradictory depictions of bellicose women. Schiller's vacillation between views of gender as fixed or fluid in his literary and philosophical works betrays his apprehension toward the mutability of gender that made the phenomenon of the violent female revolutionary possible.[32] Socially conservative gender myths about the ostensibly different yet commensurate nature of the sexes find a voice in poems such as "Würde der Frauen" ("The Dignity of Women") and "Die Geschlechter" ("The Sexes"), which privilege visions of the active, male warrior contrasted with images of the passive, virtuous domestic heroine as static and eternal.[33] At the same time this essentialist view is undermined by Schiller's 1793 essay *Über Anmut und Würde* (*On Grace and Dignity*), in which Gail K. Hart has located evidence for Schiller's acknowledgment of gender's "transferability."[34]

To neutralize the threat posed by the publicly active, armed woman, Schiller's literary women warriors affirm conservative myths about women's inherent unsuitability for the masculine pursuit of war, but they do so in very different ways. Schiller's poem "Das Lied von der Glocke," with its lyrical manifestation of savage, cannibalistic hyenas, functions as an explicit critique of revolutionary women as well as a more general criticism of the Revolution's lawless, debauched atmosphere.[35] Published originally in *Musen-Almanach für das Jahr 1800*, the poem reveals not only its author's more conventional stance on the nature of the sexes but also on the turmoil wrought by the Revolution. The poem's progression from idyllic images of a peaceful community to horrific scenes of brutality by unruly mobs and bloodthirsty women parallels the Revolution's gradual degeneration into cruelty and disorder. The first half of the poem, mirroring the structures of "Würde der Frauen" and "Die Geschlechter," reflects the early years of the Revolution and presents man and woman in their opposing spheres of activity. Man is forced into the world where he actively exerts himself in the pursuit of happiness, while woman plays devoted, industrious housewife and nurturing mother within the confines of a domestic utopia (SL, 2.1:230). This almost prelapsarian Eden is suddenly destabilized by the advent of the Revolution in which all social conventions are abandoned and even peaceful citizens are incited to violence. The depravity unleashed by the chaos is embodied by women who become brutal beasts threatening public safety and order: "Da werden Weiber zu Hyänen / Und treiben mit Entsetzen Scherz, / Noch zuckend, mit des Panthers Zähnen, / Zerreissen sie des Feindes Herz" (SL, 2.1:237; "Women into hyaenas start; / Disgustingly with horror jest; / With panther-teeth their victims' heart / They tear, yet quivering, from the breast" [SLE, 33]). Women's descent into savagery signifies that the Revolution has decimated the last bastion of civilized society. These monstrous women are the very same dutiful, mild-mannered housewives, sisters, and daughters depicted at the poem's beginning.[36]

In contrast to the brutal predators of his poem, Schiller's historical drama *Die Jungfrau von Orleans* complicates the easy distinction of the violent woman displayed in his poems as categorically dangerous and fundamentally unnatural. Although the play's message ultimately aligns with that of "Lied von der Glocke," foreclosing the possibility of women's unmediated participation in public life, the means by which Schiller accomplishes this rhetorical feat is anything but straightforward. His historical drama transports the woman warrior from her contemporary context to the battlefields of the Hundred Years' War in the conflict between France and the invading English enemy. Successfully leading the French troops to victory against the English, Johanna actively fights alongside her countrymen to expel the enemy usurper.[37] Overcoming a momentary emotional lapse, which threatens to derail her divine mission, Johanna returns to the field of battle, where she dies heroically in order to return King Charles VII to his throne, thereby restoring the feudal system of power, and along with it the king's temporarily compromised masculinity. Spared the fate of public execution suffered by the historical Joan of Arc for her gender transgressions, the play's closing scene offers Johanna a legacy as patriotic martyr and depicts the armed maiden being received with open arms by the paragon of the "eternal feminine," the Virgin Mother, thereby lending power to myths of the woman warrior as defender of the patriarchal order and domestic sanctuary.

The Nature of Transgression

The tension characterizing Naubert, Goethe, and Schiller's works is established in part by the texts' emphasis on the correlation, or contradiction, between appearance and inner "nature" of the characters. Despite the texts' assertion that the woman warrior is a woman to the core, her disconcerting appearance and refusal to comply with gender expectations cannot be easily harmonized with social conventions and notions of gender's immutability. Literary cross-dressing assumes various degrees of importance in the women's transformations to warriors—Dorothea serves as the exception because she commits no obvious sartorial violation. However, her simultaneous display of "masculine" and "feminine" traits proves just as unsettling for the poem's characters as the sight of the cross-dressing soldier in Naubert and Schiller's works. The failed masquerades of Naubert's warlike women, the hybrid appearance of Schiller's warrior maiden accessorized by sartorial signifiers of masculinity and warfare, and the robust stature and brave actions of Goethe's domestic amazon, which are tempered by feminine attire and virtues, complicate assumptions of gender as a stable and recognizable category.

The appearance of the warlike woman and her presence on the battlefield in both the material and literary worlds represents not only a transgression of the gendered division of public and private spheres but also exposes the fissures inherent in constructed myths of femininity and masculinity. For the cross-dressers Thekla and Philippe, their acts of gender dissimulation, which facilitate their entrance into their respective military conflicts, gesture toward a renegotiation of the gender paradigm only to reaffirm an essentialist position and reconfirm the male figures' masculine identity and heteronormativity as warriors, protectors, and husbands. In Goethe's epic poem, the juxtaposition of the young female refugee's heroic act of violence with the reticent future family patriarch's inaction exposes ruptures in reactionary narratives of gender determinism and raises questions about just who the future defenders of "domestic" stability will be. Schiller's warrior maiden Johanna deviates from the feminine ideal established in the play's prologue, and confirmed by the play's other female characters, by claiming and occupying a role as active, deadly warrior on the battlefield. In doing so, Johanna's violation of gender conventions and her demonstrated ability as an effective warrior, like Goethe's Dorothea, draws attention to the weakened model of masculinity predicated on the warrior identity.

Naubert's representations of warlike women in *Thekla von Thurn* and *Philippe von Geldern* turn on the ambiguity engendered by the act of cross-dressing. Most recently, Tatiana Korneeva has productively applied Madeleine Kahn's terminology "narrative transvestism" to examine the subversive potential of Naubert's writing style, which implies—or at least leaves open the possibility for—a male narrative voice to depict the lives of women in times of conflict.[38] While I agree with Korneeva's assessment that the subversive depiction of femininity in Naubert's works "points towards the process of exclusion of women from the social sphere" and that "Naubert's literary strategy of cross-dressing indicates the crisis of the binary oppositions of fixed gender identity,"[39] the failure of Naubert's male and female cross-dressers in *Thekla von Thurn* and *Philippe von Geldern* leaves the myth of gender binaries intact albeit destabilized.

Naubert establishes a parallel narrative about cross-dressing involving Thekla's sister Therese in order to contextualize and attenuate Thekla's perceived offense. Naubert's heroines hesitantly resort to cross-dressing, a move sanctioned in Thekla and Therese's case by a male authority in order to stave off male (sexual) violence at a time of impending military danger (BNT, 2:32).[40] Initially, this authorized violation appears to completely upset the "natural" order: Therese's decision to fight and die protecting her husband (BNT, 2:34) requires her to relinquish her role as mother and to orphan her son. However, even such a clear offense of gender roles elicits an equivocal reaction from the novel's staunchest conservative and proponent of the gender paradigm, Queen Maria Eleonore of Sweden:

> "Das ist groß! das ist edel!" rief sie. "Ich glaubte nicht, daß ich ihr würde verzeihen können, daß sie aus den Schranken ihres Geschlechts heraus trat, und sich in männlichem Gewand mit dem Schwert an der Seite in den Streit wagte; ein Schritt, den meines Erachtens kein Frauenzimmer aus irgend einer Ursache thun solte; aber diese Therese! ihr Tod! Ja, ich muß ihr verzeihen, muß sie bewundern!" (BNT, 2:103)

> "That is great! That is noble!" she cried. "I did not think that I would be able to forgive her for having overstepped the boundaries of her sex and ventured into the fray dressed in men's clothing with a sword at her side; a step, which in my estimation, no lady should take for any reason. But this Therese! Her death! Yes, I must forgive her; I must admire her!"

It is not Therese's sartorial violation that is deemed valorous but her death defending her husband that receives the queen's praise. Her heroic sacrifice, although ineffective—her husband dies shortly after she does—signals to

Thekla and the reader that there is no place for such warlike women, even brave wives, in the reigning gender hierarchy. Her actions are only laudable so long as they present no long-term threat to the status quo and because her sacrifice was an attempt to defend the family patriarch. Eleonore's strict adherence to the established gender dichotomy and her reaction to Thekla's own cross-dressing—she brands her both an "Ungeheur" (monster) and "Schlange" (snake) (BNT, 2:285)—reinforce the exclusion of women who transgress the "laws of Nature" from society. The reproach of the queen and her ladies to Thekla's masquerade demonstrates the social stigma of indecency and sexual impropriety that marred women caught cross-dressing as soldiers (BNT, 2:285–86).[41] Yet, the narrator's criticism of the queen's rigidity about gender roles (BNT, 2:97–98) together with the novel's repeated assertion of Thekla's preserved virtue, in spite of her semiotic slippage, only tentatively mitigates the subversive nature of the sartorial violation. The repeated condemnation of Thekla's actions by the novel's characters and her adoption of the same rigid binaries articulated by the queen suggest that Thekla upholds rather than undermines the dominant narrative of gender.

Thekla's masquerade receives the harshest condemnation from the novel's male characters, signaling that the incursion into the culture of warfare by the female cross-dresser functions as a direct assault on their masculine identities and positions of power. Both the fatherly figure Hastendorf and Thekla's eldest brother Bogeslav censure her for her perceived violation and immediately assume, like the queen, that her intentions are dishonorable. For Bogeslav, the family patriarch in the father's absence, Thekla's actions cast aspersion not only on her moral character but more importantly on the entire family's reputation. He goes so far as to declare her the "Mörderin meines Lebens!" (Murderess of my life!), a crime far worse than donning men's clothing, and accuses her of being Bernhard von Weimar's mistress (BNT, 2:225). Here too, the heroic martyr Therese, whose sacrifice Bogeslav claims is demeaned by Thekla's actions, is invoked as a comparison and criticism of cross-dressed Thekla's ostensibly ignoble demeanor. At the same time, Thekla's revelation of her secret life to her future husband Eggenberg, whom she freed from captivity while still pretending to her brother Jaromir, only inspires admiration: "Himmlisches, himmlisches Mädchen! rief er, Heldin! Engel in Menschengestalt! Retterin! Befreyerin! Wie soll ich dich nennen!" (BNT, 2:335; "Heavenly, heavenly maiden! he cried, heroine! Angel in human form! Savior! Deliverer! How shall I call you!"). Indeed, on the field of battle and as a military captive Eggenberg benefitted directly from her compassion and sense of justice, feminine virtues that could not be stifled by her men's clothing.[42]

Naubert's deployment of sartorial masquerades in *Thekla von Thurn* relies on the authority of a patriarchal figure of power to sanction such subversive behavior in order to forestall criticism. Writing *Philippe von Geldern* three years later, at the height of the revolutionary violence and invasions of German territories, Naubert strategically distances herself from what would have been viewed as far more ominous acts of disorderly conduct by women, by questioning the justifications for sartorial masquerades that appear to cause more harm than they prevent. At first, cross-dressing manifests as a necessary evil in order to stave off far greater crimes and acts of aggression: two of the novel's maternal figures, Selim's mother Zelide and Kalepin's nursemaid Raja, initiate the role reversal between Philippe and the young Turkish prince Kalepin to ensure *his* safety. Philippe's narrative attributes the unfortunate decision to gender-bend to the women's irrationality—a stark departure from Falkenberg's acknowledgment that cross-dressing has strategic advantages in *Thekla von Thurn*. However, even the harsh criticism is softened by displacing the responsibility for the women's faulty decision on the negative effects of harem culture, which Philippe laments only fosters women's illogical fantasies of intrigue and conspiracy (BNP, 2:319–20). Thus Naubert walks a fine line by appearing to disapprove of female cross-dressing that offered women access to male spheres of power previously off limits to them while simultaneously challenging what the novel presents as a misogynistic practice that perpetuates women's mental inferiority and social subordination.

As in *Thekla von Thurn*, Naubert pairs Philippe's story of cross-dressing with the counter-narrative of Kalepin's gender bending (BNP, 2:440–50) to articulate the complexities of the gender masquerade and emphasize gender's rigidity and ineluctable "nature." Philippe's disconcerting appearance and mannerisms as the young boy Kolonna unsettle men and women alike. Described as "ein seltsames Geschöpf" (BNP, 2:128; an odd creature), she finds disfavor among the women at court and the knights on the battlefield (BNP, 2:128–29, 2:334). The narrator attributes the inexplicable dislike the characters feel for Kolonna to his inability to conform to the expectations of masculinity both at court and on the battlefield. Indeed, it is Philippe's inherent feminine nature (BNP, 2:334), which cannot be suppressed and which hinders her ability to play the part of the brave young page Kolonna convincingly:

> Sittsamkeit und schüchterne Zurückhaltung, welche damahls die Grundlagen des weiblichen Anstandes ausmachten, waren ihr angebohren, eben sie waren die Ursach gewesen, warum ihr Anblick im Jünglingskleide so auffallend war, warum man nicht recht mit sich einig werden konnte, was man aus ihr machen sollte, und bey den widrigen Gefühlen, die sie erregte, so leicht ein Misfallen an ihr aufkommen ließ, das sich weder mit ihrer reizenden Figur noch mit der Gutmüthigkeit, die auf ihrem unschuldigen Gesicht lächelte, zu vertragen schien. (BNP, 2:379–80)

> Modesty and shy restraint, which formed the foundation of feminine decorum in those times, inhered in her. It was these very characteristics that were the cause for why her appearance in boy's clothing

> was so conspicuous, why one was not quite capable of agreeing upon what he should make of her. They were also the cause for why the adverse feelings, which she evoked, so easily allowed an aversion to her to develop, which appeared to agree neither with her attractive build nor the good nature that appeared across her innocent face.

Philippe's failure to pass as the young page and warrior articulates an essentialist view of gender—its corresponding duties and fates—as ingrained and inescapable. The narrator emphasizes Philippe and Kalepin's natural inclination toward their respective genders and their corresponding activities as well as their decidedly *unnatural* and unsuccessful attempts to disguise their "true" nature.

Naubert stresses the disaffection Philippe's failed masquerade produces in others to illustrate her protagonist's inherent femininity; male-to-female crossing, however, reveals a double standard for the gender benders by portraying the overall positive impression Kalepin makes as Philippe. In marked opposition to the effeminate Kolonna, the "heldenhafte" (lion-hearted) Philippe's stunning appearance and exceptional demeanor elicit only praise, adoration, and respect: "Man ahndete etwas außerordentliches in seiner Person; da nun das Außerordentliche immer viel Anziehendes hat, so durfte er sich nur zeigen, und alle Herzen waren für ihn eingenommen" (BNP, 2:441; "One sensed something extraordinary about his character; since the extraordinary always has many appealing qualities, he only needed to appear, and he won the favor of all hearts"). As the narrator notes, "Es ist bekannt, daß ein Jüngling in Mädchenkleidern immer mehr Glück macht, als eine verkleidete Dame" (BNP, 2:441; "It is a well-known fact that a boy in girl's clothing is always more successful than a disguised lady"). The hierarchy of gender traits prevails, even in instances of male-to-female transvestism that should mark its destabilization. Kalepin's successes and positive impact signal that not all cross-dressers are equal: male-to-female crossing serves to elevate a woman's perceived status and appeal, while the reverse cannot be claimed for female-to-male masquerades. Despite the affirmative effect Kalepin's appearance has on his social standing, his disguise is no more successful than Philippe's. The unsuccessful suppression of his masculine inclination—he is ultimately exposed when staging the armed rescue of his abducted childhood playmate and love interest Fräulein Hohenburg—is once more a sign of gender's immutability. Like Philippe, Kalepin's "transgression" is covered up and his gendered identity fully restored. While Philippe retreats to a cloister to fully develop the aspects of her femininity (BNP, 2:380), Kalepin is shipped off to military school "um dort ganz aus einem Mädchen in einen Helden verwandelt zu werden, und Talente, die ihm die Natur gab, durch Kunst auszubilden" (BNP, 2:450; "in order to be fully transformed from a girl to a hero and to develop the talents which Nature gave him"). As the novel demonstrates, Philippe and Kalepin's masquerades are doomed to fail from the start;

their attempts at cross-dressing foreground rather than destabilize the myth of gender's durability.

Further exposing the tension inherent in such gender narratives, Goethe's poem juxtaposes the ambiguous appearance of the domestic amazon Dorothea with her future groom Herrmann. The reader's first encounter with the male titular figure unsettles their expectations about the poem's hero when his father laments his son's shortcomings and questions Herrmann's masculinity (JG, 8:815).[43] From its outset the poem signals that this Herrmann has nothing in common with his legendary namesake, Hermann the chieftain of the Cheruski who liberated the Germanic tribes from the yoke of Roman invaders. Indeed, the name of the poem's "hero" has direct implications for the poem's gender dynamic. The combination of two linguistic signifiers of masculinity ("Herr" and "Mann") suggests a hyper-masculine title character befitting the genre. Despite the virility implied by his name and the war raging on the opposite side of the river bank, Herrmann is a man of peace, who appears to lack the characteristics of a typical young man, by his father's estimations. Already this rupture between form and content, marked by the epic poem's less than heroic male protagonist, necessitates a heroic figure to assume his place.

The appearance of Herrmann's future bride, possessing a striking physical strength and decisive demeanor, offers the reader the hero, or more pointedly heroine, for whom it has been searching. Recounting his first sight of Dorothea alongside a giant cart, Herrmann describes the impressive scene:

> Von zwei Ochsen gezogen, den größten und stärksten des Auslands,
> Neben her aber ging, mit starken Schritten, ein Mädchen,
> Lenkte mit langem Stabe die beiden gewaltigen Tiere,
> Trieb sie an und hielt sie zurück, sie leitete klüglich. (JG, 8:816)
>
> Drawn by a yoke of oxen, two big strong beasts from the Rhineland,
> And beside it walked a young woman, stepping out briskly
> And controlling the two huge beasts as she went, with a long stick,
> Drawing them on and holding them back with the skill of an expert.
> (JGE, 236–39)[44]

The young woman's imposing physical presence, emphasized by the description of the oxen and the heavy cart, appears better suited to the innkeeper's notion of ideal masculinity: Dorothea is self-assured, strong, and pragmatic while Herrmann is timid, reserved, and emotional. When placed side-by-side, the characteristics of the two figures represent an inversion of Wilhelm von Humboldt's model of gender complementarity. Dorothea's unusual appearance and behavior, however, are attributed to the chaos engendered by the political circumstances, which creates the possibility for, and perhaps even necessitates, women to assume traditionally masculine roles, especially when there is an absence of capable men.

The story of Dorothea's heroic use of "masculine" force to protect a young group of German girls from French marauders serves to confirm the ambivalent status conferred upon her by Herrmann's description. Recounting the dramatic event, a refugee known as the judge describes the womanly warrior as a study in contradictions: a member of the weaker sex, yet fierce and powerful; a girl and maiden at once brave-hearted and noble (JG, 8:851–52). The judge's use of the term "Jungfrau" (maiden) not only signals to the apothecary and pastor Dorothea's virtuous nature, it also emphasizes her protection of Germany's virtue against the hyper-sexualized aggression of the French enemy:

> Sie erblickten das Bild der schön erwachsenen Jungfrau
> Und die lieblichen Mädchen, noch eher Kinder zu heißen.
> Da ergriff sie wilde Begier; sie stürmten gefühllos
> Auf die zitternde Schar und aufs hochherzige Mädchen.
> Aber sie riß dem einen sogleich von der Seite den Säbel,
> Hieb ihn nieder gewaltig; er stürzt' ihr blutend zu Füßen.
> Dann mit männlichen Streichen befreite sie tapfer die Mädchen,
> Traf noch viere der Räuber; doch die entflohen dem Tode.
> Dann verschloß sie den Hof, und harrte der Hülfe bewaffnet.
> (JG, 8:852)
>
> [The rabble] set eyes on this maiden, a beautiful woman she'd grown to,
> And on the charming young girls, little more than children they still were.
> Then they were seized by passionate lust, they attacked in a brutal
> Frenzy the girls who stood trembling with fear, and the bravehearted maiden.
> But she immediately snatched the sword of one of them from its
> Scabbard, and struck him dead at her feet, and as he lay bleeding
> She dealt more mighty blows, most valiantly freeing the victims.
> Four more of the marauders she wounded, who fled with their bare lives.
> Then she locked up the farm and guarded it, armed, until help came.
> (JGE, 1202–10)

Goethe's scene depicting Dorothea's use of deadly force relies on extreme oppositions in order to present his warlike woman's disorderly behavior as a necessary and natural response. The stark image of the French marauder's implied sexual aggression juxtaposed with the trembling, fragile, innocent German victims clearly signals for the reader who the hero and villains are.

The extent of Dorothea's violence is limited to ensuring the safety of the nation's future wives and mothers and to securing, metaphorically, the safety of German values. This includes preserving the gender hierarchy that demands the warlike woman's eventual return to her role as dutiful wife, a hierarchy threatened and destabilized by demonstrations of female violence and self-reliance. Dorothea's threats are aimed outward at the foreign enemy in defense of domestic stability; the subversive potential of her actions are mitigated by the fact that her violence protects the domestic order which her fellow countrymen will reoccupy upon their return from war. The fact that her act of violence is committed *within* the domestic sphere—as opposed to on the battlefield—further suggests that her actions may serve to shore up existing patriarchal structures of power rather than undermine them, at least when the French are involved. Her act is neither premeditated nor one of aggression, since she only takes up a sword when there is an immediate threat and no available protection other than her own will and capable arm.

Dorothea's heroic act takes on greater significance when considered alongside the judge's narrative conflating violence and sexual desire to describe the invasion of German borders by the French:

> Nichts ist heilig ihm mehr; er raubt es. Die wilde Begierde
> Dringt mit Gewalt auf das Weib, und macht die Lust zum Entsetzen.
> Überall sieht er den Tod, und genießt die letzten Minuten
> Grausam, freut sich des Bluts, und freut sich des heulenden Jammers.
> (JG, 8:850)

> Nothing is sacred to them, they will simply seize it; in wild lust
> They must take women by force, they must make a horror of pleasure;
> Everywhere they see death, and gloat cruelly over the dying's
> Final moments, delighting in blood and in the screams of affliction.
> (JGE, 1154–57)

Goethe's poem portrays the German territories as a feminized, helpless victim in need of (male) protection against the invading, destructive desire of a foreign male aggressor.[45] Seeking revenge, the men of the village arm themselves with any available weapon, turning farm tools used to harvest the fertile soil into instruments of death soaked with French blood (JG, 8:850). Goethe's poem appropriates and reverses popularized images of revolutionary women wielding farm implements as weapons, by placing these tools in the hands of German men and turning them against the French in order to protect the "feminized" German territories. However, this gender paradigm—in which men *protect* and women *are protected*—proves untenable as the men pursue the invaders, leaving their homes and families vulnerable to further attacks, thereby creating the need for strong warlike women to do the defending.

The poem's portrayal of this warlike woman struck a chord with contemporaries, who drew a logical comparison between Goethe's German amazon and French female revolutionaries. In a 1799 essay the German philosopher

Wilhelm von Humboldt distinguishes between contemporary women's motivations for taking up arms and Dorothea's heroism, excusing her transgression as an act of necessity:

> Der weibliche Heroismus ist überhaupt, und besonders in unserer Zeit, schwer und zart zu behandeln. Zwar wäre es vielleicht möglich, auch noch jetzt eigentliche Amazonencharaktere mit dennoch rein bewahrter Weiblichkeit zu zeichnen; aber zu diesen gehört Dorothea nicht. Dorothea kann einen Mord, selbst den eines übermüthigen Feindes, nie im mindesten aus freiem Entschluß, immer nur durch die äußerste Noth getrieben, begehen, und dies springt zu klar und auffallend in die Augen.[46]

> Female heroism is in general, and specifically in our own time, a difficult matter that must be addressed delicately. Although it might be possible even still now to portray real Amazon-like characters with nevertheless perfect, preserved femininity, Dorothea does not belong to these characters. Dorothea can never commit murder of her own resolve, even murder of a wanton enemy. It must always be driven by extreme necessity. This is too clear and strikingly apparent.

Von Humboldt's apprehension about German women warriors results in the strategic distancing of Dorothea from her violent contemporaries by emphasizing the defensive rather than offensive nature of her violent act.

Like Goethe's Dorothea, Schiller's patriotic martyr Johanna appears to be the embodiment of contradictions. She remains an elusive and enigmatic chimera for the play's characters, readers, audience, and even scholars. Johanna's refusal to conform to the gender paradigm articulated by the family patriarch Thibaut coupled with her demonstration of masculine bravery and violence on the battlefield contribute to her transgressive status as woman warrior. The inability of the play's characters to accurately identify and neatly classify Johanna as decidedly feminine or masculine, angelic or demonic, patriotic or traitorous signals an epistemic crisis that threatens to further destabilize the already precarious social order. Her uncertain status is informed further by the inner conflict she faces in eschewing personal desire to perform her patriotic duty. While Johanna seeks to suppress her "true feminine nature" as a prerequisite for her admission to the battlefield, her momentary emotional lapse during her encounter with the English enemy Lionel suggests that it is an impossible demand that is doomed to failure. Moreover, Johanna's inner turmoil is presented as a choice between two opposing archetypes of femininity: the king's mistress Agnes Sorel stands as a paragon of "feminine virtue" by remaining loyal to the king in his moment of need and encouraging him to demonstrate that he is the "man" she knows him to be. The king's aberrant mother Queen Isabeau figures as the embodiment of female transgression, having forsaken her role as "nurturing mother" and proven her disloyalty by willingly turning against her own kin and country. Johanna's refusal of both options further confirms her "hybrid" status, to use a term first employed by Hart to describe the uneasiness that Johanna's cross-dressing evokes.[47] Even the play's concluding scene, in which Johanna is elevated as martyr for her selfless bravery and valorous death on the battlefield, remains ambivalent. Rather than returning to the halls of her *Landesvater* (sovereign) to be crowned with accolades for single-handedly restoring the monarchy, the armed maiden is rewarded with a patriotic death and joins the Virgin Mother, the eternal symbol of maternal femininity. Her fate signals a return to the gender status quo in which men are honorable, brave soldiers and women are devoted, obedient mothers, wives, and daughters.

The notion of feminine duty articulated by Herrmann's mother and father undergoes a dramatic reinterpretation in Schiller's *Jungfrau* in an attempt to reestablish the gender hierarchy in which men are noble warriors and respected kings and women are dedicated, nurturing helpmates. From its very outset, Schiller's play foregrounds the tension between the figure of the woman warrior and the expectations of patriarchal society. In an effort to affirm man's socially dominant position and masculine identity, which are dependent on his role as defender and protector, the play constructs an oppositional relationship between warrior specter and domestic ideal. Already in the play's prologue, Johanna's father Thibaut confers upon the woman warrior the status of unnatural Other when he denounces the king's traitorous mother Queen Isabeau as "Rabenmutter" (SJ, 9:15; "that bird of prey, his mother" [SJE, 621]).[48] She is branded as deviant for forsaking her primary duty as maternal caregiver in order to take up arms against her son (SJ, 9:16–18). Thibaut's unequivocal assessment of the queen articulates the dismay elicited by the woman warrior's presence on the battlefield, and he strives to quiet his uneasiness by retreating to less threatening gender roles that preserve the dichotomy of man-warrior and woman-housewife: "denn das Weib / Bedarf in Kriegesnöten des Beschützers, / Und treue Lieb hilft alle Lasten heben" (SJ, 9:21–23; "In times like these, women need our protection, / and true love helps to make our burdens lighter" [SJE, 621]). In this moment of unrest—it is after all the Hundred Years' War and France is struggling to unite its disparate parts against a common invading enemy[49]—the institution of marriage, sanctioned by both *Hausvater* and *Gottvater* (religious patriarch), represents a safe haven for conservative values against the disruptive effects of war.

As in Goethe's epic poem, Schiller employs the institution of marriage as a means by which to restore domestic stability and the patriarchal authority of the husband and father. The play's opening scene, followed by Thibaut's praise for his two daughters' agreement to marry and fulfill their destinies as wives and mothers (SJ, 9:43–44), establishes the drama's dominant narrative of appropriate gender roles and informs Johanna's status as unnatural because she is beyond comprehension and categorization. She neither conforms to nor can she be classified within the available models of femininity. Unlike her sisters, Johanna impedes her father's efforts to restore "normalcy" in a time of chaos by refusing her destiny as wife and mother. Her transgression of both Nature and the "father's law"[50] can only be explained as "eine schwere Irrung der Natur" (SJ, 9:62; "some serious error in Nature" [SJE, 622]) and the result of a diabolical, supernatural power (SJ, 9:80–108). Thibaut's characterization of his daughter as aberrant aligns her more closely with the unnatural mother and woman warrior Isabeau than with her sisters, who serve as standard bearers of "ideal femininity." Although Johanna's lack of conformity signals a threat to the established gender paradigm, her intended husband Raimond offers an interpretation, which elevates Johanna's nonconformity to more mythical proportions (SJ, 9:78–79). Despite Raimond's attempt to redeem Johanna's "otherness" as affirmative, it only further solidifies her position as outsider.

Johanna's fascination with matters of warfare proves far more disconcerting and disruptive to standard definitions of "femininity" than her refusal to marry. Johanna springs to life when talk turns to the most recent news of the war, including her brother-in-law's detailed description of the armor-clad Isabeau and Thibaut's renewed dismissal of the queen as unnatural and immoral.[51] She repeatedly resists efforts to force her into an appropriate feminine role: Bertrand admonishes her for showing interest in the mysterious helmet he has brought from the market (SJ, 9:191–92), and Thibaut chastises her for demanding information about the troop's position (SJ, 9:292–93). By actively asserting her claim to the helmet (SJ, 9:193), a sartorial signifier of masculinity and aggression, Johanna stakes her claim to a place on the battlefield and in the men's discussion. This act of defiance only confirms for the superstitious family patriarch his daughter's suspected deviancy suggested by her nocturnal visits to the Druid's tree (SJ, 9:80–97).

Johanna's defiance of her father's attempts at gender norming not only undermine the family patriarch's authority, but her movement into the sphere of warfare poses a threat to the structures of domination imposed from above by the sovereign and spiritual patriarchal powers. Like Thibaut, the king's ambivalent response to the description of the victory by his army with Johanna at the helm as "höchst wunderbar und seltsam!" (SJ, 9:985; Miraculous and strange! [SJE, 648]) and his skepticism that a woman warrior will deliver him to the throne: "Das ist nicht in dem Laufe der Natur" (SJ, 9:999; "That's hardly in the normal course of Nature" [SJE, 648]), position Johanna on the periphery as abnormal, unnatural. It is ultimately the Archbishop, the earthly representative of the spiritual patriarch (God the Father), who sanctions Johanna's violence for the good of France (SJ, 9:1111–14). Johanna's claims to the divine provenance of her mission are insufficient to justify her violent participation on the battlefield. The legitimacy of her actions must be confirmed by an individual with the recognized institutional authority to sanction such transgressive behavior.

Schiller further complicates the woman warrior's status by presenting her simultaneously as a perpetrator of violence and the object against which competing forces exert symbolic violence. Johanna becomes an ideological battlefield for the French and English to wage their war for the throne by imposing their visions of gendered violence onto her. The arbitrary nature of the female warrior allows her to appear to the French as ordained by God and fighting in the service of a just cause, because her aggression is aimed outward, against the invading enemy and in defense of the monarchy and its feudalist power structure. At the same time, those on the receiving end of the woman warrior's aggression retreat to the supernatural to explain the bellicose apparition, locating the source of this manifestation in the depths of hell rather than the heights of heaven (SJ, 9:1246, 1480, 1714). Still other references challenge her divine authority and deny her agency not by vilifying her per se but rather by reducing her to a figment of the fevered imagination, a harmless phantom (SJ, 9:1248, 1469, 1478, 1488, 1568). This strategy to render innocuous the enemy's greatest weapon is compounded by the English soldiers' reduction of the purported "Schreckensgöttin" (SJ, 9:1543; goddess of terror [SJE, 665]) to her mortal body and with it to her sex, thereby attempting to return her to an identifiable, knowable category within the existing paradigm over which power and control can be asserted. Johanna's steadfast refusal to submit to the category "Weib" and its associated gender attributes renders the male character's reliance on gender as a stable signifier to be tenuous at best.

Johanna's appearance, which vacillates between extremes, is a critical factor informing the characters' conflicting perceptions of the woman warrior that allows her to appear simultaneously alluring and frightening. Schiller accessorizes his heroine with martial markers of masculinity—armor, helmet, and so on. Beyond the competing descriptions of Johanna by compatriots and enemies, the play's stage directions for act 2, scene 4 ("*im Helm und Brustharnisch, sonst aber weiblich gekleidet*") ("*wearing helmet and breastplate but otherwise dressed as a woman*") and act 3, scene 4 ("*im Harnisch, aber ohne Helm, und trägt einen Kranz in den Haaren*") ("*in armour, but without a helmet, wearing a wreath in her hair*") remind us that it is a woman carrying out the brutal attacks against the enemy. However, it remains unclear whether these key references to Johanna's feminine appearance are meant to highlight the aggression of which a woman warrior is capable or to mitigate the transgressive nature of female violence committed in the name of the sovereign father and Holy Mother. Schiller erases the stain of criminality and deviancy from his heroine's cross-dressing by strategically foregrounding Johanna's sex via feminine signifiers such as her attire and long hair.[52] References to the warrior maiden's femininity are intended to diminish her transgressions: despite her violent acts, she never degenerates into an "unnatural" monster.

Nevertheless, Johanna's hybrid appearance signals an epistemic crisis with deadly implications. The same sartorial markers of Johanna's femininity leading Raimond to affirm the woman warrior's presence in the martial realm prove unreliable for the majority of the play's characters, including Raimond, who are incapable of deciphering the enigma. The paradox presented by the pairing "woman" with "warrior" proves particularly lethal for the English soldier Montgomery, who misreads the gender signs and mistakenly assumes the woman will subdue the warrior: "sie ist ein Weib, / Ob ich vielleicht durch Tränen sie erweichen kann!" (SJ, 9:1578–79; "she is a woman— / I have to see if tears have any power to move her!" [SJE, 666]). Montgomery's attempt to rescue himself calls attention to yet another inversion of gender norms: he adopts characteristically "unmasculine" mannerisms—resorting to tears, invoking images of his bride and mother, kneeling for mercy—which only elicit Johanna's scorn. Just as the battlefield is deemed no place for the average woman, Montgomery violates the code of masculine conduct accorded a warrior on the battlefield. His reliance on outward signs proves ineffective as Johanna renounces the gendered confines of her earthly body altogether—simultaneously undermining Raimond's previous assertion of her feminine breast and manly heart, which locates her firmly beyond the boundaries of the gender paradigm—and instead insists on a model of warfare that leaves no room for the heart, or any emotion for that matter (SJ, 9:1608–11, 1660–61). Johanna's rejection of her feminine exterior, followed by Montgomery's failed efforts to activate any remnant of her femininity, culminates in his death at the hands of the woman warrior. The confrontation between Johanna and Montgomery indicates an important shift in Schiller's depiction of the woman warrior from simply talking about destroying the enemy—or secondhand descriptions of Johanna's battlefield exploits—to publicly staging the woman warrior's brutality.[53]

It is tempting to read Johanna's rejection of gender and the body as a progressive gesture toward an enlightened, modern androgynous individual; however, Johanna's eschewal of personal agency for her combative actions and renunciation of her femininity make such interpretations problematic at best. Johanna's repeated insistence that she is merely the earthly vessel for an intervening higher power emphasizes the heroic woman warrior as an anomaly and undermines a sense of female agency.[54] Her miraculous transformation from shepherdess to mighty warrior maiden (SJ, 9:1655–67) reinforces the dominant gender narrative in which the default setting is man-warrior-battlefield, woman-caregiver-hearth. By displacing responsibility for her disorderly behavior onto God and the Holy Mother, Johanna's characteristically "unfeminine" and even horrifyingly violent actions are recast as divine, righteous, and sanctioned: "Erhabne Jungfrau, du wirkst Mächtiges in mir! / Du rüstest den unkriegerischen Arm mit Kraft, / Dies Herz mit Unerbittlichkeit bewaffnest du" (SJ, 9:1677–79; "Oh, Blessed Virgin, you have worked a miracle in me! / You give strength to my unwarlike arm, and arm / this heart of mine with stern implacability" [SJE, 669]). At the same time, the projection of Johanna's agency onto an external, supernatural object suggests the immutability of gender traits: although she might suppress her femininity, she cannot eradicate it entirely. It is this suppressed, inherent femininity that the king's mistress Agnes Sorel attempts to reactivate and restore to its full glory in the warrior maiden, once her mission has been accomplished.

As the play's touchstone for socially conservative gender norms, Agnes Sorel not only promotes the reclamation of Johanna's femininity but also Charles's masculinity as sovereign and warrior king. The dominating presence of Schiller's warrior women Johanna and Isabeau on the field of battle exposes the frayed fabric of the king's masculinity and reveals his weaknesses as *Landesvater* to assert his authority over *all* of his subjects. The embodiment of "ideal femininity," Agnes is selfless, loyal, maternal, and most importantly, her participation in the politics of warfare is restricted to symbolic, financial sacrifices (SJ, 9:608–13, 623–26). By promoting a conservative, contained model of femininity, Agnes simultaneously establishes the characteristics informing a "masculine ideal." When the king falters and resigns himself to defeat, Agnes reminds him of his duty to be a courageous leader: "Du wirst dich wieder finden, männlich fassen, / Mit edelm Mut dem Schicksal widerstehen, / Das grimmig dir entgegen kämpft" (SJ, 9:774–76; "You will soon be yourself again, and able / to count bravely all the blows that Fate / is dealing you" [SJE, 642]). She emphasizes his masculinity and the corresponding masculine attributes required for successful participation in the public sphere. Just as Thibaut locates the catalyst for war in the unnatural mother, so too does Agnes blame the king's emasculated state on the unnatural betrayal by his mother (SJ, 9:772–73). The king's weakness creates a vacuum justifying Johanna's manly valor as a kind of proxy; however, it simultaneously allows for the specter of the unnatural mother. The king's return to the throne necessitates Johanna's retreat from her provisional role as woman warrior. Having restored the king's masculinity and sovereign power, there is no longer room for the woman warrior in any form.

Subduing the Woman Warrior through Domesticity or Death

The gender "transgressions" committed by Naubert, Goethe, and Schiller's warlike women threaten to expose the fissures in myths of gender's immutability and render existing gender categories unstable. In order to neutralize the subversive potential implied by gender-bending warrior women, the texts offer their armed heroines two possible fates: the woman warrior who defends the German patriarchal order against a foreign enemy is either returned to the domestic sphere unharmed and more than content to resume her duties as loyal wife and nurturing mother, or she is sacrificed on the battlefield and elevated to heroic heights in death. Goethe's domestic heroine Dorothea and Naubert's reluctant cross-dressing warriors exemplify the first model. Their actions are recast as virtuous models of femininity reinforcing the dominant gender narrative. Schiller's armed maiden Johanna instantiates the second model, whose offense against social conventions, albeit sanctioned by the patriarchal order, necessitates her death be coded as heroic self-sacrifice.

The recuperation of Naubert's warrior women is predicated on Thekla and Philippe's reluctance and ineffectiveness as warriors. If cross-dressing constitutes their violation, then Thekla and Philippe's abiding aversion to their masquerades and the fact that they never kill anyone functions to ameliorate their subversive behavior.[55] Both women express their own uneasiness with the entire act of cross-dressing: Thekla is plagued by guilt and the threat of impropriety (BNT, 2:92), while Philippe's anxiety stems from her early adoption of a masculine role and lack of experience as a woman (BNP, 2:379). Commenting on Thekla's hesitation about revealing her identity, the narrator cautions female readers against disguising their true virtue lest it take on the stain of transgression (BNT, 2:108). While sartorial disguises may be sanctioned for protective purposes in times of imminent danger, it is the deceptive intentions behind the act that threaten to destabilize the gender order, the power of which rests on the ability to identify, categorize, and thereby assert power over the individual. In the end, the texts attenuate the potential for disobedience implied by the characters' transvestism by foregrounding their virtue and honor. Thekla's undisguised shock in response to her brother Bogeslav's claims of her illicit behavior serve as proof of her modesty and preserved virtue (BNT, 2:200). For Philippe, it is her confession to Selim and the narrator's insistence on her chaste demeanor that erases any wrongdoing. Similarly, Kalepin's honorable conduct, by not exploiting his unmitigated access to the object of his affection, also functions to expunge the transgressive quality of his gender bending (BNP, 2:470).

The strategic slippage in Naubert's portrayals of her gender-bending protagonists in *Thekla von Thurn* and *Philippe von Geldern* allows the narrative to diffuse gender misconduct and implications of sexual impropriety. Both Thekla and Philippe are criticized time and again by their male counterparts, more specifically by the men they love, for failing to conform to the expectations of a masculine soldier. As a literary device, this isolated "blindness" by specific characters forestalls accusations of immorality arising from the woman warrior's presence among men and allows her to assert her virtue. Thekla's companion and love interest Bernhard von Weimar finds fault with "Jaromir" for his "feminine" behavior and even expresses his dismay that Jaromir will have a feminizing effect on the entire troop (BNT, 2:155). At the same time he also expresses his fear of being emasculated, when he articulates his inexplicable attraction to the effeminate Jaromir: "Ich hasse seine Weichherzigkeit, und doch weis Gott, welch ein Gefühl mir bey seinen Thränen durch das Innerste meiner Seele dringt.—Gute, zärtliche, himmlische Seele!" (ibid; "I hate his tender-heartedness, and yet God knows, what a feeling penetrates the very core of my soul at the sight of his tears.—Good, tender, heavenly soul!"). Bernhard's ambivalent response not only highlights Thekla's unconvincing performance and inability to suppress her inherently feminine nature, it also recuperates Bernhard's potentially "unnatural" attraction to the young man as a heteronormative desire. This same sense of apprehension emerges in encounters between Selim and Philippe's male persona Kolonna (BNP, 2:254) and is similarly resolved by Philippe's unsuccessful masquerade, which allows both the novel's characters and the readers to see through the disguise knowing full well that "he" is really a "she."

The novels' simultaneous insistence on unwavering images of the masculine warrior bound to acts of aggression and prowess on the battlefield paired with assertions of gender's inherent stability and inflexibility complicates the subversive potential of Thekla and Philippe's masquerades. Thekla and Philippe's success at convincingly playing their roles as Jaromir and Kolonna is contingent on their ability to wield a weapon and to demonstrate their courage on the battlefield. In a letter to the disguised Jaromir, Bernhard insists that he can only silence rumors about his identity if he proves himself as a warrior: "Zeigt, daß ihr ein Mann seyd, Jaromir, setzet die weibische Furchtsamkeit auf die Seite, ihr versteht ja den Degen zu führen; ihr müßt inskünftige nicht allein mein beständiger Gefährte bey Hofe, sondern auch im Gefechte seyn" (BNT, 2:195; "Jaromir! Show that you are a man. Set aside the womanish timidity. You know how to wield the dagger. In the future, you must be my constant companion both at court and in battle"). Similarly, Kolonna's lack of manly determination and warrior-like attributes mortifies Selim, causing him to fear for his brother's future: "Ich muß dir sagen, daß sich dein ganzes All ändern muß, wenn du und ich in einer Welt fortkommen sollen, wo Personen, wie wir beyde, sehr rauhe Wege zu betreten haben" (BNP, 2:259; "I must tell you, that your entire being must change, if you and I are to advance in a world in which people like us have very rough paths to tread"). Kolonna's promises to change only confirm for Selim his "weiche weibische Nachgiebigkeit" (ibid; weak, womanish placableness). Time and again, Thekla and Philippe fail to live up to the expectations of the male warrior. Their inability to "overcome" their feminine nature in order to fulfill these expectations and demonstrate their bellicose qualities appears to uphold the gender paradigm in which true men are warriors and real women are objects of male desire.

By returning her gender-bending protagonists to their appropriate roles as dutiful wives and future mothers, Naubert's cross-dressing heroines only temporarily invert the gendered order. Thekla and Philippe retreat willingly to the domestic sphere of marital bliss and to their "predetermined" fates as wives and mothers. The narrator notes that Philippe's desire for "Einsamkeit und Stille" (BNP, 2:551; solitude and tranquility) suits her for the life of an oriental queen, who retreats from politics and allows her husband to rule.[56] Similarly, Thekla is reunited with her former enemy and captive Fürst von Eggenberg, with whom she will raise her orphaned nephew and start a new family. Thekla's return to the Swedish court as Fürstin von Eggenberg is presented by the narrator as a kind of sweet revenge for the injustices she had previously suffered at the hands of the queen and court (BNT, 2:404). While Naubert does not mobilize the figure of the cross-dressing woman warrior to agitate for woman's active participation in the public sphere or warfare, the ambiguity informing her virtuous heroines renders, intentionally or otherwise, reactionary gender myths unreliable. Furthermore, Naubert's novels depicting the impact of military conflict on the private lives of its characters offers a more holistic history that seeks to balance heroic exploits with warfare's violent reality. Thus, Naubert, like her warlike women, navigates extremes and tentatively explores the possibilities offered by the middle ground in her novels by blending personal and political histories.

Merging personal narratives with contemporary political turmoil, Goethe's epic poem treats with irony the emergent pre-nationalist sentiments, which are intricately bound to and informed by notions of masculinity, resulting from foreign invasion. One of the poem's ironies is the fact that the warlike woman's "transgression" is never truly a "violation." Dorothea's act of aggression is recuperated by the poem's characters as a cruel necessity of war: when men are away at war, women are forced by unusual circumstances to defend home and family. The vacuum created by the absence of capable male protectors allows for and even demands that capable women, like the domestic amazon Dorothea, fill this role, albeit only as a temporary placeholder.

The poem plays with gender myths that promote the illusion of women's power in the domestic sphere. Herrmann's offer to marry Dorothea and to give her a safe, permanent home requires she swap sword for apron. It is not only the Janus-faced Dorothea but also Herrmann's outspoken mother, who frustrates overly determined images of female domesticity. She reinforces the very myth of ideal femininity she subtly appears to resist. Confirming the image of the industrious, hardworking caretaker and homemaker (JG, 8:830), she also presents herself, and the entire female sex for that matter, as the voice of reason in contrast to the rash "nature" of men. The mother performs the role of objective mediator to mend the rift between father and son, thus demonstrating that women are just as insightful and capable as men, if not more, of solving problems (JG, 8:835). For example, she is able to discern the true motivation for Herrmann's hollow patriotism, which materializes as a desire to prove himself to his father (JG, 8:833) and in defiance of his father's refusal to allow him to marry Dorothea (JG, 8:834), rather than out of a sense of duty to the fatherland. Furthermore, the mother's support of Herrmann's decision to marry suggests a challenge to the father's authority (JG, 8:838), implying that it is the mother who knows how to finesse the familial figurehead in order to attain the desired outcome. Despite the housewife's demonstration of power, her influence is confined to domestic affairs and matters within the home, a similar fate which Dorothea appears all too willing to assume.

If Dorothea's return to the domestic realm signals an affirmation of the patriarchal stability, her continued self-reliance and confidence forces the reader to reconsider the traditionally feminine role of caretaker as well as the role of family patriarch. Refusing Herrmann's assistance at the village well, Dorothea takes the lead and Herrmann follows *behind* her, as she brings the heavy jugs of water back to the refugees (JG, 8:863). Despite her independence, Dorothea has a clear understanding of social norms and her place within society: "'Dienen lerne bei Zeiten das Weib nach ihrer Bestimmung; / Denn durch Dienen allein gelangt sie endlich zum Herrschen'" (JG, 8:864;"Service is woman's lot, and the sooner she learns it the better! / For it is only by service she ends up being the mistress / And enjoying the power that by rights is hers in the household" [JGE, 1522–25]). Invoking words such as "Schicksal" and "Bestimmung," Dorothea justifies her readiness to enter a life of service. Like Herrmann's mother, Dorothea does not resist her fate as a woman in the domestic sphere, where a good wife is one who always is active (JG, 8:830). Her views of woman's social destiny articulate the prevailing narrative of female domesticity as biological destiny.[57] However, she too glorifies the role of mother, noting that men are too weak to endure the pain and suffering that women must endure: "Zwanzig Männer verbunden ertrügen nicht diese Beschwerde, / Und sie sollen es nicht; doch sollen sie dankbar es einsehn" (JG, 8:864; "This is a burden not twenty men working together could shoulder, / And there's no reason they should; but they should take note and be thankful" [JGE, 1535–36]). Neither Herrmann's mother nor Dorothea ultimately advocate for women's participation in the public sphere; their statements about duty and service align with conservative views of female domesticity; however, they acknowledge the power women gain through their roles as wives and caretakers (JG, 8:835, 8:864). Such proclamations combined with Dorothea's ambiguity have led scholars to read her as an empowering model of femininity, which signals a positive change in the family hierarchy.[58] However, the ironic scene concluding the poem leaves the reader questioning whether Herrmann's assumption of the role as family patriarch will usher in a new era of progressive thinking or simply perpetuate the entrenched views of his father.[59]

What is clear is that the assertion of Herrmann's masculinity and authority as future *Hausvater* requires Dorothea's complete confinement within the family home. Dorothea's transformation from warlike woman to her supporting role as housewife coincides with her physical return to the domestic sphere as well as Herrmann's sudden, ironic assertion of his physical strength and role as protector. Making their way to his parent's home, Dorothea's unsteady steps contradict previous images of a strong, sturdy woman: "Sorglich stützte der Starke das Mädchen, das über ihn her hing. / Aber sie, unkundig des Steigs und der roheren Stufen, / Fehlte tretend; es knackte der Fuß, sie drohte zu fallen [. . .]" (JG, 8:870; "Careful and strong, he supported her weight as she clung close behind him; / But there were some rough steps, and the pathway was unfamiliar, / And she stumbled, missing her foothold [. . .]" [JGE, 1700–1702]). Gender roles appear to have been restored with Herrmann now depicted as "der Starke" (the strong one) while Dorothea's steps are unsure on unfamiliar ground. However, this role reversal remains tentative as Herrmann struggles "mit Mannesgefühl" (with masculine strength) against the weight of "die Heldengröße des Weibes" (JG, 8:870; her magnificent stature [JGE, 1710]). Dorothea's imposing physical presence has not diminished entirely by returning to the realm of bourgeois domesticity, just as Herrmann has not miraculously become the paragon of masculinity his father wishes for in canto 1, despite his best efforts to play the part. Herrmann adopts the role of protector, but it is a superficial gesture: he remains an unsure, timid boy, a fact that is further emphasized by the couple's appearance in the doorway to the family's home: "Ja, es schien die Türe zu klein, die hohen Gestalten / Einzulassen, die nun zusammen betraten die Schwelle" (JG, 8:873; "Even the door seemed too small to admit them, so noble of stature / Were they, as loftily now they crossed the threshold together" [JGE, 1774–75]). The text's emphasis on the astonishment of the apothecary, pastor, and parents to the imposing figure of the future housewife, which is comparable to that of the future family patriarch, casts doubt on the depiction of Herrmann as "der Starke" and his jingoist assertions in the final canto.

The poem's exploration of a gender paradigm inverted by political and social upheaval reveals its reliance on complementary gender characteristics, in which only one of the two parts can dominate at once. Herrmann's authority is illusory as long as Dorothea appears his equal. Her sudden weakness (JG, 8:882), a result of her fond reminiscence of her heroic first fiancé, creates the possibility for Herrmann to occupy the vacated role as her protector. In doing so, he positions himself as the cautious, conservative guardian of German values in contrast to the rash, revolutionary-minded soldier (JG, 8:882–83). Herrmann speaks of the stable, rational German, whose character stands in direct opposition to that of the French, including what he perceives to be his competition with Dorothea's memories of her first fiancé for her affection.[60] However, what has become all too apparent in the epic poem is that Herrmann is not a man of action but a man of peace.[61] Whereas Dorothea's first fiancé was pragmatic and motivated to action for a cause he believed in, Herrmann's decision to defend his country only emerges once his father prohibits him from marrying Dorothea (JG, 8:834). The empty patriotic sentiments he uttered to his mother in the garden resurface as he tries to assert his newfound power as husband and patriot:

> Du bist mein; und nun ist das Meine meiner als jemals.
> Nicht mit Kummer will ichs bewahren und sorgend genießen,
> Sondern mit Mut und Kraft. Und drohen diesmal die Feinde,
> Oder künftig, so rüste mich selbst und reiche die Waffen.
> Weiß ich durch dich nur versorgt das Haus und die liebenden Eltern,

O, so stellt sich die Brust dem Feinde sicher entgegen.
Und gedächte jeder wie ich, so stände die Macht auf
Gegen die Macht, und wir erfreuten uns Alle des Friedens. (JG, 8:883)

Now you are mine: and that makes what I have more mine now than ever.
I shall not own it in sorrow, an anxiously guarded possession,
But defend it with courage and strength; and if enemies threaten
Now or in the future, then arm me yourself and hand me my weapons!
For if I know you are here to look after our home and our parents,
Why, then with confidence I shall go out and confront our attackers.
And if our countrymen all felt as I do, we'd all of us rise up:
Might against might would stand, and for all of us wars would be over. (JGE, 2027–34)

Herrmann's bravado and nationalistic appeal to German readers to unite against a common enemy in defense of God, country, and family stand in striking contrast to his teary-eyed proclamations to defend his homeland, while unable to assert his decision to marry whom he chooses. Whereas previously his patriotic sentiments focused solely on the defense of his beloved land, he now feels himself instilled with the "Mut und Kraft" to go into battle to protect his family, while Dorothea remains securely confined to the home. Herrmann's patriotism presents a conservative model for German nationalism and strengthens traditional social values that maintain the gendered order of things,[62] although it is Dorothea who actually defends German values in the public sphere.

The poem's ironic and even humorous depiction of its would-be warrior Herrmann juxtaposed with the truly heroic actions of the warlike Dorothea undermines the conservative, nationalistic rhetoric espoused by its title character at the end, which seeks to firmly restore the patriarchal order. While Dorothea initially appears to uphold the narrative of female domesticity, she does not cease to be the strong woman in the private sphere that she was in the public realm. Like Herrmann's mother, Dorothea will most certainly influence the familial dynamic and power structure once she becomes Herrmann's wife: the fact that she stands up to Herrmann's father already suggests that she is unlikely to acquiesce to his or Herrmann's patriarchal posturing.

Unlike Dorothea, Johanna demands and claims a position on the battlefield as combatant and aggressor. If the depiction of Schiller's patriotic maiden Johanna, who fights and dies for king and country, appears to sanction women's violence in service of the fatherland, the potentially empowering female image is ultimately complicated by her death at the conclusion of the drama. In order to participate legitimately in the masculine, political sphere, Schiller's warrior is forced to renounce her "femininity," a transgression far too severe to permit her eventual return to the societal fold. She has overstepped, figuratively and literally, the sanctioned boundaries of public and private in her merciless pursuit and killing of the enemy.

Schiller's poem "Das Lied von der Glocke" invokes an anti-revolutionary rhetoric casting female revolutionaries as crazed Furies and bloodthirsty hyenas. Yet, in a striking turn, Johanna functions as an idealized model of bourgeois feminine *Tugend* (virtue), who not only neutralizes the threat posed by real revolutionary women but upholds the patriarchal authority to which she is subservient.[63] Removing the stigma associated with emancipatory longing, Schiller recasts Johanna as a patriotic guardian, who wards off foreign invaders, including unnatural mothers (Isabeau). Although Schiller's patriotic martyr shares a fate similar to many of her female literary counterparts, whose defiance of sociopolitical and gender norms lead to premature death in late eighteenth- and early nineteenth-century texts, her untimely passing is not depicted as punishment for her disorderly behavior; instead, her insurrectional actions and subsequent death are reframed as patriotic offerings.

By allowing Johanna's "unusual" martial conduct to be linked to her duties as shepherdess, Schiller creates the possibility for his woman warrior's transformation into a benevolent defender of the common good. Responding to Thibaut's denigration of Johanna's warlike inclination as "unnatural," Raimond repackages her aggressive demeanor in defensive terms citing her brave encounter with the *Tigerwolf* (SJ, 9:197; wolf [SJE, 626]). The play's insistence on the correlation between Johanna the shepherdess and Johanna the warrior recuperates her for the greater good without completely destabilizing the masculine identity of the warrior and protector. Rather than becoming a wild animal like the revolutionary hyenas of "Das Lied von der Glocke," she defends the fold against such attacks. Her enigmatic character, exemplified by Raimond's remark: "Denn ihre Brust verschließt ein männlich Herz" (SJ, 9:196; "she has a man's heart in that body" [SJE, 626]), signals a union of feminine appearance and masculine traits that complicates the model established by the father and implies a more flexible understanding of gender.[64] In spite of her manly heart, Johanna retains her feminine appearance, forestalling her complete degeneration into a *Mannweib* (virago) like Isabeau. Raimond's further assessment of her as "die löwenherzge Jungfrau" (SJ, 9:200; the lion-hearted maid [SJE, 626]) subtly reinforces the feminine component of the gender amalgam by privileging her virtuous nature, a characteristic shared by all the women warriors in this chapter and placed front and center by their authors. It is Johanna's retention of her femininity that allows her to be returned to the realm of the Virgin Mother at the play's dramatic conclusion and celebrated as patriot and martyr.

Schiller's play suggests that the woman warrior's presence in the public sphere during times of war is precarious and provisional at best. As the play repeatedly asserts, unusual circumstances call for unconventional yet temporary solutions (SJ, 9:3081–87); the woman warrior is not intended to be a permanent fixture on the battlefield. Johanna's status as warrior is transient, and she readily acknowledges that her destiny is not domestic bliss but a heroic death (SJ, 9:1664–67). Indeed, the precondition for Johanna's access to the realm of warfare proves an impossible demand that offers an unsettling dilemma: either Johanna fulfills her divine mission, having successfully suppressed her personal desire, and dies a martyr *or* she succumbs to the natural drives attributed to her sex and appears no better than the licentious queen Isabeau as the aberration her father claims her to be. Schiller resolves the tension implied by this precarious double bind by demonstrating the immutability of Johanna's femininity, which only *appears* to have been eradicated.

Even before her confrontation with Lionel, the battle-hardened, divinely empowered warrior has adamantly asserted that she is not to be taken at face value: she has sacrificed her claim to domestic happiness and her "earthly duty" as wife and mother in order to fight and die for the king on the battlefield. Johanna's ostensible denial of her feminine "nature" is the price of admission to the public sphere: she has swapped bridal wreath for the laurel wreath of victory (SJ, 9:413–16, 2025). Yet, she experiences a moment of doubt in which her "feminine" emotions, compassion for the enemy, threaten her ability to fulfill her mission (SJ, 9:1680–83). Johanna is apprehensive about her own deadly use of force; only an act of God, or supernatural intervention, and the belief that she is fighting a just battle can quiet these uncertainties: "Doch wenn es not tut, alsbald ist die Kraft mir da, / Und nimmer irrend in der zitternden Hand regiert / Das Schwert sich selbst, als wär es ein lebendger Geist" (SJ, 9:1684–86; "but when the need is there, there also is the strength, / and in my trembling hand, the sword unerringly / moves of its own accord, as if it were alive" [SJE, 669]). Like Dorothea, Johanna's supernatural strength and courage are activated by the necessity of the extreme situation and represent a temporary state of aggression. Even her observation that the sword behaves as if of its own volition distances Johanna from the most evident sign of her transgression: she is a dealer of death, rather than a giver of life. Ultimately, Johanna's invocation of a higher power is a renunciation of her own agency, ensuring that her "unnatural" actions can be appropriated for a greater cause, namely the restoration of the king and unity among her countrymen as ordained by God and the Virgin Mother.[65] However, Johanna's denial of her "feminine nature" proves far more problematic and requires more than the subjugation of superficial hallmarks of femininity (passivity, morality, empathy, sentimentality, etc.). Johanna's sanctioned acts of aggression demand that she defy Mother Nature herself.

The brief moment in which Johanna unexpectedly succumbs to her desire for her enemy Lionel suggests that her feminine nature is unwavering, regardless of how heroic her actions or how fervently she attempts to deny the existence of her concrete body. While Johanna establishes that she is more than capable of defending herself against the threat posed by the enemy's weapons (SJ, 9:1516–23), the same cannot be said about the threat posed by love. Johanna's vulnerability allows Lionel, the catalyst for her existential crisis, to reaffirm his identity as male warrior and protector by repositioning her as a passive object:

> Du kannst gerettet werden. Folge mir!
> Ich will dich retten, aber säume nicht.
> Mich faßt ein ungeheurer Schmerz um dich,
> Und ein unnennbar Sehnen, dich zu retten. (SJ, 9:2495–98)
>
> Yes. You can be saved.
> Follow me, and I will save you, but
> no more delay. I feel unutterable
> sorrow for you, a nameless longing
> for your safety [. . .] (SJE, 695)

Despite Johanna's clear ability to defend herself—after all she has just dispatched Montgomery—Lionel experiences an inexplicable need to impose conventional gender roles on the battlefield. His attempt to classify Johanna within the existing gender hierarchy simultaneously removes her from the battlefield as a deadly enemy, while also confirming his masculinity and prowess as the knight who tamed the fierce woman warrior.

However, it is Johanna's violation of her vow and the incursion of her personal desire into the masculine realm of politics that defuses her threat; her participation in the public sphere is no longer sanctioned and thus becomes "unnatural." She cannot remain within the public domain, and the gender boundaries must be reinforced. The patriarchal father's public condemnation of his daughter (SJ, 9:2975–76) accompanies the sovereign's banishment of the young warrior maiden (SJ, 9:3042–47), doubly damning her to a position as outsider and deviant Other. Johanna's redemption once more demands a personal sacrifice. In one last act of bravery, the armed maiden solidifies her status as "die Jungfrau" by steadfastly resisting Lionel's advances and attempting to turn his desire for her toward her advantage in order to rescue her countrymen (SJ, 9:3349–59).[66] Hearing that her king has been captured, Johanna offers an impassioned plea to God, and demonstrating supernatural strength she breaks the chains binding her, both physical and symbolic, and rushes into battle. She willingly offers herself up in order to restore the sovereign patriarchal authority that ultimately prohibits her existence within the culture of warfare.

In the final scenes of the play, Johanna dies heroically, not as a heretic burned at the stake but as a national heroine praised by king and court. She dies not with a sword in her hand but carrying the flag bestowed upon her by the divine power. Her final vision of the Virgin Mother before death recuperates her actions as an ordained mission and restores her femininity, which she was forced to renounce in her earthly quest as woman warrior:

Im Chor der Engel steht sie glänzend da,
Sie hält den ewgen Sohn an ihrer Brust,
Die Arme streckt sie lächelnd mir entgegen.
. . . .
Der schwere Panzer wird zum Flügelkleide. (SJ, 9:3538–42)

Look! Do you see the rainbow in the sky?
Heaven is opening its golden gates.
She stands in glory amid the angel choir,
her ever-living son held to her breast:
now she holds out her arms to me, and smiles.
. . . .
my heavy armour's changing—I am on wings. (SJE, 733)

Johanna's vision is not of God the Father but the Virgin Mother, performing her role as mother and caregiver by suckling the savior at her breast. The final image of the woman warrior is not that of "goddess of terror" or "devilish witch"; her return to the virtuous Virgin Mother signals the full restoration of her femininity alongside the restoration of patriarchal, feudal order.

Despite narrative strategies to reframe warlike women as unwilling combatants, defenders of domestic values, and patriotic martyrs in order to contain their destabilizing impact, the texts ultimately confirm the woman warrior's status as enigma and the unreliability of gender as a stable signifier. Naubert's novels gesture toward the preservation of existing patriarchal structures and gendered division of public and private spheres by depicting cross-dressing warriors who are never truly at home on the battlefield and who subsequently never fully relinquish their feminine identities. Yet, the author employs the figure of cross-dressing warrior in order to write a more inclusive history of events that takes into consideration the impact of warfare on the lives of women. While Thekla and Philippe resort to cross-dressing, Johanna's challenge to the gendered status quo of the battlefield manifests itself openly without disguise. Johanna's moment of weakness exposes that she is no immortal being but a woman, a woman who effectively fights and kills on behalf of her king and country, inevitably undermining the order established by the family patriarch in the play's prologue. Even as her heroic death forecloses her return to society and her dying vision in which she is elevated to saint-like status alongside the divine paragon of feminine virtue mitigates the transgression of gender norms, this *Jungfrau in Waffen* (maiden in arms) renders the gender binary uncertain. Unlike her literary counterparts, Dorothea neither commits a sartorial transgression nor does she overstep the boundaries of social propriety; yet, her equivocal status is conferred upon her by the symbiosis between feminine and masculine attributes. She is simultaneously traditional caregiver and nurturer for the displaced refugees and armed protector of defenseless virtue. The irony informing Goethe's text leaves the reader skeptical about the poem's conclusion, which returns the topsy-turvy world upright once more with Herrmann's assumption of the role as family patriarch and national patriot and the warlike Dorothea tending the hearth.

At the same time that these texts asserted the ambiguous status of the violent, warlike woman, the destabilization of the patriarchal order implied by the appearance of their heroic women on the battlefield or defending themselves against the enemy instantiated a crisis in masculinity. The phenomena of the woman warrior necessitated a renegotiation of the "masculine ideal," strictly bound to notions of man as heroic warrior and loyal patriot. This redefinition of what it meant to be a man and patriot was intimately linked with developing conservative discourses articulating pre-nationalist impulses, which took on greater importance well into the nineteenth century. Naubert, Goethe, and Schiller's texts confirm that the potentially threatening figure of the woman warrior proved critical to a reenvisioning of masculinity, a process that was already well underway even before the devastating defeat at Jena less than half a decade after Schiller's *Jungfrau* made its appearance on stage.

Chapter Four

Emancipatory Fantasies

The Woman Warrior as Liberator and (Proto-)Feminist

> Ich lebte zwei Jahre der fürchterlichsten Erbitterung, wär damals die Revolution gewesen, ich wär an die Blutstätten geeilt, ich hätte in den Reihen der Streiter gekämpft, ich hätte gemordet—um ein Gefühl zu genießen, das die starre Verzweiflung meiner Brust belebte.
>
> —Therese Huber, "An Johann Gotthard von Reinhold" (February 24, 1806)

> Schon oft hatte ich den unweiblichen Wunsch mich in ein wildes Schlachtgetümmel zu werfen, zu sterben. Warum ward ich kein Mann! ich habe keinen Sinn für weibliche Tugenden, für Weiberglükseeligkeit. Nur das Wilde Grose, Glänzende gefällt mir. Es ist ein unseliges aber unverbesserliches Misverhältniss in meiner Seele; und es wird und muß so bleiben, denn ich bin ein Weib, und habe Begierden wie ein Mann, ohne Männerkraft.
>
> —Karoline von Günderrode, "An Kunigunde Brentano" (August 29, 1801)

Just as readily as authors mobilized the rhetoric of patriotic self-sacrifice and domestic heroism in an effort to attenuate the subversive quality of the bellicose woman and contain women's role in the public sphere, authors simultaneously exploited the ambiguity of the woman warrior by deploying similar narrative strategies to explore the untapped potential of women's violent participation in political and military conflicts. In doing so, authors mined various forms of female self-sacrifice for opportunities to imagine themselves and their worlds differently, to express and realize their dreams that may have run counter to social convention, and to envision alternative models for women's active participation in the public sphere. As the texts in this chapter reveal, women writers did not present a unified front in terms of their political and social views, yet their literary fantasies of warlike women, in which personal love and patriotic duty are linked, gesture toward new forms of female existence destabilizing entrenched myths of gendered separate spheres and warfare as an exclusively masculine domain. These literary renditions of the self-sacrificing woman warrior attempt to strike a balance between the extremes of domesticated martyr and crazed Fury.[1]

Women writers Therese Huber (1764–1829), Karoline von Günderrode (1780–1806), and Caroline de la Motte Fouqué (1775–1831)[2] strategically appropriated and resignified reactionary social theories binding femininity to love in their literary portraits of the warrior woman. In conjuring unconventional forms of female agency, their texts highlight the complex and contradictory nature of gender. Huber, Günderrode, and Fouqué's female warriors destabilize the dominant narratives constructed by Fichte and his contemporaries by revealing the fissures in what otherwise might appear as a hegemonic discourse on femininity, love, and sacrifice. These acts of subversion and literary renegotiation enable Huber, Günderrode, and Fouqué to reexamine women's relationship to the public welfare of a precarious and emerging German nation. This strategic act of *mimicry*,[3] in which the authors critically employ myths of love and female self-sacrifice, forced these women writers to work within the existing patriarchal structure of power in order to rethink the prevailing gendered paradigm and to create spaces for women in the public and private affairs ultimately leading to a better society. In the works discussed below, love, be it for the familial home or political homeland, functions to validate women's entrance into and contribution to the social and political welfare of their respective societies.

However, such a narrative strategy presents a precarious double bind for the authors: by mobilizing essentialist notions of femininity, they run the risk of reinforcing the very structures they seek to exploit, expose, and subvert. As Gayatri Spivak's writings warn us, the danger of resorting to an essentialist position lies in the failure to do so strategically and thereby leaving the oppressive structures of power unexposed, unchecked, and intact.[4] In the instances of Huber, Günderrode, and Fouqué, strategic readings of the feminine models they construct open up the possibility for new, alternative forms of femininity. Despite these attempts to create opportunities for female readers to redefine themselves and their roles as women in the public sphere, these fictional heroines are always generated and constrained by myths of a "feminine ideal" produced by the male gaze and perpetuated by underlying systems of power that threaten to attenuate their subversive significance.

At the same time, the emancipatory potential contained in the figure of the warrior woman is particularly appealing to the alienated or oppressed as a means to question the discursively constructed gender myths of the time, to imagine themselves in positions of power, and to serve as a platform from which to critique the failures and shortcomings of patriarchal society. The terms "emancipation," "emancipatory," and "proto-feminist," or "pre-feminist" employed in the discussion of literary visions of women and warfare around 1800 are not intended to conjure up modern feminist notions of women's liberation movements or explicit demands for equal rights. Instead, these concepts are meant to convey the expansion of women's spheres of influence and different ways of thinking about women's existence during this historical juncture. Furthermore, by "expansion" I refer to women's increased visibility and participation in the public sphere, both as public authors and private individuals invested in the social and political security of their communities. Emancipatory and proto-feminist tendencies, therefore, do not imply agitation for equality in the sense of voting rights and the like. In some instances, the term "emancipation" simply signifies the desire for increased female agency, in whatever form it might take. Huber can be characterized as politically progressive while the same cannot be said of Fouqué, who remained a staunch supporter of feudal structures.[5] Nevertheless, their women warriors expose the fissures in the traditional gender dichotomy and the tension between woman as warrior and patriot and woman as the embodiment of the bourgeois "feminine ideal." The ambiguity inherent in such images in the Age of Goethe becomes fertile ground, particularly for women writers, to challenge gender hierarchies and spheres of activity.

While not all acts of transvestism are intentionally subversive, as I demonstrated in the case of Naubert's reluctant women warriors Thekla and Philippe, sartorial transgressions applied pressure to the gendered binarism informing social and political institutions, including the institution of warfare. Textual manifestations of cross-dressing women masquerading as male soldiers complicate and reveal as unstable the reliance on appearance as a means to accurately identify and categorize individuals and the roles they occupy based on gender, as Schiller's *Jungfrau* aptly illustrates. As I argue in my analysis of these cross-dressing women warriors, Huber, Günderrode, and Fouqué play with the gender ambiguity of their cross-dressing heroines, exploiting discursively constructed notions of "femininity" and "masculinity" in order to carve out new, empowering modes of female agency through narrative maneuvers that appropriate forms of love for subversive ends.[6] The works discussed in this chapter blur the lines between battlefield and home front and reveal the political act of war as fundamentally very personal. Simultaneously, the protagonists in these texts probe the permeability of the borders between the socially and politically embedded concepts of masculinity and femininity and embody alternative myths about gender and warfare that further secure the enigmatic status of the woman who goes to war.

Personal Revenge and Public Action

Reflecting on her tumultuous political past and unpopular political views in a letter from February 9, 1814, to family friend and Swiss journalist

Paul Usteri, Therese Huber acknowledges and acquiesces to the limitations placed on women in matters of politics and warfare: "Ich war ja Jakobinerinn und Demokratinn, und Revolutionär, aber ich wußte stez das Weib solle schweigen wenn Männer sprächen, und nie außer dem innigsten Zirkel von politik sprechen [. . .]"[7] ("I was Jacobin, Democrat, and Revolutionary, but I always knew that a woman should remain silent when men spoke and never to speak about politics outside of the most intimate circle"). However, in her most popular work *Die Familie Seldorf* (1795/96), Huber employs the literary genre of the *Familienroman* (domestic novel), a genre deemed by male contemporaries as "acceptable" for women writers of the period, as a more public medium by which to explore the interdependence between the tempered sphere of the family and the violent sphere of politics.

The French Revolution, with its claims of equality and liberty, and the resulting military campaigns that disrupted almost every aspect of daily life, played a formative role in how women writers fashioned themselves and their figures as active political participants.[8] Like many of her contemporaries, Huber opted for the novel as the vehicle by which to explore the ambivalent image of the woman warrior and to address sociopolitical aspects of the Revolution that were deemed potentially inflammatory.[9] Huber succeeded in bridging the divide between the supposedly mutually exclusive gendered domains of public and domestic not only through the act of writing but also through the subject matter of her works. Huber lived what she wrote about, namely, the belief that woman's sphere of influence was not confined to the home, but rather, that it included participation in the public realm. While the overriding theme of her stories centered on the lives of mothers and wives portrayed in domestic scenes, her first novel *Die Familie Seldorf* marked an important departure from the rest of her oeuvre by breaching the gendered public-private divide and presenting a strong female protagonist, who actively participates in the politically charged violence of the Revolution.

Huber does not limit her literary representations of women to socially accepted roles. In the protagonist Sara Seldorf, the author creates another option for women: one transcending the binary division of gender characteristics and their corresponding social roles. The rather seamless transition of her protagonist Sara from the role of daughter, sister, lover, and mother to heroic male captain of republican troops in the Vendée and back to maternal figure confronted the notion of an "ideal femininity" tethered to the domestic sphere. Huber's mobilization of the female warrior exemplifies the artificiality of prescribed gender roles and gender as a performance informed by social, historical, and political attitudes. The heroine Sara, and her male persona Captain Verrier, served as a conduit through which Huber presented the female reader with empowering, albeit temporary, alternatives to the extreme poles in the representational spectrum of warlike women while simultaneously critiquing and proposing a more humane model for the inherently brutal nature of warfare.

Unfolding amidst the turmoil of the French Revolution, the personal lives of Huber's fictional characters collide with historical events, exposing the author's extensive knowledge of the events developing across the border, which had a direct impact on her own life. Like her protagonist Sara Seldorf, Huber engaged with urgent concerns of her time, and her life and literary work reveal in a compelling manner the false dichotomy of the seemingly separate public and private spheres.[10] The daughter of philology professor Christian Gottlob Heyne, Huber grew up in the university town of Göttingen, where she became acquainted with her father's students, including her first husband, the naturalist Georg Forster, and the intellectual pursuits of his contemporaries, including Herder, Wieland, and Goethe.[11] Separating from Forster, a well-known supporter of the French Revolution and delegate to the French National Convention for the Mainz Republic, Huber fled Mainz in July 1793 when the city was reclaimed by Prussian forces. She moved her children to Switzerland and married her lover, and family friend, author and publicist Ludwig Ferdinand Huber, shortly after Forster's death in 1794. It was under Ludwig Huber's name and in his journal *Flora* that the novel *Die Familie Seldorf* was first published.[12]

Huber recognized in the Revolution's subversive atmosphere the potential to contest established gender norms and the patriarchal political hierarchy. For example, the novel's protagonist defies the National Convention's decree banning women from military participation, reflecting the real-life stories of women in the military as they were reported in French and German newspapers.[13] Furthermore, Huber openly acknowledged that she incorporated personal experiences during the Revolution into her novel.[14] Scholars have interpreted this weaving of personal and political as a means by which Huber sought to address the politics of the Revolution and Germany's response to it.[15] Barbara Becker-Cantarino even suggests Huber's fictional work is an attempt to challenge patriarchal society,[16] and I argue further that Huber's narrative is a direct criticism of the dehumanizing practice of warfare as it was waged around 1800.

As the full title of her narrative *Die Familie Seldorf: Eine Erzählung aus der Französischen Revolution* (*The Family Seldorf: A Story from the French Revolution*) suggests,[17] Huber tells the story of a family whose private life is overturned by political events. The politics of the Revolution are not confined to the public tribunals or meeting hall of the National Convention in Paris; the effects and violent ramifications of the Revolution are felt most acutely by families in both the city and the French countryside. In the first volume, Huber's novel very much keeps with the theme of woman's daily existence in the domestic sphere; Sara's relationships as daughter, sister, and lover provide the focal point of the narrative. However, the second volume marks her departure from the domestic realm of the bourgeois family and her entrance into the French Revolution. As Sara's personal relationships, with men in particular, crumble and her familial ties dissolve, she is liberated from traditional female archetypes and thrust into the revolutionary violence.

The omniscient narrator of Huber's novel recounts the story of a family whose life is interrupted by political events. The father of the Seldorf family, a German immigrant and widower who fought for the French in the American War of Independence, returns from America and settles in the French countryside with his children. Years later, Seldorf's son Theodor runs off to Paris and joins the royalist movement, against his father's wishes. Meanwhile, Sara lives happily with her father in the idyllic countryside until she meets her new neighbor Count L***.[18] The count, a royalist pretending to be a republican, seduces, impregnates, and promises to marry Sara. Upon her father's death, L. moves her to Paris, where, unbeknown to Sara, he keeps her as his mistress, since he is already married. During the storming of the Tuileries, the count inadvertently shoots at and wounds their child, forcing Sara to confront the treachery of her lover and to avenge her lost honor. Sara's attempts to kill L. ultimately fail. She lapses into a brief bout of insanity, comes to terms with the death of her child, disguises herself as a man, and joins the republican army to hunt down the count. Sara's actions on the battlefield transform her into a war hero. After being wounded, Sara is revealed to be a woman, dons women's clothing, returns to the ruins of L.'s estate, and raises the orphaned legitimate son of the count.

In her description of the Seldorf family, Huber critiques the patriarchal structure of revolutionary politics. The form and content of Huber's novel, which draws a parallel between the disruption of the patriarchal familial structure and the political order, instantiates what Lynn Hunt has characterized as the "family romance" of French revolutionary politics.[19] The novel's male characters reproduce the complex political landscape of the Revolution: the Seldorf father, an ethnic German, represents a more restrained and skeptical attitude toward the Revolution foreshadowing its violence and destruction (TH, 1:85); Sara's brother Theodor and her lover Count L. embody the views of royalist supporters; while the neighbor Berthier and his grandson Roger express pro-revolutionary sentiments that do not readily condone violence but accept it as a necessary evil (TH, 1:82). Sara's relationship to each of these male figures is characterized by her submission to their authority as representatives of the patriarchal order.

Huber's novel further serves as a challenge to the rigid gender dichotomy undergirding the patriarchal structure of family and the nation.[20] The father of the Seldorf family instructs his children on "appropriate" gender roles and stresses the reciprocal yet hierarchical relationship between masculine and feminine gender characteristics that resonate with Wilhelm von Humboldt's essays *Über den Geschlechtsunterschied* and *Über die männliche und weibliche Form*:

> Der feste, treue, eiserne Mann kann nur der sanftesten Weiblichkeit huldigen; Schwächlinge lieben Amazonen. Damit aber das Weib diesen Zauber ihres Geschlechtes besize [sic], muß ihr Herz kindlich

> bleiben, wie gebildet auch ihr Verstand sey; und unsre Achtung allein kann das Zutrauen hervorbringen, welches diese Kindlichkeit [er] hält. Fühlt das Weib nicht diesen Lohn seiner Liebenswürdigkeit, so sucht es sich von uns unabhängig zu machen, und dann wird es verächtlich. Die Natur, die uns stärker machte als sie, verträgt diese Unabhängigkeit nicht; alsdann erniedrigen wir sie dafür, gewaltsam oder listig, zu unsern Sklavinnen, und pflanzen auch alle Laster des Sklavensinnes in ihre entartete Brust. (TH, 1:26–27)
>
> The solid, loyal, iron man can only pay attention to the gentlest femininity; weaklings love amazons. In order for the woman to possess the magic of her sex, her heart must remain childlike, regardless of how educated her mind may be. Only our attention can bring out the trust, which preserves this childlike nature. If the woman does not feel the reward of her kindness, she will seek to make herself independent from us and then she becomes contemptible. Nature, which made us stronger than them, does not tolerate this independence. So then we degrade them for this independence, violently or cunningly, to be our slaves and we also plant every vice of the slave mentality in their degenerate breast.

The father rigidly organizes the gender characteristics as contrasting, yet complementary qualities. He invokes the laws of Nature, thereby replicating the rhetoric of Nature employed by eighteenth-century social theorists, when he derides deviations from or reversals of these norms as contemptible.[21] Despite the reciprocity between the sexes, Father Seldorf espouses an "ideal femininity" that infantilizes woman, thereby necessitating and perpetuating her submission to man as a form of symbolic violence. Similarly, Todd Kontje views the relationship between the sexes in Huber's novel as illustrating a form of male domination over and violence against women.[22] Sara is thus inculcated from an early age with an unrelenting doctrine promoting the idea of the "active" paternal male and "passive" childlike female that demands her willing subordination.

The establishment and perpetuation of this gendered structural violence is not restricted to the Seldorf family. Even Roger, a symbol of the Revolution's ideals, preserves the gender paradigm when he infantilizes Sara in his attempts to play protector and guardian (TH, 1:63–66). Sara does not initially resist Roger's protection and as the narrator notes, she begins to understand her father's lessons on the "gegensätzliche Abhängigkeit" (contrasting dependence) of the sexes (TH, 1:77). Gender roles and responsibilities are handed down from one generation to another: from father to son—and in this case from father to daughter—and even from grandfather to grandson—regardless of political affiliation.

If Roger's infantilization of Sara serves as a criticism of the Revolution's failures, then the count's attraction to Sara's childlike demeanor and his desire to dominate her function as a commentary on the corrupt, despotic ancien régime. He is drawn to and exploits Sara's innocence and perceived helplessness (TH, 1:178). The narrator repeatedly depicts their relationship in terms of ownership and subservience (TH, 1:264, 2:57). L. plays upon the ideals of domestic happiness that Sara's father instilled in her in order to solidify his control over Sara. In depicting a domestic utopia for Sara, he envisions very rigid boundaries for woman's role in society—a role excluding any interest or involvement in the realm of politics:

> [. . .] so sprach er ernst und fast gebieterisch über die Pflicht, welche jezt mehr wie jemals den Weibern obläge, sich vor leidenschaftlichen Meinungen über öffentliche Vorfälle zu hüten. Er äusserte den entschiedensten Widerwillen gegen allen politischen Geist an Weibern; er bat sie, niemals, was auch geschehen möchte, den zärtlichen Gatten mit dem Geschäftsmann zu verwechseln; er stellte ihr mit den reizendsten Farben der Liebe und Schmeichelei das Glük vor, sich bei ihr auszuruhen, zu erholen, an ihrer Seite Mensch zu seyn, wenn er allenthalben nur das Gespenst der Politik vor Augen gehabt hätte. (TH, 2:69–70)

> [. . .] he spoke seriously and almost imperiously about the duty, which would be incumbent upon women, now more than ever, to protect themselves against impassioned opinions about public occurrences. He expressed the most decisive aversion to women possessing any political spirit. He asked her, regardless of what should happen, never to confuse the gentle husband with the businessman. He presented to her, in the most attractive colors of love and flattery, the happiness he felt to relax with her, to recover, to be human by her side, when everywhere else he would have had the specter of politics in mind.

Sara finds comfort in the image of domestic happiness created by the count (TH, 2:70), because it is the only existence she has known. L.'s control over Sara and his ability to continue leading a double life hinges on her willing confinement within the home, which he achieves by enforcing the rhetoric of Nature Sara learned as a child.

Sara's ready acceptance of one male guardian after another can perhaps be attributed to the lack of female role models presenting alternatives to the role created for Sara by the men in her life. The only examples of feminine behavior that Sara encounters are a series of tragic victims: her deceased mother, who was trapped in a loveless marriage leading her to take a lover; her Parisian neighbor Martha, who dies of grief after losing her two children during the storming of the Tuileries; and her neighbor Nanette, who, having suffered a similar fate as Sara, loses touch with reality, murders her child, and is a shell of her former self. Although Sara experiences her own moment of temporary insanity, the desire for revenge prevents Sara from becoming another helpless, mentally unstable victim. Sara becomes her own advocate and a champion for the entire female sex. Unlike the suffering females she encounters, Sara does not endure helplessly the crimes of betrayal and exploitation L. perpetrates against her. After discovering the truth about the count and recovering from the accidental death of her child—at the hands of her father during the storming of the Tuileries—she liberates herself from her domestic prison and from the culture of female passivity into which she was indoctrinated. Huber's novel thereby resists perpetuating the eighteenth-century culture of female victimhood in its portrayal of the protagonist and instead contemplates possible forms of female agency.

This firsthand encounter with the violence of the Revolution and the resulting personal loss are the most formative experiences motivating Sara to take up arms and become an active participant in that very same violence. Initially, political interests do not factor into Sara's participation in the Revolution, and the narrator even distances Sara's personal motives for public action from the political "fanaticism" of other revolutionary women, whom the narrator refers to as "verkehrte Geschöpfe" (perverted creatures), "Abarten ihres Geschlechts" (aberrations of their sex) and "unwürdige Gemeinschaft" (dishonorable company) (TH, 2:174–75). In doing so, the narrator forestalls criticism of Sara's entrance into the masculine, political domain as unnatural or deviant. Despite the narrator's rhetorical distancing of Sara from the female revolutionaries, Sara remains an avenging angel for "beleidigt[e] Weiblichkeit" (offended femininity) (TH, 2:175), which she sees embodied in these very same women.

While the narrator's characterization of the common woman's participation in the Revolution appears harsh, the text overall conveys a sympathetic tone toward their plight. Reflecting on Sara's desire for revenge, the narrator acknowledges that the women, who initially unsettle Sara, have been driven to their actions by no fault of their own: "Diese entarteten Geschöpfe hatten Mord und Aufruhr zu ihrem Gewerbe gemacht, weil sie nur darinn erlangten, was der Mensch von der Wiege an bis zum Grabe sucht: einen Plaz im gesellschaftlichen Daseyn" (TH, 2:162; "These degenerate creatures had made murder and revolt their profession because only through these means could they achieve what the human being seeks from the cradle to the grave: a place in the social existence"). The violence perpetrated by the female revolutionaries is a direct result of the rights denied them. The narrator's assertion that these women resort to violence only as a means to gain the inalienable right to civic participation resonates with Theodor von Hippel's view that public spectacles of female revolutionaries demanding their equal treatment could have been prevented had women been granted the same rights as men from the beginning of the Revolution.[23] Due to their exclusion from rational debates, the women Sara encounters are only able to make themselves seen and heard through violence.

Strategically employing the same gendered myth of "ideal femininity" used to advocate women's exclusion from public life, Huber attempts to demonstrate women's contribution to political and social well-being. Sara's second encounter with women of the Revolution is far more political. Like the "creatures" of the September massacres, the women filling the seats of the local tribunal are depicted as enraged fanatics: "nur waren es hier meistens feine, zierliche, verkehrte Geschöpfe, die in die kalte Raserei dieses oder jenes Demagogen einstimmten, weil sie überhaupt eines Gözen bedurften, der sie aus Dankbarkeit an dem Weihrauch des blinden Haufens theilnehmen ließe" (TH, 2:174; "It was mostly refined, dainty, backwards creatures, who agreed with the cold fury of this or that demagogue, because they needed some kind of idol, who out of gratitude would allow the women to participate in the unquestioning mob's praise"). Having been denied the opportunity to develop informed political views and assert their voices in political debates, these women are forced to blindly follow a male figure to gain access to the sphere of politics. The narrator depicts the women as puppets, who cannot think for themselves; instead, they merely "nachplapperte[n]" (mimicked) the ideals proclaimed by their male counterparts. In contrast to these women, Sara distinguishes herself through her ability to think independently and her inner moral compass (TH, 2:174). Sara's transition from the domestic realm to the political does not necessitate her renunciation of her moral values and sense of compassion. The narrator's disdain for the fanatical women in the public sphere can be read in conjunction with Sara's positive example as criticizing the social and political injustices resulting from women's exclusion from the Revolution's ideals of liberty and equality. Thus, Huber turns the argument for women's exclusion from the public sphere against itself, by presenting Sara as an affirmative model of female activism, and presents a compelling argument for the sanctioned inclusion of women into the public sphere in order to prevent such fanaticism.

Love, or rather betrayed love, is the underlying motivation for Sara's decision to join in the revolutionary violence. The count's loyal support of the corrupt, crumbling monarchy gives Sara's pursuit of personal revenge a political dimension and serves as justification for her entrance into the public domain of the Revolution as an active participant: "Rache und Recht kennt und braucht auch das Weib, [. . .]; Rache und Recht geben mir allein noch Denkkraft" (TH, 2:147; "Woman also knows and needs revenge and justice, [. . .]; revenge and justice alone still give me my ability to think"). For Sara, revenge and justice are not rights reserved for men alone as she asserts her claim to seek out this vengeance via the violence of the Revolution. In fact, Sara's male counterpart Joseph is also motivated by revenge for the abuse both he and his sister Nanette experienced at the hands of the corrupt aristocracy. Thus, Sara's recourse to vengeance and violence is no different than that of the men alongside whom she fights.

The personal and political converge even more clearly when the narrator describes L.'s betrayal. As the narrator informs the reader: "Sie [Sara] hörte dort [bei Martha und Thirion], daß ihr Verderber eben so treulos an seinem Vaterland gehandelt hatte, wie an seiner Geliebten" (TH, 2:172; "She [Sara] heard there [at Martha and Thirion's], that her seducer had acted just as treasonously against his fatherland as he had against his lover"). Sara eagerly awaits the execution of the king not only because the count fought to defend the monarch the night he wounded his own child but also because his political duties superseded his duties as family patriarch (TH, 2:176). If we remember Berthier's warning that the count "ist der Feind seines Vaterlands und der Verräther seines Volks; wer die Sache der Freiheit verräth, wird sich nicht scheuen, die hülflose Unschuld aufzuopfern!" (TH, 2.66; "is the enemy of his fatherland and the traitor of his people; whoever betrays the cause of freedom, will not shy away from sacrificing the defenseless innocence"), we see that Sara's actions are not detached from the realm of revolutionary politics as others have suggested; instead, the two spheres are inextricably bound to one another.[24]

Despite the justifications presented in the novel for Sara's decision to take up arms, Huber problematizes Sara's entrance into the public violence. The Revolution provides Sara the opportunity to seek revenge while simultaneously threatening to destroy her both physically and morally.[25] Sara struggles to retain her integrity in the face of the fanaticism and bloodlust to which the baser women of the Revolution seem to succumb. Initially, Sara's striving for moral autonomy is described by the narrator as creating a schism between her actions and her "socially acceptable" role as wife and mother:

> Wie jeder Tag ihren Kopf mit neuen politischen Tollheiten füllte, so starb jeden Tag eine Faser ihres Herzens ab; selbst die Erinnerung, Tochter, Geliebte, Weib, Mutter gewesen zu seyn, äußerte sich endlich nur in heftigeren Ausbrüchen des Parteigeists auf den Tribünen der Volksgesellschaften, in den Sälen der Sektionsversammlungen—denn dorthin drängte sich jezt jene Sara, deren Stimme ehemals aus mädchenhafter Schaam lieblich zitterte, wenn sie einem fremden Knecht einen Auftrag ihres Vaters ausrichtete, dort stand sie jezt, und stürmte ihrer Partei wilden Beifall zu, oder höhnte kek die schwächeren Gegner. (TH, 2:175)

> Just as every day her head was filled with new political madness, a part of her heart died off; even the memory of having been daughter, lover, wife, mother, finally expressed itself only in fierce outbursts of party loyalty in the tribunals of the peoples' clubs, in the halls of the section gatherings—for it was toward these places that Sara now rushed. The Sara whose voice had once sweetly quivered with girlish embarrassment, when she had to give an unknown male worker an order from her father. Now she stood there and wildly applauded her support for her party, or mocked the weaker opponent.

Sara's revolutionary activism marks a striking contrast between her traditional role as a woman within the domestic sphere—characterized here by a timid, quivering girlish voice—and her outspoken presence as a woman within the male-dominated revolutionary faction. The narrator appears to present these two realms, those of the domestic and the political, as irreconcilable: women who enter into public life must forsake their "feminine" characteristics and traditional roles as mothers and wives. They are forced to adopt "masculine" attributes in order to gain entrance in the public realm. The changes Sara undergoes as she becomes more involved in revolutionary politics as well as her decision to cross-dress as a man and assume the identity of a soldier to join the republican troops would appear to support this view. However, Sara does not completely forsake her femininity nor the positive attributes associated with it: as Captain Verrier on the battlefield of the Vendée, Sara maintains and even asserts the guiding moral principles and inner values she possessed *before* entering the public realm of the Revolution. This ambiguity, instantiated by the woman warrior, disrupts gender binarism and challenges the readers' assumptions about warfare as the exclusive domain of the male soldier.

Sara's forays into cross-dressing and her success in the military campaigns of the Vendée highlight the arbitrary rigidity of gender stereotypes. Urged on by her friend Babet, Sara disguises herself as a male soldier to continue her hunt for L., who now leads royalist troops in the Vendée uprising. As Captain Verrier Sara is able to fight in the military from which women were legally banned.[26] Despite the initial teasing by fellow soldiers, who call her "den finstern Jungfernknecht" (TH, 2:249; the somber maiden servant) because of her slight build but earnest demeanor, Sara excels at the "masculine" pursuit of warfare and becomes the ideal soldier. Initially the narrator characterizes Sara's decision to take up arms as "unnatürlich" (TH, 2:250); yet, Sara's subsequent actions undermine the myth asserting as unnatural the combination of "woman" and "war." Sara becomes so adept at wielding a weapon and so fearless that she is made the commander of a platoon. Her supposed physical "limitations" as a woman do not prevent her from performing acts of bravery and strength. The narrator, by referring to Sara as "sie" (she) while she is disguised as Verrier, reminds the reader that it is not a man whose bravery wins over the loyalty of the soldiers, but a woman. Sara's success on the battlefield problematizes the "passive" and "physically weak" characteristics attributed to her gender and as Krimmer argues, Sara's successful performance as Verrier exposes the "social constructedness of gender."[27]

It has been suggested that Sara's appearance as a man in the public realm coincides with a denial of her "femininity" and the characteristics associated with her role as daughter and mother.[28] At first Sara's actions on the battlefield bear out such readings: her behavior does not differ significantly from that of her male counterparts and she participates unquestioningly in the brutality of war as conceived and practiced by patriarchal society. However, Sara neither completely renounces her "femininity" nor does she become fully "masculine"; instead, these qualities exist symbiotically, manifesting an image of the woman warrior as the embodiment of ambiguity. One moment in particular clearly demonstrates Sara's successful combination of both "feminine" and "masculine" attributes. After discovering that the count has fallen in battle, Sara's desire for revenge has been quelled. Her motto is no longer the reckless and desperate "Sieg oder Tod!" (TH, 2:263; Victory or death!); instead, it has been replaced by one of justice and compassion: "Tod den Verräthern, und Schuz den Hülflosen!" (TH, 2:276; "Death to the traitors and protection to the defenseless!"). As Verrier, Sara continues to fight to suppress the royalist revolt, a sign that her motives are no longer simply personal, but there is a noticeable shift in her actions. She is no longer a "Todesengel" (TH, 2:251; angel of death) demanding revenge; the hatred driving Sara's actions up until this point has been superseded by compassion and mercy, gender characteristics previously associated with her role as mother, daughter, and sister in the domestic sphere.

By cross-dressing and appearing as a man in the public sphere of the Revolution, Sara reinscribes the principles of the Revolution (*liberté*, *égalité*, and specifically *fraternité*) as gender-inclusive. Sara now uses her position and the respect earned as Captain Verrier to rescue victims of the civil war. Prior to the count's death, the narrator describes how Sara, having been wounded and recovered, cared for one of her fellow soldiers (TH, 2:257), suggesting she is not devoid of compassion and sense of pity.[29] She has extended her role as defender of "beleidigte Weiblichkeit" (offended femininity) to include all victims of senseless violence:

> Oft gieng sie, mit einigen Kriegsgefährten, die zu menschlich fühlten, um unbarmherzigen Feindeshaß mit Tapferkeit zu verwechseln, in feuchten kalten Nächten auf die Menschenjagd; und sie brachten bald verhungerte Kinder, Jungfrauen und Weiber, als ehrenvolle Beute zurük, und übergaben sie in dieser oder jener kleinen Stadt den mitleidigen Bürgern, die sie mit reiner Menschlichkeit aufnahmen, pflegten, verbargen, keinen Verrath von Geschöpfen befürchtend, an welchen sie Bruderpflichten erfüllten. (TH, 2:265–66)

> On damp, cold nights she often went on the hunt for people with a few of her fellow soldiers, who felt too humane to mistake merciless hatred of the enemy for bravery. They returned with nearly starved children, young girls, and old women as honorable spoils and handed them over to sympathetic citizens in this or that small city, who accepted them with pure humanity. The citizens cared for and hid them without any fear of betrayal by the creatures toward whom they had fulfilled their brotherly duties.

As this passage reveals, notions of bravery, hatred, mercy, and humanity as gendered characteristics are no longer mutually exclusive. The resurfacing of Sara's "feminine" attributes alongside and in harmony with the more "masculine" ones demonstrates that Sara has not renounced her identity as mother and nurturer entirely while participating in the public realm. In moments such as these, Sara's ability to assist the helpless victims (mostly women and children) of the Revolution justifies the suffering she endured and inflicted (TH, 2:266–67).

Huber's gender-bending protagonist probes the tension between what it means to be a soldier and to uphold Enlightenment ideals of humanity. In her critique of the bloody and merciless face of war, Huber's woman warrior models for her fellow soldiers an alternative form of warfare and patriotism that includes both bravery and compassion:

> Verriers Begleiter—so wenig eine so grosse Anzahl Menschen durch feinere Gefühle ganz zusammenhängen konnten—hatten doch schon alle das Glück des Wohlthuns, und den Stolz der Tapferkeit geschmekt, sie hatten zusammen dem Tode getrozt und das Leben von Unschuldigen gerettet, in beiden Fällen ihren braven Kapitain an ihrer Spize: sie hatten also einen menschlicheren, aber auch strengeren Begrif von ihrer Pflicht als Krieger und Patrioten. (TH, 2:273)
>
> Verrier's companions—as much as such a large number of people could be united by dignified sentiments—had already tasted the happiness of good deeds and the pride of bravery. Together they had defied death and rescued the lives of the innocent: in both cases their brave captain had led them. Thus, they had developed a more humane but also stricter sense of their duty as warriors and patriots.

Huber's female fighter depicts the ability of women to effect change and to provide justice against tyranny for all victims of oppression, be it in the form of the patriarchal aristocracy, the unfaithful lover, or the cruelty defining the institution and practice of warfare.

The positive influence Sara exerts as Verrier does not cease once her identity and sex have been revealed nor once she has retreated from the public field of battle. Upon learning that her brother Theodor is alive and standing before her as her enemy and that he is caring for the count's legitimate heir Hyppolit, Sara faints on the battlefield. Believing their captain to be seriously wounded, the soldiers quickly rip open Verrier's shirt to locate the injury, leading to an even greater surprise: "Es ist ein Weib!—Verrier ein Weib!" (TH, 2:281; "It's a woman!—Verrier is a woman!"). The soldiers' response to the discovery that their brave male captain is really a woman conveys unease and fascination. This equivocation is reinforced by both the grammatical gender of the pronoun "Es," used to refer to Verrier/Sara, and the performative speech act contained in the declaration "Es ist ein Weib!"[30] The neuter pronoun "it" captures the ambiguity of the cross-dressing woman warrior and the soldiers' inability to categorize "it" as either masculine or feminine, while the illocutionary act performed by the soldiers seeks to constitute Sara as decidedly female and thereby return her to her proper place within the bifurcated gender hierarchy in an attempt to stabilize the sphere of warfare, coded as masculine. Although the soldiers find it difficult to reconcile Sara's sex with her bravery on the battlefield, the discovery that she is a woman does not diminish their feelings of loyalty and admiration for her even though it contradicts their firmly held assumptions: "Kapitain, sagte er [ein Soldat] trozig, bis du deine Autorität bei unserm Chef niedergelegt hast, sind wir Dir Gehorsam schuldig, so wenig dein Geschlecht sich mit dieser Autorität reimt" (TH, 2:283; "Captain, he [a soldier] said defiantly, until you have relinquished your authority to our commander, we owe you obedience, even though your sex does not agree with this authority"). The soldiers' reverence for Sara and the compassion she demonstrated on the battlefield is transferred to her actions off of the battlefield as well: "sie schienen ihre ganze Achtung für Verrier, den braven Soldaten, auf Sara, das unglükliche [*sic*] Weib, übergetragen zu haben" (TH, 2:290; "they appeared to have transferred their complete respect for Verrier, the brave soldier, to Sara, the unhappy woman"). Furthermore, we find that the sense of respect for Sara's demeanor is shared by everyone who either encounters her or hears her story (TH, 2:317). If anything, the respect she commanded as their courageous and compassionate Verrier is intensified by the fact that she has defied traditional assumptions about women's nature.

Even upon her return to the domestic sphere, Sara's life and behavior are transformed by her experiences during the Revolution and carry a political undertone. Sara moves quickly to restore the outward signs of her femininity, trading in her uniform for a dress (TH, 2:290). Some scholars have criticized Huber's work as perpetuating conventional gender roles by arguing that Sara's ready acceptance to put on women's clothing implies her return to the socially prescribed role as maternal caregiver and passive victim.[31] Such criticism, however, neglects the dominant social, economic, and political realities in which Huber lived and wrote. Huber presents readers with the harsh realities encountered by women while at the same time showing that there is potential for change, but that change cannot be forced through irrational, violent actions. Sara's decision to return to women's clothing does not imply the perpetuation of the notion of woman as helpless victim or that woman is only suited for the role of mother, wife, sister, or daughter; instead, Huber's protagonist creates a new space for herself in *both* public and private life.

Sara's ability to move seamlessly between the traditionally "male" public sphere of political and martial activities and the traditionally "female" domestic sphere of child-rearing and familial responsibilities complicates constructed notions of gender and their corresponding spheres of activity.

Sara's formative experiences in the revolutionary public sphere suggest that she returns to the country estate a different woman than when she left her father's home. Sara continues to refuse her childhood friend Roger's marriage proposals—denying the dying wish of her father and thereby rejecting the patriarchal order—and remains unwed, thus retaining her autonomy even in the domestic realm. As a single woman, she is not subject to the will of a husband, brother, or father. Instead, Huber offers her protagonist an alternative beyond the patriarchal institution of marriage.[32] She opts out of the standard fate for women by choosing the path providing her the ability to decide her own fate and that of her adopted son.

Although it may be argued that Sara's return to the ruins of L.'s estate and her acceptance of a life of solitude imply woman's inescapable destiny to fulfill the traditional domestic roles as wives and mothers,[33] her return to the domestic realm is not merely a retreat to her previous life and the status quo but gestures instead toward a reconsideration of gendered roles and a reassessment of political structures. While the ruins of the estate certainly indicate that Sara's personal life is desolate and barren, her decision to plant a garden in the spring among the ruins suggests gradual rebirth and renewal: "und mit den ersten Frühlingsregen keimten da Gemüse heraus, und wilde Blumen, die sie für ihren Kleinen sorgfältig pflegte" (TH, 2:320–321; "and with the first spring rains the vegetables sprouted as did wild flowers that she carefully tended to for her little one"). Sara nurtures the sprouting seeds that symbolize a new beginning for Hyppolit, who represents the future of the Republic, and even for Sara, who gradually begins the healing process: "Es kamen jezt Stunden, wo Sara's Herz mit der Natur um sie her einstimmte—Keime, die den grausen Trümmern entsproßten!" (TH, 2:322; "There were hours when Sara's heart agreed with the Nature around her—seeds that sprung forth from the dreadful ruins!"). At the same time, this growth can be read as the end of the corrupt and dilapidated aristocracy and the beginning of democracy rising out of the ashes of the old regime, fostered and sustained by Sara's own hands. Sara's decision to raise and educate Hyppolit suggests an attempt to right the past wrongs of the aristocracy.[34] Everything Sara has learned from her experiences and sacrifices during the Revolution will be handed down to the count's son as a means by which to positively influence a generation of more tolerant and compassionate citizens. Huber's novel suggests that women do, indeed, play many critical roles in shaping the future of the nation.

Huber's story bridges the gendered public-private divide by reimagining women as both potential mothers *and* warriors as well as demonstrating the humanizing impact that women's participation on the battlefield can have on the brutality of warfare, leading to a more humane generation of future citizens and soldiers. Huber's warrior woman sows the seeds of possibility for female readers to envision an alternative, inclusive female reality, in which women can have a family *and* exercise their public voice. Like Huber, the figure of the warrior woman proved particularly appealing to Karoline von

Günderrode as a means by which she could imagine a new form of female agency beyond the borders of contemporary societal norms.

For Love of the Father(land)

Like Huber, the letters and literary works of the early Romantic poet Karoline von Günderrode created the possibility for the author, and her women readers, to escape the drudgery of her domestic routine and to live out her emancipatory fantasies in the fictional world: "Gedichte sind Balsam auf unerfüllbares im Leben; nach und nach verharscht es, und aus der Wunde deren Blut den Seelenboden tränkte hat der Geist schöne rote Blumen gezogen die wieder einen Tag blühen, an dem es süß ist der Erinnerung Duft aus ihnen zu saugen"[35] ("Poems are balm for the unrealizable in life. Little by little it forms a scab and from the wound, whose blood saturates the soul's foundation, the spirit has picked beautiful red flowers, which bloom again one day, upon which it is sweet to draw the scent of memory from them"). By seeking solace and a permanent sanctuary in her female protagonists, the oppression of her own existence is made more bearable and the "unrealizable in life" momentarily accessible.

The liberatory potential underlying Günderrode's works, her female characters in particular, and their importance for her female audience was not lost on contemporaries. In a letter dated at the end of August 1804, Günderrode's friend Lisette Nees von Esenbeck urged her to assert her public voice through writing in order to provide herself and her readers with a model of female empowerment: "Da so viele Weiber in Deiner Nähe ihre Untergeordnetheit fühlen, und Du noch immer nicht wagst gegen das Gemeine und Schlechte Dich frei und ohne Rücksicht zu erklären, wie sollten selbst die Beßren die Dich umgeben es wagen?"[36] ("Since so many women in your proximity feel their subordination, and still you do not dare to express yourself freely and without regard against the base and evil, how should even your betters, who surround you, dare?"). It was not only Günderrode's strong female figures but also the power she wielded as a writer that enabled her to influence how entire generations of women, regardless of class, viewed themselves and the roles available to them.

Although born to an aristocratic family, Karoline von Günderrode's short life was far from privileged. Her father's death when she was only six years old left the family impoverished, forcing her mother to take up a position as lady in waiting to support the family. At seventeen Günderrode, who had helped raise her siblings, was sent to live in a convent in Frankfurt, where she enjoyed a considerable degree of freedom to receive visitors and travel. Here she befriended the likes of Bettina von Arnim, Clemens Brentano, and Friederich Creuzer. With the latter she had an intimate yet unhappy affair ending in her suicide at the young age of twenty-six.[37] This series of events in combination with the strict social constraints imposed on women led Günderrode to explore the subversive potential proffered by the female protagonists she created.

Günderrode's mythical warrior women transcend the binary gender division she herself could not escape and die the heroic deaths of which she could only dream. In a letter to Bettina von Arnim from 1805, composed during Günderrode's work on *Poetische Fragmente* (*Poetic Fragments*), she gives further voice to the emancipatory potential of her literary figures: "Wenn ich nicht heldenmütig sein kann, und immer krank bin an Zagen und Zaudern, so will ich zum wenigsten meine Seele ganz mit jenem Heroismus erfüllen und meinen Geist mit jener Lebenskraft nähren die jetzt mir so schmerzhaft oft mangelt, und wo her sich alles melancholische doch wohl in mir erzeugt"[38] ("If I cannot be heroic, and I am always ill due to apprehension and indecision, then at least I will fill my soul entirely with that heroism and nourish my spirit with that vitality, which I now so painfully lack and from where everything melancholy in me perhaps stems"). Writing here about a planned, yet uncompleted project about Spartan women,[39] Günderrode viewed these mythic women as the epitome of the heroism for which she yearned. Although Günderrode's project never came to fruition, she discovered productive avenues by which to explore the liberatory connection between warfare and femininity. In her letter to Gunda Brentano, Günderrode identified her own wish to participate in battle and to die a heroic death as "unweiblich" (unfeminine).[40] Günderrode's codification of warfare and the desire to die heroically illustrates how such views of warfare as a decidedly masculine pursuit were deeply entrenched in even the most progressive individuals.

Rather than attributing Günderrode's fascination with war to her fixation with death, as some scholars have suggested, I argue the depictions of warfare and heroic death, particularly the death of the warrior woman, become outlets for reimagining women's existences. These desires find expression in the actions of her literary heroines in the poem "Darthula nach Ossian" ("Darthula According to Ossian," 1804), *Mora* (1801–02/1804), and *Hildgund* (1804/1805),[41] whose love of family and homeland lead them to risk their lives in their defense. These figures offer themselves for a greater good, a sacrifice that requires these warlike women to merge personal and political interests.

In contrast to Huber, who places her warrior woman in a contemporary political context, Günderrode transports her characters and readers to mythic pasts and distant destinations. Günderrode's construction of new myths and the creative license she takes with existing myths confront the very gender norms to which she was subjected.[42] Like many female contemporaries, Günderrode viewed a reversal of such rigid gender concepts in her own lifetime as impossible, thereby making the transference of her emancipatory fantasies onto the actions of her warrior women even more significant. Her first attempt to depict the heroic actions of a young woman warrior in her poem "Darthula nach Ossian," an adaptation of the poem "Darthula" by the bard Ossian (an alias for the Scotsman James Macpherson), envisions a young maiden, who dies bravely while trying to avenge the deaths of her father, brother, and lover. Macpherson's poem not only channeled Günderrode's own desires, but it also provided her with fertile material from which to construct her visions of the woman warrior. Darthula takes steps to seize her fate and avenge the injustices she and her family have suffered by arming herself and confronting her enemy on the battlefield.

Günderrode's poem tracks the transformation of its titular heroine, constructing a narrative of empowerment that unsettles dominant myths of women as victims in times of military conflict. Held captive by the enemy Caibar, Darthula, daughter of King Collas, attempts to flee with the aid of her lover Nathos; however, their plans unravel when unfavorable winds prevent them from setting sail. The poem's entire cast of male warriors, Collas, Darthula's brother Truthil, her lover Nathos and his brothers, die defending their homelands and trying to rescue Darthula from Caibar's clutches. However, Darthula is not a passive victim dependent on others for her rescue; instead, Darthula takes up sword and shield to defend her father and avenge her brother's death. By depicting Darthula's actions as sanctioned by the patriarchal order, Günderrode strategically lends her heroine's actions legitimacy, thereby removing the stain of transgression from her behavior: "Geh', ergreif das Schwerdt vergangner Schlachten! / Also Colla: seine Worte fachten, / Höher noch in mir des Kampfes Muth" (KGD, 1:78–80; "Go; seize the sword of past battles! / So Colla: his words stoked, / Higher still within me the courage for battle").[43] It is father/king who calls Darthula to arms and inspires her to enter the battle. Darthula's decision to fight is portrayed not only as a form of resistance against Caibar but as a means of honoring her brother by taking his place at her father's side. Darthula is unable to defend her father and he falls mortally wounded beneath her shield: "Ach! umsonst bedeckt von meinem Schilde, / Sank der Vater mir im Schlachtgefilde, / Und in heißen Thränen schwamm mein Blick" (KGD, 1:88–90; "Oh! In vain covered by my shield / The father fell in the throngs of the battle / And my gaze was flooded by hot tears").[44] Darthula, however, does not express a sense of resignation or defeat after the deaths of her father and brother; instead, she arms herself with the weapons necessary to avenge their deaths:

> Nathos! reiche mir das Schwerdt der Tapfern,
> Vater! ich will deiner würdig seyn,
> In des Stahles Treffen werd' ich gehen,
> Nimmer Caibars düstre Hallen sehen,
> Nein! ihr Geister meiner Liebe! nein! (KGD, 1:116–20)
>
> Nathos! Hand me the sword of the brave,
> Father! I want to be worthy of you.
> I will go to the encounter of steel
> Never will I seek Caibar's dark halls
> No, you spirits of my love! No![45]

It is Darthula, empowered by her loss and bound by a sense of honor, who takes up the sword this time to actively pursue her enemy and to die valiantly rather than succumb to Caibar's oppression. Inspired by her courage and readiness to die, Nathos finds himself reinvigorated and Darthula follows him into the fray, where both meet tragic ends without successfully conquering the enemy. Nathos is cut down alongside his brothers, while Darthula escapes enslavement at the hands of Caibar when she is struck by a stray arrow (KGD, 1:171–72).

Demonstrating that both men and women are equally victims of unchecked power and aggression, Günderrode levels the playing field for the sexes and argues for a reconsideration of society's gender hierarchy. In the end, neither the male warriors nor Darthula are successful in defending their homeland and defeating Caibar.[46] Despite their best efforts, the male warriors prove no match for their enemy and appear ineffectual in the one thing in which they are skilled. As for Darthula, she is never depicted as the aggressor actively fighting or killing her male enemies. In the two instances in which Darthula appears on the battlefield (KGD, 1:81–82, 1:88–90), neither suggest that she initiates combat. Despite her heroic gestures and proclamations (KGD, 1:78–80, 1:116–20), she ultimately fails to protect her father or to avenge his death by defeating Caibar.

Yet, Darthula's efforts are not futile, and her death is not in vain. Her heroic course of action, resulting in her death, can be read as a liberation from a fate as Caibar's mistress. Darthula knowingly places herself in a position of peril by joining the battle and thereby ensuring her death will be a means to freedom. The sudden mortal wound inflicted on the battlefield rescues her from her certain fate while simultaneously bestowing upon her a heroic death. Darthula's death and failure to defeat the enemy have led some scholars to read Günderrode's protagonist as emphasizing the helplessness of her warrior women;[47] however, such arguments overlook the fate Darthula shares with her father and brother, whose deaths on the battlefield are cast in heroic terms. In this sense, Darthula's death by arrow can also be interpreted as honorable and brave. Darthula's decision to take up weapons to determine her fate signals a shift away from depictions of women as vulnerable, passive victims. Her efforts to effect change and assert her will is the progressive moment and empowering thrust of Günderrode's poem. Although Darthula dies without completing her mission to destroy Caibar, her success lies in the sense of agency motivating and informing her actions on the battlefield. Unlike the numerous willing female victims of eighteenth-century literature,[48] Günderrode's warrior women go down fighting or at the very least resist submitting to their male opponents.

The themes of female resistance and sacrificial love that first emerge in an attenuated manner in "Darthula" appear more prominently in *Mora* and *Hildgund*. In *Mora*, Günderrode presents her readers with yet another heroic death, this time of the maiden Mora, who dies defending the honor of her lover King Frothal. While Mora and Darthula share a similar fate, the open ending of Günderrode's story of the Germanic warrior woman Hildgund allows for the possibility that her sacrifice, unlike that of her predecessors, may prove successful. By offering herself up to her enemy, Attila the Hun, Hildgund single-handedly assumes the burden of protecting her family and her people from destruction and oppression.

However, it is not only love *for* something that drives these women to take up arms, but it is also a *lack* of love, or unrequited love, that places them at the center of political and military conflicts. Caibar has captured and desires to make Darthula his possession, Karmor feels slighted that Mora has chosen Frothal over him, and Attila wishes to make Hildgund his bride, despite her being in love with and promised to Walther. As in the case of Darthula, Mora and Hildgund are simultaneously motivated by their lack of love for the men who desire them; thus, unrequited love is depicted here as just as powerful a motivation for heroic action as the affirmative sentiment of love.

In her analysis of Günderrode's works, Becker-Cantarino foregrounds sacrificial love and a hope for reunion in the afterlife as that which drives Günderrode's protagonists and ultimately leads to their deaths.[49] While Becker-Cantarino asserts that examples of female self-sacrifice in Günderrode's texts result in "sublimating and aestheticizing them [women] as sex objects,"[50] I suggest that Günderrode recodes the "feminine" inclination toward love and sacrifice as facilitating forms of female agency that unsettle the gender dichotomy. Even as early nineteenth-century German women's patriotic duty was being defined in terms of their roles as supportive wives and patriotic mothers, whose responsibility it was to raise future soldiers and citizens to be sacrificed in defense of the homeland, Günderrode's female warriors make the ultimate sacrifice in order to preserve the lives of their beloved husbands, brothers, sons, and fathers. While Günderrode's more conservative contemporaries presented models of female self-sacrifice necessitating women warriors to renounce their "feminine natures" as the price for participation in the public sphere of warfare, Günderrode's warrior women complicated these images of female sacrifice and recalibrated forms of female patriotism in the wake of the French Revolution and amidst the Napoleonic Wars.[51] Simultaneously, Günderrode's warriors critique social expectations that women should passively accept their destinies to languish in loveless marriages or to endure marriages of social and political convenience.[52] Günderrode's armed maidens reject the advances of the often more politically powerful and influential enemy and thereby refuse to become pawns in a political conflict. Instead, Darthula, Mora, and Hildgund seek to shape their destinies and those of their people by actively pursuing a policy of violence face-to-face with their enemy.

Composed after "Darthula nach Ossian," *Mora* further expands the image of the warrior woman embodied by Darthula and serves as a poetic tribute to the Scandinavian maiden who ultimately takes up sword and shield to fight for that which she loves most. Whereas Darthula dies before defeating Caibar, Mora dies valiantly *while* battling the enemy Karmor. The poem opens with King Frothal's bards, who foreshadow the impending tragedy. Carul sings the praises of spring and the beauty of young Mora, invoking a sense of vitality and peace (KGM, 1:7–15). The tranquility is soon disrupted when the second bard, Thormod, sings of the approaching nightfall and descending darkness; the themes of vitality and youth are quickly replaced with that of impending death and ghosts rising from their graves (KGM, 1:16–24). However, it is Mora who appears as a light leading Frothal from the darkness and providing him refuge in the bards' songs (KGM, 1:45–47). Ultimately, it will be Mora who rescues Frothal from the threat of Karmor's sword.

Mora, like Darthula, is empowered to take up arms by the sanctioning words of a male authority. In Darthula's case it is Colla, who charges his daughter to take up her slain brother's sword and to join him on the battlefield; for Mora, it is her lover and king, who instructs her to don his armor and wield his weapons. Yearning for the excitement of the hunt, Frothal asks Mora to accompany him. Sensing danger, she entreats him to remain by her side within the safe confines of their shelter. Frothal prevails and orders her to join in the hunt: "Komm zur muntern Jagd, nimm die Waffen der Könige Scandinaviens daß du glänzest im Stahle der Helden [. . .]" (KGM, 1:66–67; "Come join the hunt, take the weapons of Scandinavian kings, so that you will shine in the steel of heroes [. . .]"). Thus, Mora's cross-dressing and subsequent combative actions are legitimized by the king's command to take up arms, which symbolizes the power and authority of his forefathers. However, it is also this symbol that leads Karmor to mistake Mora for the king and to challenge her to battle.

Mora asserts her autonomy by determining to whom she will give her love and with whom she will align herself; she is not a submissive object to be claimed as a prize or possession. Exhausted from the hunt, Frothal sleeps while Mora, plagued by her ominous dreams, keeps watch. The knight Karmor, feeling jilted by Mora's union with Frothal, stumbles upon Mora and mistakes her for Frothal upon seeing the sword and shield (KGM, 1:106–7). Believing Frothal has stolen what Karmor claims was rightfully his, namely the daughter of Torlat (KGM, 1:81–84), Karmor demands that she fight him for the right to possess Mora. However, Karmor's words reveal that it is not Frothal who has deprived him of the beautiful maiden but that Mora herself has rejected his affection: "Er hat mir die Seele meines Busens geraubt, ich liebte die Tochter von Torlat, und sie wählt ihn" (KGM, 1:81–82; "He stole from me the soul of my bosom. I loved the daughter of Torlat, and she chooses him"). Mora makes explicitly clear to Karmor that it is Mora, and not Frothal, who is the cause of his unhappiness: "Sie wählt ihn, und nicht dich. Was nutzt dir der Kampf? was hilft dir der Sieg?" (KGM, 1:83–84; "She chooses him and not you. How does battle benefit you? How does victory help you?").

Rather than divulge her identity, Mora, emboldened by Karmor's claims to possess her, takes matters into her own hands. She accepts his challenge to do battle to the death for the right to possess the daughter of Torlat with the menacing battle cry: "Komm, mich dürstet nach Kampf, mein Muth jauchzt der Gefahr entgegen, komm!" (KGM, 1:90–91; "Come, I thirst for battle. My courage rejoices in the face of danger, come!"). The violent struggle is not depicted, as is the case with all of Günderrode's warrior women; however, the bards acknowledge her sacrifice for Frothal: "Frothal! sie fiel für dich" (KGM, 1:107–108; "Frothal! She fell for you"). The fact that Günderrode does not depict the battle between Mora and Karmor does not diminish Mora's heroic act. Whereas Darthula is struck down before she can even raise her sword, Mora, as we learn from the bards, dies bravely defending Frothal.

Even as Mora's death is memorialized as an act of heroism, the concluding scene of the text proves ambiguous. Rather than condemning Mora's use of violence and resulting death as a cross-dressed warrior as "unnatural," Frothal and his bards choose to build lyrical monuments to her youth and beauty, ignoring her bravery and courage altogether. Frothal commands, "Singet ihr Barden, das Lob der schönen Tochter von Torlat! singet den Ruhm des Mädchens, daß unsterblich blühe die leicht verwelkliche Schönheit" (KGM, 1:109–11; "Sing you bards, the praise of the beautiful daughter of Torlat! Sing the glory of the girl, who immortally blooms the easily withering beauty") and Carul sings, "Mora du bist gefallen in deiner Schönheit, gesunken in deiner Blüthe! lieblich warst du wie der Stern des Abends, freundlich wie die scheidende Sonne" (KGM, 1:114–15; "Mora you have fallen in your beauty, you have sunk in the prime of your life! lovely were you like the evening star, pleasant like the setting sun"). Mora's warrior prowess is superseded by her physical beauty and her function as muse meant to inspire men. Like Mora, Darthula's physical appearance is foregrounded not only by the prolific use of the word "schön" (beautiful) to describe her but also in repeated references to her flowing brown locks (KGM, 1:7–10, 51, 67, 122, 175, 185), a clear reference to her femininity that supersedes what could be characterized as her "masculine" actions on the battlefield. On the one hand, Mora's heroic act remains uncelebrated as the story concludes with Frothal, symbol of the patriarchal order, charging off to avenge her death and victimhood. Thus, Mora's sacrifice has succeeded in preserving the status quo, and war remains between men. However, Günderrode's text simultaneously presents another reading that envisions a space for women in the public sphere of warfare and in service to their homeland. The bards' emphasis on Mora's femininity mitigates the transgressive nature of her violent actions and allows Günderrode to underscore for her readers that heroism, like love, is a natural feminine attribute.

If Mora's heroic self-sacrifice gestures toward a more progressive model of female agency, then Hildgund's plot to assassinate Attila the Hun in order to protect her father/king asserts a more forceful claim for women's participation in the public sphere. In the fragment *Hildgund* themes of patriotism and political activism are established from the outset by Günderrode's conflation of fatherland and father. The dramatic work begins with the long-awaited return home of Hildgund, daughter of the Elector of Burgundy. Her return is presented as a return to the ancestral halls of her family as well as to the halls of the homeland, thereby foregrounding the union of the personal and political. This blurring of the two interests is further compounded by the greeting she receives from her father Herrich: "Dem Vaterlande nicht allein, dem Vater / Gehört der Tochter erste Freude an" (KGH, 1:10–11; "The daughter's first joy does not belong to the fatherland alone / But also to the father") and her reply: "Der Vater macht das Vaterland erst werther, / Und meine Freude theilet sich in ihm, und es" (KGH, 1:12–13; "The father makes the fatherland more valuable, / And my joy is shared with him and it"). Love for country and family are conflated in Hildgund's patriotic duty to her home(land). Her participation in the public welfare of her land and people is grounded in her familial ties to father/king. As with Günderrode's other works, we see the "family model of politics" at work;[53] rather than overthrowing the father/king, Günderrode's warrior daughters fight to defend the existing patriarchal structure from a far more sinister and oppressive external threat.

Hildgund's escape from captivity by Attila the Hun and her successful return home is not only a matter of personal interest but also has political implications. As the daughter of the Elector, Hildgund's value as an individual assumes greater meaning: her escape, although welcomed, directly impacts the well-being of the people of Burgundy. Inquiring as to how she managed to free herself from Attila's clutches, Hildgund recounts the story of her liberation initiated by her betrothed Walther. Walther advises Hildgund to steal from Attila's treasure what she deems most useful for her escape. She does not steal gold to finance their escape; instead, the objects which Hildgund carefully selects signify her first assault on Attila's power and person: she selects armor, a sword, and a shield (KGH, 1:97–99). Like Mora and Darthula, Hildgund appropriates the weapons of her enemy, the most politically powerful man in the world, in order to carry out her plans. Using these confiscated weapons, she will wield them against Attila in order to free those he has oppressed.[54] Although Walther crafts the initial plan to escape, it is neither the mortal Walther nor the gods' intervention to which Hildgund attributes her success, rather, she asserts that she freed herself by means of her own will and self-reliance: "Der Gott, der mich befreit, wohnt in dem eigenen Herzen [. . .]" (KGH, 1:104; "The god, who frees me, lives in my own heart"). It is Walther's plan but it is Hildgund alone who can carry it out. The pronouns "wir" and "uns" are used repeatedly to describe Walther and Hildgund's escape, signaling that it is not Walther who rescued the helpless Hildgund, but that they worked together to evade capture and make the successful journey home. Armed with sword and shield, Hildgund stands as Walther's equal as they successfully flee Attila's kingdom (KGH, 1:108–13).

Hildgund's agency, however, is momentarily nullified by the patriarchal order, only to be restored by Hildgund's heroic act of sacrifice. Her father attributes her safe return to Walther's bold plan and rewards his bravery by encouraging his daughter to give herself freely to Walther (KGH, 1:119). When it becomes clear that Attila will only spare Herrich's kingdom in return for Hildgund, her father once again encourages her to offer herself to Attila (KGH, 1:199–208). In the eyes of Günderrode's male figures, Hildgund at first appears to be nothing more than an object of desire to be possessed and a political pawn to be traded between men for political power and advantage. Despite her father's clear preference, the choice ultimately rests with Hildgund: "Der Tochter Wille nur kann über sie entscheiden" (KGH, 1:218; "Only the will of my daughter can determine her fate"). It is Hildgund who must make the final decision and determine not only her fate but that of her people: "Ich bin entschieden; nur in feigen Busen kämpfet / Der größere mit dem kleineren Entschluß, / Ich bin Attilas" (KGH 1:220–22; "I have decided; only in weak bosoms / Does the greater decision battle the smaller one, / I am Attila's"). Hildgund establishes herself as a defender of her fatherland while simultaneously asserting herself as an independent and active political participant.

Hildgund's fatalistic acceptance of death as inevitable is mitigated by her realization that she has the power to determine *how* she dies and she opts for the heroic and noble sacrifice (KGH, 1:246–47). She acknowledges the singularity of the plan she intends to carry out: "In meines Herzens tiefsten Gründen reifet / Die größte That, die je ein Weib gethan" (KGH, 1:240–41; "In the greatest depths of my heart matures / The greatest deed that a woman has ever accomplished") and is keenly aware of the limitations imposed on her as a woman. Hildgund views this decision to offer herself to Attila as a way of shaping her fate:

> Wie herrlich ist der Mann, sein Schicksal bildet er,
> Nur eigener Kräfte Maas ist sein Gesetz am Ziele,
> Des Weibes Schicksal, ach! ruht nicht in eigner Hand!
> Bald folget sie der Noth, bald strenger Sitte Wille,
> Kann man sich dem entziehn, was Uebermacht befiehlt?
> (KGH, 1:252–56)
>
> How magnificent is the man, who can shape his fate,
> Only the measure of his own strengths is his law in the end,
> Woman's fate, alas! rests not in her own hand!
> Soon she follows necessity, soon the strict will of convention,
> Can one elude, that which the superior power commands?

Like Goethe's Iphigenie, Günderrode's protagonist gives voice to the restrictions placed on the female sex that limit her sense of agency and the options available to her.[55] Now presented with the opportunity to transcend these limitations, Hildgund intends to liberate her countrymen:

> Mord! Ha der Name nur entsetzet,
> Die That ist recht, und kühn und groß,
> Der Völker Schicksal ruht in meinem Busen,
> Ich werde sie, ich werde mich befrein.
> Verbannt sey Furcht und kindisch Zagen,
> Ein kühner Kämpfer nur ersiegt ein großes Ziel. (KGH, 1:277–82)

> Murder! Even the name is shocking,
> The deed is right, and bold and great,
> The fate of peoples rests in my breast,
> I will free them, I will free myself
> Away with fear and childish hesitance,
> A bold warrior alone achieves a great goal.[56]

Yet, her intentions go beyond the interests of her family and people. Günderrode's text takes on greater patriotic dimensions when Hildgund promises to liberate the entire Roman Empire, represented here by Italy, from the yoke of Attila's oppression:

> Schon zuckt mein Dolch, bald wird das große Opfer bluten,
> Das, Herrscher einer Welt, ein schwaches Weib besiegt.
> . . . .
> Italien zage nicht! ich werde dich befreien,
> Der Völker Geisel fällt durch Hildegundens Hand. (KGH, 1:304–9)

> Already my dagger quivers, soon the great sacrifice will bleed,
> Who, ruler of a world, a weak woman conquers.
> . . . .
> Italy do not be apprehensive! I will liberate you,
> The scourge of the people will die by Hildgund's hand.

In more general terms, Hildgund's fight to free those subjected to Attila's tyrannical rule can be read as Günderrode's indictment of oppression, regardless of what social or political form it takes.[57] In fact, Attila is not presented in the same critical and negative terms as the tyrant Caibar. Rather, Günderrode constructs a ruler who ultimately appears fair and merciful (KGH, 1:72–73, 192–96), even if he does not uphold the principle of freedom for everyone.[58] Quite to the contrary, Attila views himself pursuing a fate determined for him by his ancestors (KGH, 1:122–26) and as righting the wrongs of other empires, particularly those of the Romans (KGH, 1:154–56). Regardless of how Attila perceives his quest to conquer the world, as the oppressor of Hildgund and her people, he must be defeated.

Unlike Darthula and Mora, the success of Hildgund's planned assassination remains controversial among scholars. Dagmar von Hoff, for example, interprets the unresolved ending as Günderrode's commentary on the futility of challenging socially prescribed gender roles.[59] However, there is no decisive conclusion to the claims that Hildgund makes, thereby freeing the reader to imagine their own ending and outcome to the warrior woman's heroic declarations. Rather than interpreting the unresolved ending as foreclosing the subversive and emancipatory potential of Günderrode's warrior, I assert that Günderrode allows for either possibility, which means that it is just as likely that Hildgund carried out this deed, particularly if the author based her character Hildgund on accounts of Attila the Hun's death, which suggest he died at the hands of his wife Ildico, as von Hoff suggests.

The tale's ambiguous ending problematized the question of female agency for early nineteenth-century readers by allowing for both the success and failure of Günderrode's heroine. The enigmatic fate of Hildgund is attenuated only by the cryptic lines "Ich folge meinem Herrn! (für sich) Ha feire nur, Tirann, / Des letzten Tages schnell entflohne Stunden" (KGH, 1:326–27; "I will follow my lord! [to herself] Ha go on and celebrate, tyrant / The quickly fleeting hours of the final day"), suggesting that Hildgund intends to carry out her plot. As Simpson and Becker-Cantarino have argued, Hildgund's pending victory over Attila does not rest on her prowess on the battlefield, as it does with Mora and Darthula; instead, she uses her "feminine" attributes to get close enough to destroy her enemy. Rather than disguise herself in men's clothing, she is "cloaked in the guise of a submissive bride."[60] Becker-Cantarino even likens Hildgund to the biblical Judith and the eighteenth-century French assassin Charlotte Corday rather than the likes of the Amazons.[61] In this instance, however, I would argue that Hildgund, like Judith, Corday, and Kleist's Amazons, employs both her powers of seduction and her bravery in an attempt to liberate herself and the world from male tyranny. Just as Hildgund plans to murder Attila in the marriage bed, so too do Kleist's Amazons free themselves from their foreign male conquerors by hiding daggers in their wedding beds. Only after murdering these men are the women free to establish an autonomous state. Because *Hildgund* remains a fragment, there is no way of conclusively ascertaining what future Günderrode intended for her heroic protagonist or the exact means by which she sought to achieve her goal. What remains clear, however, is that "feminine" cunning appears just as viable a means of defeating the enemy as engaging in hand-to-hand combat on the battlefield.

The warlike women in "Darthula," *Mora*, and *Hildgund* demonstrate the strategies by which Günderrode deployed the rhetoric of patriotism, love, and sacrifice to secure a place for women in public life.[62] Both Günderrode and Huber critically employ this gendered rhetoric of love as a narrative strategy by which to fashion their warrior women as active participants on the political stage and as valued contributors to the social and political welfare of their homelands. While the tone of their works suggests an affinity with revolutionary politics, Caroline de la Motte Fouqué mobilizes the figure of the armed woman to argue for women's service to restore and bolster the monarchy and the return to a feudal order.

Female Sacrifice as Patriotism

A staunch supporter of the monarchy and fierce opponent of the French occupation of German territories under Napoleon, Fouqué appears at first glance to stand in stark contrast to the more politically liberal Huber and Günderrode. However, when one examines the figure of the warrior woman in Fouqué's 1816 historical novel *Das Heldenmädchen aus der Vendée* (*The Heroine of the Vendée*), the similarity between these three authors begins to crystallize. Although Fouqué mobilizes her protagonist to fight for the preservation of aristocratic values, the actions and character of her heroine apply pressure to socially prescribed myths of gender. By placing the aristocratic Elisabeth La Rochefoucault in the thick of the Vendée uprising and assigning her a critical role on the battlefield between royalists and republicans, Fouqué argues for woman's place at the table in the political arena.

Like Günderrode, Fouqué was born to an aristocratic family toward the end of the eighteenth century; however, in contrast, she grew up in a financially secure home affording her the luxury of stability, a basic education, and the opportunity of marriage.[63] At the age of fifteen, in the same year the French Revolution erupted, she married a young German officer and moved to Potsdam, where she gave birth to two children over the course of the next six years. After her husband committed suicide, Fouqué married the poet Friedrich Baron de la Motte Fouqué in 1803 and settled down at her family's estate at Nennhausen in Brandenburg.[64] Here Caroline's father, Friedrich Wilhelm August von Briest, had created a haven for authors and philosophers that Caroline and Friedrich continued with their circle of Romantic friends.[65] This creative environment not only provided inspiration for Fouqué by offering her the opportunity to engage in discussion with her literary contemporaries, but it also enabled her to establish herself as an author in her own right.

Furthermore, the surrounding political climate also shaped the views expressed in her novels and essays: like many of her contemporaries, Fouqué was informed about the events unfolding across the border in France and also witnessed firsthand the violent impact of the French occupation on Prussia.[66] After the Prussian defeat at Jena in 1806, the Fouqués were forced to quarter French soldiers during the occupation, an experience which had a profound impact on Fouqué.[67] In 1813 Fouqué fully supported her husband and two sons' decision to join the Prussian Army in the fight against Napoleon in the Wars of Liberation. As scholars have observed, Fouqué's 1812 essay *Ruf an die deutschen Frauen* (*A Call to German Women*), which emerged out of the growing patriotic fervor in Prussia against the French, expresses Fouqué's knowledge of and active engagement in current political events and efforts to support an emerging nation.[68] In this essay, Fouqué ascribes German women a crucial role in this process by calling upon them to support the cause through personal sacrifice. As Wilde and others have noted, Fouqué answered Princess Marianne's 1813 call to the women of Prussia to contribute both financially and personally in support of the war effort.[69] Fouqué's essay, as well as her novel discussed below, argue for women's inclusion in the public life of the emerging nation based on what Baumgartner calls the concept of sociability. She suggests that Fouqué appropriates the conservative views about gender roles espoused by social theorists in order to argue that women are "fundamental to the welfare of the public sphere."[70] In other words, the maternal "nature" of women was no longer grounds for their exclusion from public life; rather, their roles as nurturer, caregiver, and educator justified and even necessitated women's inclusion. However, the forms of patriotic activism Fouqué envisions in *Ruf an die deutschen Frauen*, based exclusively on woman's role as wife, mother, and hearth-keeper, stands in contrast—at least on the surface—to that of her protagonist Elisabeth in her novel from 1816.

Drawing on the upheaval of the not-so-distant past, Fouqué selects the tumultuous context of the French Revolution as the stage for her historical novel *Das Heldenmädchen aus der Vendée* upon which her patriotic female protagonist makes her debut. Fouqué highlights the persecution and plight of royalist supporters under the chaotic and bloody regime of the revolutionary factions. In doing so, the author foregrounds the threat to society and the individual that is wrought by the violence of the Revolution. In *Heldenmädchen*, Fouqué criticizes the unjust oppression of the citizens of the Vendée, both aristocracy and commoners alike, and their fight against the Republic under Jacobin rule as well as the Reign of Terror carried out by the Montagnards under Robespierre. Read through the lens of Prussia's occupation by Napoleonic forces, Krimmer argues that the novel highlights Fouqué's emphasis on women's contributions to the national cause.[71] Fouqué's *Jungfrau in Waffen* (maiden in arms) symbolizes the struggle of the Vendeans and their commitment to defending the monarchy and all that it represents. Through the trope of the warrior woman, Fouqué suggests the critical role women can play in defeating the threat from abroad in order to preserve political and social stability.[72]

Fouqué's two-volume narrative, set during the royalist insurrection of 1793–94 in the western region of France known as the Vendée, tells the story of the young, orphaned aristocrat Elisabeth, whose love for king and country—as well as her brave cousin Prince Talmont—cause her to don men's clothing, take up arms, and rush headlong into the Vendée skirmishes under the assumed identity Georg von Rochefoucault. Fighting alongside Talmont and her uncle, the Duke de la Tremouille, Elisabeth is transformed by the prince and entire royalist movement into a kind of talisman. Bearing the royalist flag, Elisabeth repeatedly rallies the troops to fight and leads them fearlessly into one battle after another, with varying outcomes. By the close of the first part of the novel, the royalist forces have suffered repeated losses to the republican troops, Elisabeth has been wounded, captured by the enemy, and rescued by Talmont. In the final scenes of part 1, Talmont is taken prisoner after the defeat at Granville and executed before a revolutionary firing squad. Elisabeth vows to uphold her promise to Talmont to carry on his legacy by aiding the cause. Part 2 opens with Elisabeth, accompanied by the young priest Silvanus, on the shores of England, where she travels in search of Talmont's friend and fellow soldier Colonel Sombreuil, who is gathering English support for another royalist attack. Returning to the French coast of Burgundy, Elisabeth, Sombreuil, and a host of other historical figures occupy an island fortress, where they are ultimately besieged and defeated. After fighting valiantly in the final battle, the fates of the royalist commanders alongside whom Elisabeth appears on the battlefield foreshadow the eventual demise of the cause: Elisabeth dies on the cliffs of the island at the base of the crucifix that she and the young priest have erected, Count Damas commits suicide by riding his horse off the same cliff, and Sombreuil negotiates the surrender of his troops and sacrifices himself for their safety, only to be betrayed one last time by the National Convention, who orders his death and that of his entire army. It is only Silvanus who emerges unscathed from the conflict and is reported to have sailed to the shores of "Amerikas Freistaaten" (CMF, 2:201; America's free states).[73]

Running simultaneously to the story of Elisabeth, a.k.a. Georg, in the Vendée is the subplot involving Elisabeth's aunt, the Marquise Robillard, and the political intrigue of the republican factions. Robillard acts as a foil to Elisabeth, and her behavior repeatedly serves to cast the actions of the novel's heroine in a positive light: whereas Elisabeth engages in the military conflicts in the Vendée in hopes of achieving a favorable outcome for restoring the king to power, the marquise's strategies to rescue the monarchy via political intrigue and by joining forces with the ousted Girondist deputies are portrayed as futile and misguided.[74] Responding to the marquise's vain and irrational behavior when the duke and prince accompany the two women to the safety of Talmont's estate—the marquise packs every single possession she owns, leaving no room for Elisabeth in the carriage—the duke expounds on women's unsuitability for politics and involvement in the public sphere:

> Frauen, fuhr er, sich zu den Uebrigen wendend fort, wälzen im Geiste Staaten um, stützen oder stürzen Throne, bewaffnen ganze Völker,

> möchten Krieg und Schlacht nur sogleich vor der Thüre haben, und können den Fuß nicht über die kleinste Erdscholle setzen, ohne den ganzen, langen Schweif lächerlicher Gewohnheiten hinter sich drein zu schleppen, und so das Wespennest häuslicher Sorgen über uns auszuschütten. Zeiten wie diese passen nicht für sie. Sie träumen viel davon, aber die Wirklichkeit hat ein allzustrenges Gesicht, sie erschrecken davor. (CMF, 1:27–28)
>
> Women, he continued, turning himself toward the others, imagine revolutionizing states, support or overthrow thrones, arm entire peoples, desire to have war and battle at their doorsteps, and cannot bring themselves to step over the smallest clod of dirt, without dragging the entire, long retinue of silly habits behind them, and thereby pouring out the hornets' nest of domestic worries over us. Such times as these are not suitable for them. They dream about it a lot, but reality has an all too severe face, which frightens them.

The marquise embodies all the negative attributes ascribed to women by late eighteenth-century social theorists and mobilized to justify their exclusion from the public sphere. Elisabeth, however, due to her demeanor and actions both on and off the battlefield, stands in contrast to the marquise as an empowering model of female activism and women's patriotic contribution to the political cause and welfare of the country. She continually demonstrates that she is just as capable as her male counterparts, whether it be riding a horse (CMF, 1:30), expressing her patriotism and readiness to die for king and country (CMF, 1:25, 155–56), or charging fearlessly into battle (CMF, 1:130–31). Her display of bravery and loyalty after her first foray into battle causes the duke to alter his views on women in the public sphere: "So pries er die Frauen in ihrer reinen Selbstverleugnung, und wie dies Himmelschild sich so stark und schirmend auf ihre Brust lege, daß sie der ernsten Lebensgefahr ohne sonderliche Anstrengung trotzen. Gewiß, setzte er gerührt hinzu, ihre Waffen sind nicht von dieser Welt!" (CMF, 1:137; "And so he extolled women for their pure self-denial, and how this shield of heaven rested so heavily and protectively on their breast, that they defied the gravest deadly peril without particular effort. Indeed, he added touched, their weapons are not of this world!"). Although the novel casts Elisabeth in a far better light than the marquise, both the prince and duke attribute her extraordinary and uncharacteristically feminine bravery to a higher power. Fouqué, I argue, strategically undermines Elisabeth's agency and presence in the public sphere by emphasizing the supernatural aspect of her actions, thereby allowing her to appear passive. In doing so, the author circumvents potential negative criticism of her heroine's behavior as transgressive and instead creates a nonthreatening example of woman's participation in the public sphere of war that contributes to the defense and welfare of the nation. Furthermore, the novel's repeated references to Elisabeth as a modern Joan of Arc elevates the protagonist's actions: Elisabeth does not belong to the regular class of soldier; instead, she is imbued with supernatural significance as a guardian angel, who takes an active role in watching over the prince while simultaneously rallying his troops to do the "real" fighting (CMF, 1:100). In another instance, she is elevated above the base bloodshed of war and assigned the role of peacemaker by the prince (CMF, 1:133). In both cases, Elisabeth's relationship to the act of war remains a passive one.

Like Huber and Günderrode, Fouqué mobilizes conservative attitudes about gender, here playing off of the passive nature of the "feminine ideal" and notions of female sacrifice in order to depict a non-threatening image of women's activism in service of the country's defense. Elisabeth's love for her king, and the prince, are depicted as justifications for her entrance into the public realm of war. Fouqué justifies Elisabeth's entrance into the sphere of warfare because she defends "patriarchal values."[75] While Krimmer asserts that Elisabeth's tragic fate signals that "'Natural' gender can only be restored through the death of the cross-dressed heroine,"[76] it would be disingenuous for Elisabeth to survive the Vendée battles when all the other generals and soldiers were put to death. Elisabeth's death, I argue, does not result from her failure to transcend gender norms; rather, Fouqué portrays her warrior woman dying a heroic death like her male counterparts and making the ultimate sacrifice for the cause. Elisabeth's special status as talisman, guardian angel, and supporter, that is, as indirect, passive participant on the battlefield, creates a space for women in the affairs of the country. Her role neither requires nor involves active fighting—she is, after all, merely a flag bearer.[77] Elisabeth's own decision to take up the royalist banner and charge into battle is depicted as an unconscious decision:

> Sich selber nicht bewußt, weder denkend noch wollend, hatte Elisabeth einem neben ihr Haltenden die weiße Fahne aus der Hand gerissen. Wie ein Blitz theilte sie die Reihen. [. . .] Ihre Hand zitterte nicht, sie konnte den Schaft, an welchem das Panier befestigt war, hoch in die Luft schwingen. Verlaßt Eure Fahne nicht, Vendéer, rief sie mit klarer Engelstimme, pflanzt sie auf die Mauern von Chantonnay. Rettet die Ehre Frankreichs! Vertilgt die Gottes- und Königsleugner! Vorwärts, Vendéer! Vorwärts! Gott und der Heiland sind unter uns! (CMF, 1:130–31).

> Unaware of herself, neither thinking nor wanting to, Elisabeth had ripped the white flag out of the hand of the bearer next to her. Like lightning she parted the ranks. [. . .] Her hand did not tremble. She could swing the shaft, upon which the banner was attached, high in the air. Do not leave your flag, Vendeans, she shouted with a clear angel's voice, plant it on the walls of Chantonnay. Rescue France's

> honor! Destroy the atheists and anti-monarchists! Forward, Vendeans! Forward! God and savior are among us!

Elisabeth's actions are reflexive as opposed to calculated and intentional: it is her shared love for the fatherland that involuntarily moves her to rally the troops. Fouqué depicts female patriotism and the desire to fight for the nation's cause as natural and pure. Such a portrait of the patriotic woman warrior aligns with those of Günderrode, while patriotism for Huber's figure arises as a kind of unintentional consequence resulting from the personal motivation driving her decision to enter the public sphere of warfare.

At the heart of Elisabeth's motivation to die for the royalist cause is her love for king and country as well as her love for the prince.[78] However, like Schiller's Johanna, Elisabeth is forced to sacrifice her youthful dreams of personal love and a life of domestic bliss in order to pursue her higher calling on the battlefield. During a lull in the war, Elisabeth and the prince return to his estate to steel themselves for the next battle. With her emotions strained by the recent bloodshed, Elisabeth finds comfort in the quiet, familiar security of the domestic surroundings. At the same time, the path her life has taken gives her pause as she realizes the unalterable consequences of her actions:

> Doch jetzt in der Waffenstille, in den heimisch eig'nen Mauern des Geliebten, allein mit ihm, vom sanften Frieden der Häuslichkeit angewehet, das eine Dach all ihr Erdenglück umschließend,—jetzt brach es in ihr los, jetzt riefen tausend verworrene Stimmen in ihr: Du junges Kind! Deine Bestimmung ist dennoch verfehlt, bereuen darfst Du nichts, doch beweinen—beweinen wirst Du's lebenslang. Das Band, das Dich mit Deinem schönen Freund verbindet, ist eigener, den Lebensformen fremd gebliebener Natur geworden, die Myrthe ward zum Lorbeer in Deiner Hand, Du wandelst ihn nicht wieder um! (CMF, 1:225)

> And yet amid the ceasefire, in the familiar walls of her beloved's home, only with him, overcome by the gentle peace of domesticity, the one roof surrounding all of her earthly happiness—now it began to break free within her, now a thousand confusing voices shouted within her: you young child! Your purpose is mistaken all the same, you must not regret anything; yet, mourn—you will mourn your entire life. The band that binds you with your beautiful friend has become something of its own, unlike any living forms. The myrtle wreath was transformed into the laurel wreath in your hand; you cannot turn it back again!

In contrast to Huber's Sara, there is no way home for Elisabeth: she has exchanged the myrtle wreath of a young bride for the laurel wreath of martial victory (CMF, 1:228). On the one hand, Elisabeth processes her own actions as transgressive and "unnatural," but in the next instance she comes to terms with her fate and takes consolation in the belief that she has sacrificed her personal desire for a higher cause and will fight and die side-by-side with the prince. The prince, however, has other plans for his "angel of peace" and "messenger of peace," ordering her to complete the mission he cannot and to become his "*höheres besseres Ich!*" (CMF, 1:232; *greater better self!*). The prince and Elisabeth are bound by their patriotic love: a love that takes precedence over their own personal desires. By presenting Elisabeth's public participation as fulfilling the prince's plans, her presence on the battlefield is sanctioned by the story's patriarchal authority. Fouqué justifies woman's right to contribute, be it on the battlefield or in patriotic clubs, to the defense of the nation and the destruction of the enemy.

Fouqué, like her counterparts, avails her heroine of cross-dressing as a means by which to enter the public sphere of battle. As in Huber's *Familie Seldorf*, Elisabeth's decision to cross-dress, but also to expose her masquerade, is strategic. She disguises herself as the young soldier Georg in order to circumvent the laws and social norms preventing her from fighting alongside the prince in pursuit of their shared mission to restore the king to his throne. By revealing her heroine's "true identity" to the prince and duke, as well as to Sombreuil, Fouqué never permits her reader to fully forget that Elisabeth is a woman, whose compassion and love give her the strength and bravery necessary to fight and die for the royalist cause. Nevertheless, Elisabeth's femininity is highlighted also by the simultaneous failure of her masquerade. Even before Elisabeth reveals her identity to Sombreuil, he already discerns that he is dealing with a woman: "Schweigend lag sein Auge auf dem tief erschütterten Wesen, das so erhaben und so zart des Geschlechtes Eigenthümlichkeit unverkennbar verrieth" (CMF, 2:54; "Silently his eye rested on the deeply unsettled creature, that unmistakably betrayed so sublimely and so gently the singularity of its gender"). The success of her masquerade is undermined by her inability to completely hide or suppress her feminine emotions.[79] Yet, the revelation of Elisabeth's gender hardly troubles the male characters and only temporarily gives them cause to doubt her suitability for the battlefield (CMF, 1:155–56). In fact, after revealing her identity to Sombreuil, she allays any concerns he might have that her temporary moment of emotionality might get in the way of her mission: "wer kämpfen will, muß sich zuerst selbst bekämpfen. Ich thue es schon, ich bin gleich wieder still und gefaßt" (CMF, 2:57; "Whoever wants to fight, must first defeat themselves. I am already doing it, soon I will be calm and composed once more").

Whether woman's love for king and country took the form of personal sacrifice and volunteerism in patriotic clubs or in rallying their male counterparts to heroic deeds on the battlefield, Fouqué envisioned German women's direct contribution to the political and military defeat of their French enemies. Kontje draws the line at suggesting that Fouqué's depiction of gender roles makes her a "feminist activist who demands equal rights for all women at all times. Yet she does allow a few exceptional women to bend the rules in exceptional circumstances, provided they remain loyal to their families, act with decorum, and—as in the case of Elisabeth—do not particularly enjoy masquerading as a man."[80] While Fouqué does not demand equal rights for all women, she promotes an image of female activism by resignifying the rhetorical strategies used to condemn the warrior woman and women who asserted themselves in the political realm. By stressing the feminine nature of her heroine, Fouqué circumnavigates claims of sexual depravity and moral corruption lodged against women who sought to make themselves heard in the public sphere. And despite the affinity that Fouqué's warrior woman shares with Naubert's heroines Thekla von Thurn and Philippe von Geldern—neither are ever completely comfortable with their male personas nor are their attempts at passing truly successful—Fouqué does not return her protagonist safely to the domestic sphere of marital bliss and motherhood; instead, she offers her armed maiden a heroic death on the battlefield similar, if not more noble, than her male counterparts in the text. After all, those who flee and survive are branded as cowards, Sombreuil is hanged, and even Prince Talmont dies before a firing squad instead of fighting with his last breath for the royalist cause on the battlefield. While I agree with Krimmer's claim that Elisabeth's death as a cross-dresser restores "'natural' gender,"[81] I also read Elisabeth's death as one of heroism securing her a place in the annals of history, albeit on the losing side, next to the male royalist martyrs.

The provocative themes of love and sacrifice woven into the texts by Huber, Günderrode, and Fouqué highlight the ruptures inherent in the myth of separate spheres and complicate eighteenth- and early nineteenth-century notions that woman's "inclination" to love foreclosed her public contribution to the welfare of her country. At the same time the narrative strategies mobilized by these authors to conflate the protagonists' love of family (father, brother, lover) with patriotic love of their homeland (fatherland)[82] carefully probe the tension and inextricable link between the personal and the political. In these literary works, personal relationships and sentiments of love are transformed into the motivation and justification *for* woman's entrance into battle in defense of both personal and public interests. In reimagining woman as armed warrior, the works by Huber, Günderrode, and Fouqué present another myth of femininity that unsettles the dominant narrative of woman's inherently "passive" nature. These fictional warlike heroines betray the complexity of gender roles and their corresponding spheres of activity that appear all too often as natural and fixed in the literary works of their counterparts and in the conservative rhetoric of social theorists. In doing so, they contribute another distinct layer of meaning to the image of the violent woman that further secures the ambiguous status of the warlike woman around 1800. These new female patriots presented their authors and female readers with the chance to explore their emancipatory fantasies that remained tenuous at best in their daily lives. Indeed, warrior women such as Eleonore Prochaska (1785–1813), Anna Lühring (1796–1866), and Friederike Krüger (1789–1848), who fought to defend German territories against the French during the Napoleonic Wars, serve as striking examples of women who not only fantasized about but also altered their reality by demonstrating woman's rightful place on the battlefield in defense of her home and homeland.

Chapter Five

✦

Treasonous Transgressions

A Nation of Women Warriors and the Politics of Desire

> Es ist wahr, mein innerstes Wesen liegt darin [*Penthesilea*], und Sie haben es wie eine Seherin aufgefaßt: der ganze Schmutz zugleich und Glanz meiner Seele.
>
> —Heinrich von Kleist (HKB, 4:397–98)

In a letter to his childhood friend Adolphine von Werdeck, the controversial nineteenth-century German author and dramatist Heinrich von Kleist (1777–1811) writes of his half-sister Ulrike: "O es giebt kein Wesen in der Welt, das ich so ehre, wie meine Schwester. Aber welchen Mißgrif hat die Natur begangen, als sie ein Wesen bildete, das weder Mann noch Weib ist, u gleichsam wie eine Amphibie zwischen zwei Gattungen schwankt?" (HKB, 4:253; "There is no being in the world that I respect more than my sister. But what mistake did Nature commit, when she created a being that is neither man nor woman and which fluctuates, as it were, like an amphibian between two genera?"). This frequently quoted 1801 letter conveys Kleist's simultaneous fascination with and apprehension about his amphibolic sister, whose contradictory nature rendered unstable the author's firm belief in the immutability of gender. Ulrike's impressive display of androgynous qualities elicits her brother's utmost respect: "Wo ein Anderer überlegt, da entschließt sie sich, u wo er spricht, da handelt sie. [. . .] Wo ein andrer fühlt, da denkt sie, u wo er genießt, da will sie sich unterrichten" (HKB, 4:254; "In instances where another person deliberates, she is decisive. Where another speaks, she acts. [. . .] Where another feels, she thinks, and where another savors, she wants to inform herself").[1] Indeed, as Kleist concludes, his sister's only transgression is that she transcends the limitations of her sex. Yet at the same time, in a letter from May 1799 Kleist censures his sister for refusing to fulfill what he and conservative contemporaries asserted was woman's "höchst[e] Bestimmung" (greatest purpose) and "heiligst[e] Pflicht" (most sacred duty), namely motherhood (HKB, 4:43). In the wake of Kleist's 1801 "Kant-Krise" (Kant crisis), in which his entire foundation for rational thought and perspective had been shaken to the core, his inability to "know" his sister as either feminine or masculine—and for that matter, how to classify and categorize his own desires within the existing grid of social propriety—proved unsettling.

Kleist's correspondence has been heavily mined by literary scholars in their attempts to decipher the enigmatic author's seemingly impenetrable corpus. In particular, Kleist's letters to female contemporaries, including his fiancé Wilhelmine von Zenge, his half-sister Ulrike, and friends von Werdeck and Karoline von Schlieben, have proved particularly fertile ground for scholarly inquiries into the author's ambivalent attitude about gender at the beginning of the nineteenth century. If Kleist's letters illustrate that he shared the dominant views around 1800 about gender's polarity and the bifurcation of public and private spheres along gendered lines,[2] then the fraught depiction of gender transgressions embodied by the nation of women warriors and their defiant Amazon queen along with the unconventional, seemingly "unmanly" actions of the heroic Greek warrior in Kleist's 1808 tragedy *Penthesilea* complicates this binarism and necessitates further critical engagement.[3]

The inversion of the mythic encounter between the star-crossed warriors during the Trojan War signals a renegotiation of the intricate webs between gender and power, individual and state. This literary intervention in issues of hierarchy, domination, and rebellion is informed by the culture of warfare, which dominated the political landscape of Europe for the majority of Kleist's life. His treatment of the Penthesilea myth and depiction of transgressive forms of femininity positioned alongside unsettling images of the disarmed, vulnerable male warrior probes the ominous region between reactionary and emancipatory visions of femininity and collapses dominant narratives of masculinity.[4] By altering the fates of his warriors, Kleist not only gives voice to deep-seated apprehension about the destructive effects of warfare on the foundations of society, but more specifically he explores the complex constellation linking gender and the culture of war undergirding German society during the most critical and defining period in its gradual transformation into a modern state.[5] In Kleist's hands, Penthesilea actively asserts herself in and renders vulnerable the "masculine" political sphere of warfare, while Achilles adopts a submissive position on the battlefield unbefitting the male warrior and transgressing the rules of engagement. These violations, which result in the protagonists' deaths, call attention to the disruptive and devastating toll of war at every level of society. At the same time the internal and external conflicts emerging from the matriarchal nation of warriors reads as a cautionary tale about the dangers of unregulated passions and desires threatening to undermine entrenched social and political structures.

Kleist composed and completed *Penthesilea* between the Fourth and Fifth Coalition Wars (1806–07; 1809) during which time Napoleon's forces defeated Prussian troops and established a decisive victory over Austria, inducing the demise of the already weakened Holy Roman Empire and ushering in a period of French control of German territories.[6] While Kleist's political stance toward the Prussian military system and the ideals of the French Revolution remains a source of contention among scholars, most agree that events surrounding the Coalition Wars transformed Kleist into a staunch opponent of Napoleon and his policies.[7] Kleist's disaffection with the French occupation ultimately resulted in his "elementares Engagement für die Heimat" ("elementary engagement for the homeland").[8] As Wolf Kittler and others have readily demonstrated, many of Kleist's works can be read through the lens of political occupation and foreign usurpation resulting in the simultaneous imposition of repressive systems of power and the collapse of preexisting social structures.[9] Specifically, Elisabeth Krimmer has examined the manifestation of Kleist's vitriol for the French in politically charged works such as his essay "Katechismus der Deutschen abgefasst nach dem Spanischen, zum Gebrauch für Kinder und Alte" ("Catechism of the Germans adapted from the Spanish, for Use by Children and the Elderly," 1809) and the poems "Germania an ihre Kinder" ("Germania to Her Children," composed 1809 and first published 1813) and "Kriegslied der Deutschen" ("Battle Song of the Germans," 1809), whose political messages turn on the imagery of the feminized political body.[10] Kleist's poem "Germania an ihre Kinder" appears to promote a traditional, conservative model of maternal patriotism, in which male warriors are inspired by their love of family and "motherland" to take up arms in her defense.[11] However, the maternal Germania's call to arms simultaneously conceives of woman as instigator and advocate of death and destruction. This seemingly contradictory depiction of women's involvement in times of war permeates Kleist's dramatic vision of a matriarchal state of women warriors in *Penthesilea*. By the time Kleist had completed his tragedy *Penthesilea* in the late fall of 1807,[12] he had already accurately predicted the public's equivocal response to the violent, brutal conclusion of the play (HKB, 4:395–96). What exactly was it about this work that Kleist anticipated would evoke both horror and empathy in the reading public? In an attempt to answer this question, scholars have addressed the potentially unconventional aspects of *Penthesilea*: Kleist's challenge to the established and accepted form of the classical tragedy and aesthetics; Penthesilea's inhumane cannibalistic attack on Achilles that contravened Enlightenment ideals; and the Amazons' clear challenge to gender norms deemed acceptable by a majority of early nineteenth-century German readers, to name but only a few.[13]

More urgently, Kleist's *Penthesilea* raises questions about the conflict that emerges between the individual and the state when individuals no longer conform to and ultimately challenge social norms and established structures of power while questioning the viability of a state founded upon and sustained by a culture of warfare. Of particular interest are Penthesilea and Achilles's attempts to place personal desire above public duty to their respective states and the implications of their defiance of the strictly defined roles demanded by these competing cultures of war. Similarly, Ritchie Robertson reads Kleist's drama as "exploring the possibility of a radically different social order" while simultaneously highlighting the threat of "individual passion" to the stability of that very order.[14] Furthermore, the affinity between Kleist's depiction of the Amazon warriors and that of late eighteenth- and early nineteenth-century female revolutionaries has invited productive readings of Kleist's play within the context of the gender debates and the culture of war around 1800.[15]

My critical engagement with Kleist's new version of the Penthesilea myth is anchored around the function of myth and what his vision of the Amazon nation tells us about German society's own attitudes about gender roles and cultures of warfare at the turn of the century. At work in Kleist's drama are multiple layers of myth with varying objectives. In the most traditional sense, Kleist's tragedy draws upon Greek mythology as a literary genre for describing the customs of ancient peoples in Western civilization. At the same time, myth also operates as a strategy by which individuals attempt to apprehend the mysteries and assign order to the chaos of the world in which they live. Furthermore, myth is treated as an ideologically driven process of signification that attempts to create dominant narratives at a specific historical moment. By unpacking these layers of myth informing Kleist's depiction of this nation of women warriors, and more specifically the Amazon queen, we can begin to decipher what the author's tragic narrative conveys about the complex constellation linking the gendered individual to the state and to practices of war within the fraught context of early nineteenth-century Germany.

While scholars have suggested reading Kleist's drama as a progressive subversion of eighteenth- and nineteenth-century gender norms,[16] I argue that the fates of these women warriors, as well as the Greek hero Achilles, render such an interpretation problematic. Kleist casts his Amazon queen Penthesilea, who asserts her active female body in the political sphere, as a destructive rather than a generative force. Penthesilea's death forecloses her continued existence both in her public role as the leader of the Amazon nation as well as her role as armed combatant in the battle to sustain the matriarchal society. While the violated bodies of the Scythian women serve as the motivation for female insurrection and as bodies that refuse to be reabsorbed into the patriarchal structure, the Amazons' rebellion by establishing an independent, matriarchal state ultimately fails because the women warriors merely mimic the society and norms from which they attempted to free themselves. Furthermore, Penthesilea and Achilles's attempts to liberate themselves from their societies' rigid structures and conventions simultaneously point to the individual's struggle to assert successfully her or his will over the will of the state but also the tragic implications of a state whose existence and vitality is predicated upon the perpetuation of sanctioned acts of violence.

As French revolutionary women took to the National Convention to demand their rights, including the right to bear arms, Germans sought to stave off similar scenes by cultivating gender myths that served reactionary social and political agendas. In his investigation of the Amazon myth in Athenian culture, William Blake Tyrrell defines myth as a means by which individuals attempt to apprehend the world around them: "Myths tend to deal with sources of conflict and tension in the social order and human condition. Their function is to elicit responses to their explanations in the minds and emotions of their receptors in order to obfuscate, circumvent, or mediate those conflicts and tensions."[17] Furthermore, Tyrrell argues that the Athenian myth of the Amazons is based on a division of the public and private spheres along gendered lines, but that there is also a distinction between the female and the feminine, with the feminine being positively associated with the process of acculturation.[18] German culture around 1800 resembles in many telling ways this same gendered division of public and private life and the invention of a "feminine ideal" that is firmly located in the domestic sphere. Treatises by the likes of Fichte, Brandes, and Wilhelm von Humboldt solidified and perpetuated a gendered social hierarchy by emphasizing the purported physical and psychological differences between the sexes and branding deviations from these "norms" as unnatural and dangerous. As Simon Richter notes in his discussion of Tyrrell and Josine Blok, the Amazon myths invoked by such theorists exploited and articulated male fears of destructive female sexuality and desire.[19] Their efforts to fix gender as a stable, unchanging truth was aided, in part, by the deployment of images of violent, transgressive femininity such as scenes of unruly, cannibalistic French female revolutionaries reported by Konrad Engelbert Oelsner. Erotically charged depictions of these disobedient women emerged, not surprisingly, alongside the military conflicts and sociopolitical upheaval that spanned Kleist's brief existence.[20]

The exclusion of women from participation in the public sphere, including sites of armed conflict, has traditionally rested on a myth of "Nature." In his examination of the function of myth in contemporary society, French theorist Roland Barthes asserts the historical quality of any single myth: "Ancient or not, mythology can only have an historical foundation, for myth is a type of speech chosen by history: it cannot possibly evolve from the 'nature' of things."[21] Yet, at the same time, the power of myth relies on its ability to obfuscate its historicalness, to liberate itself from its history, and to appear as a naturalized truth, thereby "transform[ing] history into nature."[22] This process of naturalization is boundless, in that myth is always changing, mutating, and adapting in order to insinuate itself into the historical and cultural moment appearing as an always already phenomenon. Thus, myths such as "feminine" and "masculine" or "public" and "private" and the attributes associated with them remain unquestioned, readily accepted, and easily transformed into ideology. Barthes's concept of myth is useful in understanding how myths of an "ideal femininity" and an "ideal masculinity" constructed in literary, scientific, and social discourses were manifested in commonly held "truths." Not surprisingly, the proliferation of the woman warrior in German culture coincided with the destabilization of social and political norms in France, its border regions, and even within German territories west of the Rhine, such as Mainz. As I have argued, the figure of the woman warrior in the Age of Goethe served as a site of contestation in this ideological struggle to perpetuate or undermine the gender status quo and bifurcated hierarchy of public and private spheres.

The Amazon Myth in German Culture around 1800

Greek and Roman culture was held in high esteem by German scholars, authors, and artists, including Kleist. The celebrated art historian and archaeologist Johann Joachim Winckelmann's intense engagement with Greek and Roman art had profound implications for the aesthetic theories of German authors and philosophers from Gotthold Ephraim Lessing to Johann Wolfgang von Goethe. Indeed, Goethe and Schiller's entire aesthetic program emphasized harmony and humanity founded upon Goethe's interpretation of Greek antiquity that was mediated in part by Winckelmann's works.[23] Early Romantics, such as Friedrich Schlegel and Friedrich Creuzer, continued to feed and shape the German fascination with Greek myth in their essays and literary works well into the nineteenth century. But more importantly, perhaps, is the question of how Kleist exploited Greek myth to construct his own narrative about the fractured times in which he lived.

Set during the Trojan War, Kleist's *Penthesilea* envisions the mythic encounter of the Greek warrior Achilles and the Amazon queen Penthesilea. In his telling of the epic military campaign, the Trojans are embroiled in battle with the Greeks over the abduction of Helen. While on the battlefield, the Greek forces are surprised by the presence of a third group of warriors. Led by their queen, Penthesilea, the warring women have come not to aid the Trojans in their efforts to fend off the Greeks; instead, they turn their weapons against both Greek and Trojan soldiers. Unbeknownst to her warriors, and appearing to transgress Amazon law, Penthesilea has come to capture and subdue the Greek hero Achilles.[24] The drama develops as a struggle for domination between its two central figures Achilles and Penthesilea. These warriors engage in fierce back-and-forth confrontations, during which each one alternately appears on the verge of either domination or submission. Throughout the battle, the skilled combatants fall in love with one another but struggle to understand and accept their emotions. These personal desires stand in conflict with their identities as fearless warriors, the rules of military engagement and warfare, and specifically the customs of their respective cultures. Achilles's defeat at the hands—or more accurately teeth—of Penthesilea arises from a misunderstanding between the would-be lovers: Achilles feigns defeat in order to become Penthesilea's captive for the Rose Festival; however, Penthesilea misreads the signs and interprets his challenge to battle as a rejection of her affection. Blinded by the stinging betrayal, she, with her dogs of war at her side, sets upon the unarmed Achilles and devours him. The Amazon queen is driven to madness by her grief, which becomes the figurative dagger that pierces her heart, allowing her to join Achilles in death.

Kleist invents a radically new account of the mythic encounter between the star-crossed warriors that departs from the more common version found, for example, in the first book of Quintus of Smyrna's epic poem *Posthomerica*. Instead, it privileges in part the less established myth in which Penthesilea defeats the Greek hero only to be slain by him upon his resurrection. As philologist Manfred Fuhrmann has argued, Kleist's dramatic portrayal of Penthesilea is not a revision of an existing Greek mythology, because there are no myths that present the encounter between Penthesilea and Achilles in quite the same manner.[25] Even the uncommon variation of the Penthesilea myth results in her death at the hands of the reanimated hero. The ancient narrative most closely resembling Kleist's drama is one delivered by Ptolemaeus Chennus (around 100 A.D.). The sources providing Kleist information about the Amazons and Penthesilea, in other words ancient myths involving the Amazons as well as descriptions of their customs and practices, served only as a general framework for the dramatist's radical vision.[26]

Kleist and his contemporaries were well-versed in Greek mythology. More specifically, as Daria Santini's more recent investigation of the Amazon myth in German culture of the eighteenth and nineteenth centuries reveals, they were familiar with myths concerning the woman warrior.[27] In particular, Santini cites the prevalence of Penthesilea in visual culture, essays on Greek and Roman art, and encyclopedia entries on mythology encountered by these authors in their studies of antiquity.[28] Among the eighteenth-century scholarly treatments of Greek myth, Benjamin Hederich's popular encyclopedia of Greek mythology, *Gründliches Lexicon mythologicum*,[29] which includes detailed entries for the terms "Amazones" and "Penthesilea," served as a primary source for Kleist's drama.[30] Additionally, scholars have suggested that Kleist's Amazon state shares an affinity with the one described by Pompeius Trogus, pointing toward Kleist's familiarity with Marie Claude Guyon's *Histoire des Amazones* (*History of the Amazons*, 1714)—translated into German by D. J. G. Krünitz in 1763—in which Pompeius Trogus's detailed description is recounted.[31] The similarities between Kleist and Quintus of Smyrna's narratives of the Amazon queen, particularly the comparisons of Penthesilea to destructive forces of nature, also suggests Kleist's possible knowledge of his *Posthomerica*, among other sources.

Hederich's entries "Amazones" and "Penthesilea" shed light on Kleist's informed portrayal of the Amazon nation. The passage on Amazons provides extensive information—its accuracy debated by scholars—ranging from a discussion of the etymology of the name, the alleged origins of the various tribes, their weapons and clothing, and addressing the likelihood of their existence.[32] Hederich documents several possibilities for the origins of the Amazon name, including the custom of removing young girls' right breasts at birth in order to improve their use of weapons,[33] a prominent feature of Penthesilea's narration of the birth story of the Amazon nation in Kleist's tragedy.

Informative for Kleist would have been the sections Hederich dedicated to Amazon tribes' domestic customs and martial practices. Under the subsection "Lebens-Art" (Lifestyle), the reader is informed about the various myths surrounding the propagation of the tribes and the role men, or in some cases lack of men, play in Amazon society. While he acknowledges that some tribes live entirely without male members, Hederich spends the majority of this section focusing on those tribes in which men still reside:

> Sie formirten in *Asien* und *Africa* besondere Königreiche, indem sie ihre eigene Königinnen hatten, litten anbey, nach einigen, kein Manns-Volck unter sich, sondern, damit doch auch ihr Geschlecht nicht untergehen möchte, begaben sie sich zu gewissen Zeiten an die Gräntzen ihrer Länder, da denn das Manns-Volck aus den benachbarten Landschaften sich auch einfande, und sie nach ihren Willen bediendte. Wenn sie darauf niederkamen, behielten sie die Mägdgen bey sich, die Knaben aber brachten sie um a), oder gaben sie, nach andern, ihren Vätern zurück b), oder, da sie auch nach noch andern ihre eigene Männer hatten, lähmeten sie denselben doch also fort in der Kindheit dergestalt Arme und Beine, daß sie keine Waffen führen, wohl aber zu geringen und sonst knechtischen Diensten geschickt blieben c). Hingegen brannten sie denen Mägdgen auf oben besagte Art die rechte Brust weg, unterrichteten sie darauf im Jagen, Reiten, Schiessen und dergleichen Krieges-Ubungen, bis sie die Waffen auch zu führen geschickt wurden d). Jedoch sollen die in *Africa* allerdings ihre Männer gehabt haben, die aber alle das in der Haushaltung thun musten, was anderweits denen Weibern oblieget; wogegen sie thaten, was sonst der Männer Verrichtungen sind. Zuförderst wurden diese durchaus zu keinen Kriegs-Händeln gezogen, oder auf einige Weise mit zur Verwaltung des Regimentes, oder dergleichen etwas gelassen, woher sie Gelegenheit nehmen können, das Weiber-Joch vom Halse zu schütteln.[34]

> In *Asia* and *Africa* they formed special kingdoms, in which they had their own queens. According to some, they did not tolerate any menfolk among them. However, in order to ensure that their lineage did not perish, they would adjourn to the borders of their lands at certain times of the year, when the menfolk from neighboring territories would also appear, and they would make use of them according to their wishes. Afterwards, when they gave birth, they retained the girls

> but killed the boys, or, according to others, gave them back to their fathers. According to still others, since they had their own men, they crippled the boys' legs and arms in their childhood to the extent that they could not bear arms. However, they remained capable of carrying out lowly and otherwise menial tasks. In contrast, they burned off the right breast of the young girls, in the manner mentioned above, instructed them in hunting, horse riding, shooting, and similar military exercises, until they had become skilled at bearing arms. Yet, the Amazons in *Africa* are supposed to have had their own men, who were forced to do everything in the household, which otherwise would fall to the women; while the women did the activities that elsewhere are for men. First and foremost, these men were not raised in any way for the business of war, nor were they permitted to participate in the management of the regiment or the likes, in which they could seize the opportunity to shake off the yoke of the women from their necks.

As his description informs the reader, traditional gender roles, as they existed in ancient Greek society, are inverted among certain Amazon tribes and men are forced to carry out menial tasks, while the women train and harden their bodies for battle. In order to maintain this "unnatural" gendered hierarchy, the men are not only physically mutilated and thereby made incapable of participating in battle, but they are also prevented from staging an uprising to overthrow the women. Through the act of mutilation, of both the male and female bodies, the Amazons defy "Nature" and biological differences in order to assert their will and maintain their positions of power. They not only level the metaphorical playing field but they also gain the upper hand. In instances in which no men are allowed to reside among the Amazons, the women are forced to seek out mates to ensure the future of their society. As Hederich later notes, only those Amazons who have proven themselves in battle by defeating an enemy are allowed to marry and bear children. Thus, the women's reproductive rights, and indeed suitability as mothers, is dependent on their prowess as warriors in combat and ability to dominate their male opponents both militarily and sexually. Such a society stands in polar opposition to that of both Greek antiquity and early nineteenth-century Germany, which makes Kleist's selection of subject matter and his radical dramatic vision all the more striking, and perhaps terrifying for his contemporaries.

Although the encyclopedia entry for Penthesilea is less extensive than that of the Amazons, it provides details about the differing accounts of the encounter between the queen and Achilles. Hederich notes the valiant battle waged by the Amazons and their ultimate defeat by the Greeks; however, most significant for this study is his final comment in the entry, in which he cites the less-common account of Penthesilea's death found in Photius's *Bibliotheca* and attributed to Ptolemaeus Chennus: "und da sie, nach wiederum andern, den *Achillem* erst selbst erleget haben soll, soll diese auf der *Tethidis*, seiner Mutter, Bitten, wieder lebendig geworden, und sodann erst noch die *Penthesileam* wieder hingerichtet haben"[35] ("and since she, according to still others, is supposed to have first defeated *Achilles*, who, upon the pleas of *Tethidis*, his mother, was resurrected, and only then executed *Penthesilea*"). This brief, nondescript reference to Penthesilea's defeat of Achilles appears to have caught Kleist's attention and offered the dramatist the space in which to construct a truly tragic encounter for both Penthesilea and Achilles.

The examination of Hederich's encyclopedia excavates the discourses of knowledge about the Penthesilea myths accessible to Kleist, but more importantly, it highlights the information he did not have and which he invented in his provocative rendering of the myth. Existing accounts served only as a basic sketch for Kleist's portrait of the Penthesilea-Achilles encounter, and it is the elements specific to his mythologizing of the woman warrior that offer critical inroads to deciphering Kleist's complicated engagement with and attempts to apprehend his world ravaged by the chaos of warfare. A reading of *Penthesilea* through Barthes's critical lens of mythification yields new insight into the potential implications of Kleist's use and unconventional interpretation of myth for questions of gender and violence in his own historical context. With his play, Kleist draws attention to the tension between the pursuit of individual desires and the maintenance of apparatuses of power, particularly during periods of military strife. The invention of a new Penthesilea-Achilles myth, in which Kleist allows his woman warrior not only to dominate but also to destroy the Greek paragon of the masculine warrior, gives voice to the author's ambivalence toward "deviant" forms of femininity, and their unsettling implications for notions of masculinity, and indeed society as a whole.[36]

The Nexus of Gender and Myth in Kleist's *Penthesilea*

Fraught with contradictions, Kleist's *Penthesilea* collapses meaning at every level. Achilles and Penthesilea defy the rules governing the practice of war as well as the customs and will of their people in pursuit of their desire for one another. This leads them to transgress against the gender roles of their respective societies, which places them in direct conflict with their individual states and forces them outside their boundaries. Penthesilea's insurrection lies not merely in her relentless pursuit of a specific enemy; far more transgressive is her privileging of love over pure, sexual desire. While sexual desire, aggression, and conquest appear as integral components of the culture of warfare for both the Greeks and Amazons, sentiments of love cannot be reconciled easily with the warrior identity and the demands of the battlefield, an issue Schiller had similarly explored in his *Jungfrau*. For his part, Achilles breaks with Greek society in his willingness to assume a submissive position to his opponent: a miscalculation that does not end in the night of sexual bliss he anticipates, but rather in his bloody dismemberment.

Central to the tragedy are the multiple and conflicting sides of Penthesilea's personality. The multivalent warrior is at once queen of the Amazons and daughter of Mars; a fierce warrior who gains honor in defeating her male opponents in battle; a wild animal governed by primal desires in one instance, yet a compassionate woman full of "Würd'" and "Grazie" (HK, 2:2680; dignity and grace [HKE, 128]) in another. She is also a woman who longs to succumb to her feelings of love necessitating that she violate her public duty to uphold and enforce those very laws and customs. In her struggle to dominate the Greek hero, Penthesilea attempts to reconcile her conflicting identities as woman and warrior. Her inability to merge these two roles harmoniously suggests a view of gender's immutability and commensurate quality that forecloses women's attempts to occupy positions in the "masculine" sphere of warfare and simultaneously maintain their "feminine" attributes. Until she encounters Achilles, Penthesilea has never desired a man, entertained thoughts of romantic love, nor been forced to confront the discord between desire and duty. The internal struggle arises within Penthesilea when this desire, coded as natural and in line with Amazon warrior culture, is awakened and transformed into love. Her offense and subsequent death are precipitated by her inability both to confine this sexual desire to the appropriate context (Rose Festival) and to subordinate entirely her overpowering affection for the enemy on behalf of the welfare of the Amazon nation.

Kleist mobilizes the metaphor of the crazed animal to describe Penthesilea and her nation of warriors. In doing so, he signals that their presence on the battlefield represents an invasion into and a threat against a traditionally exclusive "masculine" realm of activity. Penthesilea's warrior identity is bound to predatory and animalistic characteristics: when viewed through the eyes of her male enemy, she is depicted as a ravenous wolf greedily stalking her prey (HK, 2:163–70), an enigmatic sphinx (HK, 2:207), a hyena blinded by rage (HK, 2:331), and a female centaur (HK, 2:548). The attacking bands of Amazons are described by the Greeks as a swarm of locusts descending upon the battlefield (HK, 2:542–44), destroying everything in their path. Even her own tribe of Amazons likens her to a lion poisoned by a hunter (HK, 2:799), a dog in need of restraint (HK, 2:2553–54), and a lioness stalking her kill (HK, 2:2666).[37] The depiction of these armed warriors as wild animals signifies a return to the realm of primal drives—outside the realm of reason and society—in which emotion and desire fuel an erotic power that reigns over rational thought.

The prevailing assumption of warfare as a "masculine" pursuit is at once highlighted and undercut by the intrusion of the Amazon warriors into the conflict. Odysseus's response to the perplexing appearance of Amazon warriors in the battle between Greek and Trojan forces articulates the unsettling effect the warring women have on the rigidly conceived notions of warfare:

So viel ich weiß, gibt es in der Natur
Kraft bloß und ihren Widerstand, nichts Drittes.
Was Glut des Feuers löscht, lös't Wasser siedend
Zu Dampf nicht auf und umgekehrt. Doch hier
Zeigt ein ergrimmter Feind von beiden sich,
Bei dessen Eintritt nicht das Feuer weiß,
Ob's mit dem Wasser rieseln soll, das Wasser
Ob's mit dem Feuer himmelan soll lecken. (HK, 2:125–32)

I thought till now that Nature knows but force
And counterforce, and no third power besides.
Whatever quenches fire will not bring water
Seething to a boil, nor vice versa.
Yet here appears a deadly foe of each,
Upon whose coming, fire no longer knows
Whether to leap with heaven-licking flame. (HKE, 8–9)

The army of warring women defies and challenges the Greek notion of *traditional* warfare in which two (masculine) sides engage in combat.[38] If warfare is dependent on the participation of only male combatants, then the insertion of this "third power," a seemingly unnatural element into the equation, challenges the very binary foundation of Nature, rendering not only the rules of combat but also the identity of man as warrior unreliable.

The threat to the Greek male warriors posed by the Amazons is intensified further by Penthesilea's perceived incompatibility with the traditionally "feminine" qualities of compassion and meekness. She shows no signs of mercy in her carefully crafted plan to attack Achilles. Penthesilea tells the Amazons of her strategy to submit the hero to her will by force (HK, 2:857–60). A deceptively harmless act of intimacy, the embrace, is appropriated by Penthesilea to signify the violent nature of her inner conflict and longing for Achilles. The "sanftest[e] Umarmung" (most gentle embrace) that is to be achieved "mit Eisen" (HK, 2:858–59; with iron [HKE, 38]) is an expression of Penthesilea's contradicting identities as a warrior and a woman in love. Amazon law dictates these two identities be compartmentalized and contained. Penthesilea's inner struggle represents not only a violation of this law but an incompatibility with the competing values of Greek culture.

Penthesilea's "unnatural" appearance as a skilled warrior on the public battlefield not only suggests a crisis in the culture of warfare but also indicates a rupture permeating the gendered order of the personal-private realm. In scene 15, Penthesilea explicitly establishes the gaping cultural chasm between the Greeks and Amazons by firmly positioning herself as the antithesis of the Greek "feminine ideal." While Achilles may be accustomed to being wooed "mit dem Strauß" and "dem verschämten Blick" (HK, 2:1893–94' "bouquet of flowers" and "averted eyes" [HKE, 92]), Penthesilea knows only a violent form of seduction "mit ehrnen Armen" (HK, 2:1900; with arms of bronze [HKE, 92]). This gendered role reversal in which the desiring male subject becomes the desired object redoubles the use of violence by men against women. The resignification of seduction by violent means elicits Achilles's admonishment of her Amazon customs as "unweiblich" and "unnatürlich" (HK, 2:1903; "unfeminine" and "unnatural" [HKE, 92]). Achilles designates Penthesilea as the "Other" and as that which resides outside the normative realm of patriarchal society and the male subject. By framing the Amazons as deviant, Achilles reveals the lacuna between the values forming the basis of his society and those of the Amazon nation. He resists the notion of warring women, who court their lovers in battle, because it poses a threat to the Greek definition of masculinity and heroism upon which his identity as warrior and desiring male subject has been predicated. This facilitates Kleist's structuring of the dramatic turn later in the work, whereby Achilles's desire to submit Penthesilea to his will and make her his queen leads him to assume, or more accurately to perform, the submissive role of her vanquished enemy, which runs counter to the very beliefs that define him.

If Kleist's *Penthesilea* spotlights the ways in which the Amazons challenge Achilles's notion of manhood, the author's depiction of the Amazon state also complicates the nineteenth-century German model of female passivity by portraying the women warriors' sanctioned use of violence as having both the ability to take and bestow life. To borrow the words of Krimmer, "Kleist's war is literally generative, but ultimately destructive."[39] Not only is the procreative Rose Festival reliant on the women warriors' successful use of force to capture and subdue their male enemies, but the Amazon nation arises from and is formed by a violent sexual attack on the bodies of the Scythian women. Implicit in Kleist's portrayal of the nation of women warriors is also a critique of state-sponsored warfare in which a culture and practice of violence is created to fulfill the needs of both the state and its citizens.

In Kleist's drama, the Greek hero's curiosity about the Amazons, whose practices he cannot comprehend and views as the complete antithesis of his own society's norms, creates the narrative moment in which Penthesilea recounts the origins of the Amazon nation. As in Kleist's *Der Hermannsschlacht* (1809), state building is carried out on the bodies of female victims. As Krimmer observes, both of Kleist's dramas put on full display the reciprocal relationship between civil society and the practice of war.[40] Like the violated body of the Germanic daughter Hally, whose severed limbs unite the Germanic tribes against their Roman usurper, so too do the bodies of the Scythian daughters, wives, and mothers lay the foundation for a matriarchal nation of warriors. The formation of the Amazon state emerges out of a direct assault on the Scythian population by their enemies, the Ethiopians, and as Simpson observes: "The conventional acceptance (until quite recently!) of male rape of the female fallen as an act of postwar entitlement inspires the original act of violence that set the Amazon nation in motion."[41] Annihilating the entire male population, the victors turn their aggression toward the unprotected women in order to claim violently what is their right as victors:

> Die Sieger bürgerten, barbarenartig,
> In unsre Hütten frech sich ein, ernährten
> Von unsrer reichen Felder Früchten sich,
> Und voll der Schande Maß uns zuzumessen,
> Ertrotzten sie der Liebe Gruß sich noch:
> Sie rissen von den Gräbern ihrer Männer
> Die Fraun zu ihren schnöden Betten hin. (HK, 2:1925–31)
>
> The victors insolently set up house
> In our own huts and, as barbarians will,
> Fed themselves on the fruit of our rich fields,
> And, to allot us our full measure of shame,
> Forced us to tender them a loving welcome:
> They tore the women from their husbands' graves,
> And dragged them off to share their loathsome beds. (HKE, 93)

The invaders assert their total domination by sexually assaulting the women in order to shame and eradicate the Scythian people. However, rather than giving birth to the offspring of their oppressors, the violated bodies of the Scythian women give life to a nation of women whose existence is dependent upon a culture of war against a male opponent. They do not silently endure male aggression; instead, the women adopt violent means to combat the brutal offense perpetrated against them:

> Die Betten füllten, die entweihten, sich
> Mit blankgeschliff'nen Dolchen an, gekeilt,
> Aus Schmuckgeräten, bei des Herdes Flamme,
> Aus Senkeln, Ringen, Spangen: nur die Hochzeit
> Ward, des Äthioper Königs Vexoris
> Mit Tanaïs, der Königin, erharrt,
> Der Gäste Brust zusamt damit zu küssen.
> Und als das Hochzeitsfest erschienen war,
> Stieß ihm die Kön'gin ihren in das Herz;
> Mars, an des Schnöden Statt, vollzog die Ehe,
> Und das gesamte Mordgeschlecht, mit Dolchen,
> In einer Nacht, ward es zu Tod gekitzelt. (HK, 2:1940–51)
>
> The desecrated beds began to fill
> With daggers, sharp-edged wedges cut and shaped
> From ornaments, in secret by the hearth,
> From spangles, buckles, rings; only the wedding

Of Vexoris, the Ethiopian King,
And young Tanaïs, the Queen, delayed the kiss
Each held in keeping for her captor's breast.
And when at last the wedding feast had come,
Tanaïs plunged her knife into his heart,
Mars in his stead carried out the marriage rite,
And in a night the murderers had their itch
Well satisfied, with knives, till they were dead. (HKE, 93)

There are no men left to protect and defend the Scythian women; instead, the mothers, daughters, and widows take matters into their own hands, turning whatever they can find, including their jewelry, sartorial signifiers of the vestiges of their femininity, into daggers in order to exact revenge against the bodies of their enemies. The desecrated beds in which the crimes of sexual aggression were perpetrated now serve as armories filled with the women's instruments for revenge and liberation. Moreover, the verbs Kleist uses to depict the women's murderous attack imbue the weapons with human qualities: the weapons will *kiss* the breasts of the captors, and will *tickle* the murderers to death. As Richter has observed, "we are dealing with a straightforward gender reversal: phallic daggers wielded by women penetrate and kill the feminized bodies (breast and clitoris) of the Ethiopian men."[42] Two intimate acts are thus transformed into deadly acts in the hands of these women with a generative effect: the birth of the Amazon state.

If Kleist's portrayal of armed women defending themselves, pursuing and attacking their enemies, and establishing a society independent of men appears progressive for his time, then the women's appropriation of military practices, maintenance of power hierarchies, and use of brutal force to subjugate the enemy suggests that the Amazon state merely reinforces the model of female passivity it appears to undermine. Catherine Rigby cautions us in our eagerness to read Kleist's Amazons as proto-feminists, arguing that the women's revolt is not a true act of liberation. Instead, the Amazons enact violence upon the foreign male bodies that mimics the male violence originally committed against the Scythian women. In doing so, the Amazon warriors "implicitly perpetuate the patriarchal assumption that the female is inferior to the male and that womanhood is incommensurate with independence."[43] In *Penthesilea*, Kleist depicts in graphic detail the deadly consequences of women taking up arms to defend themselves and to avenge the violence perpetrated against them. It is the women's uprising that results in the death of male warriors but also the birth of an autonomous matriarchal society that poses a threat to traditional Western patriarchal structures of power.

Kleist's rendering of the Amazons presents female agency in ambiguous and ominous terms. The Amazon body is a destructive female body that threatens the established structure of warfare on the battlefield and the structure of patriarchal society. Moreover, this body is perceived by Achilles as having been "beraubt" (HK, 2:2011; deprived [HKE, 95]) of an essential "feminine" aspect due to the Amazon practice of amputating the breast to aid in the use of weapons. The bodies of the Amazons have been distorted and can never be made whole again, or as Richter argues, Penthesilea is only made whole through her consumption and devouring of Achilles, who "has finally and entirely become the breast."[44] Thus, the Amazon body appears threatening because it challenges the norms, practices, aesthetics, and functions of the female body in the Amazon nation as well as patriarchal Greek society. Achilles's reaction to the absence of this female appendage leads him to characterize the practice as "unmenschlich" (HK, 2:2011; inhumane [HKE, 95]) and "barbarisch" (HK, 2:2014; barbaric [HKE, 95]). He projects his socially prescribed gender expectations onto the female body which refuses to conform to or be contained by these norms and is therefore characterized as deviant, foreign, and Other.

Yet, Achilles's presumption that because the Amazons are devoid of a breast, or rather because of their "bad breast" to channel Richter, they are not susceptible to the same emotions as Greek women, is undercut in the same passage by Penthesilea's reassurance that what he regards as "Der Sitz der jungen, lieblichen Gefühle" (HK, 2:2013; "The seat of kindness, tenderness, and youth" [HKE, 95]) has been safely rescued by the left breast. Like Schiller's armed maiden Johanna, Penthesilea possesses these "feminine" attributes but Amazon custom demands their sublimation to ensure the independence and survival of an autonomous state. Despite Penthesilea's perceived undermining of gender's immutability, the text insists that she is, indeed, a woman and all that it entails, albeit buried deep below the surface.

Achilles's desire to dominate Penthesilea and to make her his bride suggests an effort to tame the transgressive female body so it can be reabsorbed into a patriarchal order to serve a traditional reproductive function, namely, to bear him children and heirs to his throne:

> Du sollst den Gott der Erde mir gebären!
> . . . .
> Doch nicht nach Themiscyra folg' ich dir,
> Vielmehr du, nach der blüh'nden Phtya, mir:
> Denn dort, wenn meines Volkes Krieg beschlossen,
> Führ' ich dich jauchzend hin, und setze dich,
> Ich Seliger, auf meiner Väter Thron. (HK, 2:2230–38)

> Your child, our son, shall be the god of Earth!
> . . . .
> But I'll not follow you to Themiscyra,
> But rather you, to blooming Phthia, me:
> For once my people's war is finished, that's where
> I'll take you, caroling for joy, and seat you,
> Blessed that I am, upon my father's throne. (HKE, 103)[45]

Simultaneously, the subjugation of the fierce Amazon queen to Achilles's will and her containment within the domestic sphere as caregiver allows Achilles to lay exclusive claim to the male-dominated theater of war and reassert his position of power both as sovereign and family patriarch. Yet this reaffirmation of the male warrior identity necessitates the use of brutal force to pacify the defiant woman warrior. More specifically Kleist illustrates that martial and sexual violence are inextricably linked. Achilles boasts that he will not rest until he has conquered her by any means necessary: "ganz wie ihr Herz es wünscht, / Auf Küssen heiß von Erz im Arm zu nehmen" (HK, 2:605–6; "just as her heart desires, / I'll take her in my arms on brazen pillows" [HKE, 29–30]) and "sie, die Stirn bekränzt mit Todeswunden, / Kann durch die Straßen häuptlings mit mir schleifen" (HK, 2:614–15; "set a crown of gashes on her forehead / And dra[g] her through the streets by her sleek hair" [HKE, 29–30]). Reflecting the conflation of sexual desire and violence articulated by Penthesilea, Achilles believes himself to be giving her exactly what she desires, "ganz wie ihr Herz es wünscht." The fusion of martial violence, oppression, and sexual aggression replicates the assault initially perpetrated against the Scythian women by their Ethiopian oppressors and which fuels the women's brutal act of revenge. Ruth Angress notes the similarity between Penthesilea's violence against Achilles and Achilles's violence against Hector in Homer's *Iliad*, arguing that Penthesilea's transgression is mitigated by the fact that she merely reproduces a model constructed and practiced by patriarchal society.[46] The fact that the drama's characters condemn Penthesilea for her desecration of the enemy's body and Achilles's act gains him honor, at least in the eyes of Penthesilea, constructs a narrative of gender inequality on the battlefield.[47]

While desire equals power for both Greek and Amazon warriors, love is tantamount to treason. Penthesilea's irrevocable violation of Amazon law occurs not when she desires to dominate and submit Achilles but when that desire gives way to love and affection, which threaten to destabilize the entire basis of the matriarchal society. Even the Amazon queen's closest confidant, Prothoe, recognizes the debilitating effects of Penthesilea's love, which make her incapable of fulfilling her duty as military commander:

> Du bist, in Flammen wie du loderst, nicht
> Geschickt, den Krieg der Jungfraun fortzuführen;
> So wenig, wie, sich mit dem Spieß zu messen,
> Der Löwe, wenn er von dem Gift getrunken,
> Das ihm der Jäger tückisch vorgesetzt. (HK, 2:796–800)

> You are on fire, consumed from head to toe,
> And hence not fit to lead the maidens' war:
> Yes, no more fit than is a lion to match
> Himself against a spear, once he has drunk
> The poison cunningly set out for him. (HKE, 36)

Prothoe employs the image of the hunt to articulate the intimate relationship between amorous desire and death. However, this is not the traditional pursuit between predator and prey. Instead, the deadly blow is administered insidiously and almost unknowingly via poison, which once consumed, works its devastating effects on the body from within. In contrast, a shot of an arrow or a strike of the sword, both penetrating acts whose force originates outside the body, is deemed an honorable death.

Penthesilea appears just as ambivalent and dismayed as her fellow Amazons by the internal battle being waged between her competing and seemingly irreconcilable identities as a woman in love and a fierce warrior. Love fuels the flames of desire threatening to consume and undo Penthesilea:

> Verflucht, im blutumschäumten Mordgetümmel,
> Mir der Gedanke an die Orgien!
> Verflucht, im Busen keuscher Arestöchter,
> Begierden, die, wie losgelaßne Hunde,
> Mir der Drommete erzne Lunge bellend,
> Und aller Feldherrn Rufen, überschrei'n! (HK, 2:1216–21)
>
> A curse upon this vile, impatient haste!
> A curse upon the thought of sacred orgies
> While blood still foams around the murderous fray!
> A curse upon desires that, in the breast
> Of Mars' chaste daughters, bay like an unleashed pack
> Of hounds, drowning the brazen lungs of trumpets
> And silencing their officers' commands! (HKE, 109)

While sexual desire figures as a primal, untamed drive, it is actually love which overpowers and silences rational thought demanded by the structured, hierarchical order of war. The amorous desire she articulates has its seat in her breast, implying that it is the deadly combination of love paired with desire that make her unfit to lead her troops. Penthesilea's attempt to satisfy both is tied to the realm of the irrational and primal. Anticipating the violent consummation and fulfillment of these desires, Kleist likens the queen's pursuit to that of a pack of wild dogs in search of prey.

For the Amazons, conflict arises when the "private"/"feminine" characteristics of the warrior conflict with the "public"/"masculine" matters of the state. At odds about her love for Achilles and her duty to uphold Amazon law, Penthesilea displaces the cause of this inner turmoil:

> Ist's meine Schuld, daß ich im Feld der Schlacht
> Um sein Gefühl mich kämpfend muß bewerben?
> Was will ich denn, wenn ich das Schwert ihm zücke?
> Will ich ihn denn zum Orkus niederschleudern?

Ich will ihn ja, ihr ew'gen Götter, nur
An diese Brust will ich ihn niederziehn! (HK, 2:1187–92)

Is it my fault that on the battlefield
I have to court his feeling with a sword?
When I assault him, what is it I want?
Is it to throw him headlong into Orcus?
All that I want, eternal gods in heaven,
Is but to draw him down upon this breast! (HKE, 54–55)

Rather than locating the source of conflict within herself and in her wish to draw him to her breast, the seat of her affection, she identifies the external "cause" as the customs and laws of the Amazon state. Thus, it is the law of the Amazon nation that demands the containment of personal interests which is called into question and deemed "unnatural" and "irrational" and not the individual's pursuit of love.[48] The reassertion of social order over individual desire forestalls Penthesilea's subversive challenge to the entrenched structure of power. The Amazons respond to Penthesilea's blame by verbally positioning her outside the social norms that are linked to the realm of reason: "Sie ras't" (HK, 2:1193; She's mad [HKE, 55]), "Unglückliche!" (HK, 2:1194; Poor stricken soul! [HKE, 55]), and "Sie ist von Sinnen!" (HK, 2:1195; She's lost her senses! [HKE, 55]).[49] However, it is not only the Amazons who reject the intrusion of personal desire in the public realm; the Greeks eschew the pursuit of personal will in matters of the state and especially in warfare. Achilles is branded a madman—"Der Rasende!" (HK, 2:622, 2:2549)—by the Greeks for his unrelenting pursuit of the Amazon queen. Both the Greek and Amazon societies reject the pursuit of individual interest over that of the state, making Penthesilea and Achilles outcasts.

The tragedy involving Achilles and Penthesilea is revealed simultaneously as the failure of individuals to adhere to the norms established by their cultures but also as an implicit critique of the rules of warfare dictated by these societies. The conflict arises not from these warriors experiencing desire, but rather from their feelings of love that do not belong on the battlefield. In his engagement with Penthesilea, Kittler posits an affinity between J. G. Fichte's theories of "love" as a woman's duty and Kleist's portrayal of the Amazon queen's transgression: "Nicht Natur oder Vernunft, sondern die Macht regelt den Geschlechterkampf. Die Position Fichtes, in der die Frau dem Mann absolut unterworfen ist, ist auch für Kleist die einzige Möglichkeit, in der der Mann die Liebe überleben kann"[50] ("It is neither Nature nor reason; rather, it is power that controls the battle of the sexes. Fichte's position, in which the woman is completely subordinate to man, is also for Kleist the only possibility in which man can survive love"). I would argue further that Kleist's drama offers a view similar to that of Fichte, in so far as a woman's inclination to love makes her an unsuitable participant in the public life of the state. However, the same charges can be leveled just as easily against the male warrior Achilles, who in his desire for Penthesilea cannot maintain the boundary between his conquest of women and his conquest in battle. It is Achilles's assumption of a submissive role, both publicly on the battlefield and privately as implied by the impending Rose Festival, in order to realize his love for and to unite with Penthesilea that constitutes his transgression against Greek conventions and the institution of war. Thus the sanctioning of the warrior who openly defies the conventions of warfare by indulging his or her amorous affections or rejecting prescriptive gender roles exposes the oppressive and dehumanizing practice of warfare, which demands combatants sublimate their humanity and individuality to carry out acts of state-sanctioned violence for political interests.

Like the Greeks, the Amazons demonize anything that challenges the stability of their state and their way of life. Only outside the realm of social norms, both Greek and Amazonian, can the two warriors be united. No one is exempt, and even Achilles is punished for indulging his desire for Penthesilea that interferes with his martial duties. The ultimate penalty for challenging the status quo is complete and permanent expulsion from the social order. The deaths of the protagonists result from their rebellions against the highly structured norms of their respective societies—norms that demand both warriors occupy the dominant position over their enemy and the objects of their desire. In Penthesilea's case, she yearns to give in to her love for Achilles but refuses to do so at the risk of assuming the passive role. Achilles's attempt at rebellion manifests itself in his strategy to assume briefly the submissive role in order to dominate Penthesilea.

The warriors' quests for sexual satisfaction are intimately cloaked in the language of violence and domination. Or, as Patricia Simpson suggests, "acts of love and war articulate desire with violent conquest."[51] The star-crossed, would-be lovers' campaigns to submit each other to their will play out repeatedly and appear most prominently in the physical positioning of the body in a posture of pure submission. In their tireless efforts and repeated claims to see their opponent assume a submissive position at their feet (HK, 2:638, 844–46, 1749–50, 2246–48), Kleist describes both warriors' acts of violence in terms of intimacy. Reminiscent of Penthesilea's foremothers, the author conflates the queen's sword with an intimate act:

> Hier dieses Eisen soll, Gefährtinnen,
> Soll mit der sanftesten Umarmung ihn,
> (Weil ich mit Eisen ihn umarmen muß!)
> An meinen Busen schmerzlos niederziehn. (HK, 2:857–60)

> Comrades, this metal here
> Shall draw him with the tenderest embrace
> (Since it's with metal that I must embrace him!)
> Closely, and painlessly, unto my heart. (HKE, 38)

Implied in this fusion of inanimate tools of violence with intimacy is the message that primal, female desires, if left unchecked, become a dominating, destructive, and deadly force.

Just as Penthesilea's description of the brutal force she intends to inflict on Achilles employs the image of a violent yet tender enveloping, enfolding action, the queen's ultimate attack on her would-be lover mobilizes a similar symbolism. The penetrating thrust of the phallic sword is to be replaced with the enveloping, devouring gesture of the feminine mouth. As the warriors' struggle for domination reaches its climax in scenes 22 and 23, Penthesilea kills, dismembers, and partially consumes Achilles. This final encounter between the doomed lovers is narrated by an Amazon:

> Penthesilea,
> Sie liegt, den grimm'gen Hunden beigesellt,
> Sie, die ein Menschenschoß gebar, und reißt,–
> Die Glieder des Achills reißt sie in Stücken! (HK, 2:2594–97)

> Penthesilea,
> She's lying down, her grim dogs close beside her,
> She who was born of human loins, tearing–
> She's tearing him to pieces, limb from limb! (HKE, 125)

Whereas Germania, in "Germania an ihre Kinder," commissions her male soldiers with the violent destruction of her enemy,[52] Penthesilea surrenders to her animalistic drives and carries out the deed herself alongside her dogs, forsaking bow and arrow or sword for teeth and tongue. As the prey, Achilles's unarmed, defenseless body becomes the object of this elemental, destructive female drive.

Rather than joining themselves to one another in a sexual, generative union from which they can create a future together, the warriors are united in an act of mutual destruction. Incapable of establishing a life together within the rigid, hierarchical structure of either of their societies, Penthesilea attempts to fuse herself with Achilles by devouring him:

> Sie schlägt, die Rüstung ihm vom Leibe reißend,
> Den Zahn schlägt sie in seine weiße Brust,
> Sie und die Hunde, die wetteifernden,
> Oxus und Sphynx den Zahn in seine rechte,
> In seine linke sie; als ich erschien,
> Troff Blut von Mund und Händen ihr herab. (HK, 2:2669–74)

> She sinks—tearing the armor off his body—
> Into his ivory breast she sinks her teeth,
> She and her savage dogs in competition,

Oxus and Sphinx chewing into his right breast,
And she into his left; when I arrived,
The blood was dripping from her mouth and hands. (HKE, 128)

It is no coincidence that it is into his left breast that she sinks her teeth: Penthesilea's physical consumption and internalization of Achilles is the only means by which the two can be coupled. If we read this scene within the context of eighteenth- and nineteenth-century European ideals of androgyny, harkening back to Plato's *Symposium* in which the merging of male and female qualities into one being forms a more complete individual, Inge Stephan suggests that Kleist depicts the destructive side of the androgen myth.[53] The androgynous ideal, which allows for the unification of disparate, contradictory elements, is inverted and thereby forecloses the potential subversion of the rigid, bifurcated structure of gender. This potentially unifying act is further negated by the death of Achilles accompanied by Penthesilea's affront to the principles of humanity. Michel Chaouli and Heather Benbow have presented compelling arguments concerning Penthesilea's oral transgression as a rebellion against Enlightenment aesthetics and values. Benbow proposes that Penthesilea's oral indulgence challenges the Enlightenment's subordination of "sexuality and other appetites to the interests of the community."[54] Allowing her personal desire for Achilles to consume her, Penthesilea endangers the lives of her fellow Amazons and completely disregards the laws and customs to which she is subject. Thus, Kleist problematizes the individual's attempt to transcend society's unrelenting hierarchal system of power founded on myths of inequality and division.

In her hypnosis-like state, Penthesilea is, for all intents and purposes, already dead to the Amazons. There is nothing left for them to do but to mourn her tragic end. The Amazons eulogize Penthesilea not for her heroics on the battlefield, but instead as a gentle and kind-hearted spirit, possessing both reason and grace:

Solch eine Jungfrau, Hermia! So sittsam!
In jeder Kunst der Hände so gechickt!
So reizend, wenn sie tanzte, wenn sie sang!
So voll Verstand und Würd' und Grazie! (HK, 2:2677–80)

So fine a maiden, Hermia! So modest!
So deft at every art and handicraft!
So lovely when she danced, and when she sang!
So good of mind! Such dignity and grace! (HKE, 128)

Ironically, she is praised for her affable nature, which is likened to a nightingale, and for her respect for life (HK, 2:2683–94). The earlier depictions of a threatening Amazon warrior skilled in the use of weaponry give way to memories of her skills at singing, dancing, and doing handicrafts. This gentle "feminine" side of Penthesilea is depicted only once she no longer has to maintain her identity as a fierce warrior and once she has been excluded from the public realm. All that is left for Penthesilea is to join Achilles in death. Only in death, outside the realm of social norms, both Greek and Amazonian, can they realize their shared desire for one another.[55]

Achilles's rebellion takes the form of symbolic self-sacrifice, offering up his position of power for a vulnerable, submissive position; however, he cannot foresee that his rebellious act against Greek customs will result not in the consummation of his desire for Penthesilea during the Rose Festival, but instead in a violent death at the hands and mouth of his would-be lover. Her mouth, a potential source of pleasure, has metamorphosed into a weapon and an instrument of death. Instead of imbuing deadly, inanimate objects with human attributes, Kleist transforms Penthesilea's body into the fatal weapon that will punish Achilles and ultimately herself.

Penthesilea's inability to account for her actions further enforces the image of an unconscious and uncontainable violence inherent in these female warriors that unleashes itself upon not only the unwitting, defenseless male body but also the female body. When confronted with her bloody deed, one that horrifies even her fellow Amazons, Penthesilea is unable to clearly recall her actions: "Küßt' ich ihn tot?" (HK, 2:2977; "Did I kiss him to death?" [HKE, 145]). Violence and domination once more are depicted as and confused with intimate, physical actions: "– So war es ein Versehen. Küsse, Bisse, / Das reimt sich, und wer recht von Herzen liebt, / Kann schon das Eine für das Andre greifen" (HKE, 2:2981–83; "– So it was a mistake. A kiss, a bite, / The two should rhyme, for one who truly loves / With all her heart can easily mistake them" [HKE, 145]). Overwhelmed by grief and the horror of what she has done, Penthesilea becomes a victim at the hands of her own remorse:

> Denn jetzt steig' ich in meinen Busen nieder,
> Gleich einem Schacht, und grabe, kalt wie Erz,
> Mir ein vernichtendes Gefühl hervor.
> Dies Erz, dies läutr' ich in der Glut des Jammers
> Hart mir zu Stahl; tränk' es mit Gift sodann,
> Heißätzendem, der Reue, durch und durch;
> Trag' es der Hoffnung ew'gem Amboß zu,
> Und schärf' und spitz es mir zu einem Dolch;
> Und diesem Dolch jetzt reich' ich meine Brust:
> So! So! So! So! Und wieder! –Nun ist's gut. (HK, 2:3025–34)
>
> For now I shall descend into my breast,
> And dig a shaft, and quarry out the cold
> Ore of a feeling that annihilates.
> This ore I purify in fire of grief

To hardest steel; in poison then, of bitter,
Burning remorse, I soak it, through and through;
Now carry it toward Hope's eternal anvil,
And grind and sharpen it into a dagger;
And to this dagger now I yield my breast:
So! So! So! So! Again! – Now it is done. (HKE, 148)

Emotion, like words, becomes a deadly weapon with which Penthesilea takes her life. Just as she sank her teeth into Achilles's left breast, Penthesilea drives the sharp shaft of despair into her own heart. The deaths of these two heroic warriors symbolize their failed rebellions as individuals attempting to assert their agency and personal desires in defiance of a rigidly structured political and social order and the roles prescribed for them as servants of their states. The weapons of their revolt, namely their bodies, become the site upon and the means by which punishment for their transgressions is meted out.

While Kleist's *Penthesilea* resists being read as an endorsement of the woman warrior, and even less an approbation of the violent nineteenth-century female revolutionary, his depiction of the Amazon queen and her nation of women warriors explores the complex circuit linking gender, the individual, and love to the institution of warfare. In his radical myth of the Amazon queen and her would-be lover Achilles, Kleist navigates the tension between gender and warfare in a way that collapses any notion of stability or logic. Penthesilea and Achilles's inability to uphold fixed notions of gender, to suppress their individual desires for the good of their states, and to adhere to the cultures of war dictated by their respective societies results in dismemberment, madness, and death. Yet, even as the tragic ending of his play threatens to foreclose the subversive potential of his protagonist warriors' efforts to undermine structures of power and radically reenvision the individual's relationship to the state, the gender bending and role reversals of Penthesilea and Achilles complicate notions of both gender and war as "straightforward" and "natural."

The effects of this play on the early nineteenth-century German public were ambivalent: most reading audiences were moved either to tears or shock at the violent and tragic outcome. Kleist's drama resonated with his audience, one way or another, because it dealt with issues that were relevant to German society at the time. Kleist created a new narrative of the woman warrior attempting to confront, interpret, and come to terms with the social and political conflicts wrought by the French Revolution and the subsequent Napoleonic Wars. The unexpected ending of Kleist's tragedy offered the dramatist an outlet by which to express the ambivalence that he, and society in more general terms, experienced toward shifting gender roles that resulted from a destabilization of social norms brought about by the culture of war that permeated European society around 1800.

EPILOGUE

Reflecting critically on the culture of warfare in the wake of Napoleon's defeat and the Germans' hard-won autonomy, Prussian general and military theorist Carl von Clausewitz (1780–1831) in his posthumously published book *Vom Kriege* (*On War*, 1832) asserted that "der Krieg nicht bloß ein politischer Akt, sondern ein wahres politisches Instrument ist, eine Fortsetzung des politischen Verkehrs, ein Durchführen desselben mit anderen Mitteln" (CC, 34; "War is not merely an act of policy but a true political instrument, a continuation of political intercourse, carried on with other means" [CCE, 87]). The inherently political nature of warfare and military institutions, a tautology perhaps for today's reader, had very acute implications for issues of gender, political agency, and the waging of war around 1800. Indeed, Clausewitz's astute observation continues to be relevant for these issues in the twenty-first century. If we agree with Clausewitz that warfare is inextricably tethered to questions of power and politics, then the historical woman warrior's claim to such "political instruments" represented her attempt to exercise the right to political subjecthood and agency as a citizen sharing the burden of defending her country and fellow compatriots. Yet, Clausewitz makes not a single reference to women as combatants nor does he speculate on the implications of their presence on the battlefield for the conduct of war, despite the profusion of both historical and fictional women warriors during the bellicose period between 1789 and 1815 as well as Clausewitz's own participation in many of the military campaigns in which women were reported to have fought. How are we to reconcile this conspicuous omission by one of Prussia's leading military theorists with the German reading public's palpable fixation with the warlike woman? Was it a necessary corrective to restore order at the conclusion of the protracted conflict by returning the unruly woman to her rightful place in the domestic sphere as docile helpmate, caregiver, and nurturer? Or perhaps as a strategy to erase from the German cultural memory the trauma induced by the appearance of warrior women on the battlefield as dealers of death?

The preface accompanying Clausewitz's book offers potential insight into this striking elision and women's fraught relationship to politics and warfare. Marie von Clausewitz, née Brühl, the general's widow, penned the foreword to and oversaw the publication of her husband's unfinished life's work. Her introduction to an intellectual work on military strategy and the politics of warfare is an intricate negotiation with the established perception of these fields as the exclusive domain of men, while at the same time it evinces her critical awareness of her audience and the gender conventions governing German society in the 1830s. Attuned to the fact that Germans were still recovering from the political and social upheaval wrought by the Revolution and ensuing wars, Marie von Clausewitz carefully frames her role in the production of the book by deploying a twofold strategy of self-effacement and strategic authorial legitimation. Mindful to eschew the stain of transgression implied by her gender and the gendered subject matter of the book, she distances herself from the decidedly "unfeminine" topic in the opening lines of the preface:

> Es wird mit Recht befremden, daß eine weibliche Hand es wagt, ein Werk von solchem Inhalt wie das vorliegende mit einer Vorrede zu begleiten. Für meine Freunde bedarf es hierüber keiner Erklärung, aber auch in den Augen derer, die mich nicht kennen, hoffe ich durch die einfache Erzählung dessen, was mich dazu veranlaßte, jeden Schein einer Anmaßung von mir zu entfernen. (CC, 3)
>
> Readers will be rightly surprised that a woman should dare to write a preface for such a work as this. My friends will need no explanation; but I hope that a simple account of the circumstances that caused me to take this step will remove any impression of presumptuousness in the minds of those who do not know me. (CCE, 65)

It is this "impression of presumptuousness" which Marie von Clausewitz, like so many other women writers of the period, was compelled to ward off. Playing to the demands of the conservative audience, she dutifully proclaims her lack of expertise on the subject and consciously rejects any claim to authorship of a work, which she notes is "weit über [ihrem] Horizont" (CC, 3; "far beyond [her] intellectual horizon" [CCE, 65]).

Working in concert with this strategy of self-effacement is Marie von Clausewitz's invocation of her role as devoted wife duty-bound to fulfill her husband's greatest wish. She conjures forth images of childbirth to portray the process involved in publishing Clausewitz's book, a process in which she assumes a supporting role as a kind of maternal literary midwife: "Nur als eine teilnehmende Begleiterin will ich demselben bei seinem Eintritt in die Welt zur Seite stehen" (CC, 3; "Only as a sympathetic companion do I want to help its entry into the world" [CCE, 65]). Thus, Marie von Clausewitz conflates her role as editor with a role deemed more socially acceptable for a woman by linking it to the role of caregiver and nurturer. Together, these strategies enabled her to circumvent criticism of her otherwise "unfeminine" pursuit.

Yet in the same instance that she claims her intellectual inadequacies, she actively undermines this maneuver of self-effacement by claiming the authority to speak about matters beyond her gendered ambit:

> Diese Stelle darf ich wohl in Anspruch nehmen, da mir auch bei dessen Entstehung und Ausbildung eine ähnliche vergönnt wurde. Wer unsere glückselige Ehe gekannt hat und weiß, wie wir *alles* miteinander teilten, nicht allein Freude und Leid, sondern auch jede Beschäftigung, jedes Interesse des täglichen Lebens: der wird begreifen, daß eine Arbeit dieser Art meinen geliebten Mann nicht beschäftigen konnte, ohne auch mir genau bekannt zu sein. (CC, 3)

> I may claim this role since I was granted a similar function in the creation and development of the work. Those who knew our happy marriage and knew that we shared *everything*, not only joy and pain but also every occupation, every concern of daily life, will realize that a task of this kind could not occupy my beloved husband without at the same time becoming thoroughly familiar to me. (CCE, 65)

Like the wives, fiancés, or sisters of most male authors and intellectuals of the period—one need only consider the names Gottsched, Schlegel, and von Arnim—Marie von Clausewitz was a sounding board for her husband's ideas, a critical reader of his manuscripts, and an active collaborator in the formation of his ideas. Thus, just as Marie von Clausewitz placates her critics by downplaying her informed interest in and extensive knowledge of politics and warfare, she problematizes the assertions of an impenetrable gendered boundary between public matters and domestic duties, thereby claiming a space for women in matters of politics and war. The example of Marie von Clausewitz not only illustrates the resurgence of a reactionary gender discourse during the conservative period of restoration following the wars of occupation, but more importantly her preface demonstrates women's continued attempts to complicate the illusion of gendered separate spheres while at the same time attempting to claim a space for themselves in the public life of politics and war.

The perceived transgression of gendered boundaries delimiting public and private, political and domestic, violence and pacifism, intellectual inquiry and dilettantism, which Marie von Clausewitz attempts to mitigate in her preface to *Vom Kriege* is but one of many instantiations of female transgression the woman warrior came to exemplify in the German imagination around 1800. As the standard bearer for all unruly women, the woman warrior embodied the most extreme articulation of female resistance and agitation against the narrow confines of bourgeois society. Carl von Clausewitz's perhaps intentional omission of the woman warrior from his critical analysis of warfare therefore may well have been an effort to close rather than revisit an unsettling chapter in German history that threatened to spark renewed attention to questions of violent women, political agency, and martial participation.

If warfare is inherently political, then literary representations of warfare, and by extension representations of the warrior woman, are not merely fictional interventions in the horrors and brutality of combat, the loss of human life, or the organization of mass violence. The business of representing women who go to war assumes a decidedly political nature. As the chapters in this book have demonstrated, the ambiguous status of the woman warrior in the Age of Goethe is the product of complex, ideologically charged negotiations with both fictional and historical women as agents of violence. The varied narrative strategies employed by men and women writers, and the literary community as a whole, constructed layers of myth about warlike women's fraught relationship to social and political structures in crisis. These dissonant literary portraits of the unruly, violent woman refract in many telling ways the precarious existence of German-speaking territories in the crumbling Holy Roman Empire and its people in the wake of the revolutionary turmoil, amidst struggles for liberation from foreign oppressors, and in attempts to articulate a shared national identity. New myths invented by eighteenth- and early nineteenth-century German society about women and warfare in an effort to contain, pacify, or exploit the disorderly female body simultaneously confirmed the artificiality of gender and positioned the woman warrior as a site of semiotic contestation in the restructuring and stabilization of German society.

Armed Ambiguity's investment in uncovering how various discourses work to exploit the tension between forms of power and the representation of women as warriors in the social, political, and martial crises of the late eighteenth and early nineteenth centuries may prove informative for discussions about the dynamic connections linking gender, representation, politics, and warfare in periods of conflict well into the twenty-first century. While a solid foundation has already been laid for critical inquiries into literary instantiations of violent women at decisive historical moments of German culture in crisis, such as 1848, 1871, 1914, 1933, the late 1960s, and the early 1970s,[1] gendered social and political discourses constructing narratives about German women warriors of the new millennium demand more concentrated scholarly attention. The 2001 admission of women to all levels and branches of the German Bundeswehr (Federal Armed Forces), including combat positions, has unleashed new assaults on the fundamental structure and values of German society that have trained their sights once more on the female warrior.[2]

Modern German Culture in Crisis: New Myths of Women and Warfare

The modern German female soldier, not unlike her fictional and historical predecessors, has become a site of negotiation in the restructuring and modernization of the German military. More than two centuries after French women asserted their right to take up arms in defense of their Republic,

German women in the military today find themselves confronted with new gendered myths of what it means to be a woman and a warrior. These renewed debates about the relationship between gender and warfare, and indeed gender and politics, signal social and political crises specific to the modern era and age of technological advancement. Innovations in weaponry and warfare have enabled both men and women to assume new roles in military conflicts, both on and off the battlefield, mitigating to a certain extent issues of physical strength and endurance demanded of soldiers in previous centuries. Competing agendas in the reorganization of German civil society within a global world have been brought to bear once more on the bodies of women, both symbolic and material.

Contemporary debates on women's participation in active combat roles in military institutions resonate with and are informed in significant ways by the gender myths mobilized at the end of the eighteenth century. Recent discussions about women's unmitigated access to all levels of the military in both Germany and the United States have reactivated anxieties about the juxtaposition of gender and warfare, and more specifically about women and perpetrators of violence, while simultaneously unmasking the social prescriptions underlying attitudes about what it means to be a man or a woman. Opponents of this historic shift tend to cite ostensible differences as the primary justification for women's exclusion from direct combat.[3] The official integration of women into fighting forces challenges long-standing notions about warfare and martial violence as exclusively masculine domains. Gender stereotypes perpetuating the dichotomy of the active man versus the passive woman remain entrenched in the constitution and the organizational structure of Germany's military institution.[4] After all, the admission of women to the German military was a decision imposed and enforced from *outside* by the European Court of Justice and was not a decision initiated by a strong majority within the German government or military.[5] In her decades-long work with the Sozialwissenschaftliches Institut der Bundeswehr (Bundeswehr Institute of Social Sciences), sociologist Ruth Seifert has documented the attitudes held by male and female soldiers toward the gradual (forced) integration of women into the military as well as the concepts of masculinity bound to the warrior identity. She argues that the conservative rhetoric employed by politicians and the reactionary attitudes held by a large portion of German society toward the issue of women and the military dictate a policy of separate but equal status between the sexes.[6]

The tension characterizing the relationship between politics, warfare, and gender received critical attention long before the Bundeswehr's official admission of women to combat roles in 2001. Already in the 1970s the feminist activist and journalist Alice Schwarzer called attention to official forms of gender discrimination and policies of oppression as they concerned women and the armed forces. In her 1978 *EMMA* editorial "Frauen ins Militär" ("Women into the Military"), Schwarzer argued that women's limited participation in the German military was "eine reine Machtfrage" ("a pure question of power").[7] For Schwarzer, a lifelong pacifist, the pursuit of universal peace and the use of military violence were not mutually exclusive but rather inextricably linked: "Ich meine: Frauen und Frieden—ja. Aber die Bemühung um Frieden sollte eine menschliche und nicht nur eine 'weibliche' Qualität sein. Und von der Möglichkeit, den eigenen Frieden auch selbst verteidigen und notfalls sogar erkämpfen zu können—davon können und dürfen Frauen sich nicht länger ausschließen lassen!" ("I mean: women and peace—yes. But the bid for peace should be a human and not only a 'feminine' quality. As to the possibility of being able to defend and in times of need to even fight for one's own peace—women can and must no longer allow themselves to be excluded!"). Seeking to transcend the gendered rhetoric of peace movements and military institutions, Schwarzer advocated for women's seat at the war table and on the front line by arguing that these two seemingly antagonistic pursuits were, in fact, interdependent. The pursuit of peace and the preservation of individual rights and security often require acts of aggression, which according to Schwarzer's logic, should be a shared burden for *all* citizens.[8]

Twenty-two years after the publication of her controversial editorial, Schwarzer revisited the question of women in the German military in light of the 2000 European Court ruling with a renewed call for all ranks of the German Armed Forces to be opened to women.[9] Despite the notable progress on issues of women's equality achieved over the course of two decades, Schwarzer voiced her skepticism about the court's decision fundamentally altering centuries of entrenched attitudes about traditional gender roles: "Eine wirkliche Integration von Frauen in die Armee würde das Herz der Männerbünde und den Kern der Geschlechterrollen erschüttern: die Rolle vom Mann als wehrhafter Täter und der Frau als wehrloses Opfer"[10] ("True integration of women in the army would unsettle the heart of male societies and the essence of gender roles: the role of man as protective agent and woman as defenseless victim"). Yet it is precisely this mindset, Schwarzer claims, which makes the integration of women into the military, and indeed all institutions of power, imperative not only for the prospect of peace but also for gender equality. As Schwarzer and others have observed, women's increased presence and participation in military conflicts across the globe have not eradicated the need for women to continually assert their rightful claim to a position on the battlefield as soldiers but also to a seat at the "political table" as engaged citizens.

Despite the heated debate about women's presence in the military more than a decade after the first women assumed combat duties, female soldiers still only constitute less than 10 percent (19,000) of the Bundeswehr's 186,000 active military force as of January 2014.[11] While the number of female soldiers continues to increase each year, the percentage of women in the military remains lower than the Bundeswehr's goal of 15 percent. This statistic must be interpreted in the larger context of recent military reforms, including the 2011 suspension of the *Wehrpflicht* (compulsory military service). Fewer young German men are volunteering for military service, which has resulted in a marked drop in the overall size of Germany's military.[12] Troop deployment to war-torn regions as well as a lack of public support for Germany's participation in the conflicts in the Middle East may also contribute to this growing disinterest in military service.

In order to combat the ever-shrinking size of the military resulting from the abolishment of compulsory military service, Bundeswehr officials have unleashed a full-scale media blitz in an effort to drum up interest. Seeking to capitalize on the relatively untapped resource of young potential female soldiers, the German military leveled its recruiting sights on women with its 2011 ad campaign "Frauen werben Frauen" ("Women Recruiting Women"). In an article posted on the Bundeswehr's official website, the report proudly touts the military's newest initiative, taking special care to emphasize the involvement of female soldiers as consultants in the development of these gender-specific ads.[13] Yet even in this campaign by and for women, prevailing myths about the perceived gender differences between men and women color the campaign and its representation of women and women warriors. Expressing his support for the campaign, the article cites the director of the Ministry of Defense's personnel division, Major General Wolfgang Born: "Frauen haben ganz eigene Qualitäten und Stärken, von denen wir als Bundeswehr gerne mehr profitieren möchten"[14] ("Women have very specific qualities and strengths, from which we as the Bundeswehr would very much like to benefit"). Despite his best intentions, the military official's remarks reinforce the same overdetermined narratives of "separate but equal" that proponents of gender equality have sought to erase and which continue to plague the culture of the military institution.

Further compounding the perceived gap between the sexes and entrenched views of gender difference is the article's pat observation, "schließlich wissen Frauen am besten, was Frauen wollen" ("after all, women know best what women want"). By emphasizing women's role in efforts to recruit other women, the Bundeswehr campaign promotes the illusion that dominant, patriarchal narratives of femininity have been replaced by "real" women's visions of what it means to be a warrior, and a woman for that matter. Yet, such assertions that "women know women best" assume a cohesive, homogenous, universalizing view of Woman that denies individuality, despite the campaign's explicit emphasis on diversity. More importantly, it invests the notion of self-representation with a fallacious sense of agency and authority, obfuscating the underlying structures of power and domination implicated in acts of representation. At stake in this campaign are the larger questions of what such visual narratives reveal about German women and their relationship to the issue of military service and indeed the role of the modern woman warrior in the twenty-first century, more than two centuries after their French counterparts first demanded their rights to take up arms in defense of their country. Do ads created by women for women create new narratives about gender and military conflict or do they perpetuate prevailing attitudes? In what ways might these modern woman warriors assert, either intentionally or unknowingly, new forms of domination and control?

The Bundeswehr's campaign "Frauen werben Frauen" consists of three primary images, all portraying the same woman in three similar scenes and accompanied by texts describing the various military and civilian career opportunities offered by the armed forces.[15] In each ad the future woman warrior is depicted in a domestic setting against the backdrop of a shoe rack filled with a variety of fashionable and sensible footwear. The trim, athletic female model is manicured, wearing makeup, and has her hair pulled back in a stylish but practical ponytail, conveying the embodiment of the modern career woman. While two of the three images present the female recruit in her combat fatigues lacing up her boots in preparation for duty, the third image speaks to the non-combat options of military service by depicting the model in form-fitting civilian clothes.[16] Each poster is marked with orange tags establishing an association between a specific activity or career—or as one could argue, a facet of the woman's identity—and certain pairs of shoes. For example, a pair of hot pink stilettos are accompanied with the tag "Feiern mit den Mädels" (partying with the girls), while business casual pumps carry the tag "Verwaltungsfachangestellte" (administrative assistant). In both posters, the combat boots convey the young recruit's combat-readiness with the tags "Arbeitszeit" (work time) and "Fallschirmjägerin" (paratrooper). The activities, like the shoes, attempt to strike a balance by suggesting that the modern woman warrior can be exactly that: a woman and a warrior. Underlying and informing these representations of the modern woman warrior and the claim that she can have it all—a successful career in the military without having to compromise her "femininity"—are assumptions stigmatizing women who opt for non-traditional careers in the historically exclusive masculine institution of the military. As literary representations of the woman warrior at the end of the eighteenth and early nineteenth centuries have revealed, images of the woman warrior that emerge during intense periods of crisis—whether they are political, economic, social, or martial in nature—activate a complex array of deep-seated anxieties about women as agents of death that disrupt seemingly stable notions of gender, martial violence, and structures of power.

These seemingly innocuous, and perhaps well-intentioned, posters, which seek to assert a progressive identity of the modern female soldier that is both appealing to potential recruits and non-threatening to the civilian population, are in fact engaged in the very act of mythmaking and power struggle the campaign gives the impression of avoiding. At the same time, these ads simply replace old myths with new fictions of what it means to be a woman who actively engages in "sanctioned" forms of violence for the fatherland. Perhaps more troubling is the campaign's lack of diversity and variety in representing women. The use of the same model, the same motif, and the same assertion of one specific form of femininity signals a disparity between the intended message of diversity, variety, and female empowerment, and the images the campaign mobilizes. Instead, the images establish a *new* myth of femininity and the ideal woman warrior, thereby marginalizing women who do not conform to or embody this new norm. Furthermore, the images selected by women soldiers to appeal to potential women recruits do not depict the modern warrior actively engaged in any of the duties she is expected to perform. Indeed, the model's static poses—sitting, kneeling, or gazing motionless at her reflection in the mirror—convey her inaction. The posters' failure to show the female recruit armed, driving a tank, manning a fighter jet, or tending to a fellow soldier's wounds on the battlefield obfuscates entirely the image of women at war and engaged in violent military encounters. While such conspicuous omissions could be attributed to the Bundeswehr's overall avoidance of the realities of war in their recruiting efforts, by suppressing portrayals of the woman as warrior, the campaign's authors retreat to nonthreatening images that avoid the anxieties underlying notions of women as active combatants and aggressors.

Implied by the campaign's motto "Frauen werben Frauen" are the problematic assumptions that women have the authority to speak for themselves and for other women, but also that self-representation is more authentic than other forms of representation and thereby immune to exploitation or manipulation. However, feminist scholar Rey Chow cautions against the illusion of empowerment and agency proffered by such acts of self-representation: "Presumed to be direct and unmediated, the act of referring to oneself has taken on the aura of 'representation' that paradoxically transcends the limits of representation, a 'representation' that, no matter how trivial and self-aggrandizing, is morally justifiable because it is (thought to be) *non-representational*. Furthermore, self-representation is now equated with the expression of truth."[17] If, as Chow and others concerned with the politics of representation have claimed, attempts to speak or represent one's self are always already mediated by, bound to, and simultaneously risk replicating dominant narratives,[18] then images and modes of self-representation of the woman warrior implied by slogans such as "women recruit women" implicate similar systems of power and symbolic violence at work in eighteenth- and nineteenth-century myths of women warriors.

My critical engagement with literary visions of women warriors and the narrative strategies employed to construct them has been invested in an examination of *how* and *what* myths of gender and warfare convey about German society's fluctuating attitudes toward the nexus between power and gender in moments of social and political crisis. The issues of gender, power, and agency, which dictated the literary renegotiations with women and men's roles in the emerging public sphere around 1800, amidst the culture of war dominating and irrevocably altering the European continent, remain active ideological battlegrounds in the struggle to represent the woman warrior today. Representations and self-representations of the modern warring woman continue to figure as both the means by which society attempts to reconcile its ambivalence toward women as agents of violence as well as symbolic bodies upon which society inscribes its narratives about gender, power, and the waging of war. As women's participation in global military conflicts increases and continues to challenge traditional notions of what it means to be a warrior, defender, protector, and aggressor, critical investigations into cultural representations of these women warriors will remain imperative in efforts to expose the underlying structures of power at work in the mobilization of discourses on gender and violence to dictate who has access to "political instruments" of power and agency, whether they are institutions of warfare, agencies of political diplomacy, or strategies of (self-)representation.

NOTES

Introduction

1. I use the terms "German" and "Germany" as shorthand for the geographical and cultural landscape of disparate territories forming the Holy Roman Empire of the German nation at the turn of the eighteenth to the nineteenth century.

2. Karen Hagemann, "Heldenmütter, Kriegerbräute und Amazonen. Entwürfe 'patriotischer' Weiblichkeit zur Zeit der Freiheitskriege," in *Militär und Gesellschaft im 19. und 20. Jahrhundert*, ed. Ute Frevert (Stuttgart: Klett-Cotta, 1997), 198–99.

3. Such a study must, out of necessity, limit its scope and narrow its focus at the risk of excluding potentially relevant works. For this reason, critical research undertaken by scholars such as Helen Watanabe-O'Kelly expand on representations of the warlike woman not taken up in the discussion here and help to present a more holistic view of the woman warrior's trajectory across centuries. Yet not even the extensive anthologies dedicated to the topic can make the claim to be exhaustive and to this end, more scholarly attention is needed. See, among others, Sarah Colvin and Helen Watanabe-O'Kelly, ed., *Women and Death 2: Warlike Women in the German Literary and Cultural Imagination since 1500* (Rochester, N.Y.: Camden House, 2009); and Helen Watanabe-O'Kelly, *Beauty or Beast? The Woman Warrior in the German Imagination from the Renaissance to the Present* (Oxford: Oxford University Press, 2010).

4. Roland Barthes, *Mythologies*, trans. Annette Lavers (New York: Farrar, Straus & Giroux, 1972), 109 (my emphasis).

5. See Isabel V. Hull, who offers a cogent analysis of the reciprocal relationship between gender, sexuality, and legislation in eighteenth-century Germany in *Sexuality, State, and Civil Society in Germany, 1700–1815* (Ithaca, N.Y.: Cornell University Press, 1996).

6. My critical use of the term "Woman" signals my investment in problematizing and reconsidering how essentialist representations of "Woman," "Man," "feminine," "masculine," "femininity," and "masculinity" were deployed in the service of a hegemonic narrative of power and control. While I do not ascribe to the notion of a cohesive, natural concept of woman or man, this was, indeed, an essential fixture of the bourgeois gender myth constructed and promoted around 1800. However, I am interested in the fissures, tensions, and contradictions emerging from such reductionist myths, which engender productive spaces to examine how representations of "femininity" or "masculinity" are negotiated.

7. Genevieve Lloyd, "Selfhood, War and Masculinity," in *Feminist Challenges: Social and Political Theory*, ed. Carole Pateman and Elizabeth Gross (Boston: Northeastern University Press, 1987), 64. See also the insightful study of the complex, evolving relationship between gender, military service, and the process

of nation-building in Ute Frevert, "Citizen Soldiers: General Conscription in the Nineteenth and Twentieth Centuries," in *Enlightened War: German Theories and Cultures of Warfare from Frederick the Great to Clausewitz*, ed. Elisabeth Krimmer and Patricia Anne Simpson (Rochester, N.Y.: Camden House, 2011), 219–37; "German Conceptions of War, Masculinity, and Femininity in the Long Nineteenth Century," in *Women and Death 2: Warlike Women in the German Literary and Cultural Imagination since 1500*, ed. Sarah Colvin and Helen Watanabe-O'Kelly (Rochester: Camden House, 2009), 169–85; and *Die kasernierte Nation: Militärdienst und Zivilgesellschaft in Deutschland* (Munich: C. H. Beck, 2001).

8. Indeed, in Plato's dialogues *Republic* and *Laws*, women who demonstrate warlike attributes are deemed just as capable of becoming "guardians" of the state as their male counterparts. See especially book 5 of *Republic* and book 6 of *Laws* in *The Collected Dialogues of Plato, Including the Letters*, ed. Edith Hamilton and Huntington Cairns (Princeton, N.J.: Princeton University Press, 1961). For a history of the woman as warrior, see Colvin and Watanabe-O'Kelly, ed., *Women and Death 2*; Frevert, *Die kasernierte Nation*; Karen Hagemann and Ralf Pröve, *Landsknechte, Soldatenfrauen und Nationalkrieger: Militär, Krieg und Geschlechterordnung im historischen Wandel* (New York: Campus, 1998); Peter H. Wilson, "German Women and War, 1500–1800," *War in History* 3, no. 2 (1996): 127–60; and Jean Bethke Elshtain, *Women and War* (Chicago: University of Chicago Press, 1987). Of particular interest for this book is the scholarship focusing on female soldiers fighting during the Revolutionary and Napoleonic Wars, including Karen Hagemann, "Female Patriots: Women, War and the Nation in the Period of the Prussian-German Anti-Napoleonic Wars," *Gender & History* 16, no. 2 (August 2004): 397–424, and Hagemann, "'Heroic Virgins' and 'Bellicose Amazons': Armed Women, the Gender Order and the German Public during and after the Anti-Napoleonic Wars," *European History Quarterly* 37 (2007): 507–27; and Claudia Opitz, "Von Frauen im Krieg zum Krieg gegen Frauen. Krieg, Gewalt und Geschlechterbeziehungen aus historischer Sicht," *L'Homme: Zeitschrift für Feministische Geschichtswissenschaft* 3, no. 1 (1992): 31–44.

9. Claudia Honegger's excellent study *Die Ordnung der Geschlechter: Die Wissenschaften vom Menschen und das Weib* (Frankfurt: Campus, 1991) provides an extensive critical engagement with treatises on gender from a number of emerging fields during the period in question. See also Thomas Laqueur, *Making Sex: Body and Gender from the Greeks to Freud* (Cambridge, Mass.: Harvard University Press, 1990).

10. Karin Hausen posits a direct correlation between the shift in notions of gender and the emergence of the middle class, which relocated the center of economic life from private to public spaces, in her influential essay "Die Polarisierung der 'Geschlechtscharaktere'—Eine Spiegelung der Dissoziation von Erwerbs- und Familienleben," in *Sozialgeschichte der Familie in der Neuzeit Europas*, ed. Werner Konze (Stuttgart: Klett, 1976), 370.

11. Honegger, *Ordnung*, 146. Similarly, historian Laqueur has argued that the eighteenth century signaled a shift in thinking about gender from a model that theorized gender as a continuum to one which privileged a divergent view of gender traits. Laqueur, *Making Sex*, 8. Laqueur, Honegger, and Londa Schiebinger have faced criticism in recent decades for neglecting eighteenth-century examples of gender's transformability. In her discussion of the female cross-dresser

in the eighteenth and nineteenth centuries, literary scholar Elisabeth Krimmer complicates the notion of a sequential paradigm shift. Elisabeth Krimmer, *In the Company of Men: Cross-Dressed Women around 1800* (Detroit: Wayne State University Press, 2004), 10. However, as historian Karen Harvey astutely observes, Laqueur acknowledges the coexistence of the one-sex and two-sex models well into the twentieth century, although Harvey notes such admissions are few and far between. Karen Harvey, "The Century of Sex? Gender, Bodies, and Sexuality in the Long Eighteenth Century," *The Historical Journal* 45, no. 4 (2002): 901–2.

12. Pierre Roussel, *Physiologie des weiblichen Geschlechts*, trans. Christian Friedrich Michaelis (Berlin: Vieweg, 1786), 16.

13. Ernst Brandes, *Ueber die Weiber* (Leipzig: Weidmanns Erben und Reich, 1787), 39.

14. Wilhelm von Humboldt, "Über den Geschlechtsunterschied und dessen Einfluß auf die organische Natur," in *Werke in Fünf Bänden*, ed. Andreas Flitner and Klaus Giel, vol. 1, *Schriften zur Anthropologie und Geschichte* (Stuttgart: J.G. Cotta'sche Buchhandlung, 1960), 285.

15. For Humboldt's assertion of the "pure" form, see Wilhelm von Humboldt, "Über die männliche und weibliche Form," in *Werke in Fünf Bänden*, ed. Andreas Flitner and Klaus Giel, vol. 1, *Schriften zur Anthropologie und Geschichte* (Stuttgart: J.G. Cotta'sche Buchhandlung, 1960), 297. See also Gail K. Hart's assessment of Humboldt in "Re-Dressing History: Mother Nature, Mother Isabeau, the Virgin Mary, and Schiller's *Jungfrau*," *Women in German Yearbook* 14 (1999): 95. On the gender debates and the androgynous ideal around 1800, see Catriona MacLeod, *Embodying Ambiguity: Androgyny and Aesthetics from Winckelmann to Keller* (Detroit: Wayne State University Press, 1998), 51.

16. Johann Gottlieb Fichte, "Grundlage des Naturrechts nach Principien der Wissenschaftslehre," in *J.G. Fichte—Gesamtausgabe*, ed. Reinhard Lauth and Hans Gliwitzky, vol. 4, *Werke 1797–1798* (Stuttgart-Bad Cannstatt: Frommann-Holzboog, 1970), 100.

17. Fichte, "Grundlage," 4.133–34.

18. English translations are from Johann Gottlieb Fichte, *Foundations of Natural Right: According to the Principles of the Wissenschaftslehre*, ed. Frederick Neuhouser, trans. Michael Baur (Cambridge, Eng.: Cambridge University Press, 2000).

19. Theodor Gottlieb von Hippel, *Über die bürgerliche Verbesserung der Weiber* (Frankfurt am Main: Syndikat, 1977), 102–3.

20. Theodor Gottlieb von Hippel, *On Improving the Status of Women*, trans. Timothy F. Sellner (Detroit: Wayne State University Press, 1979), 108–9. I have modified the translation.

21. Michel Foucault's notion of *episteme* and his focus on scientific and political discourses of the body in the eighteenth century is particularly informative for my analysis of the woman warrior. See, among others, Michel Foucault, *The Order of Things: An Archaeology of the Human Sciences* (New York: Vintage Books, 1994) and *Discipline and Punish: The Birth of the Prison* (New York: Vintage Books, 1995).

22. Schiebinger cites French female anatomist Marie Thiroux d'Arconville's 1759 depiction of the female skeleton for helping substantiate claims that

women's skulls, and therefore brains, were smaller than those of men. However, in 1796 German anatomist Samuel Thomas von Soemmerring provided a competing illustration, which disputed such claims by presenting woman's skull as larger. Londa Schiebinger, *The Mind Has No Sex? Women in the Origins of Modern Science* (Cambridge, Mass.: Harvard University Press, 1989), 207.

23. Barthes, *Mythologies*, 129. Barthes further contends that myth's primary function is to "transform history into nature."

24. Judith Butler, *Bodies That Matter: On the Discursive Limits of "Sex"* (New York: Routledge, 1993), 8.

25. Judith Butler, *Excitable Speech: A Politics of the Performative* (New York: Routledge, 1997), 14.

26. Butler, *Excitable Speech*, 15.

27. Stacy Alaimo and Susan J. Hekman, ed., *Material Feminisms* (Bloomington: Indiana University Press, 2008), 6.

28. The redefinition of gender roles has been attributed to additional causes such as the rise of women's writing; *Empfindsamkeit* (the literary movement characterized by sentimentality); the separation of residence from place of work; and scientific advancements, to name only a few. See for instance Laqueur, *Making Sex*; and Harvey, "Century of Sex."

29. While journals enjoyed greater liberties when it came to reporting on the events of the Revolution, newspapers in territories such as Prussia were subject to more stringent censorship laws. For a more in-depth discussion of censorship laws and the press in Prussia, see Gert Hagelweide, "Publizistischer Alltag in der preußischen Provinz zur Zeit der Französischen Revolution," in *Französische Revolution und deutsche Öffentlichkeit: Wandlungen in Presse und Alltagskultur am Ende des achtzehnten Jahrhunderts*, ed. Holger Böning (Munich: K.G. Sauer, 1992), 251–66.

30. German responses to the French Revolution have been documented extensively. See, among others, the extensive collection of cultural artifacts in Friedrich Eberle and Theo Stammen, ed., *Die Französische Revolution in Deutschland: Zeitgenössische Texte deutscher Autoren Augenzeugen, Pamphletisten, Publizisten, Dichter und Philosophen* (Stuttgart: Philipp Reclam, 1989); Thomas P. Saine, *Black Bread—White Bread: German Intellectuals and the French Revolution* (Columbia, S.C.: Camden House, 1988); the collection of realia in Horst Günther, ed., *Die Französische Revolution: Berichte und Deutungen deutscher Schriftsteller und Historiker* (Frankfurt am Main: Deutscher Klassiker Verlag, 1985); Klaus Epstein, *The Genesis of German Conservatism* (Princeton, N.J.: Princeton University Press, 1966); and G. P. Gooch, *Germany and the French Revolution* (New York: Russell and Russell, 1966).

31. As Alain Ruiz notes, it is rare to find travelogues written in the early years of the Revolution by individuals opposed to the ideals of the Revolution, with the exception of August von Kotzebue. Ruiz, "Deutsche Reisebeschreibungen über Frankreich im Zeitalter der Französischen Revolution (1789–1799): Ein Überblick," in *Reiseberichte als Quellen europäischer Kulturgeschichte: Aufgaben und Möglichkeiten der historischen Reiseforschung*, ed. Antoni Mączak and Hans Jürgen Teuteberg (Wolfenbüttel: Herzog August Bibliothek, 1982), 237. See also, for example, the correspondence series by Johann Heinrich Campe, "Briefe aus Paris zur Zeit der Revolution geschrieben," in Günther, *Berichte und Deutungen*,

9–102; and Konrad Engelbert Oelsner, "Historische Briefe über die neuesten Begebenheiten in Frankreich," *Minerva* 3 (1792): 515–75, which map the trajectory of the Revolution's degeneration from idealistic principles into the realities of violence and bloodshed that informed the average German's gradual disillusionment.

32. Perhaps the most prominent example of the French occupation of German territories was the city of Mainz, located west of the Rhine River, which served repeatedly as a battleground for competing French and German military interests. The Republic of Mainz was short-lived and quickly reverted back to German control after only four months under French occupation in 1793. Most notable among the Mainz Jacobins was the naturalist and professor Georg Forster, who represented the German republic in France's National Convention only to die in exile in Paris after Prussian forces retook the city.

33. Epstein, *German Conservatism*, 458. See also W. Daniel Wilson, *Goethes Weimar und die Französische Revolution: Dokumente der Krisenjahre* (Cologne: Böhlau, 2004), 48–49; and Jeffrey L. High, "Schiller, 'Merely Political Revolutions,' the Personal Drama of Usurpation and Wars of Liberation," in *Schiller: National Poet—Poet of Nations: A Birmingham Symposium*, ed. Nicholas Martin (Amsterdam: Rodopi, 2006), 231–32.

34. See, for example, Friedrich Schiller's 1795 treatise *Über die ästhetische Erziehung des Menschen in einer Reihe von Briefen* (*Letters on the Aesthetic Education of Man*). The example of Schiller is perhaps most striking, since the ideas expressed in his 1782 Sturm und Drang drama *Die Räuber* (*The Robbers*) made him an icon for French revolutionaries. Indeed, he was awarded the title "citoyen français" by the National Convention in 1792 for the "revolutionary" ideals espoused in his play, which he neither publicly accepted nor declined. Some scholars have read Schiller's silence as a direct result of his precarious status in Weimar. See Manfred Windfuhr, "Evolution oder Revolution?: Goethes und Schillers Stellung zur französischen Revolution," in *Literatur: Verständnis und Vermittlung*, ed. Joseph A. Kruse, Monika Salmen, and Klaus-Hinrich Roth (Düsseldorf: Cornelsen, 1991), 104; and Jutta Linder, "Schillers Schweigen: Das Verhalten des Dichters zu Beginn der Französischen Revolution," *Jahrbuch der Brüder Grimm-Gesellschaft* 13–14 (2003–04): 127–32.

35. See, for example, Forster's 1793 correspondence with estranged wife Therese Huber and his *Parisische Briefe*, excerpts of which have been reprinted in *Charlotte Corday: Ein Buch der REPUBLIK*, ed. Petra Nettelbeck and Uwe Nettelbeck (Nördlingen: Delphi, 1987).

36. Epstein, *German Conservatism*, 443. Epstein notes that the revolt's instigator, Christian Benjamin Geissler, had taken special interest in news reports documenting the French women's insurrectionary actions.

37. See chapter 1 for a more in-depth treatment of these historical events and discussion of press reports documenting the women's requests and treatment. See also Dominique Godineau, *The Women of Paris and Their French Revolution*, trans. Katherine Streip (Berkeley: University of California Press, 1998); Darline G. Levy and Harriet B. Applewhite, "Women and Militant Citizenship in Revolutionary Paris," in *Rebel Daughters: Women and the French Revolution*, ed. Sara E. Melzer and Leslie W. Rabine (Oxford: Oxford University Press, 1992), 79–101; and Susanne Petersen, *Marktweiber und Amazonen: Frauen in der Französischen Revolution* (Cologne: Pahl-Rugenstein, 1989).

38. Hippel, *Verbesserung*, 123.

39. Natalie Zemon Davis, "Women on Top: Symbolic Sexual Inversion and Political Disorder in Early Modern Europe," in *The Reversible World: Symbolic Inversion in Art and Society*, ed. Barbara A. Babcock (Ithaca, N.Y.: Cornell University Press, 1978), 154–55.

40. Katharine Kittredge, introduction to *Lewd and Notorious: Female Transgressions in the 18th Century*, ed. Katharine Kittredge (Ann Arbor: University of Michigan Press, 2003), 1.

41. Ruth-Ellen Boetcher Joeres's work on ambiguity and representation in the nineteenth century similarly asserts the importance of studying the anti-ideal, the deviant Other, the peripheral, and the abnormal as these intersect with women writers. See Ruth-Ellen Boetcher Joeres, *Respectability and Deviance: Nineteenth-Century German Women Writers and the Ambiguity of Representation* (Chicago: University of Chicago Press, 1998).

42. Rudolf Dekker and Lotte van de Pol, "Republican Heroines," *History of European Ideas* 10 (1989): 361.

43. Hagemann, "Heldenmütter," 196–97.

44. Krimmer, *Company*, 43.

45. For Marjorie Garber, cross-dressing "offers a challenge to easy notions of binarity, putting into question the categories of 'female' and 'male,' whether they are considered essential or constructed, biological or cultural." Marjorie Garber, *Vested Interests: Cross-Dressing and Cultural Anxiety* (New York: Routledge, 1992), 10. However, Garber has come under fire for what critics, including Anne McClintock, consider her essentialist view of transvestism's subversive power. See Krimmer, *Company*, 14–15.

46. Krimmer, *Company*, 31. As one of the first and most substantive investigations into cross-dressing in German culture of the eighteenth and early nineteenth centuries, Krimmer's book proves invaluable to a discussion of gender ambiguity and the woman warrior.

47. Garber, *Vested Interests*, 17. As part of the transgressive, destabilizing potential of cross-dressing, Garber submits that literary transvestism may signal a crisis in other categories beyond gender: "Category crises can and do mark displacements from the axis of *class* as well as from *race* onto the axis of gender." Garber's correlation between cross-dressing and "epistemic crisis" has proven useful for eighteenth-century scholars like Krimmer and myself, who draw a correlation between the political and social crises generated by the Revolution and those pertaining to gendered identity. Krimmer, *Company*, 13.

48. For a substantive study on the aesthetics of androgyny in the nineteenth century, see MacLeod, *Embodying Ambiguity*. Surprisingly, MacLeod only mentions Kleist in a brief discussion of the fictional figures Kleist and Günderrode in Christa Wolf's *Kein Ort: Nirgends*.

49. See, for example, the insighful and seminal collection of essays by Inge Stephan and Sigrid Weigel in *Die verborgene Frau: Sechs Beiträge zu einer feministischen Literaturwissenschaft* (Berlin: Argument, 1988).

50. See Inge Stephan, "'Da werden weiber zu Hyänen . . .': Amazonen und Amazonenmythen bei Schiller und Kleist," in *Inszenierte Weiblichkeit: Codierung der Geschlechter in der Literatur des 18. Jahrhunderts* (Weimar: Böhlau, 2004), 113–32. Although Stephan's interpretation has been criticized, most

recently by Carola Hilmes and Anett Kollmann, as too narrow and failing to consider broader influences (political, cultural, philosophical, etc.) on the literary constructions of violent women, her readings remain rich resources for feminist investigations of the trope of the woman warrior. See Carola Hilmes, "'Wer bist du, wunderbares Weib?' Kleists *Penthesilea*," in *Die femme fatale im Drama: Heroinen—Verführerinnen—Todesengel*, ed. Jürgen Blänsdorf (Tübingen: Francke, 1999), 59–79; and Anett Kollmann, *Gepanzerte Empfindsamkeit: Helden in Frauengestalt um 1800* (Heidelberg: Universitätsverlag Winter, 2004), 146–47.

51. See, for example, Viktoria Schmidt-Linsenhoff and Christina Klausmann, ed., *Sklavin oder Bürgerin? Französische Revolution und neue Weiblichkeit 1760–1830* (Marburg: Jonas Verlag, 1989); Inge Stephan, Sigrid Weigel, and Ruth Henry, ed., *Die Marseillaise der Weiber: Frauen, die Französische Revolution und ihre Rezeption* (Hamburg: Argument-Verlag, 1989); Helga Grubitzsch et al., ed., *Frauen, Literatur, Revolution* (Pfaffenweiler: Centaurus Verlagsgesellschaft, 1992); and Kollmann, *Gepanzerte Empfindsamkeit.* Furthermore, I am indebted to the extensive, careful documentation by French and German historians of women's participation in the political and military spaces of the French Revolution, Revolutionary Wars, and Napoleonic Wars. See Hagemann, "Female Patriots"; Godineau, *Women of Paris*; Helga Grubitzsch, Hannelore Cyrus, and Elke Haarbusch, ed., *Grenzgängerinnen: Revolutionäre Frauen im 18. und 19. Jahrhundert: Weibliche Wirklichkeit und männliche Phantasien* (Düsseldorf: Schwann, 1985); Petersen, *Marktweiber*; and Joan Landes, *Women and the Public Sphere in the Age of the French Revolution* (Ithaca, N.Y.: Cornell University Press, 1988) and Landes, *Visualizing the Nation: Gender, Representation, and Revolution in Eighteenth-Century France* (Ithaca, N.Y.: Cornell University Press, 2001).

Chapter One

1. The terms "Frauenzimmer" and "Weib(er)" originally referred to woman in general. In the eighteenth century, the word "Weib" continued to refer to woman in the broadest sense, but its meaning was dependent on context and could be used pejoratively. "Frauenzimmer" connoted a woman of higher moral and social standing, something "fein" (delicate) and "gebildet" (refined). See *Deutsches Wörterbuch von Jacob Grimm und Wilhelm Grimm*, s.vv. "Frauenzimmer," "Weib," http://woerterbuchnetz.de/DWB/. See also Ute Frevert, *"Mann und Weib, und Weib und Mann": Geschlechter-Differenzen in der Moderne* (Munich: Beck, 1995). Like the use of *citoyenne* in late eighteenth-century France, the German use of "Bürgersfrau" [*sic*] or "Bürgerin" referred to the "passive" female citizen, who was not granted the same legal rights as "active" male citizens. See Johann Christoph Adelung, ed., *Grammatisch-kritisches Wörterbuch der Hochdeutschen Mundart, mit beständiger Vergleichung der übrigen Mundarten, besonders aber der Oberdeutschen*, s.vv. "Bürgerin," "Weib," http://lexika.digitale-sammlungen.de/adelung/online/angebot. On the "passive" citizen in revolutionary France, see Godineau, *Women of Paris*, 100, 282.

2. See Silvia Bovenschen, *Die imaginierte Weiblichkeit: Exemplarische Untersuchungen zu kulturgeschichtlichen und literarischen Präsentationsformen des Weiblichen* (Frankfurt am Main: Suhrkamp, 1979).

3. Sigrid Weigel has observed that women act as surfaces upon which the male author projects his desires and fears. See Sigrid Weigel, "Die geopferte Heldin und das Opfer als Heldin: Zum Entwurf weiblicher Helden in der Literatur von Männern und Frauen," in *Die verborgene Frau: Sechs Beiträge zu einer feministischen Literaturwissenschaft* (Berlin: Argument, 1988), 141; as well as Inge Stephan, "Bilder und immer wieder Bilder: Überlegungen zur Untersuchung von Frauenbildern in männlicher Literatur," in *Die verborgene Frau: Sechs Beiträge zu einer feministischen Literaturwissenschaft* (Berlin: Argument, 1988), 15–34, and Susanne Zantop, "Crossing the Border: The French Revolution in the German Literary Imagination," in *Representing the French Revolution*, ed. James A.W. Heffernan (Hanover, N.H.: University Press of New England, 1992), 213–33.

4. Elaborating on the process of mythification, Pierre Bourdieu points to the mechanisms by which *symbolic power*, also referred to as *symbolic violence*, is exerted insidiously over and confirmed by the very person subjected to its will. Central to this process is what Bourdieu calls *habitus*, or the historically constituted "system of structured, structuring dispositions," which serves as the vehicle by which individuals are inculcated with ideas, beliefs, and values. The durability of these dispositions, ingrained in the very core of each human being, enables myth to appear as Nature, as an eternal truth. In this way, violent female revolutionaries and patriotic ladies become victims and perpetrators of myth's violence by signifying the very same reactionary social agendas that seek to contain these women within the confines of the domestic, familial realm. See Pierre Bourdieu, *The Logic of Practice*, trans. Richard Nice (Stanford, Calif.: Stanford University Press, 1990), 52.

5. Helga Brandes, "'Über die Revolutionssucht deutscher Weiber': Frauenbilder in der deutschen Publizistik um 1800," in Brandes, "*Der Menschheit Hälfte blieb noch ohne Recht*," 152.

6. Brandes, "Revolutionssucht," 150, 147. See also Brandes, "Literary Market and the Journal, Medium of the Enlightenment," in *German Literature of the Eighteenth Century: The Enlightenment and Sensibility*, ed. Barbara Becker-Cantarino (Rochester, N.Y.: Camden House, 2005), 79.

7. It was common practice for newspapers from different regions to reprint reports from one another. In fact, there is a high rate of transference between the *Vossische* and *Spenersche Zeitungen* as well as newspapers such as the *Kaiserlich privilegirte Hamburgische neue Zeitung*. Many reports published in German newspapers were taken straight from French newspapers. For further discussion of news transference, see Hagelweide, "Publizistischer Alltag"; and Rolf Reichardt, "Probleme des kulturellen Transfers der Französischen Revolution in der deutschen Publizistik 1789–1799," in Böning, *Französische Revolution und deutsche Öffentlichkeit* (Munich: K. G. Saur, 1992), 91–148.

8. Ursula E. Koch, Ute Nawratil, and Detlef Schröter, "Sommer 1789: Französische Revolution und preußische Zeitungsberichte," in Böning, *Französische Revolution und deutsche Öffentlichkeit*, 209 and 244. Although it is well known that the general tone of reports in the *HSZ* remained sympathetic to the Revolution until 1793 and that the *VZ* was, for the most part, impartial throughout, their reports of revolutionary women do not differ significantly in content. See Axel Schumann, "Berliner Presse und Französische Revolution: Das Spektrum der Meinungen unter preußischer Zensur 1789–1806" (doctoral thesis, Technische

Universität Berlin, 2001), 50, http://opus4.kobv.de/opus4-tuberlin/frontdoor/index/index/docId/323/.

9. See Jürgen Wilke, "Die Zeitung," in *Von Almanach bis Zeitung: Ein Handbuch der Medien in Deutschland 1700–1800*, ed. Ernst Fischer, Wilhelm Haefs, and York-Gothart Mix (Munich: C. H. Beck, 1999), 397; Schumann, "Berliner Presse," 50; and Ernst Fischer, Wilhelm Haefs, and York-Gothart Mix in the introduction to *Von Almanach bis Zeitung*, 9.

10. Wolfgang Kaschuba, "Revolution als Spiegel: Reflexe der Französischen Revolution in der deutscher Öffentlichkeit und Alltagskultur um 1800," in Böning, *Französische Revolution und deutsche Öffentlichkeit*, 384.

11. Christoph Martin Wieland, "Unparteyische Betrachtungen über die dermalige Staats-Revolution in Frankreich," *Der Neue Teutsche Merkur* 2 (1790): 51–53.

12. However, not even Wieland was immune to the subjective tendencies inherent in reporting the Revolution, as is evident in his treatment of the French female assassin Charlotte Corday discussed in chapter 2.

13. According to Martin Welke, women accounted for only a relatively small percentage of readers who had access to political material. However, those privileged few, whose homes served as meeting places for intellectual circles, often in university towns, gained access to political news and debates which influenced their own writing and literary works. Therese Huber, Dorothea Schlözer, and Caroline Schelling are among the women Welke acknowledges as forming the exception to the rule. "Die Presse und ihre Leser: zur Geschichte des Zeitungslesens in Deutschland von den Anfängen bis zum frühen 19. Jahrhundert," in *Als die Post noch Zeitung machte*, ed. Klaus Beyrer und Martin Dallmeier (Giessen: Anabas, 1994), 142. Huber and Caroline de la Motte Fouqué stand out in particular for the political subject matter of their novels *Die Familie Seldorf* and *Das Heldenmädchen aus der Vendée* respectively. See chapter 4 for a discussion of images of the warrior women constructed in these texts.

14. Stuart A. Kane, "Wives with Knives: Early Modern Murder Ballads and the Transgressive Commodity," *Criticism* 38, no. 2 (1996): 223.

15. Kane, "Wives with Knives," 232.

16. Martin Welke, "Zeitung und Öffentlichkeit im 18. Jahrhundert: Betrachtungen zur Reichweite und Funktion der periodischen deutschen Tagespublizistik," *Presse und Geschichte* (1977): 82; and Welke, "Presse und ihre Leser," 142. Welke also observes that there were objections to the dissemination of newspapers to the lower classes, particularly peasants, because news of the Revolution in the hands of the uneducated was viewed as a threat to political and social order. See Welke, "Zeitung und Öffentlichkeit," 88; and "Gemeinsame Lektüre und frühe Formen von Gruppenbildungen im 17. und 18. Jahrhundert: Zeitungslesen in Deutschland," in *Lesegesellschaften und bügerliche Emanzipation: Ein europäischer Vergleich*, ed. Otto Dann (Munich: C. H. Beck, 1981), 29–53.

17. Katharine Kittredge suggests that the generalization of women who participated in "transgressive" activities is a direct result of their classification as "female antitype[s]." Kittredge, introduction to *Lewd and Notorious*, 7.

18. *VZ*, July 30, 1789.

19. "Aufstand in Paris; Vereinigung des Königs mit der Nation; Zurückberufung des Herrn Necker und des alten Ministerium," *Historisch-politisches Magazin, nebst litterarischen Nachrichten* 6 (1789): 107.

20. *HSZ*, February 15, 1791.
21. *VZ*, February 15, 1791.
22. Stephan, "Amazonenmythen," 118.
23. *VZ*, October 20, 1789.
24. Ibid.
25. "Neue Revolution in Frankreich: Verlegung der königl. Residenz," *Historisch-politisches Magazin, nebst litterarischen Nachrichten* 6 (1789): 443.
26. Ibid.
27. Ibid.
28. "Paris, den 16. Oktober," in *VZ*, October 27, 1789.
29. For an insightful look at historical cross-dressing women around 1800, see Dekker and van de Pol, "Republican Heroines."
30. Zemon Daves, "Women on Top," 181–82. Caroline de la Motte Fouqué depicts the events mentioned in this report and criticizes the men's attempts to carry out crimes and elude arrest in the guise of women in her novella *Laura: Eine Begebenheit aus der Französischen Revolution*, in *Erzählungen*, vol. 2 (Jena: Bei August Schmid, 1821), 208. Todd Kontje reads this scene within the context of Fouqué's political conservatism, noting that the sight of male cross-dressers would have seemed even "more perverse" than women's cross-dressing and only further reinforced Fouqué's rejection of the Revolution and its negative impact on societal norms. Todd Kontje, *Women, the Novel, and the German Nation 1771–1871: Domestic Fiction in the Fatherland* (Cambridge, Eng.: Cambridge University Press, 1998), 106.
31. *VZ*, August 28, 1792.
32. Ibid.
33. Joseph Hansen, ed. *Quellen zur Geschichte des Rheinlandes im Zeitalter der Französischen Revolution 1780–1801*, vol. 2, *1792–93* (Bonn: Peter Hanstein, 1933), 320.
34. The most famous example is of course Friedrich Schiller's poem "Das Lied von der Glocke," in which women morph into bloodthirsty hyenas. See my discussion of Schiller's portrait of violent female revolutionaries alongside the heroic martyr Johanna from *Die Jungfrau von Orleans* in chapter 3. See also Stephan, "Amazonenmythen."
35. Oelsner, "Historische Briefe," 515.
36. Revenge functions as justification for Sara Seldorf, the protagonist of Therese Huber's novel *Die Familie Seldorf*, to take up arms and to participate in the political and military upheaval of the Revolution.
37. The motif of the consuming, devouring force of uncontainable female sexuality resurfaces most strikingly in the frenzied cannibalistic attack on the Greek warrior Achilles by the Amazon queen Penthesilea in Heinrich von Kleist's tragedy *Penthesilea*, which is analyzed in greater detail in chapter 5.
38. "Unbekannte Züge und Anecdoten zu den Pariser Mord-Scenen im September 1792," *Minerva* 14 (1793): 191.
39. For further "corroboration" of such reports, see also Richard Twiss, "Reise nach Paris: Im Jahr 1792," trans. Johann Wilhelm von Archenholz, *Minerva* 6 (1793): 514.
40. *HSZ*, March 24, 1792.

41. Johann Wilhelm von Archenholz, "Historische Nachrichten vom neuern Frankreich," *Minerva* 2 (1792): 117–18.

42. *VZ*, February 28, 1792.

43. For example, see Brandes, *Ueber die Weiber*, 43, 44. "Documented" anatomical characteristics of the female body such as a smaller, more fragile skeleton, tenuous nerves, ligaments and joints, a proclivity toward overheating, and even skull (i.e. brain) size were all cited as evidence of women's physical and mental inferiority, preventing them from meeting the demands of the public sphere.

44. *VZ*, August 9, 1792.

45. For an analysis of women on the public stage in eighteenth-century Germany, see Wendy Arons, *Performance and Femininity in Eighteenth-Century German Women's Writing: The Impossible Act* (New York: Palgrave Macmillan, 2006); and Mary Helen Dupree, *The Mask and the Quill: Actress-Writers in Germany from Enlightenment to Romanticism* (Lewisburg, Pa.: Bucknell University Press, 2011).

46. *VZ*, June 4, 1793.

47. *VZ*, January 15, 1793.

48. *VZ*, July 4, 1793.

49. See the report from Paris dated August 30 in *VZ*, September 11, 1792.

50. The mobilization of women for war by the Mainz Jacobins stands in stark contrast with the Mainzer Jakobinerclub's policy prohibiting women from becoming official members. Women could fight and sacrifice their lives for their political beliefs, yet they were banned from exercising the same political rights as their male counterparts.

51. Stephan, "Amazonenmythen," 118.

52. *VZ*, April 10, 1790.

53. *HSZ*, June 8, 1790.

54. See the report from Paris on June 25 in *VZ*, July 6, 1790.

55. For further discussion of the paradox of women embodying the Revolution's principles yet denied the rights of citizenship their very images signified, see Landes, *Visualizing the Nation*.

56. See respectively the report from Paris dated September 9 in *HSZ*, September 22, 1792 and one from Paris dated September 7 in *VZ*, September 22, 1792.

57. *VZ*, September 20, 1792.

58. See Hagemann, "Female Patriots" and "Heldenmütter."

Chapter Two

The opening epigraphs read as follows: "Fused together one sees here the ideals / Of beguiling femininity and masculinity. In / The *spirit of Brutus* in the most beautiful form." Heinrich Zschokke, *Charlotte Corday oder die Rebellion von Calvados. Ein republikanisches Trauerspiel in vier Akten. (Aus den Zeiten der französischen Revolution.) In Jamben* (Stettin: Bei Johann Sigismund Kaffke, 1794), 48. "Only in contradiction / Does my self appear with my inner *self*." Engel Christine Westphalen, *Charlotte Corday. Tragödie in 5 Akten mit Chören* (Hamburg: Hoffmann, 1804), 129.

1. Certainly the media coverage of the violent and highly political acts committed in the 1970s by Ulrike Meinhof, Gudrun Ensslin, and other female members of the Rote Armee Fraktion (Red Army Faction) dwarfs the German Corday

reception by comparison. See, for example, Clare Bielby, *Violent Women in Print: Representations in the West German Print Media of the 1960s and 1970s* (Woodbridge, Eng.: Boydell and Brewer, 2012) and Sarah Colvin, "Witch, Amazon, or Joan of Arc? Ulrike Meinhof's Defenders, or How to Legitimize a Violent Woman," in Colvin and Watanabe-O'Kelly, *Women and Death* 2, 250–72.

2. Regarding the eighteenth-century German reception of Corday, see, for example, Petra and Uwe Nettelbeck's collection of journal reports, essays, and etchings in *Charlotte Corday*.

3. In both trial proceedings and the letter to Barbaroux published by the press, Corday is reported to have commented on Marat's nationality. In Corday's letter, translated and reprinted in Christian Ulrich Detlev von Eggers's *Deutsches Magazin*, the passage reads: "dem Himmel sey Dank; er ist kein gebohrner Franzose" ("thank heaven; he is not a Frenchman by birth"). Konrad Georg Friedrich Elias von Schmidt-Phiseldeck, trans., "Aktenstücke, Charlotte Corday betreffend," *Deutsches Magazin* 6 (December 1793): 1382. In Johann Wilhelm von Archenholz's reproduction of trial documents in his journal *Minerva*, a similar statement reads: "Glücklicherweise war er kein Franzose" ("fortunately he was not a Frenchman"). "Briefe und Verhör der Charlotte Corday," *Minerva* 7 (1793): 295.

4. See, among others, Joachim Heinrich Campe's letters from Paris in which the pedagogue and publisher describes the bloodlust and cruelty of the French women: "die Weiber in Paris und, wie es nach verschiedenen Vorfällen in den Provinzen das Ansehen hat, das ganze weibliche Geschlecht in Frankreich dem männlichen an Kultur, an Mäßigung und Sittlichkeit nachsteht und, sooft es zu Gewalttätigkeiten kommt, sich fast immer durch Blutdurst und Grausamkeiten auszeichnet [. . .]" (Campe, "Briefe aus Paris" 88; "The women of Paris and, as it appears based on various incidents in the provinces, the entire female sex in France is inferior to the male sex in terms of culture, moderation, and whenever it comes to violence, the female sex is almost always characterized by bloodlust and cruelty"). Susanne Zantop suggests that opinions such as Campe's were representative of the general sentiment among Germans and that women's "intrusion into a 'male' sphere" threatened established patriarchal norms and the sanctity of the family in Europe. Zantop, "Crossing the Border," 220.

5. Inge Stephan, "'Die erhabne Männin Corday': Christine Westphalens Drama *Charlotte Corday* (1804) und der Corday-Kult am Ende des 18. Jahrhunderts," in *"Sie, und nicht wir,"* ed. Arno Herzig, Inge Stephan, and Hans G. Winter, vol. 1, *Die Französische Revolution und ihre Wirkung auf Norddeutschland* (Hamburg: Dölling & Galitz, 1989), 182. Stephan refers here to the debate over the justification for or against the *Widerstandsrecht* (right of resistance), which proved the sticking point for almost all conservatives in their assessment of Corday's murder of Marat.

6. Stephan, "Corday-Kult," 186.

7. Other such disillusioned revolutionary enthusiasts included Adam Lux, Jean Paul, Konrad Engelbert Oelsner, Friedrich Gottlieb Klopstock, and Johann Wilhelm Ludwig Gleim, among others. For a discussion of their reactions to the bloody turn of the Revolution, see Stephan, "Corday-Kult"; and Arnd Beise, *Charlotte Corday: Karriere einer Attentäterin* (Marburg: Hitzeroth, 1992).

8. Georg Forster, "Georg Forster Briefe," in Günther, *Berichte und Deutungen*, 693–94.

9. Forster, "Briefe," 726.

10. Ibid.

11. Susanne Kord, *Murderesses in German Writing, 1740–1860: Heroines of Horror* (Cambridge, Eng.: Cambridge University Press, 2009), 5–6.

12. Kord, *Murderesses*, 11.

13. Foucault, *Discipline and Punish*, 25.

14. Marat suffered from a painful skin condition contracted during his imprisonment in the early years of the Revolution. In order to alleviate the discomfort, he often conducted business while taking baths.

15. For historical assessments on the renegotiation of masculinities and citizenship, see among others Karen Hagemann, "The Military and Masculinity: Gendering the History of the Revolutionary and Napoleonic Wars, 1792–1815," in *War in an Age of Revolution, 1775–1815*, ed. Roger Chickering and Stig Förster (Cambridge, Eng.: Cambridge University Press, 2010), 331–52; Alan Forrest, Karen Hagemann, and Jane Rendall, ed., *Soldiers, Citizens and Civilians: Experiences and Perceptions of the Revolutionary and Napoleonic Wars, 1790–1820* (New York: Palgrave Macmillan, 2009); and Alan Forrest, "Citizenship and Masculinity: The Revolutionary Citizen-Soldier and His Legacy," in *Representing Masculinity: Male Citizenship in Modern Western Culture*, ed. Stefan Dudink, Karen Hagemann, and Anna Clark (New York: Palgrave Macmillan, 2007), 111–29.

16. See Foucault on the public spectacle of punishment as a (re)assertion of sovereign power. As such, trials and executions as public ceremonies function "not only as a judicial, but also as a political ritual." *Discipline and Punish*, 47.

17. After her death, medical examiners performed an autopsy and determined that Corday was, as she had claimed, a virgin at the time she murdered Marat. Thus, the physical dissection served to restore, at least for some, Corday's virtue and thereby the virtue of her independent act.

18. Bronfen dissects how depictions of social sacrifice involving the feminine body serve as sites of contestation "for a preservation of existing cultural norms and values or their regenerative modification." Bronfen, *Over Her Dead Body: Death, Femininity and the Aesthetic* (New York: Routledge, 1992), 181.

19. Stephan, "Corday-Kult," 200. Stephan was the first scholar to argue that German writers' apotheosis of Corday allowed them to remove the stain of criminality and social transgression from her violent act. Stephan, "Corday-Kult," 186. See subsequently Beise, *Attentäterin*; Erika Süllwold, "'Charlotte Corday' in Hamburg: Christine Westphalens Drama von 1804," in Brandes, *"Der Menschheit Hälfte blieb noch ohne Recht,"* 88–112; and Dagmar von Hoff, *Dramen des Weiblichen: Deutsche Dramatikerinnen um 1800* (Opladen: Westdeutscher Verlag, 1989).

20. See also Stephan, who argues that Corday's act was tolerated, if not sanctioned, among revolutionary supporters, not least because it was perceived as restoring rather than toppling the original revolutionary order and principles. Stephan, "Corday-Kult," 186.

21. "Warnung für einer abscheulichen Mode," *Journal des Luxus und der Moden*, November (1793): 552.

22. "Warnung," 552.

23. The full passage reads: "Liebenswürdige Weiblichkeit, die beym Geräusche der Waffen, und einem blitzenden Stahle erblaßt, nur diese macht Ihnen die Herzen der Männer geneigt, die das wilde funkelnde Auge und das verzerrte Gesichte

einer Bacchantin verscheucht." ("Amiable femininity, which grows pale at the sound of weapons and flashing steel, only this form of femininity inclines the hearts of men toward you and banishes the wild, sparkling eye and the distorted face of a bacchant"). Playing off the gender debates and idealized constructions of femininity at the end of the eighteenth century, the writer Therese Huber, discussed in chapter 4, places a similar sentiment in the mouth of her novel's father figure in *Die Familie Seldorf*: "Der feste, treue, eiserne Mann kann nur der sanftesten Weiblichkeit huldigen; Schwächlinge lieben Amazonen." ("The firm, constant, unyielding man can only revere the gentlest femininity; weaklings love amazons"). Therese Huber, *Die Familie Seldorf*, ed. Magdalene Heuser, 2 vols. (Hildesheim: Georg Olms, 1989), 1:26.

24. Within the larger German reception of Corday, Beise argues that it is "das 'väterliche' Motiv" (the "paternal" motif) and patriotic love of the assassin that is repeatedly mobilized by Corday's defenders in order to justify her transgression. Beise, *Attentäterin*, 31.

25. Themes of self-sacrifice and female patriotism collide with the figure of the woman warrior in works by men and women writers problematizing woman's place in the public life of the emerging German nation. See chapters 3 and 4 for analyses of the deployment of female self-sacrifice by competing interests.

26. While scholars have focused extensively on the demonization of Corday in the "Warnung" article, K---k's response on the point of her exemplarity has received little attention and deserves to be quoted here at some length.

27. K---k, "Ueber Charlotte Corday, die Mörderin Marats, mit Bezug auf einen Aufsatz im Journal des Luxus und der Moden vom November 1793; unter dem Titel: Warnung für(vor) einer abscheulichen Mode," *Deutsche Monatsschrift* 2 (1794): 63–64.

28. Bronfen, *Dead Body*, 181.

29. "Warnung," 552.

30. Ibid.

31. K---k, "Mörderin Marats," 62.

32. See, for example, Johann Wilhelm Ludwig Gleim's series of poems dedicated to Corday unapologetically and emphatically asserting the young French woman's martyrdom and Marat's depravity. In all three texts, the poet raises Corday's noble act of heroism above those of Judith, Brutus, and Cato. Johann Wilhelm Ludwig Gleim, "Charlotte Corday," *Minerva* 8 (1793): 1–4.

33. Wieland's commentary, "Ein Paar Anmerkungen des Herausgebers über Scharlotte Korday" ("A Few Comments by the Publisher on Charlotte Corday"), accompanies the main article "Scharlotte Korday" but as a separate section. All references to Wieland's commentary will appear under the article's main title and author. —tz, "Scharlotte Korday, Nebst einem Anhang über Scharlotte Korday von Christoph Martin Wieland," *Der Neue Teutsche Merkur* 3 (1793): 68–98.

34. —tz, "Scharlotte Korday," 76.

35. Ibid., 81 (my emphasis).

36. Compare Beise, who cites Wieland's remark about Corday's sex to make the case that the issue of gender is only of nominal interest for the broader German Corday reception. *Attentäterin*, 21, 70.

37. Only three years after Corday's assassination of Marat, Fichte had asserted unequivocally that women who demanded the right to participate in public life

did so only out of vanity and desire for fame: "Sie suchen Celebrität bei ihrem Leben, und nach ihrem Tode in der Geschichte" (Fichte, *Grundlage*, 4.131; "they seek celebrity during their lives, and after death in history" [Baur, 300]), behavior which Fichte claimed diminished woman's morality and dignity. More critically, Fichte locates this quest for glory in women's inherent nature to love, a drive to which all other inclinations are subordinate and which similarly informs her virtue (ibid.). Following this logic to its extreme conclusion, even public acts of violence committed by women are inextricably linked to women's bodies and their predisposed natures. If, as Fichte asserts, a woman's every action is dictated by her inclination to love and to sacrifice herself for that love, then depictions of Corday as a patriotic martyr circulating in the German press rely on both the sex and gender of the female assassin to inform their literary treatment of the offender.

38. Wieland dismisses the fanatical tone characterizing translations of Corday's letters as embellishment by well-meaning publishers and translators. He refers here specifically to the excerpts in the "Scharlotte Korday" essay, but his criticism could also be leveled at authors such as Archenholz, who translated and published Corday's letters in his journal *Minerva.*

39. I have chosen to translate "Kaltblütigkeit" along the lines of "sangfroid" in order to convey the calm and composed demeanor exuded by Corday at her trial and execution as reported by the press. To translate it as "cold-bloodedness" would connote reproach, which I suggest does not exist by the conclusion of Wieland's commentary.

40. Stephan, "Corday-Kult," 182–83.

41. The story of the Israelites' rescue from the Canaanites is portrayed in the Book of Judges and depicts how the young Hebrew Yael murdered Sisera, commander of King Jabin's army, with a hammer and nail to the head in her tent. More familiar is the story of Judith's decapitation of the Assyrian general Holofernes in order to save the Israelites. Unlike Yael, Judith's story is laden with erotic undertones and implications that Judith seduced Holofernes in order to murder him. As such, visual and literary culture has privileged a sexually laden image of the Hebrew heroine, and in the nineteenth century, Judith came to exemplify the model of transgressive femininity as femme fatale. For cultural representations of Judith in the German tradition, see Watanabe-O'Kelly, *Beauty or Beast?* 112–44.

42. Translations of documents pertaining to Corday's case appeared in von Eggers's *Deutsches Magazin* 6 (1793). Archenholz published another set of translations among which were the letters Corday wrote in order to gain access to Marat, as well as the letters to Barbaroux and her father. As I have already noted, Wieland took exception to the exaggerated tone in the published translations of Corday's letters and provided his readers with what he deemed a more accurate translation.

43. Von Schmidt-Phiseldeck, "Aktenstücke," 1384.

44. Ibid.

45. "Briefe und Verhör," 298.

46. Corday's critique appears even sharper in the versions of letters to her father published in *Minerva*: "O ihr unglücklichen Republikaner! muß euch ein Weib den Weg zu erhabenen Handlungen zeigen" ("Briefe und Verhör," 288; "Oh you unhappy republicans! Must a woman show you the way to noble action").

See also the enthusiastic eulogy in Wieland's *Merkur*: "Erbärmliche Republikaner! Mußte ein Weib euch die Bahn zu Großthaten zeigen?" (—tz, "Scharlotte Korday," 75; "Wretched republicans! Must a woman have shown you the path to mighty deeds?"). These remarks do not appear in the documents published in von Eggers's *Deutsches Magazin*, nor does Wieland include them in his translation of her letter to her father. This inconsistency and inclusion of such a striking critique in some journals while absent in others highlights the ambivalent response of the German public to an act of violence perpetrated by a woman.

47. I refer here to Bakhtin's term "dialogism" taken up and adapted by Julia Kristeva in her articulation of "intertextuality" to communicate the constellations of meaning linking myths across historical and cultural spaces. In this sense, images of the biblical heroines Yael or Judith that take hold of the cultural imagination around 1800 cannot be emptied entirely of their previous meanings. These traces of meaning persist and the very historicity of such forms is what allows them to be appropriated and adapted readily for any specific historical context, or as Barthes notes, "mythical speech is made of material which has *already* been worked on so as to make it suitable for communication." Barthes, *Mythologies*, 110. In the case of Corday and the legacy of self-sacrificing female heroism, these semiotic traces prove critical to orienting the eighteenth-century reader to the greater significance of Corday's act of patriotism and her literary apotheosis.

48. Watanabe-O'Kelly, *Beauty or Beast?* 142.

49. For a biographical account of Zschokke, see Werner Ort, *Heinrich Zschokke (1771–1848): Eine Biographie* (Baden: hier + jetzt, 2013); and Holger Böning, *Heinrich Zschokke und sein "Aufrichtiger und wohlerfahrener Schweizerbote": Die Volksaufklärung in der Schweiz* (New York: Peter Lang. 1983). For Westphalen, see Süllwold, "Westphalens Drama"; and Stephan, "Corday-Kult." For a discussion of Hamburg as an independent, politically progressive city amidst the revolutionary conflicts, see among others Jost Hermand, "The Jacobins of Hamburg and Altona (in memoriam Walter Grab I)," in *Patriotism, Cosmopolitanism, and National Culture: Public Culture in Hamburg, 1700–1933*, ed. Peter Uwe Hohendahl (Amsterdam: Rodopi, 2003), 133–41.

50. In Westphalen's work alone the following references appear within the span of fifteen pages: "Engel" (angel) 217, 219, 220, 221, 22; "Heilige" (saint) 217; and "Göttliche" (the divine) 232.

51. Be, review of *Charlotte Corday: Tragödie in fünf Acten, mit Chören, Mit einem Kupfer*, by Engel Christine Westphalen, *Neue Allgemeine Deutsche Bibliothek* 101, no. 1 (1805): 180. Westphalen published her works under the pseudonym Angelika. On the challenges faced by eighteenth- and nineteenth-century women dramatists, see Susanne Kord, *Ein Blick hinter die Kulissen: Deutschsprachige Dramatikerinnen im 18. und 19. Jahrhundert* (Stuttgart: J. B. Metzlersche Verlagsbuchhandlung, 1992); von Hoff, *Dramen des Weiblichen*; and Arons, *Performance and Femininity*. On German women writers and anonymity during this period, see Kord, *Sich einen Namen machen* (1996); and Helen Fronius, *Women and Literature in the Goethe Era: (1770–1820): Determined Dilettantes* (Oxford: Clarendon, 2007). See also Stefanie Hilger, who sees an affinity between Corday's incursion into the masculine realm of politics and Westphalen's invasion of the male-dominated domain of drama. Hilger, "The Murderess on Stage: Christine Westphalen's *Charlotte Corday* (1804)," in *Women and Death*

3: *Women's Representations of Death in German Culture since 1500*, ed. Clare Bielby and Anna Richards (Rochester, N.Y.: Camden House, 2010), 73.

52. Eg, review of *Charlotte Corday, oder die Rebellion von Calvados: Ein republicanisches Trauerspiel in vier Acten. (Aus den Zeiten der französischen Revolution), In Jamben*, by Heinrich Zschokke, *Neue allgemeine deutsche Bibliothek* 17, no. 2 (1795): 340.

53. Westphalen, *Corday*, 5–6.

54. Zschokke, *Rebellion von Calvados*, 1. Beise argues that Zschokke's use of the terms "Schwärmerei" (excessive enthusiasm) and "Schwärmerin" (enthusiast or dreamer) are not meant pejoratively but that Zschokke reappropriates them as "eine bestimmte Art von Wirklichkeitsaneignung, besser gesagt -bewältigung, durch und in der Kunst, speziell der Literatur" ("a certain way of appropriating reality, or better said a way of overcoming reality, by means of and in forms of art, specifically literature") in order to affirm Corday's motivations. Beise, *Attentäterin*, 40.

55. See the report from Paris dated July 29 in *VZ*, August 10, 1793.

56. Zschokke, *Rebellion von Calvados*, 1.

57. Westphalen, *Corday*, 14.

58. Stephanie Hilger argues that Westphalen's positioning of Corday as a witness to the Revolution's violence allows Corday's decision to murder Marat to appear as informed and not irrational. See Hilger, "Murderess on Stage," 82.

59. Compare Karin Baumgartner, who argues that Corday's impetus for murder remains abstract, "as she has not been affected personally by the Revolution." Baumgartner, *Public Voices: Political Discourse in the Writings of Caroline de la Motte Fouqué* (New York: Peter Lang, 2009), 99.

60. Lynn Hunt offers an insightful discussion of the French Revolution's destabilizing effects on patriarchal systems of power at both the state and family levels in *The Family Romance of the French Revolution* (Berkeley: University of California Press, 1992). See also Peter Uwe Hohendahl on the literary renegotiation of masculinities amidst German military defeats during the Revolutionary and Napoleonic Wars in "Krise der Männlichkeit im späten 18. Jahrhundert: Ein Problemskizze," *Zeitschrift für Germanistik* 12, no. 2 (2002): 275–86.

61. See Baumgartner, who examines early nineteenth-century German women writers' reassessment of masculinity in the wake of the devastating defeat by French forces at the Battle of Jena in 1806 through an analysis of Westphalen's collection of patriotic songs *Gesänge der Zeit* (*Songs of the Time*, 1815). Baumgartner reads Westphalen's work as mounting a critique of German masculinity as a direct result of the military's continued losses, which lead to Napoleon's occupation of German territories. She also asserts that Westphalen's songs envisioned forms of armed female activism in the service of the homeland. Baumgartner, "Valorous Masculinities and Patriotism in the Texts of Early Nineteenth-Century German Women Writers," *German Studies Review* 31, no. 2 (2008): 129–30.

62. Von Hoff, *Dramen des Weiblichen*, 93, 105.

63. See also Hilger, who argues the importance of Westphalen's selection of Cato, Socrates, *and* Arria as stressing the legacy of politically active women and that bravery is not limited to a male tradition. At the same time, Westphalen opts out of referencing the biblical heroine Judith and thereby erases the mark

of impropriety associated with her beheading of Holofernes. Hilger, "Murderess on Stage," 82.

64. Zschokke, *Rebellion von Calvados*, 5.

65. For Zschokke's Corday, civil war literally appears as a war within a family: "Brüder werden ihre Brüder / Ermorden, Väter ihre Söhne!" (HZ, 43; "Brothers will murder their brothers, / Fathers will murder their sons!"). All further citations from Zschokke that include italics appear in the original.

66. Compare Beise, *Attentäterin*, 38–39. Beise reads the emancipatory tendency of Zschokke's work as his new contribution to the Corday reception in Germany; however, he stops short of suggesting that Zschokke's drama was intended to incite real change or agitate for women's active political participation.

67. By establishing a personal tie between Corday and the Mainzer deputy, whose public defense of the assassin cost him his life, Hilger argues that Westphalen carefully creates an *Identifikationsmöglichkeit* (possibility for identification) for her German readers to the French murderess. Hilger, "Murderess on Stage," 76.

68. I refer here again to Fichte's appendix on family right in his treatise *Grundlage des Naturrechts*, in which he articulates a theory of woman's inextricable nature to love and sacrifice herself for man. See chapters 3 and 4 for more detailed treatments of Fichte's theories and their implications for representations of women warriors.

69. See similarly Hilger, "Murderess on Stage," 79; and Süllwold, "Westphalens Drama," 102, who view Luchs's characteristics as evidence of Westphalen's inversion of the gender paradigm.

70. Von Hoff, *Dramen des Weiblichen*, 93. See also Stephan, "Corday-Kult," 198.

71. Indeed, the drama's male characters Luchs and Lagarde only take note of Corday as an object of desire and admiration *after* she has murdered Marat and is unattainable.

72. On the femme fatale in the nineteenth century, see Carola Hilmes, *Die Femme fatale: Ein Weiblichkeitstypus in der nachromantischen Literatur* (Stuttgart: Metzler, 1990).

73. Corday uses the metaphor of illness and infection to characterize the devastation of a civil war and the means to eradicate it:

Allein der *Bürgerkrieg*,
Der Bürgerkrieg, Corbigni, ist Verwesung
Des Staats; ein Gift, das diesen blühnden Körper
Von innen aus zerstört; die Banden
Zerfrißt, die ihn umfassen, und die Theile
Des schönen Ganzen aus einander treibet.
Wer ist der *Arzt*, der Frankreich rettet?
Ich will ihn lieben, will anbeten ihn
Wie meinen Gott! (HZ, 54)

Only the *civil war*,
The civil war, Corbigni, is decay
Of the State; a poison, which destroys this thriving body
From the inside outward; the ties

It devours, which surround it, and the parts
Of the glorious whole it drives apart.
Who is the *physician,* who will save France?
I want to love him, want to worship him
As my God!

74. Corbigni's change of heart and willingness to carry out the attack on Marat only arises when he realizes that Corday will murder Marat on her own. His impetus to act is not a newfound patriotic loyalty; rather, his motivation remains his desire to possess Corday: "Höll' und Tod, es geht nicht! / Was kümmert mich das Vaterland, die Welt, / Wenn diese Welt ihr Kleinod für mich nicht / Mehr hat" (HZ, 99; "Hell and death, it will not work! / What does the fatherland, the world matter to me, / If this world no longer holds this treasure / For me").

75. Von Hoff, *Dramen des Weiblichen*, 81. Von Hoff cites the parallel example of Günderrode's dramatic heroine Hildgund, which I discuss in detail in chapter 4.

76. See also Corday's remark after Robert's departure: "Keine / Minute länger, und ich war——ein Weib!" (HZ, 116; "Not / A minute more, and I was——a woman!").

77. Renatus Karl von Senckenberg also depicts Corday stabbing Marat to death in his 1797 documentary-style drama *Charlotte Gorday oder die Ermordung Marats dramatisirt: Carolina Cordaea Epos* (St. Ingbert: Röhrig Universitätsverlag, 1999). For an analysis of this text, see Beise, *Attentäterin*, 45–48.

78. In this regard, I disagree with Beise, who recognizes the emancipatory potential inherent in Zschokke's affirmative portrayal of Corday as an empowered agent of change but argues that Zschokke's drama forecloses the potential for Corday to be read as agitating for female emancipation because his audience knows that it is only a work of fiction. See Beise, *Attentäterin*, 45.

79. Süllwold, "Westphalens Drama," 98.

80. Westphalen, *Corday*, 111–12.

81. In a similar strategy, Westphalen constructs political debates between the play's male characters (Antoine, father Corday, Luchs, and Lagarde) about who is the true villain of the Revolution to confirm Charlotte's decision to target Marat.

82. Westphalen draws a parallel between Marat and the sixteenth-century head of the Catholic Church, Pope Sixtus V (1520–1590), an accomplished reformer who was known for his severity and strictness, including the use of public executions, in order to restore order in the Papal States. See Richard McBrien, *Lives of Popes: The Pontiffs from St. Peter to John Paul II* (San Francisco: HarperCollins, 1997), 292–94.

83. Westphalen uses the following expressions to convey Corday's internal turmoil: "*Mit Abscheu*"; "*Mit Befremdung*"; and "*Sie hält erschrocken inne. / Mit Abscheu*" (CW, 129; In disgust; In disconcertment; and Horrified, she pauses. / In disgust).

84. Baumgartner, *Public Voices*, 97.

85. See similarly Kord, *Kulissen*, 126.

86. See also Hilger for a comparison between the original trial proceedings and Westphalen's staged scene. "Murderess on Stage," 78–79.

87. See Baumgartner, *Public Voices*, 98; and Hilger, "Murderess on Stage," 77.

88. See Beise, who reads Westphalen's drama through the lens of Schiller's dramatic aesthetic and with Schiller's *Die Jungfrau von Orleans*. Beise, *Attentäterin*, 95–101.

89. See also Stephan, who interprets Corday's declaration as evidence of Corday's status as an independent, active subject. "Corday-Kult," 197.

90. Süllwold suggests that Lagarde's newfound patriotic fervor and vision of the Republic post-Corday embodies Westphalen's "gesellschaftliche Utopie" (societal utopia). Süllwold, "Westphalens Drama," 103. However, Lagarde's continued inaction and implied inability to realize such a vision leaves the utopian ideal exactly that, an imaginary, unattainable state.

91. Süllwold, "Westphalens Drama," 104.

92. Kord argues that Westphalen places greater weight on the pure motives driving Corday's deed than on the success of her action. Critical to Corday's deification is not "*wie* sie handelt, sondern *daß* sie handelt, macht Charlotte zur Heldin und ihr Leben nacherzählenswert" ("*how* she acts, rather, *that* she acts, which makes Charlotte into a heroine and her life worth retelling"). Kord, *Kulissen*, 128.

93. Certainly the issue of authenticity is one that is both complex and fraught with contradictions. What or who is the authentic Corday? Is it her own self-stylized image constructed for public consumption? Is it the image that is mediated through translation of language and ideological agendas of publishers and reporters? While it is impossible to know who this authentic Corday is, I apply the term with this critical awareness in mind.

94. Zschokke alters slightly Corday's statements in letters to her father and Barbaroux as they appeared in Archenholz's *Minerva*: "Sie wissen, daß nur das Verbrechen, nicht aber das Schaffot beschimpft" ("You know, that it is only crime, and not the scaffold, which affronts"). To Barbaroux, Corday is reported to have written: "ich hoffe noch am nämlichen Tage in den Elisäischen Feldern mit Brutus und einigen andern Alten zusammen zu treffen" ("Briefe und Verhör," 288, 293; "I hope to encounter on that certain day Brutus and a few other ancients in the Elysian Fields").

95. In the trial documents, the statements Corday made in court appear as: "aber den Franzosen fehlt es an Geist und Energie, Republicaner zu seyn. [. . .] Ich sehe in der Versammlung des Convents unwissende und feige Memmen, die da dulden, daß einige wenige Bösewichter die Menschheit mit Füssen treten, und den Bürgerkrieg anzünden" ("Briefe und Verhör," 298; "but the Frenchmen are lacking in spirit and energy in order to be republicans. [. . .] I see in the assembly of the National Convention ignorant and faint-hearted cowards, who tolerate that a few miscreants trample humanity with their feet and ignite civil war").

Chapter Three

1. Epstein, *German Conservatism*, 675. As Epstein has readily pointed out, the parochial structure of the Holy Roman Empire around 1800 made *Staatspatriotismus* (regional patriotism) rather than *Reichspatriotismus* (national patriotism) far more prevalent (244).

2. Ibid., 451.

3. Krimmer, *Company*, 43.

4. I have chosen to use the spelling of the name Herrmann as it appeared in the play's first edition. Beginning with the 1808 Cotta edition, the spelling was changed to Hermann.

5. See, for example, Sigrid Weigel, "Der schielende Blick: Thesen zur Geschichte weiblicher Schreibpraxis," in *Die verborgene Frau: Sechs Beiträge zu einer feministischen Literaturwissenschaft* (Berlin: Argument, 1988), 83–137

6. Pierre Bourdieu, *Masculine Domination*, trans. Richard Nice (Stanford, Calif.: Stanford University Press, 2001), 40.

7. Data collected in the University of Innsbruck's online database for the historical novel upsets this long-held assumption documenting that more men than women published novels in the eighteenth and nineteenth centuries. See Anita Runge, "Schweizerische Geschichte in Familiengeschichten: *Elisabeth, Erbin von Toggenburg* von Benedikte Naubert (1756–1819)," in *Familiengeschichten: Biographie und familiärer Kontext seit dem 18. Jahrhundert*, ed. Christian von Zimmermann and Nina von Zimmerman (New York: Campus, 2008), 34. See the database for historical novels compiled by Kurt Habitzel and Günter Mühlberger, "Projekt Historischer Roman," Institut für Germanistik der Universität Innsbruck, http://www.uibk.ac.at/germanistik/histrom.

8. Among others, see Waltraud Maierhofer, "Das späte 18. Jahrhundert: Benedikte Naubert: *Thekla von Thurn* (1788)—Bernhard von Weimars Page wider Willen," in *Hexen—Huren—Heldenweiber: Bilder des Weiblichen in Erzähltexten über den Dreißigjährigen Krieg* (Cologne: Böhlau, 2005), 96. See also Jeannine Blackwell, "Die verlorene Lehre der Benedikte Naubert: Die Verbindung zwischen Phantasie und Geschichtsschreibung," in *Untersuchungen zum Roman von Frauen um 1800*, ed. Helga Gallas and Magdalene Heuser (Tübingen: M. Niemeyer, 1990), 153.

9. Kurt Scheinert, *Benedikte Naubert: Ein Beitrag zur Entstehungsgeschichte des historischen Romans in Deutschland* (Berlin: Kraus Reprint, 1969), 26.

10. Naubert published an impressive number of historical novels, countless fairy tales, essays, and translations. Due to Naubert's anonymity as an author, even the most conservative estimate of thirty novels indicates just how prolific a writer she was, particularly given the staggering length of her novels.

11. See Ak, review of *Philippe von Geldern, oder Geschichte Selims des Sohns Amurat. Zwey Theile*, by Benedikte Naubert, *Neue Allgemeine Deutsche Bibliothek* (1793): 460. On the gender of Naubert's readership, see Anita Runge, "Gattung und Geschlecht—Zusammengestellt von Anna Fleig und Helge Meise—Konstruktionen von Geschichte und Geschlecht im Geschichtsroman deutschsprachiger Autorinnen um 1800: Das Beispiel Benedikte Naubert (1756–1819)," *Das Achtzehnte Jahrhundert* 29, no. 2 (2005): 230.

12. Benedikte Naubert, *Geschichte der Gräfin Thekla von Thurn oder Scenen aus dem dreyssigjährigen Kriege* (Leipzig: Weygandsche Buchhandlung, 1788), 1:VIII.

13. Naubert's surviving correspondence, with the exception of two letters, covers only the period between 1805 and 1818, after the publication of the novels considered in this chapter.

14. See also Watanabe-O'Kelly, *Beauty or Beast?* 218. Frauke Reitemeier suggests that Naubert's narrators take a critical stance on rebellions and revolts by

the masses. Reitemeier, *Deutsch-englische Literaturbeziehungen: Der historische Roman Sir Walter Scotts und seine deutschen Vorläufer* (Munich: Ferdinand Schöningh, 2001), 52.

15. Maierhofer, "Page wider Willen," 73.

16. Only general references to the novel appear in works about the author and the genre of the historical novel. See, for example, Reitemeier, *Literaturbeziehungen*, 58–68. See also Christine Touaillon, *Der deutsche Frauenroman des 18. Jahrhunderts* (Bern: Peter Lang, 1979), 349. As an exception, see the study of homoerotic undercurrents in the novel in Dino Heicker, *Gespenster und Geschlechter: Homoerotik in der europäischen Schauerliteratur* (Hamburg: MännerschwarmSkript, 2004), 101–4.

17. The majority of the novel's characters (Philippe, Amurat, Mahomed, Ladislav, etc.) are based loosely on historical figures; however, Naubert appears to have conflated the sultans Mehmed II (1432–1481), Selim I (1470–1520), and Selim III (1761–1808) in the novel's male protagonist Selim. For detailed histories of the Ottoman Empire and military conflicts, see Halil İnalık, *The Ottoman Empire: The Classical Age, 1300–1600* (New York: Praeger, 1973); and more recently Colin Imber, *The Ottoman Empire, 1300–1650: The Structure of Power* (New York: Palgrave Macmillan, 2009).

18. Naubert's spelling of the name Kolonna is inconsistent. It appears as both Kollonna and Kolonna throughout the novel. I have chosen to use the spelling Kolonna. Similarly, she spells Mohamed as Mahomed. I have opted to keep the original spelling as it appeared in the first edition.

19. Recent scholarship on the woman warrior has tended to overlook Dorothea, most likely because she does not fit characteristics commonly associated with warlike women (cross-dressing, presence on the public battlefields as soldier, etc.).

20. For Goethe's attitudes toward rebellion and revolution, see W. Daniel Wilson, *Goethes Weimar* and *Das Goethe-Tabu: Protest und Menschenrechte im klassischen Weimar* (Munich: Deutscher Tanschenbuch, 1999).

21. Johann Wolfgang von Goethe, "Bedeutende Fördernis durch ein einziges geistreiches Wort," in *Sämtliche Werke: Briefe, Tagebücher, und Gespräche*, ed. Dorothea Kuhn, vol. 24, *Schriften zur Morphologie* (Frankfurt am Main: Deutscher Klassiker, 1987), 597. Reiner Wild suggests that Goethe's attempts to come to terms with the Revolution were not just about the political events but also about the possibility of using literature in order to express the experience of the Revolution. Wild, "Naivität und Terror: Die Französische Revolution im Urteil des klassischen Weimar," in *Schreckensmythen–Hoffnungsbilder: Die Französische Revolution in der deutschen Literatur*, ed. Harro Zimmermann (Frankfurt am Main: Athenäum, 1989), 52.

22. In a letter to Johann Heinrich Meyer dated December 5, 1796, Goethe states that the action of the drama occurs during August 1795. Goethe, *Samtliche Werke: Briefe, Tagebücher, und Gespräche*, ed. Christoph Brecht and Waltraud Wiethölter, vol. 8, *Die Leiden des Jungen Werthers, Die Wahlverwandtschaften, Kleine Prosa, Epen* (Frankfurt am Main: Deutscher Klassiker, 1987), 1199. See Wiethölter's commentary on the genesis of *Herrmann und Dorothea* for likely inspirations for the figure Dorothea, including Goethe's encounter with refugees while accompanying Duke Carl August during the First Coalition in 1792–93,

which are documented in *Campagne in Frankreich* (1822). Goethe, *Sämtliche Werke*, 8:1195–1198.

23. Frank C. Ryder and Benjamin Bennett, "The Irony of Goethe's *Hermann und Dorothea*: Its Form and Function," *PMLA* 90, no. 3 (May 1975): 436.

24. In addition to Ryder and Bennett, Peter Morgan observes that Dorothea is the only figure who is never the object of irony. Morgan, *Critical Idyll: Traditional Values and the French Revolution in Goethe's "Hermann und Dorothea"* (Columbia, S.C.: Camden House, 1990), 93.

25. Hohendahl, "Krise der Männlichkeit," 276. Hohendahl's essay cites the critical period between 1806 and 1815 as decisive for the emergence of new masculine identities closely bound to the archetypes of soldier/warrior and public servant (277). However, Hans Peter Herrmann's analysis of the Herrmann motif in eighteenth-century literature argues that even as early as the 1740s notions of masculinity and warfare were being reconceptualized. See Herrmann, "Arminius und die Erfindung der Männlichkeit im 18. Jahrhundert," *Der Deutschunterricht* 47 (1995): 32–47.

26. Lesley Sharpe, *Schiller and the Historical Character: Presentation and Interpretation in the Historiographical Works and in the Historical Dramas* (Oxford: Oxford University Press, 1982), 7.

27. Friedrich Schiller, *Werke: Nationalausgabe*, ed. Helmut Koopmann and Benno von Wiese, vol. 20, *Philosophische Schriften* (Weimar: Böhlau, 1962), 218. English translation of *On the Pathetic*, in *Friedrich Schiller: Essays*, ed. Walter Hinderer and Daniel O. Dahlstrom, trans. Daniel O. Dahlstrom (New York: Continuum, 1993), 66. References to Schiller's works are from *Werke: Nationalausgabe*. Quotations of prose texts and poetry are identified by volume and page number; quotations of his verse drama are indicated by volume and line number.

28. See, for example, Gail K. Hart, "Re-Dressing"; and Elisabeth Krimmer, *The Representation of War in German Literature: From 1800 to the Present* (New York: Cambridge University Press, 2010).

29. See the commentary for Schiller's *Wallenstein* as well as correspondence between Schiller and Christian Körner, most notably November 2, 1788, and April 17, 1797. Correspondence between Schiller and the publisher Johann Friedrich Cotta (May 1, 1795 and May 12, 1795) also suggest Schiller's familiarity with Naubert's *Neue Volksmärchen der Deutschen* (*New German Folktales*). For *Wallenstein*, see Schiller, *Werke: Nationalausgabe*, ed. Hermann Schneider and Lieselotte Blumenthal, vol. 8, *Wallenstein* (Weimar: Böhlau, 1949). For Schiller's correspondence and familiarity with Naubert's works, see *Werke: Nationalausgabe*, ed. Günter Schulz and Lieselotte Blumenthal, vol. 35, *Briefwechsel: Briefe an Schiller 25. 5. 1794–31. 10. 1795* (Weimar: Böhlau, 1964).

30. Wild suggests that beginning with the storming of the Tuileries (August 10, 1792), Germans had grown disenchanted with the general trends toward revolutionary violence. Wild, "Naivität und Terror," 59. For scholarship concerning Schiller's stance on the early years of the Revolution, see Jeffrey L. High, *Schillers Rebellionskonzept und die Französische Revolution* (Lewiston, N.Y.: Mellen, 2004); Jutta Linder, "Schillers Schweigen"; Manfred Windfuhr, "Evolution oder Revolution?: Goethes und Schillers Stellung zur Französischen Revolution," in *Literatur: Verständnis und Vermittlung*, ed. Joseph A. Kruse, Monika Salmen,

and Klaus-Hinrich Roth (Düsseldorf: Cornelsen, 1991), 97–110; and Ulrich Karthaus, "Schiller und die Französische Revolution," *Jahrbuch der deutschen Schillergesellschaft* 33 (1989): 210–39.

31. High, "Drama of Usurpation," 220, 235.

32. See also Hart, "Re-Dressing"; and Ariane Martin, "Johannas 'männlich Herz' im Zwiespalt: Geschlechterdifferenz als tragischer Konflikt in Schillers *Jungfrau von Orleans*," *Der Deutschunterricht* 6 (2004): 75–85.

33. The very structure of Schiller's "Würde der Frauen," with alternating stanzas and differing meter and form, reproduces the oppositional, commensurate view of femininity and masculinity articulated in Wilhelm von Humboldt's treatise *Über den Geschlechtsunterschied*. Although von Humboldt praised Schiller's poem as "ein göttliches Stück" (Schiller, *Werke*, 35:328; a divine work), the Romantics Friedrich and August Wilhelm Schlegel were less generous in their assessment of the poem. August Wilhelm Schlegel suggested it should be read backwards and created a parody titled "Schillers Lob der Frauen" ("Schiller's Praise of Women"). See Friedrich Schlegel, *Kritische Friedrich-Schlegel-Ausgabe*, ed. Hans Eichner, vol. 2, bk. 2, *Charakteristiken und Kritiken II, (1802–1829)* (Munich: Ferdinand Schöningh, 1975), XIII–XIV.

34. Hart, "Re-Dressing," 96.

35. See also the letter to Schiller from his fiancé Charlotte von Lengefeld, dated November 13, 1789, in which she recounts secondhand accounts of female cannibalism in the streets of Paris. Schiller, *Werke: Nationalausgabe*, ed. Siegfried Seidel, vol. 33, bk. 1, *Briefe an Schiller 1781–1790* (Weimar: Böhlau, 1989), 410–11.

36. Despite the favorable reception Schiller's poem received by his close circle of friends, including Wilhelm von Humboldt, Körner, and Goethe, the Schlegels once again derided his unrealistic depiction of women. See Caroline Schlegel's letter to her daughter Auguste Böhmer, in which she states that reading Schiller's poem caused people to fall off their chairs in laughter. Caroline Schlegel-Schelling, *"Lieber Freund, ich komme weit her schon an diesem frühen Morgen": Caroline Schlegel-Schelling in ihren Briefen*, ed. Sigrid Damm (Darmstadt: Luchterhand, 1981), 190.

37. Jeffrey L. High reads Schiller's later historical dramas, including *Jungfrau*, within the political climate of warfare and foreign occupation around 1800. He notes that Schiller's work on *Jungfrau* commenced around the time of French occupation of southern German territories and that his "metanarratives" on occupation and insurrection "invoke German prospects for nationhood" in his contemporary readers. High, "Drama of Usurpation," 235, 238. See also David Pugh, "Schiller and Revolution," in *The French Revolution and the Age of Goethe*, ed. Gerhart Hoffmeister (Hildesheim: Olms, 1989), 31–50. In this sense, Johanna can be read as a defender of the *German* domestic good.

38. See Tatiana Korneeva, "Cross-Dressing Strategies in Benedikte Naubert's Fairy Tale Novella *Der kurze Mantel*," *German Life and Letters* 65, no. 3 (July 2012): 281–94. Korneeva's assessment is based on Naubert's strategy of "literary cross-dressing" in the fairy tale novella *Der kurze Mantel* (*The Cloak*, 1789–92) and the historical novel *Barbara Blomberg, vorgebliche Maitresse Kaiser Karls des Fünften* (*Barbara Blomberg, Alleged Mistress of Charles V*, 1790).

39. Korneeva, "Cross-Dressing Strategies," 293, 294.

40. Thekla's first masquerade as a soldier, an idea which initially excites her, ultimately results in rampant rumors that threaten to disgrace her family. Her brother-in-law, Colonel Falkenberg, authorizes her second masquerade as a defensive move to protect her and her sister Therese from General Tilly's impending attack on Magdeburg.

41. As Watanabe-O'Kelly notes, Naubert repeatedly emphasizes the assumption that a woman who cross-dresses and goes to war does so "out of lust to be near the man she loves." Watanabe-O'Kelly, *Beauty or Beast?* 216. However, Thekla and Philippe repeatedly pass these tests of their virtue.

42. There is certainly a parallel between Naubert's Thekla and Therese Huber's protagonist Sara Seldorf, whose presence on the battlefield serves to humanize warfare and the male soldier. However, none of the male warriors exposed to the "humanizing" influences of Thekla or Philippe demonstrates a transformation to more compassionate warriors, and the novels' narrators remain silent on this aspect of women's presence amidst the military conflicts.

43. Notation of citations from *Herrmann und Dorothea* indicate volume and page number.

44. All translations of *Herrmann und Dorothea* are indicated by line number.

45. Irmgard Wagner, "*Herrmann und Dorothea* in the Context of Kant and Voß: A Question of Peace and Patriarchy," *Goethe Yearbook* 9 (1999): 178. In this regard, Goethe's portrayal of the French attack on German territories anticipates and perhaps shapes the imagery deployed in Kleist's patriotic, and decidedly anti-French, poems "Germania an ihre Kinder" ("Germania on her Children") and "Kriegslied der Deutschen" ("Battle Song of the Germans," 1809) as well as his tragedy *Penthesilea*, in which the birth of the Amazon nation is presented as a direct result of sexual aggression by a foreign usurper.

46. Wilhelm von Humboldt, "Ueber Göthe's *Herrmann und Dorothea*," in *Gesammelte Werke* (Berlin: G. Reimer, 1843), 4:95.

47. Hart, "Re-Dressing," 100.

48. Notations of English translations refer to page number. While MacDonald translates "Rabenmutter" as "that bird of prey, his mother," I propose the translation "unnatural mother" to capture Queen Isabeau's deviant status within Thibaut's gender model.

49. See also High, *Schillers Rebellionskonzept*; and Pugh, "Schiller und Revolution."

50. See Edward T. Larkin's emphasis on the father in "Reading Schiller's *Die Jungfrau von Orleans* with Lacan: In the 'Name-of-the-Father' and of the Daughter," *Monatshefte* 96, no. 2 (2004): 199–219.

51. Anett Kollmann has argued that Isabeau presents a positive model of women in the public sphere, because her engagement in political events is unmediated. Kollmann, *Gepanzerte Empfindsamkeit*, 114. While I agree with Kollmann's assessment of Isabeau as a new model of the politically active woman, her presence within the political realm is neither legitimized nor tolerated by patriarchal society. Isabeau does not offer the same emancipatory potential as the women warriors of Huber, Günderrode, and Fouqué's works.

52. Hart, "Re-Dressing," 120. Despite natural affinities to the historical Joan of Arc, Johanna deviates from her counterpart in several important features, including her appearance. See Watanabe-O'Kelly, *Beauty or Beast?* 148–56;

Krimmer, *Representation of War*, 37–44; and Inge Stephan, "Hexe oder Heilige? Zur Geschichte der Jeanne d'Arc und ihrer literarischen Verarbeitung," in *Die verborgene Frau: Sechs Beiträge zu einer feministischen Literaturwissenschaft* (Berlin: Argument, 1988), 54–58.

53. The majority of dramatic texts involving women warriors, including those treated in this book, avoid depicting female aggression and violence on stage; instead, they resort to descriptions of the battle by other characters in real time, such as in Kleist's *Penthesilea*.

54. Karl S. Guthke argues Johanna's mission is not primarily motivated by religious fervor but by patriotism and politics. As he perceptively notes, it is Johanna who invokes God to justify her actions and not God who has chosen Johanna. Guthke, "'Die Jungfrau von Orleans': Sendung und Witwenmachen," in *Schiller heute*, ed. Hans-Jörg Knobloch and Helmut Koopmann (Tübingen: Stauffenburg, 1996), 122–23.

55. In *Philippe von Geldern*, the true warrior woman is Hermione, the daughter of Emperor Constantine, who disguises herself as a soldier in order to protect her father. Her death is also depicted heroically, allowing her transgression to be recuperated for a noble cause. Naubert, *Philippe von Geldern*, 1:159–60.

56. Although Kalepin dies at the end of the novel, he does so from wounds sustained on the battlefield, implying a death suitable for a warrior. BNP, 2:548–549.

57. Barbara Becker-Cantarino reads Dorothea in the larger context of Goethe's literary female characters as confirming Goethe's conservative view of women's role in society. Becker-Cantarino, "Goethe and Gender," in *The Cambridge Companion to Goethe*, ed. Lesley Sharpe (Cambridge, Eng.: Cambridge University Press, 2002), 188.

58. See, for example, Wagner, "Peace and Patriarchy," 179; Katharina Mommsen, "Goethe as a Precursor of Women's Emancipation," in *Goethe Proceeding: Essays Commemorating the Goethe Sesquicentennial at the University of California, Davis*, ed. Clifford A. Bernd (Columbia, S.C.: Camden House, 1984), 55; and Gerhard Kluge, "*Herrmann und Dorothea*: Die Revolution und Herrmanns Schlußrede-zwei 'schmerzliche Zeichen'?" *Goethe-Jahrbuch* 109 (1992): 64.

59. Wagner, "Peace and Patriarchy," 184.

60. Scholars have debated the inspiration for Goethe's first fiancé: Peter Morgan suggests Mainzer Jacobin and naturalist Georg Forster. Morgan, "Aufklärung, Revolution und Nationalgefühl: der Topos des Jakobiners und die Frage deutscher Identität in Goethes 'Herrmann und Dorothea,'" in *Grenzen, Traditionen, Vergleiche: Akten des VIII. Internationalen Germanisten-Kongresses, Tokyo*, ed. Eijirō Iwasaki (Munich: Iudicium, 1991), 80. Thomas Saine presents a compelling case for German Jacobin Adam Lux in "Charlotte Corday, Adam Lux, and *Hermann und Dorothea*," in *Exile and Enlightenment: Studies in German and Comparative Literature*, ed. Uwe K. Faulhaber et al. (Detroit: Wayne State University Press, 1987), 87–96.

61. For a reading advancing Herrmann's agency, see Morgan, *Critical Idyll*, 62–63. For Herrmann and pacifism, see Saine, "Adam Lux," 382. See also Ryder and Bennett, who view the contradiction between Herrmann's words and actions as an example of poetic irony. Ryder and Bennett, "Form and Function," 442.

62. Morgan, "Topos des Jakobiners," 87.

63. Stephan, "Amazonenmythen," 126.

64. Martin, "Geschlechterdifferenz," 79. See also Hart, "Re-Dressing," 102.

65. See also Stephan, "Amazonenmythen," 124.

66. Heinrich Zschokke deploys a similar strategy in his portrayal of Charlotte Corday, who uses her suitor Corbigni's desire for her in an attempt to convince him to murder Marat. See chapter 2 for an analysis of this scene.

Chapter Four

Huber's epigraph reads: "I lived two years of the most dreadful bitterness, if there had been the Revolution at the time, I would have rushed to the sites of bloodshed, I would have fought in the columns of fighters, I would have murdered—in order to savor a feeling that revived the numb despair of my breast." Quoted in Andrea Hahn, ed., *Die reinste Freiheitsliebe, die reinste Männerliebe: Ein Lebensbild in Briefen und Erzählungen zwischen Aufklärung und Romantik* (Berlin: Henssel, 1989), 148. Günderrode's epigraph reads: "I have often had the unfeminine wish to throw myself into the wild tumult of battle, to die—why wasn't I born a man? I have no sense for feminine virtues, for the bliss of women. Only the wild, grand, and shining pleases me. It is a wretched but incorrigible disparity in my soul; and it will and must remain so, for I am a woman and have desires like a man without his strength." The original German quote appears in Max Preitz, "Karoline von Günderrode in ihrer Umwelt II: Karoline von Günderrodes Briefwechsel mit Friedrich Karl und Gunda von Savigny," *Jahrbuch des freien deutschen Hochstifts* (1964): 171. The English translation is taken from Patricia Anne Simpson, *The Erotics of War in German Romanticism* (Lewisburg, Pa.: Bucknell University Press, 2006), 105–6. In this letter to Kunigunde Brentano (August 29, 1801), Günderrode expresses her lifelong desire to free herself from the social bonds that held her captive and for the right to die a heroic death that was reserved for men.

1. The narrative strategies these authors deploy in their depictions of the female warrior evince a striking affinity with those mobilized by the authors in chapters 2 and 3. Indeed, the very fluidity and polyvalent nature of the rhetorically constructed warlike woman allowed her to be easily appropriated and reframed by writers for competing purposes. One could place Fouqué alongside Naubert, Goethe, and Schiller just as readily as one might argue reading Goethe or Naubert together with Huber and Günderrode. Such juxtapositions might yield further productive discussions on the myth of the warlike woman. The subtle distinctions separating these authors' literary attempts to make sense of the enigmatic woman warrior are ones of gradation rather than stark opposition. I have chosen to position Fouqué next to Huber and Günderrode to allow her work to be read through a critical lens challenging notions that aristocratic women writers unquestioningly supported the gendered status quo. At the same time, this deliberate grouping is intended to provoke a reconsideration of the complex ways in which class, gender, and politics inform representations of disorderly women in public life.

2. Further references to Caroline de la Motte Fouqué are listed simply as Fouqué.

3. See, for example, Luce Irigaray's notion of mimesis to subvert essentialist views of "the feminine." As Irigaray advocates, "One must assume the feminine role deliberately. Which means already to convert a form of subordination into

an affirmation, and thus to begin to thwart it. [. . .] To play with mimesis is thus, for a woman, to try to recover the place of her exploitation by discourse, without allowing herself to be simply reduced to it." Irigaray, *This Sex Which Is Not One* (Ithaca, N.Y.: Cornell University Press, 1985), 76.

4. Gayatri Chakravorty Spivak, "In a Word: Interview," in *Outside in the Teaching Machine* (New York: Routledge, 1993), 5. See also Spivak, "Can the Subaltern Speak?," in *Marxism and the Interpretation of Culture*, ed. Cary Nelson and Lawrence Grossberg (Urbana: University of Illinois Press, 1988).

5. Baumgartner, *Public Voices*, 18.

6. See Dekker and van de Pol's documentation of historical cross-dressers during the French Revolution and Revolutionary Wars in "Republican Heroines."

7. Therese Huber, *Briefe*, ed. Magdalene Heuser et al. (Tübingen: Niemeyer, 1999–2011), 5:437. Huber's quote is couched as a response to the increasingly nationalistic sentiment in Germany during the War of the Sixth Coalition. More specifically, she criticizes what she views as staunchly conservative women's desires for only the most sensational, biased news about Napoleon's atrocities to confirm their own uninformed political views of the French enemy. Becker-Cantarino notes Huber's strategic self-fashioning as dutiful housewife and mother to stave off criticism of her literary pursuits. Becker-Cantarino, "Revolution im Patriarchat: Therese Forster-Huber (1764–1929)," in *Out of Line/Ausgefallen: The Paradox of Marginality in the Writings of Nineteenth-Century German Women*, ed. Ruth-Ellen B. Joeres and Marianne Burkhard (Amsterdam: Rodopi, 1989), 242.

8. Mechthilde Vahsen, *Die Politisierung des weiblichen Subjekts: Deutsche Romanautorinnen und die Französische Revolution (1790–1820)* (Berlin: E. Schmidt, 2000), 45–72.

9. See Helmut Peitsch, "Die Revolution im Familienroman: Aktuelles politisches Thema und konventionelle Romanstruktur in Therese Hubers *Die Familie Seldorf*," *Jahrbuch der Deutschen Schiller-Gesellschaft* 28 (1984): 259; and Helga Meise, "Politisierung der Weiblichkeit oder Revolution des Frauenromans? Deutsche Romanautorinnen und die Französische Revolution," in *Les Femmes et la Revolution Française: Actes du Colloque International, 12–13–14 Avril 1989, Université de Toulouse-Le Mirail*, ed. Marie-France Brive (Toulouse: Presses Universitaires du Mirail, 1989), 75.

10. For further details about Huber's life, see Barbara Becker-Cantarino, *Schriftstellerinnen der Romantik: Epoche—Werke—Wirkung* (Munich: C. H. Beck, 2000); Gerhart Söhn, *Frauen der Aufklärung und Romantik: Von der Karschin bis zur Droste* (Düsseldorf: Gruppelo, 1998); Jeannine Blackwell, "Marriage by the Book: Matrimony, Divorce, and Single Life in Therese Huber's Life and Works," in *In the Shadow of Olympus: German Women Writers Around 1800*, ed. Katherine R. Goodman and Edith Waldstein (Albany: State University of New York Press, 1992), 137–56; and Blackwell, "Therese Huber," in *German Writers in the Age of Goethe, 1789–1832*, ed. James N. Hardin and Christoph E. Schweitzer (Detroit: Gale, 1989), 187–92; and Magdalene Heuser, "Nachwort" to *Die Familie Seldorf*, by Therese Huber (Hildesheim: Georg Olms, 1989).

11. Söhn, *Frauen der Aufklärung*, 172.

12. Huber claimed authorship of *Die Familie Seldorf* in 1811. Heuser, "Nachwort," 2:350.

13. Scholars have argued convincingly for reading Sara with the French female revolutionary Théroigne de Méricourt. See Helga Grubitzsch, "Théroigne de Méricourt—Revolutionärin, Minerva oder Hure der Nation? Lebenswirklichkeit und biographische Legenden einer revolutionären Frau," in *Frauenmacht in der Geschichte*, ed. Jutta Dalhoff, Uschi Frey, and Ingrid Schöll (Düsseldorf: Schwann, 1986), 210; and Renate Haas, "Therese Huber: Teilemanzipation und Schriftstellerinnenkarriere durch die Französische Revolution," in *Freiheit, Gleichheit, Weiblichkeit: Aufklärung, Revolution und die Frauen in Europa*, ed. Marieluise Christadler (Opladen: Leske & Budrich, 1990), 92n36.

14. Hahn, *Freiheitsliebe*, 143; and Elisabeth Krimmer, "Female War Stories: Violence and Trauma in Works by Therese Huber and Caroline de la Motte-Fouqué," *Internationales Jahrbuch der Bettina-von-Arnim-Gesellschaft* 17 (2005): 126–27.

15. Peitsch, "Familienroman," 259; and Carola Hilmes, "'Die Familie Seldorf'—Ein Revolutionsroman," in *Skandalgeschichten: Aspekte einer Frauenliteraturgeschichte* (Königstein: Ulrike Helmer Verlag, 2004), 55.

16. Becker-Cantarino, "Revolution im Patriarchat," 236.

17. The subtitle was not added until the 1831 edition.

18. Future reference to Count L*** will appear simply as L. or the count.

19. See Hunt, *Family Romance*.

20. Huber was well-versed in the contemporary debates and even maintained regular correspondence with Wilhelm von Humboldt (Huber, *Briefe*, 1:606), including a discussion of his theories on complementary gender characteristics, with which Huber apparently disagreed. Haas, "Teilemanzipation," 78.

21. Seldorf's disdain for any transgression of these gender "norms" is reminiscent of Ernst Brandes's treatise *Ueber die Weiber*. As Brandes's step-niece, Huber no doubt would have been familiar with the views expressed in his work and its place within the gender debates of the late eighteenth century. On Huber's relationship to Brandes, see Haas, "Teilemanzipation," 91n31.

22. Kontje, *Domestic Fiction*, 69.

23. Hippel, *Verbesserung*, 123.

24. See also Meise, "Politisierung der Weiblichkeit," 71; and Hilmes, "Revolutionsroman," 56.

25. See, for example, Stephanie Hilger, "Sara's Pain: The French Revolution in Therese Huber's *Die Familie Seldorf* (1795–1796)," in *Contemplating Violence: Critical Studies in Modern German Culture*, ed. Stefani Engelstein and Carl Niekerk (New York: Rodopi, 2011), 35–48.

26. As of April 30, 1793, the National Convention had decreed women's participation in the armed forces to be illegal and henceforth barred.

27. Krimmer, *Company*, 52.

28. See, for example, Baumgartner, *Public Voices*, 94; Becker-Cantarino, "Revolution im Patriarchat," 249–51; and Hilmes, "Revolutionsroman," 57.

29. See similarly Watanabe-O'Kelly, *Beauty or Beast?* 222.

30. I draw here on J. L. Austin's theory of speech acts and illocutionary acts as "performatives" that bring into existence the very things they declare. See Austin's *How to do Things with Words* (Cambridge, Mass.: Harvard University Press, 1962). It should also be noted that "Es" can refer also to the neuter noun "das Weib."

31. See, for example, Inge Stephan, "Revolution und Konterrevolution: Therese Huber's Roman 'Die Familie Seldorf' (1795/96)," in *Der deutsche Roman der Spätaufklärung: Fiktion und Wirklichkeit*, ed. Harro Zimmermann (Heidelberg: Winter, 1990), 193.

32. Baumgartner, *Public Voices*, 96. See also Watanabe-O'Kelly, who reads the open ending of *Die Familie Seldorf* as resisting the "conventional view of matrimony as woman's destiny." *Beauty or Beast?* 221.

33. See Sigrun Schmid, *Der 'selbstverschuldeten Unmündigkeit' entkommen: Perspektiven bürgerlicher Frauenliteratur* (Würzburg: Königshausen & Neumann, 1999), 91; Inge Stephan, "On Gender Wars and Amazons: Therese Huber on Terror and Revolution," in Krimmer and Simpson, *Enlightened War*, 179; Becker-Cantarino, "Poetische Freiheit, Revolution und Patriarchat: Über Therese Hubers Roman 'Die Familie Seldorf,' " in Brandes, *"Der Menschheit blieb noch ohne Recht,"* 72; and Anke Gilleir, "On the Presentation of the Body in the Work of Therese Huber and Johanna Schopenhauer," in *Harmony in Discord: German Women Writers in the Eighteenth and Nineteenth Centuries*, ed. Laura Martin (New York: Peter Lang, 2001), 224. Stephan goes so far as to describe Sara as a living corpse, incapable of affection. Stephan, "Revolution und Konterrevolution," 183.

34. Compare Kontje, *Domestic Fiction*, 62; and Krimmer, "War Stories," 129.

35. Bettine von Arnim, *Werke und Briefe*, ed. Walter Schmitz and Sibylle von Steindorff (Frankfurt am Main: Deutscher Klassiker Verlag, 1986), 1:536.

36. Max Preitz, "Karoline von Günderrode in ihrer Umwelt I: Briefe von Lisette und Christian Nees von Esenbeck, Karoline von Günderrode, Friedrich Creuzer, Clemens Brentano und Susanne von Heyden," *Jahrbuch des freien deutschen Hochstifts* (1962): 250.

37. For detailed Günderrode biographies, see Margaret C. Ives, "Karoline von Günderrode (1780–1806): The 'Tian' Legend," in *Sappho in the Shadows: Essays on the Work of German Women Poets of the Age of Goethe (1749–1832), with Translations of Their Poetry into English*, ed. Anthony J. Harper and Margaret C. Ives (New York: Peter Lang, 2000), 87–98; Becker-Cantarino, *Schriftstellerinnen*, 199–225; Margarete Susman, *Frauen der Romantik: Mit zahlreichen Abbildungen und einem Nachwort von Barbara Hahn* (Frankfurt am Main: Insel, 1996), 168–200; Xu Pei, *Frauenbilder der Romantik: Annette von Droste-Hülshoff, Clemens Brentano, Joseph von Eichendorff, Heinrich Heine* (Düsseldorf: Gruppelo, 1997), 78–95; Birgit Weißenborn, ed., *"Ich sende Dir ein zärtliches Pfand": Die Briefe der Karoline von Günderrode* (Frankfurt am Main: Insel, 1997), 7–39; and Lucia Maria Licher, *Mein Leben in einer bleibenden Form aussprechen: Umrisse einer Ästhetik im Werk Karoline von Günderrode (1780–1806)* (Heidelberg: Universitätsverlag C. Winter, 1996).

38. Von Arnim, *Werke und Briefe*, 535.

39. Ives, "Karoline von Günderrode," 93.

40. See the Günderrode epigraph at the beginning of this chapter, in which Günderrode, inspired by her reading of Ossian's poem "Darthula," gives voice to desires deemed unseemly for women around 1800.

41. The dates for the works by Günderrode are based on Walter Morgenthaler's critical notes: where two dates are listed, the first date is the general time frame for the creation of the text followed by the first date of publication.

42. Compare Becker-Cantarino, "The 'New Mythology': Myth and Death in Karoline von Günderrode's Literary Work," in Bielby and Richards, *Women and Death 3*, 67.

43. All references to Günderrode's works are listed as volume and line number in which they appear in Karoline von Günderrode, *Sämtliche Werke und ausgewählte Studien*, ed. Walter Morgenthaler (Basel: Stroemfeld/Roter Stern, 1990–91).

44. The English translation is taken from Krimmer, *Company*, 136.

45. Translation from Krimmer, *Company*, 136.

46. See Krimmer, *Company*, 136.

47. Ibid., 135.

48. Von Hoff, *Dramen des Weiblichen*, 15.

49. Becker-Cantarino, "Myth and Death," 52.

50. Ibid., 68.

51. Weißenborn observes there is little reference to Günderrode's political leanings in her correspondence. *Briefe*, 18. An 1804 letter from Savigny to Günderrode is cited in which he teases her about her "ordentlich republikanische Gesinnungen" (proper republican attitudes). Preitz, "Umwelt II," 195. Licher argues that Günderrode's protagonist conveys her support for the unrealized ideals of the Revolution. Licher, *Umrisse einer Ästhetik*, 50.

52. Simpson, *Erotics of War*, 107.

53. Hunt, *Family Romance*, xiv.

54. See similarly Judith Purver, "Revolution, Romanticism, Restoration (1789–1830)," in *A History of Women's Writing in Germany, Austria and Switzerland*, ed. Jo Catling (Cambridge, Eng.: Cambridge University Press, 2000), 79; and von Hoff, *Dramen des Weiblichen*, 100.

55. Simpson likewise notes the affinities between Günderrode's Mora and Hildgund and Goethe's Iphigenie. Simpson, *Erotics of War*, 120, 122.

56. The English translation appears in Simpson, *Erotics of War*, 122.

57. More specifically, Licher reads Hildgund as the torchbearer of the revolutionary principles and a freedom fighter and Attila as a placeholder for Napoleon, the oppressor of the German people. Licher, *Mein Leben*, 146. See also Becker-Cantarino, *Schriftstellerinnen*, 214.

58. Licher, *Umrisse einer Ästhetik*, 138.

59. Von Hoff, *Dramen des Weiblichen*, 99.

60. Simpson, *Erotics of War*, 123.

61. Becker-Cantarino, *Schriftstellerinnen*, 212.

62. See also Simpson, *Erotics of War*, 120.

63. For detailed Fouqué biographies, see Erich P. Hofacker, Jr., "Caroline de la Motte Fouqué," in Hardin and Schweitzer, *German Writers in the Age of Goethe*, 78–83; and Jean T. Wilde, *The Romantic Realist: Caroline de la Motte Fouqué* (New York: Bookman Associates, 1955).

64. Fouqué's first husband's drinking and gambling habits had driven her to return home to her family and to seek a divorce. During this marriage, it is suspected that Fouqué engaged in an affair with the Prussian officer von Lehndorff, resulting in the birth of her daughter Klara in the late 1790s. Despite her conservative political background, such an affair would suggest Fouqué was socially progressive. Wilde, *Romantic Realist*, 31. Indeed, the unconventional intimate

relationships of Huber, Günderrode, and Fouqué reveal the tension between the myth of bourgeois virtue and daily life.

65. Nennhausen became a meeting place for the likes of Jean Paul, August Wilhelm Schlegel, Ludwig Tieck, and Johann Gottlieb Fichte, among others. Wilde, *Romantic Realist*, 121–60.

66. During both marriages, Fouqué spent time at the court in Berlin, where she had befriended among others Princess Marianne, wife of Prince Wilhelm and sister-in-law to the king of Prussia, Friedrich Wilhelm III. She would have been privy to the latest news, and also gossip, about the events surrounding the French Revolution and the subsequent Wars of Liberation. Furthermore, her second husband Friedrich de la Motte Fouqué had participated in the 1794 campaign and his family had direct ties to the royalist supporters of the Vendée insurrection.

67. See, for example, Fouqué's letter to Karl Varnhagen von Ense from November 11, 1813, in which she recounts the trauma suffered by the family during the French occupation in Karl August Varnhagen von Ense, *Biographische Portraits: Nebst Briefen von Koreff, Clemens Brentano, Frau von Fouqué, Henri Campan und Scholz* (Leipzig: Brockhaus, 1871), 145. However, more horrific than her personal loss are the deaths of the soldiers and simultaneously the principles of freedom: "Ich flehete wie eine Besessene zu Gott, und könnte etwas den Himmel spalten, mein Schmerzensschrei wäre hindurchgedrungen!" (ibid; "I pleaded to God like a woman possessed. If it were possible for something to split open the heavens, my cry of pain would have penetrated through it").

68. Krimmer, "War Stories," 131.

69. Wilde, *Romantic Realist*, 93.

70. Baumgartner, *Public Voices*, 81. See also Krimmer, *Company*, 174, 177; and Todd Kontje, "Gender-Bending in the Biedermeier," *Women in German Yearbook* 12 (1996): 64.

71. Elisabeth Krimmer, "Officer and Lady: Pants and Politics in Caroline de la Motte-Fouqué's *Das Heldenmädchen aus der Vendee* (1816)," *Studies in Eighteenth-Century Culture* 30 (2001): 166.

72. See similarly Krimmer, "Officer and Lady," 177.

73. References to Fouqué's novel refer to volume and page number.

74. The expelled and persecuted Girondist deputy Barbaroux makes a cameo appearance, as do Jacobins Robespierre, Saint-Just, and Danton. Even Marat's young assassin Charlotte Corday is mentioned in connection with Barbaroux, and Fouqué uses the rumoured association between Barbaroux and Corday to introduce the news of Marat's assassination at a woman's hand into her novel. Indeed, Fouqué similarly portrays Corday's great sacrifice as a challenge to men's bravery and masculinity, when she has Barbaroux exclaim: "Was leben wir denn noch, [. . .] und verkriechen uns wie Elende in Wäldern und Höhlen, wenn die Welt keine Seele mehr hat wie diese [Corday]!" (CMF, 1:119; "Why do we still live, [. . .] and crawl away like the wretched into forests and caves, if the world has no other souls like this [Corday]!").

75. Krimmer, "Officer and Lady," 171.

76. Ibid., 177.

77. Here we see a clear affinity between Fouqué's Elisabeth and Schiller's Johanna. Both bear the banner for the restoration of the monarch; however, Schiller's Johanna actively fights and kills in the name of the sovereign.

78. See also Kontje, "Gender-Bending," 60; and Baumgartner, *Public Voices*, 108–9.

79. Krimmer, "Officer and Lady," 173.

80. Kontje, "Gender-Bending," 60–61.

81. Krimmer, "Officer and Lady," 177.

82. It should be noted that the word "patriot," derived from Greek *patriōtēs*, foregrounds the correlation between personal and political in the stem of the word associated with *patḗr*.

Chapter Five

1. Androgynous attributes gained popularity in literary lives and works during the age of *Empfindsamkeit* and took on even greater significance in the era of German Romanticism. See, for example, MacLeod, *Embodying Ambiguity*. Notations of citations for Kleist's correspondence refer to volume and page number, while notations of citations from *Penthesilea* indicate volume and line number. All translations of *Penthesilea* are noted with page numbers.

2. Sigrid Scheifele, *Projektionen des Weiblichen: Lebensentwürfe in Kleists Penthesilea* (Würzburg: Königshausen & Neumann, 1992), 234–39. See also Stephan, who finds evidence for Kleist's conflicted notions of his own sexual identity in letters to his half-sister Ulrike. Stephan, "Amazonenmythen," 127. Specifically, Stephan addresses speculation surrounding Kleist's close relationship with Ernst von Pfuel, with whom he served in the Prussian army.

3. Compare Paul Kluckhohn, who dismisses the connection between Kleist's conservative stance toward women's emancipation and the "Amazonenproblem" (Amazon problem) in his drama. Kluckhohn, "Penthesilea," in *Heinrich von Kleist Aufsätze und Essays*, ed. Walter Müller-Seidel (Darmstadt: Wissenschaftliche Buchgesellschaft, 1987), 46. As Stephan and others have demonstrated, reading Kleist's Amazons through the lens of his relationship with his real-life amazon sister and other "emancipated" women of his time has proven productive in establishing Kleist's engagement with dominant gender discourses and emancipatory desires around 1800. Stephan, "Amazonenmythen."

4. See Hohendahl, "Krise der Männlichkeit."

5. See Krimmer for a discussion of Kleist's critique of warfare in *Die Hermannsschlacht* and *Penthesilea*. She argues that Kleist rejects war as a rational pursuit by depicting its violence and inhumanity which are displaced onto the bodies of women. Krimmer, *Representation of War*, 47. See also Krimmer, "The Gender of Terror: War as (Im)Moral Institution in Kleist's *Hermannsschlacht* and *Penthesilea*," *The German Quarterly* 81, no. 1 (Winter 2008): 75.

6. It was also during this time that Kleist had been captured by the French and imprisoned in Fort Joux and Châlons-sur-Marne under suspicion of being a spy. Kleist, *Sämtliche Werke*, 2:677.

7. Dirk Grathoff, *Kleist: Geschichte, Politik, Sprache. Aufsätze zu Leben und Werk Heinrich von Kleists* (Opladen: Westdeutscher Verlag, 1999), 175. Grathoff also stresses the importance of the young Kleist's disenchantment with and later renunciation of the Prussian military complex as an institution of tyranny and oppression (179).

8. Jochen Schmidt, *Heinrich von Kleist: Die Dramen und Erzählungen in ihrer Epoche* (Darmstadt: Wissenschaftliche Buchgesellschaft, 2003), 38.

9. Wolf Kittler, *Die Geburt des Partisanen aus dem Geist der Poesie: Heinrich von Kleist und die Strategie der Befreiungskriege* (Freiburg: Rombach, 1987), 226.

10. See Krimmer, "Gender of Terror," 70–71.

11. See also Julie Koser, "Rebellious Bodies: The Human Form as Site of Social and Political Conflict in Heinrich von Kleist's *Die Hermannsschlacht* and *Penthesilea*," in *Rebellion and Revolution: Defiance in German Literature, History and Art*, ed. Melissa Etzler and Priscilla Layne (Newcastle upon Tyne, Eng.: Cambridge Scholars Publishing, 2010), 63–64.

12. Kleist completed the drama in 1807 and published a portion of it as a fragment in the first edition of his literary journal *Phöbus* in 1808 before its full publication later that year by Cotta.

13. For scholarship addressing the classical tragedy and aesthetics, see Hinrich Seeba's commentary in the Deutscher Klassiker edition. HK, 2:752–53; Ortrud Gutjahr, "Iphigenie–Penthesilea–Medea: Zur Klassizität weiblicher Mythen bei Goethe, Kleist und Grillparzer," in *Frauen: MitSprechen MitSchreiben*, ed. Marianne Henn and Britta Hufeisen (Stuttgart: Hans-Dieter Heinz, 1997), 228; Roger Paulin, "Kleist's Metamorphoses: Some Remarks on the Use of Mythology in *Penthesilea*," *Oxford German Studies* 14 (1983): 35–36; Inge Stephan, "Mignon und Penthesilea: Androgynie und erotischer Diskurs bei Goethe und Kleist," in *Inszenierte Weiblichkeit: Codierung der Geschlechter in der Literatur des 18. Jahrhunderts* (Cologne: Böhlau, 2004), 180; Schmidt, *Dramen und Erzählungen*, 107–10; Michel Chaouli, "Devouring Metaphor: Disgust and Taste in Kleist's *Penthesilea*," *The German Quarterly* 69, no. 2 (1996): 125–43; and Heather Merle Benbow, "'Weil ich der raschen Lippe Herr nicht bin': Oral Transgression as Enlightenment Disavowal in Kleist's *Penthesilea*," *Women in German Yearbook* 22 (2006): 151–55. For scholarship on Kleist's critique of the Enlightenment and his "Kant Crisis," see Benbow, "Oral Transgression"; Hinrich Seeba, "The Eye of the Beholder: Kleist's Visual Poetics of Knowledge," in *A Companion to the Works of Heinrich von Kleist*, ed. Bernd Fischer (Rochester, N.Y.: Camden House, 2003), 103–22; Catherine E. Rigby, *Transgressions of the Feminine: Tragedy, Enlightenment and the Figure of the Woman in Classical German Drama* (Heidelberg: Winter, 1996); and Christoph Türcke, "Liebeserklärung an den Amoklauf: Menschheit und Tierheit in Kleists *Penthesilea*," *Einspruch* 5 (1987): 39–44. For a discussion of gender, see among others Erika Berroth, *Heinrich von Kleist: Geschlecht—Erkenntnis—Wirklichkeit* (New York: Peter Lang, 2003); Jost Hermand, "Kleists *Penthesilea*: Im Kreuzfeuer geschlechtsspezifischer Diskurse," *Monatshefte* 87, no. 1 (Spring 1995): 34–47; Sigrid Lange, *Die Utopie des Weiblichen im Drama Goethes, Schillers und Kleists* (New York: Peter Lang, 1993); Stephan, "Amazonenmythen"; and Ruth Angress, "Kleist's Nation of Amazons," *Beiträge zur Germanistik* 1 (1978): 5–28.

14. Ritchie Robertson, "Women Warriors and the Origin of the State: Zacharias Werner's *Wanda* and Heinrich von Kleist's *Penthesilea*," in Colvin and Watanabe-O'Kelly, *Women and Death 2*, 75. See also Peter Horn, "'Penthesilea': The Revival of a Greek Myth as an Endorsement of Kleist's Social and Political Ideals," *English Studies in Africa* 18 (January 1975): 99–106.

15. The first scholar to establish the connection between Kleist's Amazons and the amazons of the French Revolution was Stephan, "Amazonenmythen." Carola Hilmes dismisses, hastily I argue, the legitimacy of such a reading as inadequate.

Hilmes, "'Wunderbares Weib?'" 71. Meanwhile, the overwhelming majority of scholarship on this issue supports Stephan's reading as well as the link between Kleist's Amazon nation and the amazons of the French Revolution. For scholarship supporting Stephan's reading see Lange, *Utopie des Weiblichen*; Eleanor E. ter Horst, *Lessing, Goethe, Kleist, and the Transformation of Gender: From Hermaphrodite to Amazon* (New York: Peter Lang, 2003); Scheifele, *Projektionen des Weiblichen*; and Türcke, "Liebeserklärung."

16. Benbow, "Oral Transgression," 159.

17. William Blake Tyrrell, *Amazons: A Study in Athenian Mythmaking* (Baltimore: Johns Hopkins University Press, 1984), xiv.

18. Ibid., xv.

19. Simon Richter, *Missing the Breast: Gender, Fantasy, and the Body in the German Enlightenment* (Seattle: University of Washington Press, 2006), 221. However, as I argue, it is not Penthesilea's desire that is transgressive or deviant. Rather, it is her love for Achilles, which she is incapable of suppressing, that violates both Amazon law and the law of the battlefield.

20. As Thomas Laqueur has demonstrated, the advent of the French Revolution and subsequent decades of warfare were only one factor contributing to the appearance of myths that propagated the view of gender's commensurability, what he terms the emergence of the "two-sex model," and the social subordination of woman by means of scientific and social theories. See Laqueuer, *Making Sex*.

21. Barthes, *Mythologies*, 110.

22. Ibid., 129.

23. See for example Goethe's essay, *Winckelmann und sein Jahrhundert* (*Winckelmann and His Century*) as well as Goethe's drama *Iphigenie auf Tauris* (*Iphigenie in Tauris*) in *Sämtliche Werke*, the latter of which embodies the ideals of Weimar Classicism and its celebration of the "golden age" of antiquity. See also Schiller's *Über die ästhetische Erziehung des Menschen*, in which he bestows upon art the power to morally educate and better the individual.

24. In Kleist's drama, Amazon custom demands that the women warriors only take those enemies who fall to them in battle randomly as lovers for the Rose Festival. Penthesilea leads her people to war with the explicit intention of acquiring Achilles, which her deceased mother and queen Otrere revealed to her on her deathbed. However, Robertson has argued that Penthesilea does not transgress Amazon law by pursuing Achilles, since her action is sanctioned by the maternal figure and can be read as an attempt to replace her dead mother with the man her mother ordered her to pursue. Robertson, "Women Warriors," 76.

25. Manfred Fuhrmann, "Christa Wolf und Kleist's *Penthesilea*: Der Amazonen-Mythos und das Problem des Matriarchats," *Neohelicon* 25, no. 2 (1998): 169. My use of the term "invention" follows Fuhrmann's suggestion that Kleist's drama is not a reworking of an existing myth but rather the creation of a new myth (175). Also referred to as *The Trojan Epic*, Quintus of Smyrna's account is perhaps the most extensive and detailed of any depiction of Achilles and Penthesilea's encounter.

26. Fuhrmann, "Problem des Matriarchats," 170, 172.

27. See Watanabe-O'Kelly, *Beauty or Beast?*; and Renate Rolle, who traces the Amazon myth from its roots in antiquity to modern German society in "Amazonen in der archäologischen Realität," *Kleist-Jahrbuch* (1986): 38–62.

28. Daria Santini, "The German Reception of the Amazon Myths from Hederich to Bachofen," in Colvin and Watanabe-O'Kelly, *Women and Death 2*, 17. For a detailed list of European paintings and operas that thematize the Amazon myth, see Seeba's commentary on sources in Kleist, *Sämtliche Werke* 2:690–91.

29. The first edition of Hederich's encyclopedia appeared 1724. The popularity of his *Lexicon* is evidenced by its multiple reprints: it was reprinted three times (1741, 1770, and 1781) in the eighteenth century alone.

30. See also Santini, "German Reception"; Paulin, "Metamorphoses"; and Robertson, "Women Warriors" for further discussions of the entries on the Amazons and Penthesilea in Hederich's compendium.

31. Fuhrmann, "Problem des Matriarchats," 171, 25ff. See also Doris Claudia Borelbach, *Mythik-Rezeption in Heinrich von Kleists Dramen* (Würzburg: Königshausen & Neumann), 53–56; and Kluckhohn, "Penthesilea," 37.

32. See for example Rolle, "Realität."

33. Benjamin Hederich, *Gründliches Lexicon mythologicum / nebst einem genealogicum mythistoricum* (Leipzig: Gleditsch, 1724), 181. Among the sources Hederich cites for his Amazon entry are Diodore of Sicily, Vergil, Seneca, Apollonius of Rhodes, Herodotus, and Justin. Interestingly, although Hederich includes Quintus of Smyrna in his bibliography, he does not consult his *Posthomerica* for his entry on the Amazons nor Penthesilea. See also Richter, who reads the missing breast of the Amazon as a signifier of female transgression: "As the missing breast, the Amazon breast is the bad breast in its most extreme form, a point that is not difficult to grasp; not only the refusing breast, the breast of which the infant is deprived, but also the militant and persecuting breast." Richter, *Missing the Breast*, 217.

34. Hederich, *Lexicon*, 182–83.

35. Ibid., 1549. Hederich gives Ptolemaeus Chennus as the source for this myth, whose credibility is dismissed in Photius's *Bibliotheca*. Fuhrmann, "Problem des Matriarchats," 170.

36. Beyond the unsettling implications Kleist's rendering of the violent woman warrior may have had on social conventions, Krimmer suggests that Kleist's strategic linking of gender and extreme forms of violence can be read as a critique of the practice of war as a "rational and political act." Krimmer, *Representation of War*, 147.

37. The comparison of the Amazons to predatory animals is, perhaps, not altogether unusual given that the entry under Amazons in Hederich's lexicon refers to their practice of cloaking themselves in the skins of snakes, particularly the African tribes. Kleist retains and incorporates this reported practice into his myth.

38. See also Maximilian Nutz, "Lektüre der Sinne: Kleists 'Penthesilea' als Körperdrama," in *Heinrich von Kleist: Studien zu Werk und Wirkung*, ed. Dirk Grathoff (Opladen: Westdeutscher, 1998), 168.

39. Krimmer, *Representation of War*, 55.

40. Ibid., 59.

41. Simpson, *Erotics of War*, 147.

42. Richter, *Missing the Breast*, 229.

43. Rigby, *Transgressions*, 164.

44. Richter, *Missing the Breast*, 241.

45. I disagree with Agee's translation of the first line, which should convey, as it does in the German, the sense of a command that does not allow for dissent.

Instead, I suggest the following: "You shall bear me the god of the Earth!" In the original, there is no sense that the child will belong to Penthesilea, as Agee's translation implies.

46. Angress, "Nation of Amazons," 6.

47. Simpson asserts a similar view when she concedes that Kleist's drama "reproduces precisely the bourgeois structures of gender that the 'imaginative proposal' of the play would, on the surface, deny." Simpson, *Erotics of War*, 138.

48. Scholars have argued that Kleist's portrayal of the Amazon nation as "unnatural" was intentional and that Penthesilea's violent transgression demonstrates what happens when women are forced to submit to "unfeminine" and "unnatural" laws. See respectively Schmidt, *Dramen und Erzählungen*, 117; and Kittler, *Geburt des Partisanen*, 185. Yet, Angress cautions readers against hastily dismissing the Amazon nation and its norms as irrational and unnatural, and she notes that the Amazon nation is based on a social contract and that the violent birth of their nation "is a story of male conquest like many others." Angress, "Nation of Amazons," 11. Indeed, Kittler appears to assert a similar view when he observes that the Amazon nation is built as a memorial to the fallen and dead husbands. Kittler, *Geburt des Partisanen*, 182. The precarious double bind of such interpretations, however, rests in the validation of the patriarchal model of nation building by means of violence and domination.

49. Caroline Neubaur views Penthesilea's break with Amazon law and its cultural norms as a transgression of the public/private divide in "Penthesilea und die Kategorie des Grässlichen," in *Kleist-Jahrbuch*, ed. Günter Blamberger (Stuttgart: J. B. Metzler, 2003), 211.

50. Kittler, *Geburt des Partisanen*, 199–200.

51. Simpson, *Erotics of War*, 129.

52. Krimmer, "Gender of Terror," 78.

53. Stephan, "Mignon und Penthesilea," 185.

54. Benbow, "Oral Transgression," 146.

55. Studies which have applied postmodern, feminist readings to Kleist's play have created a space for further analysis of the psychological complexity of Penthesilea. Lilian Hoverland cites Luce Irigaray's theories of the feminine to address Penthesilea's inability to reconcile her own conflicting identities and to overcome the masculine-feminine divide. Hoverland views the impossible "desire for oneness," which drives Penthesilea's actions, as the basis for the tragic death of both Achilles and Penthesilea. Hoverland, "Heinrich von Kleist and Luce Irigaray: Visions of the Feminine," in *Gestalt und Gestaltend: Frauen in der deutschen Literatur* (Amsterdam: Rodopi, 1980), 75. In her Lacanian analysis of *Penthesilea,* Ingrid Stipa notes that the labels applied to Penthesilea (as *Sphinx*, *Kentauerin*, *Megär*, *Hyäne*, etc.) "exclude Penthesilea from the realm of reason long before the actual mad scenes toward the end" and signify a shift from the "male" symbolic realm to the "feminine" realm of the imaginary. Stipa, "Kleist's *Penthesilea*: From Misapprehension to Madness," *Seminar* 27, no. 1 (1991), 34.

Epilogue

1. For women and revolutionary moments disrupting the reactionary, conservative politics of nineteenth- and early twentieth-century Germany, see as examples Helga Grubitzsch, Hannelore Cyrus, and Elke Haarbusch, ed., *Grenzgängerinnen:*

Revolutionäre Frauen im 18. und 19. Jahrhundert. Weibliche Wirklichkeit und männliche Phantasien (Düsseldorf: Schwann, 1985); Grubitzsch et al., *Frauen, Literatur, Revolution* (Pfaffenweiler: Centaurus-Verlagsgesellschaft, 1992). For the periods of World War I and II, see Klaus Theweleit's pioneering work *Männerphantasien* (Frankfurt am Main: Verlag Roter Stern, 1977–78); as well as Claudia Koonz, *Mothers in the Fatherland: Women, the Family and Nazi Politics* (New York: St. Martin's, 1987). For the period of the late 1960s and early 1970s, see Colvin, "Witch, Amazon, or Joan of Arc?" and Bielby, *Violent Women in Print*. These are, of course, only a fraction of the scholarly works published on these transformative junctures in modern German history.

2. Women's participation in combat units is a direct result of the January 11, 2000, European Court of Justice ruling, which declared that Article 12a paragraph 4 of Germany's constitution discriminated against women by excluding them from voluntary participation in combat roles. Prior to the court's ruling, women had served in the *Sanitätsdienst* (medical services) and *Militärmusikdienst* (military band) since the mid-1970s. The revision made to the constitution does not promote women's combat participation; it simply restricts women from being *forced* to participate in active combat.

3. See, for example, German press coverage of recent scandals surrounding controversial statements about women in the military published in the Bundeswehr-Universität München's student magazine *Campus* and the Marine officers' magazine *MarineForum* reported in *SpiegelOnline*'s articles. Björn Hengst, "Frauenfeindliche Thesen: Bundeswehr-Uni fürchtet Unterwanderung von rechtsaußen," *SpiegelOnline.de*, July 20, 2011, available at http://www.spiegel.de; "Bundeswehr-Uni: Professoren warnen vor Rechtsruck in Studentenzeitschrift," *SpiegelOnline.de*, July 22, 2011, available at http://www.spiegel.de; "Tod auf der 'Gorch Fock': Marine-Magazin verunglimpft Frauen an Bord," *SpiegelOnline.de*, July 8, 2011, available at http://www.spiegel.de; and Maria Holzmüller, "Bundeswehr: Rechtsruck im Uni-Magazin: Rechter Aktivist leitet Zeitung an Bundeswehr-Uni," *Süddeutsche.de*, July 14, 2011, available at http://www.sueddeutsche.de.

4. Maja Apelt, "'Die Integration der Frauen in die Bundeswehr ist abgeschlossen,'" *Soziale Welt* 53 (2002): 330.

5. Apelt, "'Integration,'" 330. See also Ruth Seifert, "Soldiers and Mothers in the German Bundeswehr: Constructions of Gender and Service under Arms," in Colvin and Watanabe-O'Kelly, *Women and Death* 2, 186, 195.

6. Seifert, "Mothers and Soldiers," 187–95. Apelt makes a similar argument in her analysis of the Bundeswehr's Zentrum Innere Führung (Center for Internal Management) and its initiatives to facilitate the integration of women into the military. "Integration," 332–34.

7. "Frauen ins Militär," *EMMA*, June 1, 1978, available at http://www.emma.de. Responding to debates among male politicians about constitutional reforms concerning conscientious objection to compulsory military service, Schwarzer framed her agitation for women's active role in the armed forces as an issue of power, control, and equality.

8. She reiterates this complex, seemingly paradoxical constellation even more clearly in a 2002 *EMMA* editorial on the question of compulsory military service for female soldiers, when she states: "Die Frage von Krieg und Frieden ist eng

verknüpft mit den Machtverhältnissen zwischen den Geschlechtern. [. . .] Je wehrhafter also die Frauen werden und je einfühlsamer die Männer, umso größer sind die Chancen für Gleichheit und damit Frieden: zwischen den Geschlechtern wie den Völkern." ("The question of war and peace is intimately connected with the power relations between the sexes. [. . .] The better able women are to defend themselves and the more empathetic men become, the greater the chances are for equality and with it peace: between the sexes as well as nations.") Alice Schwarzer, "Editorial von Alice Schwarzer: Rechte & Pflichten: Wehrdienst für Frauen? Pflichtjahr für beide Geschlechter? Oder alles lassen, wie es ist?," *EMMA*, May 1, 2002, available at http://www.emma.de.

9. In the follow-up to her 1978 article "Frauen ins Militär," Schwarzer notes the debates and strong criticism she faced from fellow feminists and peace activists, who viewed women's role in the military as a perpetuation of patriarchal violence and oppression, which stood in direct opposition to women's ostensibly inherent stake in peace movements and the eradication of the military-industrial complex.

10. Alice Schwarzer, "Frauen und Militär: Vor der Kaserne," *EMMA*, March 1, 2000, available at http://www.emma.de.

11. Susanne Lopez and Frank Bötel, "Gelebte Normalität: Frauen in der Bundeswehr," *Bundeswehr.de*, last modified July 16, 2014, available at http://www.bundeswehr.de.

12. Compounding the anemic troop sizes are recent reports revealing the high turnover rates of voluntary recruits due in part to a general dissatisfaction with the military structure and prevailing culture of the Bundeswehr. See, for example, the series of articles in *Der Spiegel*'s online magazine from 2011–13, among others "Wehrreform: Freiwilling zum Bund? Nein, danke!," *SpiegelOnline.de*, April 21, 2011; "Hohe Abbrecherquote: Jeder dritte Bundeswehr-Freiwillige gibt auf," *SpiegelOnline.de*, January 2, 2013; "Wehrdienst: Bundeswehr findet immer weniger Freiwillige," *SpiegelOnline.de*, August 16, 2013; and "Wehrbeauftragter: Soldaten beschweren sich mehr als je zuvor über die Bundeswehr," *SpiegelOnline.de*, October 22, 2013. All are available online at http://www.spiegel.de.

13. Susanne Lopez, "Anzeigen-Kampagne: Frauen werben für Frauen," *Bundeswehr.de*, last modified December 3, 2013, available at http://www.bundeswehr.de.

14. Ibid.

15. The images analyzed are from the Bundeswehr article concerning the ad campaign. Accompanying the images in the Bundeswehr article are captions, or speech bubbles. See Lopez, "Anzeigen-Kampagne." In the published ads, each of the three images is accompanied by a text highlighting a different facet of the carrier opportunities offered by the military: military assignments both at home and abroad; civilian assignments and career paths; and a combination of military and civilian training options. The controversy and criticism surrounding the most recent incarnation of the Bundeswehr ad campaign, as this book goes to press, has been highlighted by media outlets such as the investigative journal *SpiegelOnline*. See Anna Reimann, "Werbung für die Streitkräfte: Bundeswehr blamiert sich mit Frauen-Kampagne," *SpiegelOnline.de*, October 2, 2014, available at http://www.spiegel.de.

16. The third image included in the campaign, not analyzed in detail here, portrays the female soldier in her fatigues and only features her from the neck

down. However, the women's shoes featured in the background, the carefully manicured nails of the hands tying the combat boots, and the accompanying text clearly signal to the viewer the gender of the soldier and the intended recipient of the campaign's message.

17. Rey Chow, "Gender and Representation," in *Feminist Consequences: Theory for the New Century*, ed. Elisabeth Bronfen and Misha Kavka (New York: Columbia University Press, 2001), 44–45.

18. Ibid., 46.

WORKS CITED

Ak [pseud.]. Review of *Philippe von Geldern, oder Geschichte Selims des Sohns Amurat. Zwey Theile*, by Benedikte Naubert. *Neue Allgemeine Deutsche Bibliothek* (1793): 459–60.

Alaimo, Stacy, and Susan J. Hekman, ed. *Material Feminisms*. Bloomington: Indiana University Press, 2008.

Angress, Ruth. "Kleist's Nation of Amazons." *Beiträge zur Germanistik* 1 (1978): 5–28.

Apelt, Maja. "Die Integration der Frauen in die Bundeswehr ist abgeschlossen." *Soziale Welt* 53 (2002): 325–44.

Archenholz, Johann Wilhelm von. "Historische Nachrichten vom neuern Frankreich." *Minerva* 2 (1792): 97–140.

Arnim, Bettine von. *Werke und Briefe*. Vol. 1, *Clemens Brentano's Frühlingskranz: Die Günderode*. Edited by Walter Schmitz. Frankfurt am Main: Deutscher Klassiker Verlag, 1986. *Digitale Bibliothek Deutscher Klassiker*.

Arons, Wendy. *Performance and Femininity in Eighteenth-Century German Women's Writing: The Impossible Act*. New York: Palgrave Macmillan, 2006.

"Aufstand in Paris; Vereinigung des Königs mit der Nation; Zurückberufung des Herrn Necker und des alten Ministerium." *Historisch-politisches Magazin, nebst litterarischen Nachrichten* 6 (1789): 101–13.

Austin, J. L. *How to Do Things with Words*. Cambridge, Mass.: Harvard University Press, 1962.

Babcock, Barbara A., ed. *The Reversible World: Symbolic Inversion in Art and Society*. Ithaca, N.Y.: Cornell University Press, 1978.

Bakhtin, Mikhail. *Rabelais and His World*. Translated by Helene Iswolsky. Bloomington: Indiana University Press, 1984.

Barthes, Roland. *Mythologies*. Translated by Annette Lavers. New York: Farrar, Straus and Giroux, 1972.

Baumgartner, Karin. *Public Voices: Political Discourse in the Writings of Caroline de la Motte Fouqué*. New York: Peter Lang, 2009.

———. "Valorous Masculinities and Patriotism in the Texts of Early Nineteenth-Century German Women Writers." *German Studies Review* 31, no. 2 (2008): 325–44.

Be [pseud.]. Review of *Charlotte Corday. Tragödie in fünf Acten, mit Chören. Mit einem Kupfer*, by Engel Christine Westphalen. *Neue Allgemeine Deutsche Bibliothek* 101, no. 1 (1805): 179–84.

Becker-Cantarino, Barbara. "Goethe and Gender." In *The Cambridge Companion to Goethe*, edited by Lesley Sharpe, 179–92. Cambridge, Eng.: Cambridge University Press, 2002.

———. "The 'New Mythology': Myth and Death in Karoline von Günderrode's Literary Work." In *Women and Death 3: Women's Representations of Death in German Culture since 1500*, edited by Clare Bielby and Anna Richards, 51–70. Rochester, N.Y.: Camden House, 2010.

———. "Poetische Freiheit, Revolution und Patriarchat: Über Therese Hubers Roman 'Die Familie Seldorf.'" In *"Der Menschheit Hälfte blieb noch ohne Recht": Frauen und die Französische Revolution*, edited by Helga Brandes, 64–73. Wiesbaden: Deutscher Universitäts Verlag, 1991.

———. "Revolution im Patriarchat: Therese Forster-Huber (1764–1929)." In *Out of Line/Ausgefallen: The Paradox of Marginality in the Writings of Nineteenth-Century German Women*, edited by Ruth-Ellen B. Joeres and Marianne Burkhard, 235–53. Amsterdam: Rodopi, 1989.

———. *Schriftstellerinnen der Romantik: Epoche—Werke—Wirkung*. Munich: C. H. Beck, 2000.

Beise, Arnd. *Charlotte Corday: Karriere einer Attentäterin*. Marburg: Hitzeroth, 1992.

Benbow, Heather Merle. "'Weil ich der raschen Lippe Herr nicht bin': Oral Transgression as Enlightenment Disavowal in Kleist's *Penthesilea*." *Women in German Yearbook* 22 (2006): 145–66.

Berding, Helmut. "Die Ausstrahlung der Französischen Revolution auf Deutschland." In *Französische Revolution und deutsche Öffentlichkeit: Wandlungen in Presse und Alltagskultur am Ende des achtzehnten Jahrhunderts*, edited by Holger Böning, 3–16. Munich: K. G. Saur, 1992.

Berlinische Nachrichten von Staats- und gelehrten Sachen. Berlin: Haude & Spener, 1790–93.

Berroth, Erika. *Heinrich von Kleist: Geschlecht—Erkenntnis—Wirklichkeit*. New York: Peter Lang, 2003.

Bielby, Clare. *Violent Women in Print: Representations in the West German Print Media of the 1960s and 1970s*. Woodbridge, Eng.: Boydell and Brewer, 2012.

Bielby, Clare, and Anna Richards, ed. *Women and Death 3: Women's Representations of Death in German Culture since 1500*. Rochester, N.Y.: Camden House, 2010.

Blackwell, Jeannine. "Benedikte Naubert." In *Bitter Healing: German Women Writers from 1700 to 1830: An Anthology*, edited by Jeannine Blackwell and Susanne Zantop, 203–6. Lincoln: University of Nebraska Press, 1990.

———. "Die verlorene Lehre der Benedikte Naubert: Die Verbindung zwischen Phantasie und Geschichtsschreibung." In *Untersuchungen zum Roman von Frauen um 1800*, edited by Helga Gallas and Magdalene Heuser, 148–59. Tübingen: M. Niemeyer, 1990.

———. "Marriage by the Book: Matrimony, Divorce, and Single Life in Therese Huber's Life and Works." In *In the Shadow of Olympus: German Women Writers Around 1800*, edited by Katherine R. Goodman and Edith Waldstein, 137–56. Albany: State University of New York Press, 1992.

———. "Therese Huber." In *German Writers in the Age of Goethe, 1789–1832*, edited by James N. Hardin and Christoph E. Schweitzer, 187–92. Detroit: Gale, 1989.

———. "Weibliche Gelehrsamkeit oder die Grenzen der Toleranz: Die Fälle Karsch, Naubert und Gottsched." In *Lessing und die Toleranz: Beiträge der vierten internationalen Konferenz der Lessing Society in Hamburg vom 27. bis 29. Juni 1985*, edited by Peter Freimark, Franklin Kopitzsch, and Helga Slessarev, 325–35. Detroit: Wayne State University Press, 1986.

Böning, Holger, ed. *Französische Revolution und deutsche Öffentlichkeit: Wandlungen in Presse und Alltagskultur am Ende des achtzehnten Jahrhunderts.* Munich: K. G. Saur, 1992.

———. *Heinrich Zschokke und sein "Aufrichtiger und wohlerfahrener Schweizerbote": Die Volksaufklärung in der Schweiz.* New York: Peter Lang, 1983.

Borelbach, Doris Claudia. *Mythos-Rezeption in Heinrich von Kleists Dramen.* Würzburg: Königshausen & Neumann, 1998.

Bourdieu, Pierre. *The Logic of Practice.* Translated by Richard Nice. Stanford, Calif.: Stanford University Press, 1990.

———. *Masculine Domination.* Translated by Richard Nice. Stanford, Calif.: Stanford University Press, 2001.

———. *Outline of a Theory of Practice.* Translated by Richard Nice. Cambridge, Eng.: Cambridge University Press, 1977.

Bovenschen, Silvia. *Die imaginierte Weiblichkeit: Exemplarische Untersuchungen zu kulturgeschichtlichen und literarischen Präsentationsformen des Weiblichen.* Frankfurt am Main: Suhrkamp, 1979.

Brandes, Ernst. *Ueber die Weiber.* Leipzig: Weidmanns Erben und Reich, 1787.

Brandes, Helga. *"Der Menschheit Hälfte blieb noch ohne Recht": Frauen und die Französische Revolution.* Edited by Helga Brandes. Wiesbaden: Deutscher Universitäts Verlag, 1991.

———. "The Literary Market and the Journal, Medium of the Enlightenment." In *German Literature of the Eighteenth Century: The Enlightenment and Sensibility*, edited by Barbara Becker-Cantarino, 78–102. Rochester, N.Y.: Camden House, 2005.

———. "'Über die Revolutionssucht deutscher Weiber': Frauenbilder in der deutschen Publizistik um 1800." In Brandes, *"Der Menschheit Hälfte blieb noch ohne Recht,"* 146–63.

"Briefe und Verhör der Charlotte Corday." *Minerva* 7 (1793): 286–302.

Bronfen, Elisabeth. *Over Her Dead Body: Death, Femininity, and the Aesthetic.* New York: Routledge, 1992.

"Bundeswehr-Uni: Professoren warnen vor Rechtsruck in Studentenzeitschrift." *SpiegelOnline.de.* July 22, 2011. http://www.spiegel.de.

Butler, Judith. *Bodies That Matter: On the Discursive Limits of "Sex."* New York: Routledge, 1993.

———. *Excitable Speech: A Politics of the Performative.* New York: Routledge, 1997.

———. *Gender Trouble: Feminism and the Subversion of Identity.* New York: Routledge, 1990.

Campe, Joachim Heinrich. "Briefe aus Paris zur Zeit der Revolution geschrieben." In *Die Französische Revolution: Berichte und Deutungen deutscher Schriftsteller und Historiker*, edited by Horst Günther, 9–102. Frankfurt am Main: Deutscher Klassiker Verlag, 1985. *Digitale Bibliothek Deutscher Klassiker.*

Chaouli, Michel. "Devouring Metaphor: Disgust and Taste in Kleist's *Penthesilea.*" *The German Quarterly* 69, no. 2 (1996): 125–43.

Chickering, Roger, and Stig Förster, ed. *War in an Age of Revolution, 1775–1815.* Cambridge, Eng.: Cambridge University Press, 2010.

Chow, Rey. "Gender and Representation." In *Feminist Consequences: Theory for the New Century*, edited by Elisabeth Bronfen and Misha Kavka, 38–57. New York: Columbia University Press, 2001.

Clausewitz, Carl von. *On War*. Edited by Beatrice Heuser. Translated by Michael Howard and Peter Paret. Princeton, N.J.: Princeton University Press, 1989.

———. *Vom Kriege: Hinterlassenes Werk*. Munich: Ullstein, 1980.

Colvin, Sarah. "Witch, Amazon, or Joan of Arc? Ulrike Meinhof's Defenders, or How to Legitimize a Violent Woman." In *Women and Death 2: Warlike Women in the German Literary and Cultural Imagination Since 1500*, edited by Sarah Colvin and Helen Watanabe-O'Kelly, 250–72. Rochester, N.Y.: Camden House, 2009.

Colvin, Sarah, and Helen Watanabe-O'Kelly, ed. *Women and Death 2: Warlike Women in the German Literary and Cultural Imagination Since 1500*. Rochester, N.Y.: Camden House, 2009.

Davis, Natalie Zemon. "Women on Top: Symbolic Sexual Inversion and Political Disorder in Early Modern Europe." In *The Reversible World: Symbolic Inversion in Art and Society*, edited by Barbara A. Babcock, 147–190. Ithaca, N.Y.: Cornell University Press, 1978.

Dekker, Rudolf, and Lotte van de Pol. "Republican Heroines." *History of European Ideas* 10 (1989): 353–63.

Dorsch, Nikolaus, ed. *"Sich rettend aus der kalten Würklichkeit": Die Briefe Benedikte Nauberts: Edition, Kritik, Kommentar*. New York: Peter Lang, 1986.

Dupree, Mary Helen. *The Mask and the Quill: Actress-Writers in Germany from Enlightenment to Romanticism*. Lewisburg, Pa.: Bucknell University Press, 2011.

Eberle, Friedrich, and Theo Stammen, ed. *Die Französische Revolution in Deutschland: Zeitgenössische Texte deutscher Autoren Augenzeugen, Pamphletisten, Publizisten, Dichter und Philosophen*. Stuttgart: Philipp Reclam, 1989.

Eg [pseud.]. Review of *Charlotte Corday, oder die Rebellion von Calvados. Ein republicanisches Trauerspiel in vier Acten*, by Heinrich Zschokke. *Neue allgemeine deutsche Bibliothek* 17, no. 2 (1795): 339–41.

Elshtain, Jean Bethke. *Women and War*. Chicago: University of Chicago Press, 1987.

Ense, Karl August Varnhagen von. *Biographische Portraits: Nebst Briefen von Koreff, Clemens Brentano, Frau von Fouqué, Henri Campan und Scholz*. Leipzig: Brockhaus, 1871.

Epstein, Klaus. *The Genesis of German Conservatism*. Princeton, N.J.: Princeton University Press, 1966.

Fichte, Johann Gottlieb. *Foundations of Natural Right: According to the Principles of the Wissenschaftslehre*. Edited by Frederick Neuhouser. Translated by Michael Baur. Cambridge, Eng.: Cambridge University Press, 2000.

———. "Grundlage des Naturrechts nach Principien der Wissenschaftslehre." In *J.G. Fichte—Gesamtausgabe*, edited by Reinhard Lauth and Hans Gliwitzky. Vol. 4, *Werke 1797–1798*, 1–166. Stuttgart-Bad Cannstatt: Frommann-Holzboog, 1970.

———. "Reden an die deutsche Nation." In *J.G. Fichte—Gesamtausgabe*, edited by Reinhard Lauth, Erich Fuchs, Peter Karlfried Schneider, and Josef Beeler-Port. Vol. 10, *Werke 1808–1812*, 97–298. Stuttgart-Bad Cannstatt: Frommann-Holzboog, 2005.

Fischer, Ernst, Wilhelm Haefs, and York-Gothart Mix. "Einleitung: Aufklärung, Öffentlichkeit und Medienkultur in Deutschland im 18. Jahrhundert." In *Von Almanach bis Zeitung: Ein Handbuch der Medien in Deutschland 1700–1800*, edited by Ernst Fischer, Wilhelm Haefs, and York-Gothart Mix, 9–23. Munich: C. H. Beck, 1999.

Forrest, Alan. "Citizenship and Masculinity: The Revolutionary Citizen-Soldier and His Legacy." In *Representing Masculinity: Male Citizenship in Modern Western Culture*, edited by Stefan Dudink, Karen Hagemann, and Anna Clark, 111–29. New York: Palgrave Macmillan, 2007.

Forrest, Alan, Karen Hagemann, and Jane Rendall, ed. *Soldiers, Citizens and Civilians: Experiences and Perceptions of the Revolutionary and Napoleonic Wars, 1790–1820*. New York: Palgrave Macmillan, 2009.

Forster, Georg. "Briefe." In *Die Französische Revolution: Berichte und Deutungen deutscher Schriftsteller und Historiker*, edited by Horst Günther, 597–774. Frankfurt am Main: Deutscher Klassiker Verlag, 1985. *Digitale Bibliothek Deutscher Klassiker*.

Foucault, Michel. *Discipline and Punish: The Birth of the Prison*. New York: Vintage Books, 1995.

———. *The Order of Things: An Archaeology of the Human Sciences*. New York: Vintage Books, 1994.

Fouqué, Caroline de la Motte. *Das Heldenmädchen aus der Vendée*. 2 vols. Leipzig: Gerhard Fleischer der Jüngere, 1816.

———. *Laura: Eine Begebenheit aus der Französischen Revolution*. In *Erzählungen*, 169–235. Jena: Bei August Schmid, 1821.

———. *Ruf an die deutschen Frauen: Die Einnahmen zum patriotischen Zwecke*. Berlin: Hitzig (in commission), 1813.

Frevert, Ute. "Citizen-Soldiers: General Conscription in the Nineteenth and Twentieth Centuries." In *Enlightened War: German Theories and Cultures of Warfare from Frederick the Great to Clausewitz*, edited by Elisabeth Krimmer and Patricia Anne Simpson, 219–37. Rochester, N.Y.: Camden House, 2011.

———. *Die kasernierte Nation: Militärdienst und Zivilgesellschaft in Deutschland*. Munich: C. H. Beck, 2001.

———. "German Conceptions of War, Masculinity, and Femininity in the Long Nineteenth Century." In Colvin and Watanabe-O'Kelly, *Women and Death 2*, 169–85.

———. *"Mann und Weib, und Weib und Mann": Geschlechter-Differenzen in der Moderne*. Munich: Beck, 1995.

Fronius, Helen. *Women and Literature in the Goethe Era (1770–1820): Determined Dilettantes*. Oxford: Clarendon, 2007.

Fuhrmann, Manfred. "Christa Wolf und Kleist's *Penthesilea*: Der Amazonen-Mythos und das Problem des Matriarchats." *Neohelicon* 25, no. 2 (1998): 155–76.

Garber, Marjorie. *Vested Interests: Cross-Dressing and Cultural Anxiety*. New York: Routledge, 1992.

Gilleir, Anke. "On the Presentation of the Body in the Work of Therese Huber and Johanna Schopenhauer." In *Harmony in Discord: German Women Writers in the Eighteenth and Nineteenth Centuries*, edited by Laura Martin, 207–35. New York: Peter Lang, 2001.

Gleim, Johann Wilhelm Ludwig. "Charlotte Corday." *Minerva* 8 (1793): 1–4.

Godineau, Dominique. *The Women of Paris and Their French Revolution*. Translated by Katherine Streip. Berkeley: University of California Press, 1998.

Goethe, Johann Wolfgang von. *Sämtliche Werke: Briefe, Tagebücher, und Gespräche*. Edited by Dieter Borchmeyer et. al. 45 vols. Frankfurt am Main: Deutscher Klassiker, 1985–2013.

———. *Verse Plays and Epic*. Edited by Cyrus Hamlin and Frank Ryder. Translated by David Luke. New York: Suhrkamp, 1987.

Gooch, G. P. *Germany and the French Revolution*. New York: Russell and Russell, 1966.

Grathoff, Dirk. *Kleist: Geschichte, Politik, Sprache: Aufsätze zu Leben und Werk Heinrich von Kleists*. Opladen: Westdeutscher Verlag, 1999.

Grubitzsch, Helga. "Théroigne de Méricourt—Revolutionärin, Minerva oder Hure der Nation? Lebenswirklichkeit und biographische Legenden einer revolutionären Frau." In *Frauenmacht in der Geschichte*, edited by Jutta Dalhoff, Uschi Frey and Ingrid Schöll, 206–17. Düsseldorf: Schwann, 1986.

Grubitzsch, Helga, Hannelore Cyrus, and Elke Haarbusch, ed. *Grenzgängerinnen: Revolutionäre Frauen im 18. und 19. Jahrhundert: Weibliche Wirklichkeit und männliche Phantasien*. Düsseldorf: Schwann, 1985.

Grubitzsch, Helga, Maria Kublitz, Dorothea Mey, and Ingeborg Singendonk-Heublein, ed. *Frauen, Literatur, Revolution*. Pfaffenweiler: Centaurus-Verlagsgesellschaft, 1992.

Günderrode, Karoline von. *Sämtliche Werke und ausgewählte Studien*. Edited by Walter Morgenthaler. 3 vols. Basel: Stroemfeld/Roter Stern, 1990–91.

Günther, Horst, ed. *Die Französische Revolution: Berichte und Deutungen deutscher Schriftsteller und Historiker*. Frankfurt am Main: Deutscher Klassiker Verlag, 1985. *Digitale Bibliothek Deutscher Klassiker*.

Guthke, Karl S. "'Die Jungfrau von Orleans': Sendung und Witwenmachen." In *Schiller heute*, edited by Hans-Jörg Knobloch and Helmut Koopmann, 115–30. Tübingen: Stauffenburg, 1996.

Gutjahr, Ortrud. "Iphigenie–Penthesilea–Medea: Zur Klassizität weiblicher Mythen bei Goethe, Kleist und Grillparzer." In *Frauen: MitSprechen MitSchreiben*, edited by Marianne Henn and Britta Hufeisen, 223–43. Stuttgart: Hans-Dieter Heinz, 1997.

Haas, Renate. "Therese Huber: Teilemanzipation und Schriftstellerinnenkarriere durch die Französische Revolution." In *Freiheit, Gleichheit, Weiblichkeit: Aufklärung, Revolution und die Frauen in Europa*, edited by Marieluise Christadler, 75–92. Opladen: Leske & Budrich, 1990.

Hagelweide, Gert. "Publizistischer Alltag in der preußischen Provinz zur Zeit der Französischen Revolution." In Böning, *Französische Revolution und deutsche Öffentlichkeit*, 251–66.

Hagemann, Karen. "Female Patriots: Women, War and the Nation in the Period of the Prussian-German Anti-Napoleonic Wars." *Gender & History* 16, no. 2 (August 2004): 397–424.

———. "Heldenmütter, Kriegerbräute und Amazonen: Entwürfe 'patriotischer' Weiblichkeit zur Zeit der Freiheitskriege." In *Militär und Gesellschaft im 19. und 20. Jahrhundert*, edited by Ute Frevert, 174–200. Stuttgart: Klett-Cotta, 1997.

———. "'Heroic Virgins' and 'Bellicose Amazons': Armed Women, the Gender Order and the German Public during and after the Anti-Napoleonic Wars." *European History Quarterly* 37 (2007): 507–27.

———. "The Military and Masculinity: Gendering the History of the Revolutionary and Napoleonic Wars, 1792–1815." In *War in an Age of Revolution, 1775–1815*, edited by Roger Chickering and Stig Förster, 331–52. Cambridge, Eng.: Cambridge University Press, 2010.

Hagemann, Karen, Gisela Mettele, and Jane Rendall, ed. *Gender, War and Politics: Transatlantic Perspectives, 1775–1830*. New York: Palgrave Macmillan, 2010.

Hagemann, Karen, and Ralf Pröve, ed. *Landsknechte, Soldatenfrauen und Nationalkrieger: Militär, Krieg und Geschlechterordnung im historischen Wandel*. New York: Campus, 1998.

Hansen, Joseph, ed. *Quellen zur Geschichte des Rheinlandes im Zeitalter der Französischen Revolution 1780–1801*. Vol. 2, *1792–1793*. Bonn: Peter Hanstein, 1933.

Hardin, James N., and Christoph E. Schweitzer, ed. *German Writers in the Age of Goethe, 1789–1832*. Detroit: Gale, 1989.

Hart, Gail K. "Re-Dressing History: Mother Nature, Mother Isabeau, the Virgin Mary, and Schiller's *Jungfrau*." *Women in German Yearbook* 14 (1999): 91–107.

Harvey, Karen. "The Century of Sex? Gender, Bodies, and Sexuality in the Long Eighteenth Century." *The Historical Journal* 45, no. 4 (2002): 899–916.

Hausen, Karin. "Die Polarisierung der 'Geschlechtscharaktere'—Eine Spiegelung der Dissoziation von Erwerbs- und Familienleben." In *Sozialgeschichte der Familie in der Neuzeit Europas*, edited by Werner Konze, 363–93. Stuttgart: Klett, 1976.

Hederich, Benjamin. *Gründliches Lexicon mythologicum / nebst einem genealogicum mythistoricum*. Leipzig: Gleditsch, 1724.

Heicker, Dino. *Gespenster und Geschlechter: Homoerotik in der europäischen Schauerliteratur*. Hamburg: MännerschwarmSkript, 2004.

Hengst, Björn. "Frauenfeindliche Thesen: Bundeswehr-Uni fürchtet Unterwanderung von recthsaußen." *SpiegelOnline.de*. July 20, 2011. http://www.spiegel.de.

Hermand, Jost. "The Jacobins of Hamburg and Altona (in memoriam Walter Grab I)." In *Patriotism, Cosmopolitanism, and National Culture: Public Culture in Hamburg, 1700–1933*, edited by Peter Uwe Hohendahl, 133–41. Amsterdam: Rodopi, 2003.

———. "Kleists *Penthesilea*: Im Kreuzfeuer geschlechtsspezifischer Diskurse." *Monatshefte* 87, no. 1 (Spring 1995): 34–47.

Herrmann, Hans Peter. "Arminius und die Erfindung der Männlichkeit im 18. Jahrhundert." *Der Deutschunterricht* 47 (1995): 32–47.

Heuser, Magdalene. "Jakobinerin, Demokratin und Revolutionär: Therese Hubers 'kleiner winziger Standpunkt' als Weib um 1800." In *Sklavin oder Bürgerin? Französische Revolution und neue Weiblichkeit 1760–1830*, edited by Viktoria Schmidt-Linsenhoff, 143–57. Frankfurt am Main: Jonas, 1989.

———. "Nachwort" to *Die Familie Seldorf*, by Therese Huber, edited by Magdalene Heuser. Vol. 2, 347–89. Hildesheim: Georg Olms, 1989.

High, Jeffrey L. "Schiller, 'Merely Political Revolutions,' the Personal Drama of Usurpation and Wars of Liberation." In *Schiller: National Poet—Poet of Nations: A Birmingham Symposium*, edited by Nicholas Martin, 219–40. Amsterdam: Rodopi, 2006.

———. *Schillers Rebellionskonzept und die Französische Revolution*. Lewiston, N.Y.: Mellen, 2004.

Hilger, Stephanie M. "The Murderess on Stage: Christine Westphalen's *Charlotte Corday* (1804)." In Bielby and Richards, *Women and Death 3*, 71–87.

———. "Sara's Pain: The French Revolution in Therese Huber's *Die Familie Seldorf* (1795–1796)." In *Contemplating Violence: Critical Studies in Modern German Culture*, edited by Stefani Engelstein and Carl Niekerk, 35–48. Amsterdam: Rodopi, 2011.

Hilmes, Carola. "'Die Familie Seldorf'–Ein Revolutionsroman." In *Skandalgeschichten: Aspekte einer Frauenliteraturgeschichte*, 54–59. Königstein: Ulrike Helmer Verlag, 2004.

———. *Die Femme fatale: Ein Weiblichkeitstypus in der nachromantischen Literatur*. Stuttgart: Metzler, 1990.

———. "'Wer bist du, wunderbares Weib?' Kleists *Penthesilea*." In *Die femme fatale im Drama: Heroinen–Verführerinnen–Todesengel*, edited by Jürgen Blänsdorf, 59–79. Tübingen: Francke, 1999.

Hippel, Theodor Gottlieb von. *On Improving the Status of Women*. Translated by Timothy F. Sellner. Detroit: Wayne State University Press, 1979.

———. *Über die bürgerliche Verbesserung der Weiber*. Frankfurt am Main: Syndikat, 1977.

Hofacker, Erich P., Jr. "Caroline de la Motte Fouqué." In Hardin and Schweitzer, *German Writers in the Age of Goethe*, 78–83.

Hoff, Dagmar von. "Dramatische Weiblichkeitsmuster zur Zeit der Französischen Revolution: Dramen von Autorinnen um 1800." In *Die Marseillaise der Weiber: Frauen, die Französische Revolution und ihre Rezeption*, edited by Inge Stephan and Sigrid Weigel, 74–88. Hamburg: Argument, 1989.

———. *Dramen des Weiblichen: Deutsche Dramatikerinnen um 1800*. Opladen: Westdeutscher Verlag, 1989.

Hoffmeister, Gerhart, ed. *The French Revolution and the Age of Goethe*. Hildesheim: Olms, 1989.

"Hohe Abbrecherquote: Jeder dritte Bundeswehr-Freiwillige gibt auf." *SpiegelOnline.de*. January 2, 2013. http://www.spiegel.de.

Hohendahl, Peter Uwe. "Die Krise der Männlichkeit im späten 18. Jahrhundert: Ein Problemskizze." *Zeitschrift für Germanistik* 12, no. 2 (2002): 275–86.

———. *Patriotism, Cosmopolitanism, and National Culture: Public Culture in Hamburg 1700–1933*. Amsterdam: Rodopi, 2003.

Holzmüller, Maria. "Bundeswehr: Rechtsruck im Uni-Magazin: Rechter Aktivist leitet Zeitung an Bundeswehr-Uni." *Süddeutsche.de*. July 14, 2011. http://www.sueddeutsche.de.

Honegger, Claudia. *Die Ordnung der Geschlechter: Die Wissenschaften vom Menschen und das Weib*. Frankfurt: Campus, 1991.

Horn, Peter. "'Penthesilea': The Revival of a Greek Myth as an Endorsement of Kleist's Social and Political Ideals." *English Studies in Africa* 18 (January 1975): 99–106.

Horst, Eleanor E. ter. *Lessing, Goethe, Kleist, and the Transformation of Gender: From Hermaphrodite to Amazon*. New York: Peter Lang, 2003.

Hoverland, Lilian. "Heinrich von Kleist and Luce Irigaray: Visions of the Feminine." In *Gestalt und Gestaltend: Frauen in der deutschen Literatur*, 57–82. Amsterdam: Rodopi, 1980.

Huber, Therese. *Briefe*. Edited by Magdalene Heuser, Andrea Kiszio, Corinna Bergmann-Törner, and Petra Wulbusch. 5 vols. Tübingen: Niemeyer, 1999–2011.

———. *Die Familie Seldorf*. Edited by Magdalene Heuser. 2 vols. Hildesheim: Georg Olms, 1989.

———. *Therese Huber: Die reinste Freiheitsliebe, die reinste Männerliebe: Ein Lebensbild in Briefen und Erzählungen zwischen Aufklärung und Romantik*. Edited by Andrea Hahn. Berlin: Henssel, 1989.

Hull, Isabel V. *Sexuality, State, and Civil Society in Germany, 1700–1815*. Ithaca, N.Y.: Cornell University Press, 1996.

Humboldt, Wilhelm von. "Über den Geschlechtsunterschied und dessen Einfluß auf die organische Natur." In *Werke in Fünf Bänden*. Vol. 1, *Schriften zur Anthropologie und Geschichte*, 268–95. Edited by Andreas Flitner and Klaus Giel. Stuttgart: J. G. Cotta'sche Buchhandlung, 1960.

———. "Über die männliche und weibliche Form." In *Werke in Fünf Bänden*. Vol. 1, *Schriften zur Anthropologie und Geschichte*, 296–336. Edited by Andreas Flitner and Klaus Giel. Stuttgart: J. G. Cotta'sche Buchhandlung, 1960.

———. "Ueber Göthe's *Herrmann und Dorothea*." In *Gesammelte Werke*. Vol. 4, 1–268. Berlin: G. Reimer, 1843.

Hunt, Lynn. *The Family Romance of the French Revolution*. Berkeley: University of California Press, 1992.

Imber, Colin. *The Ottoman Empire, 1300–1650: The Structure of Power*. New York: Palgrave Macmillan, 2009.

İnalık, Halil. *The Ottoman Empire: The Classical Age, 1300–1600*. New York: Praeger, 1973.

Irigaray, Luce. *This Sex Which Is Not One*. Ithaca, N.Y.: Cornell University Press, 1985.

Ives, Margaret C. "Karoline von Günderrode (1780–1806): The 'Tian' Legend." In *Sappho in the Shadows: Essays on the Work of German Women Poets of the Age of Goethe (1749–1832), with Translations of Their Poetry into English*, edited by Anthony J. Harper and Margaret C. Ives, 87–98. New York: Peter Lang, 2000.

Joeres, Ruth-Ellen B. *Respectability and Deviance: Nineteenth-Century German Women Writers and the Ambiguity of Representation*. Chicago: University of Chicago Press, 1998.

K---k. [pseud.]. "Ueber Charlotte Corday, die Mörderin Marats, mit Bezug auf einen Aufsatz im Journal des Luxus und der Moden vom November 1793; unter dem Titel: Warnung für (vor) einer abscheulichen Mode." *Deutsche Monatsschrift* 2 (1794): 53–64.

Kane, Stuart A. "Wives with Knives: Early Modern Murder Ballads and the Transgressive Commodity." *Criticism* 38, no. 2 (1996): 219–37.

Karthaus, Ulrich. "Schiller und die Französische Revolution." *Jahrbuch der deutschen Schillergesellschaft* 33 (1989): 210–39.

Kaschuba, Wolfgang. "Revolution als Spiegel: Reflexe der Französischen Revolution in der deutscher Öffentlichkeit und Alltagskultur um 1800." In Böning, *Französische Revolution und deutsche Öffentlichkeit*, 381–98.

Kittler, Wolf. *Die Geburt des Partisanen aus dem Geist der Poesie: Heinrich von Kleist und die Strategie der Befreiungskriege.* Freiburg: Rombach, 1987.

Kittredge, Katharine. Introduction to *Lewd and Notorious: Female Transgression in the 18th Century*, edited by Katharine Kittredge, 1–17. Ann Arbor: University of Michigan Press, 2003.

Kleist, Heinrich von. *Penthesilea.* Translated by Joel Agee. New York: Perennial, 1998.

———. *Sämtliche Werke und Briefe.* Edited by Hans Rudolf Barth, Ilse-Marie Barth, Hinrich C. Seeba, Klaus Müller Salget, and Stefan Ormanns. 4 vols. Frankfurt am Main: Deutscher Klassiker, 1987–97.

Kluckhohn, Paul. "Penthesilea." In *Heinrich von Kleist Aufsätze und Essays*, edited by Walter Müller-Seidel, 35–50. Darmstadt: Wissenschaftliche Buchgesellschaft, 1987.

Kluge, Gerhard. "*Herrmann und Dorothea*: Die Revolution und Herrmanns Schlußrede-zwei 'schmerzliche Zeichen'?" *Goethe-Jahrbuch* 109 (1992): 61–68.

Koch, Ursula E., Ute Nawratil, and Detlef Schröter. "Sommer 1789: Französische Revolution und preußische Zeitungsberichte." In Böning, *Französische Revolution und deutsche Öffentlichkeit*, 199–250.

Kollmann, Anett. *Gepanzerte Empfindsamkeit: Helden in Frauengestalt um 1800.* Heidelberg: Universitätsverlag Winter, 2004.

Königlich Privilegirte Berlinische Zeitung von Staats und gelehrten Sachen. Berlin: Voss, 1789–93.

Kontje, Todd. "Gender-Bending in the Biedermeier." *Women in German Yearbook* 12 (1996): 53–69.

———. "Under the Spell of the Father: Patriarchy versus Patriotism in Therese Huber's *Die Familie Seldorf*." *Seminar* 28, no. 1 (February 1992): 17–32.

———. *Women, the Novel, and the German Nation 1771–1871: Domestic Fiction in the Fatherland.* Cambridge, Eng.: Cambridge University Press, 1998.

Koonz, Claudia. *Mothers in the Fatherland: Women, the Family and Nazi Politics.* New York: St. Martin's, 1987.

Kord, Susanne. *Ein Blick hinter die Kulissen: Deutschsprachige Dramatikerinnen im 18. und 19. Jahrhundert.* Stuttgart: J. B. Metzlersche Verlagsbuchhandlung, 1992.

———. *Murderesses in German Writing, 1740–1860: Heroines of Horror.* Cambridge, Eng.: Cambridge University Press, 2009.

———. *Sich einen Namen machen: Anonymität und weibliche Autorschaft 1700–1900.* Stuttgart: Metzler, 1996.

Korneeva, Tatiana. "Cross-Dressing Strategies in Benedikte Naubert's Fairy Tale Novella *Der kurze Mantel*." *German Life and Letters* 65, no. 3 (July 2012): 281–94.

Koser, Julie. "Rebellious Bodies: The Human Form as Site of Social and Political Conflict in Heinrich von Kleist's *Die Hermannsschlacht* and *Penthesilea*." In

Rebellion and Revolution: Defiance in German Literature, History and Art, edited by Melissa Etzler and Priscilla Layne, 62–88. Newcastle upon Tyne, Eng.: Cambridge Scholars Publishing, 2010.

Krimmer, Elisabeth. "Female War Stories: Violence and Trauma in Works by Therese Huber and Caroline de la Motte-Fouqué." *Internationales Jahrbuch der Bettina-von-Arnim-Gesellschaft* 17 (2005): 123–35.

———. "The Gender of Terror: War as (Im)Moral Institution in Kleist's *Hermannsschlacht* and *Penthesilea*." *The German Quarterly* 81, no. 1 (Winter 2008): 66–85.

———. *In the Company of Men: Cross-Dressed Women around 1800*. Detroit: Wayne State University Press, 2004.

———. "Officer and Lady: Pants and Politics in Caroline de la Motte-Fouqué's *Das Heldenmädchen aus der Vendée* (1816)." *Studies in Eighteenth-Century Culture* 30 (2001): 165–81.

———. *The Representation of War in German Literature: From 1800 to the Present*. New York: Cambridge University Press, 2010.

Krimmer, Elisabeth, and Patricia Anne Simpson, ed. *Enlightened War: German Theories and Cultures of Warfare from Frederick the Great to Clausewitz*. Rochester, N.Y.: Camden House, 2011.

Krug, Michaela. *Auf der Suche nach dem eigenen Raum: Topographien des Weiblichen im Roman von Autorinnen um 1800*. Würzbug: Königshausen & Neumann, 2004.

Landes, Joan. *Visualizing the Nation: Gender, Representation, and Revolution in Eighteenth-Century France*. Ithaca, N.Y.: Cornell University Press, 2001.

———. *Women and the Public Sphere in the Age of the French Revolution*. Ithaca, N.Y.: Cornell University Press, 1988.

Lange, Sigrid. *Die Utopie des Weiblichen im Drama Goethes, Schillers und Kleists*. New York: Peter Lang, 1993.

Laqueur, Thomas. *Making Sex: Body and Gender from the Greeks to Freud*. Cambridge, Mass.: Harvard University Press, 1990.

Larkin, Edward T. "Reading Schiller's *Die Jungfrau von Orleans* with Lacan: In the 'Name-of-the-Father' and of the Daughter." *Monatshefte* 96, no. 2 (2004): 199–219.

Lehnert, Gertrud. *Maskeraden und Metamorphosen: Als Männer verkleidete Frauen in der Literatur*. Würzburg: Königshausen & Neumann, 1994.

Levy, Darline Gay, and Harriet B. Applewhite. "Women and Militant Citizenship in Revolutionary Paris." In *Rebel Daughters: Women and the French Revolution*, edited by Sara E. Melzer and Leslie W. Rabine, 79–101. Oxford: Oxford University Press, 1992.

Levy, Darline Gay, Harriet Branson Applewhite, and Mary Durham Johnson, ed. *Women in Revolutionary Paris 1789–1795*. Urbana: University of Illinois Press, 1980.

Licher, Lucia Maria. "'Der Völker Schicksal ruht in meinem Busen': Karoline von Günderrode als Dichterin der Revolution." In Brandes, "*Der Menschheit Hälfte blieb noch ohne Recht*," 113–32.

———. *Mein Leben in einer bleibenden Form aussprechen: Umrisse einer Ästhetik im Werk Karoline von Günderrode (1780–1806)*. Heidelberg: Universitätsverlag C. Winter, 1996.

Linder, Jutta. "Schillers Schweigen: Das Verhalten des Dichters zu Beginn der Französischen Revolution." *Jahrbuch der Brüder Grimm-Gesellschaft* 13–14 (2003–04): 115–32.

Lloyd, Genevieve. "Selfhood, War and Masculinity." In *Feminist Challenges: Social and Political Theory*, edited by Carole Pateman and Elizabeth Gross, 63–76. Boston: Northeastern University Press, 1987.

Lopez, Susanne. "Anzeigen-Kampagne: Frauen werben für Frauen." *Bundeswehr .de*. Last modified December 3, 2013. http://www.bundeswehr.de.

Lopez, Susanne, and Frank Bötel. "Gelebte Normalität: Frauen in der Bundeswehr." *Bundeswehr.de*. Last modified July 16, 2014. http://www.bundeswehr.de.

Lorentzen, Lois Ann, and Jennifer Turpin, eds. *The Women and War Reader*. New York: New York University Press, 1998.

Lux, Adam. "Ueber Charlotte Corday, von Luchs." *Minerva* 7 (1793): 302–12.

MacLeod, Catriona. *Embodying Ambiguity: Androgyny and Aesthetics from Winckelmann to Keller*. Detroit: Wayne State University Press, 1998.

Maierhofer, Waltraud. "Das späte 18. Jahrhundert: Benedikte Naubert: *Thekla von Thurn* (1788)—Bernhard von Weimars Page wider Willen." In *Hexen—Huren—Heldenweiber: Bilder des Weiblichen in Erzähltexten über den Dreißigjährigen Krieg*, 67–100. Cologne: Böhlau, 2005.

Martin, Ariane. "Johannas 'männlich Herz' im Zwiespalt: Geschlechterdifferenz als tragischer Konflikt in Schillers *Jungfrau von Orleans*." *Der Deutschunterricht* 6 (2004): 75–85.

Martin, Laura. *Benedikte Nauberts Neue Volksmärchen der Deutschen: Sturkturen des Wandels*. Würzburg: Königshausen & Neumann, 2006.

McBrien, Richard. P. *Lives of the Popes: The Pontiffs from St. Peter to John Paul II*. San Francisco: HarperCollins, 1997.

Meise, Helga. *Die Unschuld und die Schrift: Deutsche Frauenromane im 18. Jahrhundert*. Frankfurt am Main: Helmer, 1992.

———. "Politisierung der Weiblichkeit oder Revolution des Frauenromans? Deutsche Romanautorinnen und die Französische Revolution." *Les Femmes et la Revolution Française: Actes du Colloque International, 12–13–14 Avril 1989, Université de Toulouse-Le Mirail*, edited by Marie-France Brive, 67–85. Toulouse: Presses Universitaires du Mirail, 1989.

Mommsen, Katharina. "Goethe as a Precursor of Women's Emancipation." In *Goethe Proceedings: Essays Commemorating the Goethe Sesquicentennial at the University of California, Davis*, ed. Clifford A. Bernd, 51–65. Columbia, S.C.: Camden House, 1984.

Morgan, Peter. "Aufklärung, Revolution und Nationalgefühl: Der Topos des Jakobiners und die Frage deutscher Identität in Goethes 'Herrmann und Dorothea.'" In *Grenzen, Traditionen, Vergleiche: Akten des VIII. Internationalen Germanisten-Kongresses, Tokyo*, edited by Eijirō Iwasaki, 78–88. Munich: Iudicium, 1991.

———. *The Critical Idyll: Traditional Values and the French Revolution in Goethe's "Hermann und Dorothea."* Columbia, S.C.: Camden House, 1990.

Naubert, Benedikte. *Geschichte der Gräfin Thekla von Thurn oder Scenen aus dem dreyssigjährigen Kriege*. 2 vols. Leipzig: Weygandsche Buchhandlung, 1788.

———. *Philippe von Geldern. Oder Geschichte Selims, des Sohns Amurat*. 2 vols. Leipzig: Weygandsche Buchhandlung, 1792.

Nettelbeck, Petra, and Uwe Nettelbeck. *Charlotte Corday: Ein Buch der REPUBLIK*. Nördlingen: Delphi, 1987.

Neubaur, Caroline. "*Penthesilea* und die Kategorie des Grässlichen. " In *Kleist-Jahrbuch*, edited by Günter Blamberger, 199–217. Stuttgart: J. B. Metzler, 2003.

"Neue Revolution in Frankreich: Verlegung der königl. Residenz von Versailles nach Paris." *Historisch-politisches Magazin, nebst litterarischen Nachrichten* 6 (1789): 440–54.

Nutz, Maximilian. "Lektüre der Sinne: Kleists 'Penthesilea' als Körperdrama." In *Heinrich von Kleist: Studien zu Werk und Wirkung*, edited by Dirk Grathoff, 163–85. Opladen: Westdeutscher, 1998.

Oelsner, Konrad Engelbert. "Historische Briefe über die neuesten Begebenheiten in Frankreich." *Minerva* 3 (1792): 515–75.

Opitz, Claudia. "Der Bürger wird Soldat—und die Bürgerin . . . ?" In *Sklavin oder Bürgerin? Französische Revolution und Neue Weiblichkeit 1760–1830*, edited by Viktoria Schmidt Linsenhoff, 38–54. Frankfurt: Jonas, 1989.

———. "Von Frauen im Krieg zum Krieg gegen Frauen. Krieg, Gewalt und Geschlechterbeziehungen aus historischer Sicht." *L'Homme: Zeitschrift für Feministische Geschichtswissenschaft* 3, no. 1 (1992): 31–44.

Ort, Werner. *Heinrich Zschokke (1771–1848): Eine Biographie*. Baden: hier + jetzt, 2013.

Paulin, Roger. "Kleist's Metamorphoses: Some Remarks on the Use of Mythology in *Penthesilea*." *Oxford German Studies* 14 (1983): 35–53.

Pei, Xu. *Frauenbilder der Romantik: Annette von Droste-Hülshoff, Clemens Brentano, Joseph von Eichendorff, Heinrich Heine*. Düsseldorf: Gruppelo, 1997.

Peitsch, Helmut. "Die Revolution im Familienroman: Aktuelles politisches Thema und konventionelle Romanstruktur in Therese Hubers *Die Familie Seldorf*." *Jahrbuch der Deutschen Schiller-Gesellschaft* 28 (1984): 248–69.

Petersen, Susanne. *Marktweiber und Amazonen: Frauen in der Französischen Revolution*. Cologne: Pahl-Rugenstein, 1989.

Plato. *The Collected Dialogues of Plato, Including the Letters*. Edited by Edith Hamilton and Huntington Cairns. Princeton, N.J.: Princeton University Press, 1961.

Preitz, Max. "Karoline von Günderrode in ihrer Umwelt I: Briefe von Lisette und Christian Nees von Esenbeck, Karoline von Günderrode, Friedrich Creuzer, Clemens Brentano und Susanne von Heyden." *Jahrbuch des freien deutschen Hochstifts* (1962): 208–306.

———. "Karoline von Günderrode in ihrer Umwelt II. Karoline von Günderrodes Briefwechsel mit Friedrich Karl und Gunda von Savigny." *Jahrbuch des freien deutschen Hochstifts* (1964): 158–235.

Projekt Historischer Roman. Institut für Germanistik der Universität Innsbruck. http://www.uibk.ac.at/germanistik/histrom.

Pugh, David. "Schiller und Revolution." In *The French Revolution*, edited by Gerhart Hoffmeister, 31–50. Hildesheim: Olms, 1989.

Purver, Judith. "Revolution, Romanticism, Restoration (1789–1830)." In *A History of Women's Writing in Germany, Austria and Switzerland*, edited by Jo Catling, 68-87. Cambridge, Eng.: Cambridge University Press, 2000.

Quintus. *The Trojan Epic: Posthomerica*. Translated by Alan James. Baltimore: Johns Hopkins University Press, 2004.

Reichardt, Rolf. "Probleme des kulturellen Transfers der Französischen Revolution in der deutschen Publizistik 1789–1799." In Böning, *Französische Revolution und deutsche Öffentlichkeit*, 91–148.

Reimann, Anna. "Werbung für die Streitkräfte: Bundeswehr blamiert sich mit Frauen-Kampagne." *SpiegelOnline.de*. October 2, 2014. http://www.spiegel.de.

Reitemeier, Frauke. *Deutsch-englische Literaturbeziehungen: Der historische Roman Sir Walter Scotts und seine deutschen Vorläufer*. Munich: Ferdinand Schöningh, 2001.

Richter, Simon. *Missing the Breast: Gender, Fantasy, and the Body in the German Enlightenment*. Seattle: University of Washington Press, 2006.

Rigby, Catherine E. *Transgressions of the Feminine: Tragedy, Enlightenment and the Figure of the Woman in Classical German Drama*. Heidelberg: Winter, 1996.

Robertson, Ritchie. "Women Warriors and the Origin of the State: Zacharias Werner's *Wanda* and Heinrich von Kleist's *Penthesilea*." In Colvin and Watanabe-O'Kelly, *Women and Death 2*, 61–85.

Rolle, Renate. "Amazonen in der archäologischen Realität." *Kleist-Jahrbuch* (1986): 38–62.

Roussel, Pierre. *Physiologie des weiblichen Geschlechts*. Translated by Christian Friedrich Michaelis. Berlin: Vieweg, 1786.

Ruiz, Alan. "Deutsche Reisebeschreibungen über Frankreich im Zeitalter der Französischen Revolution (1789–1799): Ein Überblick." In *Reiseberichte als Quellen europäischer Kulturgeschichte: Aufgaben und Möglichkeiten der historischen Reiseforschung*, edited by Antoni Mączak and Hans Jürgen Teuteberg, 229–51. Wolfenbüttel: Herzog August Bibliothek, 1982.

Runge, Anita. "Gattung und Geschlecht—Zusammengestellt von Anna Fleig und Helge Meise—Konstruktionen von Geschichte und Geschlecht im Geschichtsroman deutschsprachiger Autorinnen um 1800: Das Beispiel Benedikte Naubert (1756–1819)." *Das Achtzehnte Jahrhundert* 29, no. 2 (2005): 222–40.

———. "Schweizerische Geschichte in Familiengeschichten: *Elisabeth, Erbin von Toggenburg* von Benedikte Naubert (1756–1819)." In *Familiengeschichten: Biographie und familiärer Kontext seit dem 18. Jahrhundert*, edited by Christian von Zimmermann and Nina von Zimmerman, 29–44. New York: Campus, 2008.

Ryder, Frank C., and Benjamin Bennett. "The Irony of Goethe's *Hermann und Dorothea*: Its Form and Function." *PMLA* 90, no. 3 (May 1975): 433–46.

Saine, Thomas P. *Black Bread-White Bread: German Intellectuals and the French Revolution*. Columbia, S.C.: Camden House, 1988.

———. "Charlotte Corday, Adam Lux, and *Hermann und Dorothea*." In *Exile and Enlightenment: Studies in German and Comparative Literature*, edited by Uwe K. Faulhaber, Jerry Glenn, Edward P. Harris, and Hans-Georg Richert, 87–96. Detroit: Wayne State University Press, 1987.

Santini, Daria. "The German Reception of the Amazon Myths from Hederich to Bachofen." In Colvin and Watanabe-O'Kelly, *Women and Death 2*, 15–27.

Scheifele, Sigrid. *Projektionen des Weiblichen: Lebensentwürfe in Kleists Penthesilea*. Würzburg: Königshausen & Neumann, 1992.

Schiebinger, Londa. *The Mind Has No Sex? Women in the Origins of Modern Science*. Cambridge, Mass.: Harvard University Press, 1989.

Schiller, Friedrich. *Das Lied von der Glocke.* Translated by Thomas James Arnold. London: D. Nutt, 1842.

———. "On the Pathetic." In *Friedrich Schiller: Essays*, edited by Walter Hinderer and Daniel O. Dahlstrom, translated by Daniel O. Dahlstrom, 45–69. New York: Continuum, 1993.

———. *Schiller: Five Plays.* Translated by Robert David MacDonald. London: Oberon Books, 1998.

———. *Werke: Nationalausgabe.* Edited by Julius Petersen, Hermann Schneider, Gerhard Fricke, Lieselotte Blumenthal, Benno von Wiese, Norbert Oellers, and Siegfried Seidel. 42 vols. Weimar: Böhlau, 1943–2013.

Schlegel, Friedrich. *Kritische Friedrich-Schlegel-Ausgabe.* Edited by Ernst Behler, Jean-Jacques Anstett, and Hans Eichner. 35 vols. Munich: Ferdinand Schöningh, 1958–2006.

Schlegel-Schelling, Caroline. *"Lieber Freund, ich komme weit her schon an diesem frühen Morgen": Caroline Schlegel-Schelling in ihren Briefen.* Edited by Sigrid Damm. Darmstadt: Luchterhand, 1981.

Schmid, Sigrun. *Der "selbstverschuldeten Unmündigkeit" entkommen: Perspektiven bürgerlicher Frauenliteratur.* Würzburg: Königshausen & Neumann, 1999.

Schmidt, Jochen. *Heinrich von Kleist: Die Dramen und Erzählungen in ihrer Epoche.* Darmstadt: Wissenschaftliche Buchgesellschaft, 2003.

Schmidt-Linsenhoff, Viktoria, and Christina Klausmann, ed. *Sklavin oder Bürgerin? Französische Revolution und neue Weiblichkeit 1760–1830.* Marburg: Jonas Verlag, 1989.

Schmidt-Phiseldeck, Konrad Georg Friedrich Elias von, trans. "Aktenstücke, Charlotte Corday betreffend." *Deutsches Magazin* 6 (December 1793): 1353–90.

Schreinert, Kurt. *Benedikte Naubert: Ein Beitrag zur Entstehungsgeschichte des historischen Romans in Deutschland.* Berlin: Kraus Reprint, 1969.

Schumann, Axel. "Berliner Presse und Französische Revolution: Das Spektrum der Meinungen unter preußischer Zensur 1789–1806." Dissertation. Technische Universität Berlin, 2001. http://opus4.kobv.de/opus4-tuberlin/frontdoor/index/index/docId/ 323/. PDF file.

Schwarzer, Alice. "Editorial von Alice Schwarzer: Rechte & Pflichten: Wehrdienst für Frauen? Pflichtjahr für beide Geschlechter? Oder alles lassen, wie es ist?" *EMMA*. May 1, 2002. http://www.emma.de.

———. "Frauen ins Militär." *EMMA* (June 1, 1978). http://www.emma.de.

———. "Frauen und Militär: Vor der Kaserne." *EMMA* (March 1, 2000). http://www.emma.de.

Seeba, Hinrich. "The Eye of the Beholder: Kleist's Visual Poetics of Knowledge." In *A Companion to the Works of Heinrich von Kleist*, edited by Bernd Fischer, 103–22. Rochester, N.Y.: Camden House, 2003.

Seifert, Ruth. "Soldiers and Mothers in the German Bundeswehr: Constructions of Gender and Service under Arms." In Colvin and Watanabe-O'Kelly, *Women and Death 2*, 186–208.

Senckenberg, Renatus Karl von. *Charlotte Gorday oder die Ermordung Marats dramatisirt: Carolina Cordaea Epos.* St. Ingbert: Röhrig Universitätsverlag, 1999.

Sharpe, Lesley. *Schiller and the Historical Character: Presentation and Interpretation in the Historiographical Works and in the Historical Dramas*. Oxford: Oxford University Press, 1982.

Simpson, Patricia Anne. *The Erotics of War in German Romanticism*. Lewisburg, Pa.: Bucknell University Press, 2006.

Söhn, Gerhart. *Frauen der Aufklärung und Romantik: Von der Karschin bis zur Droste*. Düsseldorf: Gruppelo, 1998.

Spivak, Gayatri Chakravorty. "Can the Subaltern Speak?" In *Marxism and the Interpretation of Culture*, edited by Cary Nelson and Lawrence Grossberg, 271–316. Urbana: University of Illinois Press, 1988.

———. "In a Word: Interview." In *Outside in the Teaching Machine*, 1–24. New York: Routledge, 1993.

Stephan, Inge. "Bilder und immer wieder Bilder: Überlegungen zur Untersuchung von Frauenbildern in männlicher Literatur." In *Die verborgene Frau: Sechs Beiträge zu einer feministischen Literaturwissenschaft*, 15–34. Berlin: Argument, 1988.

———. "'Da werden Weiber zu Hyänen . . .': Amazonen und Amazonenmythen bei Schiller und Kleist." In *Inszenierte Weiblichkeit: Codierung der Geschlechter in der Literatur des 18. Jahrhunderts*, 113–32. Weimar: Böhlau, 2004.

———. "'Die erhabne Männin Corday': Christine Westphalens Drama *Charlotte Corday* (1804) und der Corday-Kult am Ende des 18. Jahrhunderts." In *"Sie und nicht wir,"* edited by Arno Herzig, Inge Stephan, and Hans G. Winter. Vol. 1, *Die Französische Revolution und ihre Wirkung auf Norddeutschland*, 177–205. Hamburg: Dölling & Galitz, 1989.

———. "Hexe oder Heilige? Zur Geschichte der Jeanne d'Arc und ihrer literarischen Verarbeitung." In *Die verborgene Frau*, 35–66.

———. "Mignon und Penthesilea: Androgynie und erotischer Diskurs bei Goethe und Kleist." In *Inszenierte Weiblichkeit: Codierung der Geschlechter in der Literatur des 18. Jahrhunderts*, 165–86. Weimar: Böhlau, 2004.

———. "On Gender Wars and Amazons: Therese Huber on Terror and Revolution." In *Enlightened War: German Theories and Cultures of Warfare from Frederick the Great to Clausewitz*, edited by Elisabeth Krimmer and Patricia Anne Simpson, 175–91. Rochester, N.Y.: Camden House, 2011.

———. "Revolution und Konterrevolution: Therese Huber's Roman 'Die Familie Seldorf' (1795/96)." In *Der deutsche Roman der Spätaufklärung: Fiktion und Wirklichkeit*, edited by Harro Zimmermann, 171–94. Heidelberg: Winter, 1990.

Stephan, Inge, and Sigrid Weigel. *Die verborgene Frau: Sechs Beiträge zu einer feministischen Literaturwissenschaft*. Berlin: Argument, 1988.

Stephan, Inge, Sigrid Weigel, and Ruth Henry, ed. *Die Marseillaise der Weiber: Frauen, die Französische Revolution und ihre Rezeption*. Hamburg: Argument-Verlag, 1989.

Stipa, Ingrid. "Kleist's *Penthesilea*: From Misapprehension to Madness." *Seminar* 27, no. 1 (1991): 27–38.

Süllwold, Erika. "'Charlotte Corday' in Hamburg: Christine Westphalens Drama von 1804." In Brandes, *"Der Menschheit Hälfte blieb noch ohne Recht,"* 88–112.

Susman, Margarete. *Frauen der Romantik: Mit zahlreichen Abbildungen und einem Nachwort von Barbara Hahn*. Frankfurt am Main: Insel, 1996.

Theweleit, Klaus. *Männerphantasien.* 2 vols. Frankfurt am Main: Verlag Roter Stern, 1977–78.

"Tod auf der 'Gorch Fock': Marine-Magazin verunglimpft Frauen an Bord." *SpiegelOnline.de.* July 8, 2011. http://www.spiegel.de.

Touaillon, Christine. *Der deutsche Frauenroman des 18. Jahrhunderts.* Bern: Peter Lang, 1979.

Türcke, Christoph. "Liebeserklärung an den Amoklauf: Menschheit und Tierheit in Kleists *Penthesilea.*" *Einspruch* 5 (1987): 39–44.

Twiss, Richard. "Reise nach Paris: Im Jahr 1792." Translated by Johann Wilhelm von Archenholz. *Minerva* 6 (1793): 486–536.

Tyrrell, William Blake. *Amazons: A Study in Athenian Mythmaking.* Baltimore: Johns Hopkins University Press, 1984.

—tz [pseud.]. "Scharlotte Korday, Nebst einem Anhang über Scharlotte Korday von Christoph Martin Wieland." *Der Neue Teutsche Merkur* 3 (1793): 68–98.

"Unbekannte Züge und Anecdoten zu den Pariser Mord-Scenen im September 1792." *Minerva* 14 (1793): 185–228.

Vahsen, Mechthilde. *Die Politisierung des weiblichen Subjekts: Deutsche Romanautorinnen und die Französische Revolution (1790–1820).* Berlin: E. Schmidt, 2000.

Wagner, Irmgard. "*Herrmann und Dorothea* in the Context of Kant and Voß: A Question of Peace and Patriarchy." *Goethe Yearbook* 9 (1999): 166–85.

"Warnung für einer abscheulichen Mode." *Journal des Luxus und der Moden* (November 1793): 551–56.

Watanabe-O'Kelly, Helen. *Beauty or Beast? The Woman Warrior in the German Imagination from the Renaissance to the Present.* Oxford: Oxford University Press, 2010.

"Wehrbeauftragter: Soldaten beschweren sich mehr als je zuvor über die Bundeswehr." *SpiegelOnline.de.* October 22, 2013. http://www.spiegel.de.

"Wehrdienst: Bundeswehr findet immer weniger Freiwillige." *SpiegelOnline.de.* August 16, 2013. http://www.spiegel.de.

"Wehrreform: Freiwillig zum Bund? Nein, danke!" *SpiegelOnline.de.* April 21, 2011. http://www.spiegel.

Weigel, Sigrid. "Der schielende Blick: Thesen zur Geschichte weiblicher Schreibpraxis." In *Die verborgene Frau*, 83–137.

———. "Die geopferte Heldin und das Opfer als Heldin: Zum Entwurf weiblicher Helden in der Literatur von Männern und Frauen." In *Die verborgene Frau*, 138–53.

Weißenborn, Birgit, ed. *"Ich sende Dir ein zärtliches Pfand": Die Briefe der Karoline von Günderrode.* Frankfurt am Main: Insel, 1997.

Welke, Martin. "Die Presse und ihre Leser: zur Geschichte des Zeitungslesens in Deutschland von den Anfängen bis zum frühen 19. Jahrhundert." In *Als die Post noch Zeitung machte: Eine Pressegeschichte*, edited by Klaus Beyrer and Martin Dallmeier, 140–47. Giessen: Anabas, 1994.

———. "Gemeinsame Lektüre und frühe Formen von Gruppenbildungen im 17. und 18. Jahrhundert: Zeitungslesen in Deutschland." In *Lesegesellschaften und bürgerliche Emanzipation: Ein europäischer Vergleich*, edited by Otto Dann, 29–53. Munich: C. H. Beck, 1981.

———. "Zeitung und Öffentlichkeit im 18. Jahrhundert: Betrachtungen zur Reichweite und Funktion der periodischen deutschen Tagespublizistik." *Presse und Geschichte* (1977): 71–99.

Westphalen, Engel Christine. *Charlotte Corday. Tragödie in 5 Akten mit Chören. Mit einem Kupfer*. Hamburg: B. G. Hoffmann, 1804.

———. *Gesänge der Zeit: Zum Besten der Hanseatischen Krieger*. Hamburg: B. G. Hoffmann, 1815.

Wieland, Christoph Martin. "Unparteyische Betrachtungen über die dermalige Staats-Revolution in Frankreich." *Der neue Teutsche Merkur* 2 (1790): 40–69.

Wild, Reiner. "Naivität und Terror: Die Französische Revolution im Urteil des klassischen Weimar." In *Schreckensmythen–Hoffnungsbilder: Die Französische Revolution in der deutschen Literatur*, edited by Harro Zimmermann, 47–80. Frankfurt am Main: Athenäum, 1989.

Wilde, Jean T. *The Romantic Realist: Caroline de la Motte Fouqué*. New York: Bookman Associates, 1955.

Wilke, Jürgen. "Die Zeitung." In *Von Almanach bis Zeitung: Ein Handbuch der Medien in Deutschland 1700–1800*, edited by Ernst Fischer, Wilhelm Haefs, and York-Gothart Mix, 388–402. Munich: C. H. Beck, 1999.

———. *Literarische Zeitschriften des 18. Jahrhunderts*. 2 vols. Stuttgart: Metzler, 1978.

Wilson, Peter H. "German Women and War, 1500–1800." *War in History* 3, no. 2 (1996): 127–60.

Wilson, W. Daniel. *Das Goethe-Tabu: Protest und Menschenrechte im klassischen Weimar*. Munich: Deutscher Taschenbuch, 1999.

———. *Goethes Weimar und die Französische Revolution: Dokumente der Krisenjahre*. Cologne: Böhlau, 2004.

Windfuhr, Manfred. "Evolution oder Revolution?: Goethes und Schillers Stellung zur französischen Revolution." In *Literatur: Verständnis und Vermittlung*, edited by Joseph A. Kruse, Monika Salmen, and Klaus-Hinrich Roth, 97–110. Düsseldorf: Cornelsen, 1991.

Wolf, Christa. *Kein Ort: Nirgends*. Berlin: Aufbau Verlag, 1979.

Zantop, Susanne. "Crossing the Border: The French Revolution in the German Literary Imagination." In *Representing the French Revolution*, edited by James A. W. Heffernan, 213–33. Hanover, N.H.: University Press of New England, 1992.

Zschokke, Heinrich. *Charlotte Corday oder die Rebellion von Calvados. Ein republikanisches Trauerspiel in vier Akten. (Aus den Zeiten der französischen Revolution.) In Jamben*. Stettin: Bei Johann Sigismund Kaffke, 1794.

INDEX